Swimming
Into the 21st Century

Cecil M. Colwin

Illustrated by Cecil M. Colwin

Leisure Press
Champaign, Illinois

Library of Congress Cataloging-in-Publication Data

Colwin, Cecil.
    Swimming into the 21st century / Cecil M. Colwin.
      p. cm.
    Includes bibliographical references.
    ISBN 0-88011-436-3
    1. Swimming. 2. Swimming--Training. 3. Swimming--Physiological
aspects. I. Title. II. Title: Swimming into the twenty-first
century.
    GV837.C784   1991
    797.2'1--dc20   90-28869
                                         CIP

ISBN: 0-88011-436-3

Figure 5.1, page 95, by Robert B. Colwin.
Photo on back cover by Leon S. Colwin.

Developmental Editors: Sue Ingels Mauck, Peggy Rupert, and John Robert King
Managing Editor: Julia Anderson
Assistant Editor: Valerie Rose Hall
Copyeditor: Bruce Bethell
Proofreader: Karin Leszczynski
Indexer: Margaret M. Colwin
Production Director: Ernie Noa
Typesetters: Angela Snyder and Kathy Fuoss
Text Design: Keith Blomberg
Text Layout: Denise Lowry and Tara Welsch
Cover Design: Jack Davis
Cover Photo: Dave Black
Computer-Generated Illustrations: David Gregory and Tom Janowski
Printers: Braun-Brumfield and United Graphics

Leisure Press books are available at special discounts for bulk purchase for sales promotions, premiums, fundraising, or educational use. Special editions or book excerpts can also be created to specification. For details, contact the Special Sales Manager at Leisure Press.

Printed in the United States of America

10 9 8 7 6 5 4 3 2 1

Leisure Press
A Division of Human Kinetics Publishers, Inc.
Box 5076, Champaign, IL 61825-5076
1-800-747-4457

Canada Office:
Human Kinetics Publishers, Inc.
P.O. Box 2503, Windsor, ON N8Y 4S2
1-800-465-7301 (in Canada only)

UK Office:
Human Kinetics Publishers (UK) Ltd.
P.O. Box 18
Rawdon, Leeds LS19 6TG
England
(0532) 504211

Australia Office:
Human Kinetics Publishers (Australia)
P.O. Box 80
Kingswood, SA 5062
(08) 374 0433

To the memory of Walter Schlueter and Howard Firby, two of the great creative coaches of this century; to my wife, Margaret, and our ''first team,'' Leon, Robert, and Pauline; and to all who swam for the Bulldogs and helped make coaching so fulfilling a career.

Contents

Preface

"Like as the waves make towards the pebbled shore,
So do our minutes hasten to their end,
Each changing place with that which goes before
In sequent toil all forwards do contend . . ."

William Shakespeare

The approaching end of the millenium presents an opportune time to view competitive swimming in perspective. The word "perspective" implies a knowledge of where the sport has been, where it is now, and where it is likely to go in the future. That is precisely what this book attempts to provide.

Amid the information explosion of recent years and the changing face of international sport, it remains possible to distinguish the *still evolving* themes that have been responsible for the progress of competitive swimming:

1. The search for improved stroke techniques
2. The development of improved training methods
3. The application of science to the search for swimming knowledge
4. The role of the human dynamic

Accordingly, I have divided the text into four parts to cover the areas identified above. These four parts are each treated in the context of past, present, and future.

Part I traces the development of swimming techniques from the early efforts of the pioneers to the more sophisticated procedures of modern biomechanics.

The text breaks new ground in describing how, by studying the flow reactions created by the swimming stroke, fluid dynamic principles can be used to understand, analyze, and improve stroke mechanics. Through this knowledge, I compare the propulsive mechanisms used by human swimmers with those used in nature. I note how the butterfly stroke, derived from the propulsion of the dolphin, has so far been our most successful adaptation from nature. I then discuss whether we can successfully borrow further examples from nature, especially in the areas of transitional and functional shaping.

The text elaborates on transitional and functional shaping of the hands and arms to create ideal flows as a new approach to stroke technique. In addition, it shows how swimmers can be taught to anticipate the distinct flow reactions caused by functional shaping to enhance their "feel of the water" and thereby improve propulsive efficiency.

Part II covers the history of swimming training methods and the principles of modern training practice, relating in depth the origin of interval training on the running track and its adaptation to swimming by the Australians, leading to the astonishing success of their Olympic team at Melbourne in 1956.

The basic principles involved in applying the training work load are discussed in detail, particularly the physiological effects of varying work:rest ratios and how they result in three main types of training: aerobic, anaerobic, and sprint. The helpful and harmful effects of these three types of training are discussed in a simple but profound manner by Nort Thornton, one of the United States' most outstanding coaches.

The continuing—and often exasperating—search for a selective method of applying the training work load is a recurring theme. In this connection, I discuss the use of heart-rate and lactate testing in assessing the intensity of exercise at different rates of speed. I also describe the periodization of the training program as a method of balancing the training emphasis in accordance with seasonal requirements, and provide an outline of the seasonal program together with a section on the effects of altitude training. Tapering, or peaking, a swimmer for competition is often a daunting challenge, even for the most experienced coach. The principal considerations involved in this vital phase of the competitive season are elaborated. (Preparation for specific events and how prominent coaches approach this phase of preparation are included in a special appendix at the end of the book.)

Part III deals with swimming research in the 20th century; Forbes Carlile and Richard Telford contribute "Selected Topics on Swimming Research."

Forbes Carlile is the doyen of Australian swimming coaches and a celebrated pioneer of scientific research in swimming. Like James Counsilman, Carlile is a scientist-coach who has produced many famous swimmers and Olympic champions and made significant contributions to swimming knowledge. His research has included such important areas as the prerace warm-up, the study of adaptation to stress, and the concept of the precompetition taper, which has been adopted worldwide. In fact, he coined the term "taper" as it is used to describe the final stages of training preparation.

Carlile's section "Selected Topics on Swimming Research" is of necessity a subjective survey based on his assessment of what research has been the most significant. His lively mind traces a sure and comprehensive path through the history of swimming research. He identifies the researchers and their most important work in a lucid, unique, and wide-ranging synthesis of a century of scientific investigation.

Richard Telford heads the department of physiology and applied nutrition at the Australian Institute of Sport in Canberra and was physiologist to the Australian Olympic teams in 1984 and 1988. Telford is probably the only physiologist in the Western world to have worked alongside national team coaches and swimmers on an ongoing basis, which he did for 8 years.

Telford is eminently equipped to write on monitoring swimmers' responses to training and on the projects carried out to answer questions that arose in the process ("Physiology and Swimming at the Australian Institute of Sport"). Significantly, the question asked before embarking on any project was, Does this *directly* help the swimmer? In this context alone, Telford's work is very much in the nature of "applied" research and, as such, an important example of successful coach-scientist cooperation in the working situation.

Part IV takes up the story of modern competitive swimming, its tremendous worldwide growth in popularity, and the important developments that have contributed to the expansion of the sport. The text spans the panorama of competitive swimming, from its spawning ground in mid–19th-century England with its great North Country swimmers, many of whom swam for money purses, to the modern multilevel national development programs.

Part IV also covers the development of the great Australian tradition in swimming, beginning with the construction of the first swimming pool in the 1870s and continuing to the reorganization of that country's national swimming program in the late 20th century. An account follows of the outstanding record and great contribution to world swimming by the United States, the giant of world swimming, in terms of technical knowledge, coaching experience, excellence, and a long roster of brilliant Olympic champions.

The account of the growth of the national program concept describes and analyzes the sudden and remarkable rise to supremacy by the Japanese swimmers in the 1930s and continues with an examination of the state-sponsored East German program that was consistently successful for many years—right up to the reunification of Germany on October 2, 1990. The former East German structure, including its talent identification and training programs, is analyzed in detail.

In the final chapter, I discuss the possible future course of competitive swimming as it moves into the 21st century. I touch on the need for meaningful research and for coach and scientist to cooperate and become more familiar with each other's disciplines. Finally, I stress the importance of the human element in making plans work and elaborate on the vital need for innovative and imaginative leadership in shaping the future of competitive swimming.

Acknowledgments

This book was made possible through the direct and indirect help of a great number of people. I wish to express my most sincere thanks to all of them, although their number precludes my naming more than a few.

Colleagues and Contributors

Edward Atraghji, formerly of the Canadian Aeronautical Establishment, for all he has taught me about flow visualization and for his helpful suggestions on the treatment of the fluid dynamic content of this text.

Forbes Carlile and Richard Telford for their invaluable contribution of "Selected Topics on Swimming Research"; Forbes Carlile for writing the section on swimming in Australia; James Counsilman for the use of his historical stroboscope photographs, Figures 8.2 and 8.3, and his Olympic Coaches' Questionnaire; William "Buck" Dawson for writing on the history of American swimming.

Richard Deal, owner and publisher of *Swimming World* and *Swimming Technique*; Robert Ingram, editor of *Swimming World*, and Mark Muckenfuss, former editor of *Swimming Technique*, for permission to include extracts from these two authoritative magazines, particularly the many training programs of top coaches and top swimmers.

John Leonard, executive director of the American Swimming Coaches Association (A.S.C.A.), for permitting the use of extracts from the *World Clinic Year Books* and other A.S.C.A. publications and for writing on the A.S.C.A. educational and coaching certification programs.

Nick Thierry, editor and publisher of *Swim Canada* magazine and secretary of the Interna-

tional Swimming Statisticians' Association, for permission to use extracts from *Swim Canada*; for preparing the world record tables of the second half of the 20th century; and for locating certain source references.

Nort Thornton, head swimming coach of the University of California at Berkeley, for permission to use his excellent article, "A Few Thoughts on Training," from *ASCA Magazine*.

Thomas Kirk Cureton for permission to use materials from chapter 4 of *How to Teach Swimming and Diving* (1934), published by Association Press, New York, and to use the chapter footnotes as a framework in compiling my chronological bibliography of the history of the swimming strokes.

Resource Specialists

I am particularly grateful to those who guided me to valuable sources of information that I otherwise would have missed:

Liana Van der Bellen, Chief of the Rare Books Division of the National Library of Canada, gave me invaluable assistance in researching the works of Thevenot (1620-1692) and Olaus Magnus (1490-1557), and even placed before me original books by the two, both in pristine condition.

Dave Kelly of the Library of Congress in Washington, DC, and Harry McKown, reference associate of the North Carolina Collection, Wilson Library, The University of North Carolina at Chapel Hill. Both went to great lengths to provide references on the early development of American swimming; I express my deepest appreciation to both for their courtesy and cooperation.

Greg Blood, Australian National Sports Information Center, and Marion Boyd, Reference Department of Canada Institute for Scientific and Technical Information, for their ready and courteous reference expertise.

Mardyth Hewitt of the National Library of Canada and Michelle Robichaud of the Library of Parliament provided expertise in locating William Byrd's diary.

I owe a special debt of gratitude to the staff at the Sport Information Resource Centre (SIRC) in Ottawa, one of the world's major sport libraries, particularly to Gilles Chiasson, president and chairman of the board, and reference librarians Janice Pereira, Linda Wheeler, Christine Lalande, and Katherine MacKellar.

Marion Washburn, resource specialist at the International Swimming Hall of Fame, gave able and willing assistance on many occasions.

Swimming Canada Natation gave permission to reprint materials from *An Introduction to Swimming Coaching* (Colwin, 1977) published by the Canadian Amateur Swimming Association (est. 1970), Ottawa, Ontario.

William Sweetenham, former head swimming coach, Australian Institute of Sport, Canberra, granted permission to reproduce a recorded conversation we had in Canberra in May 1987.

Mark Muckenfuss, former editor of *Swimming Technique*, Tim Welch, head swimming coach of the University of Notre Dame, and Peggy Rupert, developmental editor of Human Kinetics Publishers, contributed reviews of the manuscript and constructive suggestions.

Fred Wilt, Olympic runner, Sullivan award winner, and acknowledged authority on track training, kindly reviewed chapter 6, "The Influence of Track Training on Swimming," and checked it for accuracy.

Robert Schleihauf granted permission to prepare and publish drawings adapted from illustrations in "Swimming Propulsion: A Hydrodynamic Analysis" (Schleihauf, 1977) and "Swimming Skill: A Review of Basic Theory" (Schleihauf, 1986) and to reprint the wire frame computer printouts that he kindly supplied for this purpose.

James G. Hay gave permission to reprint the picture of his analog watch and to quote from pages 70 and 71 of *Starting, Stroking and Turning* (James G. Hay, Editor, 1986).

The Citizen, Ottawa, for permission to reprint extracts from "The Ancient Olympics: A Run for The Money" by Trevor Hodge, January 9, 1988.

Ron Gilchrist, First Essex Productions, gave permission to make adaptive drawings of the technique of Mary T. Meagher from slides taken from the instructional film by Ernest Maglischo and Don Gambril and produced by First Essex Productions.

Mary T. Meagher granted permission to make adaptive drawings of her swimming stroke.

Cornell University Press, Ithaca, New York, gave permission to use the extract from 1st-century Roman poet, Manilius, as contained in *Sport in Greece and Rome*.

Kamel Sayedh provided photocopying services.

My association with Human Kinetics Publishers during the 6 years this book has been in preparation has been uniquely enjoyable. I have rarely worked with professionals in any field who have brought such enthusiasm, expertise, and efficiency to everything they do. I express my appreciation to publisher Rainer Martens, acquisitions editor Vic MacKenzie, and my first developmental editors, Sue Mauck and Peggy Rupert, for their interest and guidance during the early stages of preparing a long text—particularly when the much-sought light at the end of the tunnel was slow to appear. I also appreciate very much the advice of art director Keith Blomberg and the expert efforts of sales director Brian Holding and direct response manager Linda Glazier. I also extend thanks to managing editor Julia Anderson, who ensured the book's smooth progress through the final production stages.

I would be extremely remiss if I failed to mention the valuable assistance and advice of developmental editor John Robert King, who made an important contribution to the final format of the book. I am indeed fortunate to have had the ready assistance of this immensely talented gentleman who not only had a natural feel for the overall concept but also brought to the project unusual dedication, patience, expertise, and unfailing good humor. I owe him a great debt of gratitude.

Prologue

In forming a perspective of competitive swimming, especially its main disciplines, we should realize that it has been an organized sport for only about 150 years.

During a long career coaching international swimmers and a one-time tenure as national technical director of Canadian swimming, I have seen many trends come and go. Some were periodically recycled, dressed in different garb and presented as new ideas; others proved to be important and useful tools that previously had been overlooked.

I learned about competitive swimming in the late 19th century from my father, who swam the English overarm sidestroke at the University of Manchester nearly 100 years ago. At that time, the great swimmers from the north of England, such as Nuttall, Tyers, and Derbyshire, led the world, and organized competitive swimming was still in its infancy. He described to me how the leading swimmers of the time, intuitively rather than by design, developed stroke techniques that produced ever-increasing speed. In 1907, he saw the first great American swimmer, Charles Daniels, compete in Manchester and break the 100-yard world record in what was then a phenomenal time of 55-2/5 seconds.

With interest and enthusiasm thus aroused, I came under the guidance and tutelage of coach James D. Allett-Green—popularly known as Jimmy Green—first as a swimmer and then as a student coach. He was the first of many swimming pioneers I was to meet. In the 1920s, Green had studied swimming under two great pioneer stroke technicians, Louis de B. Handley of the Women's Swimming Association of New York and William Bachrach of the Illinois Athletic Club, Chicago, who coached Johnny Weissmuller, the man acknowledged to be the greatest swimmer in the first half of the century.

Green was a typical product of the "Golden Age of Sport." He was the most colorful character I've met in a sport that has produced many. His two pets, a parrot (usually perched on his shoulder) and a lion cub (until it grew too big) were familiar figures on the pool deck. In World War I, Green had been a pilot in the Royal Flying Corps. He always insisted that there was "nothing so akin to swimming as flying." He regularly illustrated the point by comparing swimming movements with those of propellers, wings, ailerons, and rudders. It is amazing to think that, even in those days, he was so close to the truth about the dynamics of swimming propulsion.

Green was the pioneer of swimming coaching in South Africa and one of the three great stroke technicians I've known. (The other two were Walter Schlueter of the United States and Howard Firby of Canada.) The man was uncanny; he could tell what you were thinking while you swam and also what pressure sensations you were receiving from the water. He was a brilliant and natural analyst of movement. He could pick out a fault within seconds. He would give a piercing whistle to stop you, and then he would start the correction. Usually, he corrected just one item and the rest of the stroke automatically fell into place. His natural ability to analyze human movement was not confined to swimming, however; golfers, tennis players, and other sports people regularly sought his assistance.

I was fortunate in that Green took an interest in me. He was undoubtedly the greatest influence in my career. In often vivid fashion, he convinced me that sheer speed could result from good stroke mechanics. He taught me how to teach stroke technique. It was entirely through his teaching, encouragement, and influence that I became a coach.

Early in my career, I was privileged to coach the great-grandson of Joey Nuttall. Nuttall was reputed to have been undefeated for 21 years using the English overarm sidestroke and was the greatest English professional champion in the late 19th century. Nuttall's family still possessed a scrapbook of that famous swimmer, and I was allowed to take notes from it. The collection of old newspaper and magazine clippings contained graphic accounts both of Nuttall's great races and of the techniques used by the individual contestants. They swam in various courses of different sizes—canals, ponds, and rivers, as well as in the old so-called swimming baths. There were many descriptions of the bets and prizes for which they competed. The resulting amateur-professional feud led to the drafting of the amateur laws, later adopted by Federation Internationale de Natation Amateur (F.I.N.A.) (the international governing body of swimming), and the subsequent schism between the "gentlemen amateur" swimmers of the South and the professional swimmers of the North.

With the unusually strenuous training undertaken by the Japanese in the 1930s came the growing realization of how much hard work the human body could absorb. Probably the biggest influence in this field was that of the 1928, 1932, and 1948 U.S. Olympic Coach, Robert Kiphuth of Yale University, who pioneered supplementary land-training exercises for swimmers and who was a tough, authoritarian conditioner of athletes. His books, *Swimming* (1942) and *How To Be Fit* (1950) were best-sellers of the time and influenced an entire generation of swimmers and coaches throughout the world. Kiphuth's early use of "wind sprints" was the precursor of interval training and today's much more strenuous training programs.

In 1952, Kiphuth invited me to visit Yale to observe his methods. Kiphuth told me that in 1917, when he was a young physical-training instructor at Yale, he was asked to coach the university's swimming team. He noticed that, although many swimmers were technically excellent, they simply lacked the power to carry through the fatigue stages of a race. Motivated by his desire to strengthen the muscles used in swimming, Kiphuth set about designing a system of land training for swimmers.

Attendance at his land-training sessions was completely voluntary, but supplementary training proved so successful that athletes from other sports came in the hope of deriving similar results. Kiphuth discovered that not only did the exercises improve performance but they did so more quickly than an equivalent time spent training in the water.

I "tested" these exercises by daily participation in the team training sessions in the Payne Whitney Gymnasium (known throughout the world of swimming as "Kiphuth's Cathedral of Sweat") along with Olympians and world-record holders such as John Marshall, James McLane, and Wayne Moore, then world renowned as "The Three M's." Each session lasted 1 hour and consisted of three 20-minute periods comprising free exercises, pulley weights, and throwing the 16-pound medicine ball.

During my stay in the United States, I studied the American swimming system at many levels of development and was present at Yale in 1952 for the publication of the first issue of *Swimming World and Junior Swimmer* (then only a mimeographed journal), edited by Kiphuth and his assistant, Peter Daland. The magazine became an important vehicle for the new age-group program that had just been started by Beth Kaufman, Carl Bauer, and Peter Daland. This program was to greatly accelerate the growth of American swimming. It was copied throughout the world and caused a great expansion of the sport in many countries.

I also witnessed what was then a new training method called "wind sprints." John Marshall, the Australian Olympic swimmer and Yale student who at the time held every world freestyle record from 200 to 1500 meters, swam a set of thirty 50-yard swims each in 30 seconds after doing the leadoff lap in 28 seconds. He rested 30 seconds between each 50-yard swim. Of course, these times bear no comparison with today's standards, but at the time, those present believed they had witnessed an unusual achievement. They were not to know until later that this was the beginning of interval training for swimming. In his letters home, Marshall described the new method, and a group of innovative Australian coaches developed interval swimming both from Marshall's description and from methods that had been used on the running track for about 20 years. The development of interval training by the Australians was to prove to be the greatest single reason for their Olympic supremacy in 1956.

Although Kiphuth made many notable contributions to swimming, his greatest gift was an abstract one. Through sheer force of intellect and the example he set, he created an image of the swimming coach other than the then-current one of a bathrobe-clad "swimming bum." Kiphuth was also a strong influence in the development of swimming in Japan and was treated with great deference and respect in that country. On one occasion, when Kiphuth and an American team emerged at Osaka station, over 100,000 people thronged the streets to welcome them. He was a national hero in Japan.

Although I had arrived at Yale rather full of the dogmatic assurance of youth, I learned many lessons from Kiphuth, the most important of which was that the human organism could absorb much more arduous work than most people at the time thought possible. It quickly became obvious to me that American swimmers of that era were superior to most of the world chiefly because they worked twice as hard as the swimmers of any other nation. I returned home and, in the face of much local criticism, worked my small team of young swimmers very hard. Soon they were rewarded by winning every berth but one on the 1956 Olympic team. The women's 4×100 meter freestyle relay team, the members of which had trained together at home, came third behind Australia and the U.S.A., and Natalie "Toy" Myburgh, who had broken the world 100-yard freestyle record earlier in the year, reached the final of the 100-meter freestyle. For this rapid improvement, I had Bob Kiphuth to thank.

By 1960, when the Rome Olympics ended, there were signs that swimming knowledge had spread around the world and that great swimmers could now be expected to emerge from any country, so long as they were prepared to do the necessary work. I remember Kiphuth's comment soon after the Australian success at the 1956 Melbourne Olympic Games:

There's really no great secret to success in swimming providing you are prepared to work very hard at it, and by hard work I don't just mean any old kind of hard work—it must be hard work combined with a modicum of intelligence.

It was to be 14 years before I returned to America. When my swimmers competed at the American outdoor championships in Lincoln, Nebraska, in August 1966, I first met James "Doc" Counsilman. Prior to that, we had con-

ducted an infrequent correspondence. In 1963, he had sent me a collection of his writings that probably formed the schematic for his book *The Science of Swimming* (1968), which appeared 5 years later and took the swimming world by storm. About the same time, he had also sent me four pages of notes, still in my possession and now beginning to turn yellow with age, on "Mechanical and Physiological Principles Applicable to Physical Education Activities."

In these notes, he dealt with such topics as energy costs, forces, and linear and angular velocities and illustrated how the laws of physics could be applied to the analysis of stroke mechanics. It was not difficult to detect behind the notes a man of great creativity and originality whose mind was being directed to a methodical and unrelenting analysis of swimming techniques in a manner never before attempted. However, when we met, my instant impression was of a practical pool-deck coach with a fine insight into human nature and a subtle way of handling his swimmers. I liked the way he spoke to his swimmers, and I could tell that he was very close to them. Above all else, he was a fine inspirational coach and as sensitive to the aspirations and emotions of his swimmers as a photographic plate is to light.

Counsilman's contributions to competitive swimming are legion. There is hardly a phase of the sport that has escaped his attention and not been dramatically improved by his influence. His classic book, *The Science of Swimming*, showed the value of a scientific approach to the coaching of swimming. The book had immediate credibility because its author was also an outstanding coach at the pinnacle of his career, with a long and illustrious record of producing world-record holders and Olympic champions.

Shortly before World War II, a development commenced in sport that grew in momentum and thrust in the 1950s and continues to spread to still more countries. This was the growth of national development programs, sponsored by the state, the private sector, or both. Included in this trend was the reappearance (from classical times) of what best can be described as the "state athlete."

The development of national, state-sponsored systems should be distinguished from previous, isolated national efforts such as those of the successful Japanese swimmers in the 1930s or the Australians in 1956. By comparison, the typical multilevel national development system is vast and comprehensive and often will involve central control of every facet of a country's sport, including millions of dollars in funding.

In 1950, the year after the GDR (East Germany) was established as a state, the *Hochschule für Körperkultur* (University for Physical Culture) was founded in Leipzig. It became the scientific center for determining how to maximize athletic performance. Most of the 7,000 graduates remained in the East German sport system, working as doctors, coaches, and teachers until the reunification of Germany in 1990.

Based on the obvious criterion of consistently producing fine results, the GDR's had been the most successful of the formal state-sponsored programs in swimming and in several other sports, too. Although the programs of other countries have proved their ability to achieve success from time to time, their results have not been nearly as consistent and predictable as those of the former GDR.

When the concept of state-sponsored sport spread to Canada, I was appointed national technical director of the Canadian Swimming Association in 1973. In retrospect, this experience was in distinct contrast to my earlier experiences in Australia and South Africa, where swimming was part of the national sporting tradition and the air was thick with swimming talk, not an artificially created environment for breeding exotic hothouse plants.

In splendid isolation, the new sport bureaucrats of Canada relentlessly proliferated paper. In dozens of offices reigned this love for classifying, systematizing, and putting out reams of statistics on just about anything. Through this process, any series of events or ideas was given the allure of a plan, theory, or basic, immutable truth. My first impression of the scene has remained the abiding one: a preponderance of sports administrators who appeared to live by The Great Plan Design, with little or no understanding of the importance of the human dynamic.

In the final analysis, innovative leadership and the ability to keep abreast of change are vital to the continuing success of any national program. The best leaders are usually highly innovative. Those who always copy others inevitably are followers instead of leaders. In this book, I discuss the nature of creativity, the phenomenon of the "inspired hunch," and whether coaches and administrators can *learn* to be innovative.

One purpose of this book is to provide a guide to help you develop your own methods, based on what you presently believe to be true. Future truth grows from or is "attached" to the truth we know today. Try to reduce the truth you find, the knowledge you gain, to its most simple components; then it will be ready to be applied.

Although this text identifies what I believe to be possible keys to future developments, I have not been so presumptuous as to attempt to predict the future. Instead, I have chosen to leave most topics open-ended, so that you, the reader, may form your own assumptions. If, as a result, you should find in the following pages material that stimulates you to innovative thought, then I shall have achieved my purpose.

C.M.C.
Ottawa, Ontario

PART I

SWIMMING PROPULSION

As "land-confirmed" beings, our initial swimming movements are crude, comparatively ineffective, and far from compatible with true efficiency in water. The simple truth is that swimming is both an *adopted* and an *adapted* sport for humans. The human physique is basically quite ungainly for the purpose. We must not only adjust our land-type breathing for use in water but also alter the normal use of our limbs to propel ourselves through it.

Although humans are not ideally endowed by nature to be highly proficient swimmers, improved technique can produce surprisingly facile and dexterous propulsion. The discovery of this explains the almost obsessive fascination with stroke techniques in the early years of swimming development.

Old-time coaches—"swimming masters," or "professors of swimming," as they sometimes called themselves—often exuded an aura of secrecy. "Come and be coached by me and I'll teach you technique," they would say. "You see, swimming is really nothing more than pull-ing and kicking, but it's done in this certain way and *that* is . . . technique!"

But eventually, intelligent swimmers expected to be told *why* they were being advised to use a particular method. They became tired of the clichés, the old "hand-me-downs," the platitudes and the folklore that had become part of the repertoire of many a so-called swimming professor.

For many, the improvement of swimming skill became an interesting and fascinating intellectual exercise as well as a test of physical ability. More often than not, "clues" leading to improved methods were observed in the techniques of great natural athletes. The term "natural athlete" is worth proper understanding. Broadly stated, it means an athlete who does the right thing naturally, as part of one's true nature. Yet the progress of many a natural athlete was stifled by the imposition of techniques that interfered with the swimmer's natural movement inclination. Of course, much was heard about the coaches' successes but little about their failures.

1

To say that the study of swimming was always an intellectual exercise would be incorrect. Entire nations climbed on the bandwagons of leading swimmers of the moment regardless of whether the athletes were successful because of their techniques or despite them. In this way, on at least two occasions in the history of technical development, swimmers of an entire generation followed what proved to be a path to nowhere.

For the first 100 years of organized competitions, the racing strokes evolved through trial and error. The early development was slow and spasmodic. Gradually, we learned the importance of streamlining—that we swim faster by decreasing drag. The advent of the crawl stroke highlighted another fundamental: A swimmer must produce continuous propulsion to keep velocity as even as possible.

In this section, I present the evolution of the racing strokes from a perspective different from the familiar accounts. The focus is on how the fundamentals of swimming technique came to be recognized and adopted. The writings of the day show how people often incorrectly rationalized the acceptance of new techniques. I will show how they repeated conceptual errors that experience should have taught them to avoid. We, too, should ask ourselves whether we tend to perpetuate pet theories. We should question everything—especially the myths by which we live.

Conversely, whenever someone had a workable, or even profound, idea, it usually took a long time to win acceptance. The history of swimming holds many examples of the old adage, "Be right too soon and your word will be ignored; be right too late and everyone is bored." For example, the sidestroke swimmers of the 19th century knew that turning the body to the side reduced water resistance, but rolling the body in crawl swimming was considered a fault for no less than 50 years, until it was given credit for at least part of the Australian world dominance in the 1950s. Actually, the victorious Japanese crawl swimmers at the 1932 Olympics had also used considerable body roll. But at the time, swimmers from the rest of the world refused to adopt body roll technique and stubbornly continued to swim with a flat body position. They attributed the Japanese ability to roll without setting up resistance to streamlined shoulders, which they claimed were a characteristic of the Japanese physique. Therefore, it was argued, a Japanese swimmer could use body roll with impunity, but a Westerner who copied it would do so at peril.

Another classic example of delayed progress was the failure to recognize an additional important principle discovered by the Japanese. Back in the 1930s, they had realized that it was more efficient to swim with long strokes at a high tempo. Today, "distance per stroke" is considered to be an important index of swimming efficiency.

History abounds with stories of how people came close to discovering important new truths about swimming but either did not recognize the clues or were slow to follow up. For a long time, the pursuit of swimming knowledge followed no specific course. In fact, this desultory approach existed before scientific methods were first used to analyze stroke mechanics.

During the second half of the 20th century, James Counsilman and Robert Schleihauf, both of the United States, made contributions of great significance. Their research caused a major reassessment of theory and a finer insight into swimming propulsion. Counsilman (1969, 1971; Counsilman & Brown, 1970), through his work on the Bernoulli effect, found the key to understanding the nature of propulsive movements. Schleihauf (1974, 1977, 1979), by accurate measurement of hand placements and use of vector analysis, showed the range of propulsive forces developed in the four swimming styles.

Counsilman (1980) showed that hand speed constantly increases during the arm pull of all four competitive strokes. However, at one point in the pull, the hand actually decelerates, causing a dip in the hand-speed curve.

Ernest Maglischo (1983) used three-dimensional motion picture photography and digitizing techniques to show distinct periods of acceleration and deceleration of forward speed during a stroke cycle. Maglischo posed the important question: "When are these periods of deceleration normal and when do they indicate stroke defects?"

Following on Maglischo's study, David Costill (1987) conceived a video-computer system that provided instant analysis of a swimmer's velocity at different points in the stroke. The system combines the use of a video camera with the *swim meter* invented by Albert Craig and David Pendergast (1979). (The mechanical parts of the swim meter were designed and built by Gerald F. Harris.) A computer synchronizes the video image with a velocity graph and superimposes the two on a video display. This information eventually may help swimmers time their strokes with greater accuracy, particularly when they know the relationship between the propulsive forces they develop and the fluctuating velocities within the stroke cycle. At present, we remain in comparative ignorance about this important *practical* aspect of swimming propulsion. The continuing challenge will be to reduce often complex scientific information to a simple, easily taught format.

Even in the late 20th century, many coaches have not yet realized that, to obtain the full benefit of the new scientific concepts, an entirely different approach to the teaching of stroke mechanics is required. This is especially true of the interaction between the swimming stroke and the water.

Eventually, we must employ fluid dynamic principles if we are to develop more effective propulsive mechanisms than those based on present concepts. We have only just begun to toy with the beginnings of this science as it applies to human swimming. A strong foundation for future progress will be laid only when biomechanical and fluid dynamic research proceed in tandem.

We need to acquire a better understanding of how the *water* reacts to swimming strokes. To this end, I discuss the potential applications of fluid dynamic principles. After several years of observing the flow reactions caused by world-class swimmers, I became convinced that the coaching of stroke mechanics has been incorrectly based on emulating the actions of mechanical propellers instead of those foil-type mechanisms more akin to natural flight and fish propulsion.

Although there are obvious anatomical differences limiting the extent to which humans can approximate these mechanisms, with some surprise I came to realize that the techniques of talented swimmers, probably unknown to the swimmers themselves, do borrow several important principles from nature; chief among these are the directional changes made by the hand as it develops the flow circulation necessary to enable predominant lift-force propulsion. A skilled swimmer manipulates the flow with remarkable efficiency and swirls it around the hand, simply by quick changes of posture, direction, and speed. The arm, and particularly the hand, is used with great dexterity, much like an elongated flipper, which, as we shall see, also incorporates some of the attributes of a wing or a fin.

Chapter 1

The Quest for Speed

For just as the dolphin glides through the water on swift fins, now rising above the surface and now sinking to the depths, and piles up waves and sends them off in circles, just so will each person born under the sign of the Dolphin fly through the waves, raising one arm and then the other in slow arcs.

Manilius, first-century Roman poet

This passage, written in the 1st century, waxes lyrical on the pleasures of swimming. One can envisage a scene 2,000 years ago: a balmy day, a buoyant sea, and a skilled swimmer performing, yes, a type of crawl stroke. Across the centuries a fellow enthusiast conveys with words his love of the water and his fascination with swimming propulsion. His reference to dolphin swimming was prophetic in the extreme, because imitating the dolphin action is the most successful adaptation humans have made from nature to their own swimming propulsion. And he must have had sharp eyes, for he describes not only technique but even the reacting vortex flows in the water, an unusual observation even today.

Humans have enjoyed swimming for thousands of years. Early recorded history suggests that people living along the warm Mediterranean swam with considerable skill.

The Origin of the Crawl

Translations from ancient Greece and Rome speak of swimmers using alternating overarm motions. There is little doubt that a type of crawl stroke existed long ago.

Then, during the Middle Ages, swimming fell into disuse throughout Europe because of the belief that outdoor bathing helped to spread the epidemics that so often swept the continent. When people did swim, they preferred a form of breaststroke to keep their faces out of the water. It was not until the second half of the 19th century that the prejudice against swimming was largely overcome.

So the crawl was "lost" for centuries, although it is believed that oceanic peoples have always swum with overarm strokes. But in Western culture, it was not until the start of the 20th century that the stroke reappeared.

The Influence of the Sea on the First Crawl Swimmers

Crawl stroke evolution appears to have started where people habitually swam in buoyant sea water. In the modern era, the early crawl development initially resulted from the influence of Alick Wickham, a native of the British Solomon Islands who migrated to Australia in 1898. Wickham's unusual overarm stroke was noticed by the Cavill family of Australian "swimming professors," who further developed the method in the sea water enclosure at Lavender Bay in Sydney harbor.

The possible effect of saltwater buoyancy on the adoption of above-water arm recovery has been overlooked. Although this line of thought can be only speculative, it is reasonable to suppose that the added buoyancy of salt water provided the stability that made out-of-water arm movements easier and less tiring for swimmers using unskilled techniques. And perhaps when these early swimmers participated in their allied recreation of surfing, the momentum of the surging ocean surf had imbued in them a need to propel with fast continuous movements, which they then subconsciously transferred to their experiments with the early crawl stroke.

Body surfing provides a possible clue to the origin of the crawl. The body surfer uses rapid alternate overarm strokes to catch the impetus of a fast-cresting wave. Then, with head down, the surfer pulls both arms through to the hips, often adding a flutter kick to ensure that the wave's full momentum has been secured.

The idea of the flutter kick and the alternate overarm came from the South Sea Islands. The Australian pioneers were quick to spot the clues, and they put them together in an entirely new form of swimming. The crawl was a marvel of ingenuity and much faster than any previous technique.

The crawl stroke brought not only increased speed but also better knowledge of the fundamentals that produce efficiency. Because studying the thinking behind the development of the crawl is the quickest way to understand these fundamentals, I have devoted this chapter to the evolution of the crawl stroke, but the same fundamentals apply to all swimming strokes. In fact, they led to the introduction of two other strokes, the backstroke and the butterfly. The common application of speed swimming fundamentals to butterfly, backstroke, and breaststroke is discussed in chapter 2.

The Evolution of Swimming Fundamentals

The evolution of the crawl stroke is the history of the human effort to swim better and faster by improving the actual technique of swimming. This development has been ably recorded by several outstanding authorities and especially so in the classic descriptions by Steedman (1867), Wilson (1883), Thomas (1904), Sinclair and Henry (1908), Cureton (1934), and Carlile (1963).

The English Overarm Sidestroke

When organized competitive swimming started in the 19th century, the sidestroke was the standard racing style. Both arms remained submerged throughout, and the legs performed a wide scissor kick with opening and closing movements that resembled walking. Swimmers found they could reduce resistance by recovering one arm over the water instead of underwater. This stroke was known as the English overarm sidestroke (Figure 1.1).

Figure 1.1 The English overarm sidestroke. *Note.* From Sachs (1912, p. 134). Adapted by permission.

The Trudgen Stroke

The idea for a double overarm stroke came from observing the unusual technique of John Trudgen, which became the basic arm stroke of the crawl. The difficulty with the trudgen stroke was that it lacked continuity; in fact, it was very jerky, because it timed one breaststroke kick to every two arm strokes. An attempt was made to overcome this handicap by combining the scissor kick of the sidestroke with the trudgen arm action. The kick, originally performed with considerable knee bend, was narrowed and the legs were held straighter, but the timing of the side scissor kick still prevented a continuous arm action (Figure 1.2).

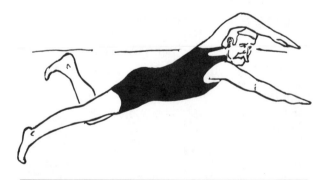

Figure 1.2 The trudgen stroke.

The Crawl Stroke

Following the introduction of the double overarm stroke, it was noticed that a continuous stroke could be performed easily by not kicking

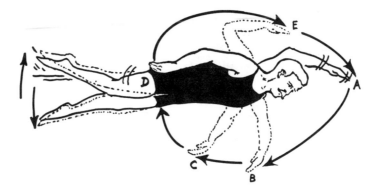

Figure 1.3 The crawl stroke. *Note.* From Sachs (1912, p. 145). Adapted by permission.

at all. Eventually, a new leg action, the flutter kick, fitted well with an alternate overarm action, and the crawl stroke was born (Figure 1.3).

Trial and Error

Studying the history of stroke development shows not only the underlying themes in the pursuit of speed but also how the early pioneers were so often near the truth but failed to realize it. This study demonstrates how swimming gradually became more technical and how certain trends were used and then discarded, only to be accepted again later. This process is typical of empirical learning, the trial and error approach, which has always been part of human experience and still is. Indeed, our understanding of swimming technique remains far from complete; the sport is still evolving and the search for improved technique continues.

Analyzing the technical information that history provides shows how the basic principles of swimming propulsion gradually became clearer. This progress was effected not only by great, talented athletes but also by those prepared to reason out the problems of speed and efficiency. A study of the history of swimming reveals a tendency to continually repeat mistakes, to the detriment of progress.

We need to learn how to recognize such pitfalls. Problems should be solved by methodical analysis while still not neglecting to follow the "inspired hunch." As we study the progress of swimming, it repeatedly becomes evident that the answer to a problem may lie down a side track and not necessarily on a straight line between points A and B.

Difficulties in Evaluating Stroke Technique

Dr. Thomas K. Cureton (1934), generally acknowledged as "the father of swimming research," identifies the difficulties the early swimmers and coaches had evaluating which methods worked and which did not:

It is a well-known fact that the majority of instructors have had little training in mechanics or in methods of objective observation. A common fault is that of championing some style or form in preference to another with little as a basis for accurate comparison.

In many cases the basis is nothing more than the fact that a popular winner used that style. The world has always followed the champion. The popular literature is full of works written by champions who were supreme in their time. We have seen the majority of these works forgotten. Few champions have the background necessary to explain the mechanical action of the strokes or the physiology of training to which a large degree of any competitive success must be attributed.

Precise knowledge of these elements is not very common at the present time. Swimming has attracted the attention of few men of science. *The results attained by those who have worked upon the scientific aspects of the sport have been very poorly understood by the practical teachers* [italics mine]. Testing methods to determine the major faults in stroke technique have been practically unknown. (p. 86)

Basic Principles

Nevertheless, swimmers gradually learned that efficient technique was concerned mainly with increasing propulsion while decreasing the resistance of the water to the swimmer's forward movement. They also came to realize the importance of efficient timing to keep the stroke as continuous as possible. These remain the known basic principles of swimming, although our knowledge of swimming strokes has become much more refined since midcentury due to scientific investigation.

Breaststroke's 400-Year Dominance

Although Nicolaus Wynman wrote the first book on swimming, *Colymbetes, Sive de Arte Natandi Dialogus et Festivus et Iucundus lectu* (published in 1538 by H. Steiner of Ingolstadt, Bavaria), an earlier book, *The Boke Named the Governour*, by Sir Thomas Elyot (published in London by Thomas Berthelet in 1531), discussed swimming as an important part of the education of gentlemen. Copies of *The Boke Named the Governour*, 258 folios, are housed in Cambridge University Library and the British Museum.

Wynman's book, *Colymbetes*, describes breaststroke as the stroke "which all must learn as the scientific stroke" (Wynman, 1538). Within the next 50 years, two more books of note followed. One by Olaus Magnus (1555), archbishop of Uppsala, Sweden, discussed swimming prominently among the other customs of northern people. The other, by Sir Everard Digby (1587), was *De Arte Natandi* (*The Art of Swimming*), published in England but written in Latin. Both books advocated breaststroke in preference to the more primitive forms of swimming that existed at the time (Cureton, 1934). Of interest to historians is the fact that Digby was executed in 1606 along with seven fellow conspirators for his part in the Gunpowder Plot to blow up King James I and the parliament.

In 1699, *The Art of Swimming*, by the French writer Melchisedech Thevenot, was published in London by Dan Brown, D. Midurnter, T. Leigh, and Robert Knaplock. The original version, *L'Art de Nager*, had been published in Paris by T. Moette in 1696. The book was first published several years after Thevenot's death on October 29, 1692. Thevenot described swimming "as an old sport which hitherto had not received the investigation necessary to improve in efficiency." During Thevenot's time, breaststroke was still considered as the scientific stroke in Europe (Cureton, 1934) (Figure 1.4). Thevenot's book was regarded as the authorita-

Figure 1.4 In 17th century Europe the breaststroke was considered to be "the scientific stroke which all should learn." Thevenot (1699, p. 53) recommended that people practice the breaststroke pull while standing in hip-deep water.

tive work on scientific swimming, as it was called then, and was reprinted in 1764 and 1772.

In recognition of Thevenot's preeminence among swimming authors during a century when swimming was considered a health hazard, Thevenot was inducted into the International Swimming Hall of Fame in 1990, nearly 300 years after his book was published.

Although Ralph Thomas (1904) claimed that Thevenot in his famous book had plagiarized Digby's work, written a century before, the prestigious British Library Catalogue simply states that Thevenot's book was "adapted" from Digby's *De Arte Natandi*. The latter explanation would appear to be a more plausible one, particularly as Thevenot was a minor celebrity of his day, a highly respected and distinguished Oriental scholar and a founder of the French Academy of Sciences. As librarian of the Royal Library (from 1684), he collected many valuable books and manuscripts, of which he published a catalog, *Bibliotheca Thevenotiana*.

As swum during the 16th and 17th centuries, the breaststroke was performed with the head held high and completely out of the water (Thevenot, 1699). Instead of using a frog kick, propulsion was applied with the insteps and not the soles of the feet (Muths, 1798).

Early in the 19th century, breaststroke swimmers adopted a frog kick in which the ankles were dorsi-flexed and propulsion was developed by pressing the soles of the feet against the water (Counsilman, 1968). A debate followed as to whether using the soles of the feet in the frog kick yielded more propulsion than spreading the legs and then straightening them before closing in a tight wedge (Thomas, 1904).

These historical discussions of how to use the legs and feet in the most efficient method for the breaststroke may mark the beginning of technical thinking and a growing interest in improving propulsion. Understanding the positive effect that could be achieved by a slight change of technique was (and is) significant; this ability later was to prove an important characteristic of a capable coach.

The Advent of the "Swimming Professors"

For the best part of 400 years, as far as can be ascertained, the breaststroke was the most common method of swimming. It provided stability and was ideal for swimming with head high in rough or polluted water. By the early 19th century, the breaststroke had been formed into a distinct pattern, and all over Europe, standardized methods were developed for teaching it.

I mention this point because, over and over in the history of swimming development, some people have fallen into the trap of trying to mold all technique into a distinct pattern, a neat synthesis, whether or not suitable to the individual. This proclivity has often stifled progress. Strangely enough, along with this trend, there also has been the tendency to jump on the bandwagon of the day's leading champion and copy that person's technique. The answer, obviously, is to find the technique that best suits individual physique and natural movement inclination; to put it another way, we now know that there is an acceptable range of effective propulsive movements, the choice of which will vary from person to person (Schleihauf, 1986).

The start of the 19th century saw the advent of the "swimming professors," who devised all sorts of teaching methods, some of which can be classified only as exotic. Their "treatises" advocated the teaching of swimming by means of a variety of preliminary land drills and gymnastics. Many other swimming drills, skills, and sculling stunts were noted. To say the least,

several of the described methods were eccentric if not weird.

Early Teaching Methods in Europe

Much of the early apparatus devised for teaching swimming we now know to have been unnecessary. The German swimming teachers, particularly, were keen on using devices to help their pupils learn the strokes on land. The procedures could not have provided a pleasurable experience. One method involved dangling the learner from parallel bars by two sets of chains slung under the chest and abdomen. Another favorite method, used during this early period in the École de Natation in France, consisted of positioning the swimmer across a box or bench and then applying manual assistance, both front and rear. One instructor guided the feet and another the hands.

Swimming in the South Seas

While Europeans were pursuing these laborious methods in their gymnasiums, the indigenous peoples of the South Seas were swimming the overarm strokes. In 1849, Sidney Howard, an American, published a book in New York, *The Science of Swimming as Taught and Practiced in Civilized and Savage Countries*, in which he referred to de la Perouse's trip around the world in 1785. Captain de la Perouse said that the Indians, or natives, of Easter Island (one of the South Sea Islands) were remarkable swimmers using overhand strokes.

The Transition From Breaststroke to Sidestroke

It is easy to imagine how the sidestroke evolved from the breaststroke. In effect, the early underarm sidestroke was really the breaststroke swum with the body turned on its side. Swimmers found that by turning on the side they encountered less water resistance. Sachs (1912) says,

It is necessary to cleave the water with the head or shoulder in order to avoid undue resistance. The first action of the swimmer is to turn from his breast on to his side, and he will notice that his resistance is reduced by almost half; his position in the water becomes that of a racing boat as compared with a punt or a barge. But he must be careful. If the change of stroke is to be the means of increasing his speed, he must be sure that his propelling power is at least as great as it was when he was on his breast. The thing must be thought out. (p. 133)

At first, the sidestroke was swum with both arms in the water on both pull and recovery; this was known as the underarm sidestroke. It was preeminent as a racing stroke from about 1855 for 15 to 20 years.

With the advent of organized swimming championships in England in 1871, the quest for speed encouraged swimmers to improve their stroke efficiency (Sinclair, 1909). The desire for technical improvement was increased by the fact that, until 1906, there were no separate events for different strokes. Except for the breaststroke, which was sometimes swum as a novelty item, swimmers competing in a single race used any stroke they liked (Counsilman, 1968).

The Jarvis Kick

With the advent of the English overarm sidestroke, racers abandoned the underarm stroke (Cureton, 1934). Sinclair (1909) diagrams overarm sidestroke technique (see Figure 1.5) and writes that

> the great exponents of the art of swimming were the Englishmen, Nuttall and Tyers, and none of the other nations had any known swimmers capable of extending them. . . . The kick of the improved stroke which these swimmers used was a marvellous screw like the leg kick [scissors kick]

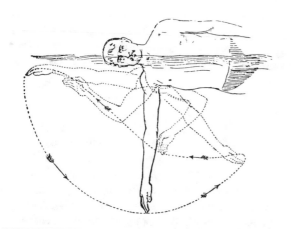

Figure 1.5 Early chart showing the mechanics of the sidestroke (Sinclair & Henry, 1908, p. 81).

which also gained for J.A. Jarvis such marked supremacy in England. (p. 83)

J.A. Jarvis won many English championships with the use of what came to be known as the "Jarvis kick." Jarvis was the "first to discover that certain movements of the feet themselves were of definite assistance in giving power to the English side-overarm stroke and of improving its speed" (Sachs, 1912, pp. 139-140). H.D. Faith of the Otter Club (Sachs, 1912) describes Jarvis's kick in a small brochure entitled *The Over-Arm Side Stroke*:

> The swinging forward of the top leg makes the water around the leg wash forward in the direction the leg is swinging. In the case of the under leg a back wash is created. As the legs are whipped together the top leg, coming back, meets and grips the water which is still being washed forward, and the under leg, coming forward, meets the wash going backward, the screw-like action of the legs giving a continuous grip of the water and making the stroke a continuation of screw and wedge. (p. 140)

Faith's description indicates how advanced the skill of lucid stroke analysis had become. Perhaps of even greater interest is that Faith gives one of the few references to the flow reactions of the water that exist in the historical literature.

The adoption of the English overarm sidestroke showed awareness of the importance of decreasing resistance in proportion to propulsion. The emphasis on the leg action was carried over from breaststroke swimming, and the indications are that, at this stage, a full appreciation of the arms' potential for propulsion still did not exist. Nor did there appear to be much concern about developing a more continuous mode of progression, other than the fact that sidestroke swimmers were inclined to insert an extra tiny wedge (Jarvis) or flutter kick (Nuttall) into the closing phase of their leg actions.

William Wilson, in his classic work, *The Swimming Instructor* (1883), describes the method of the improved English overarm sidestroke (see Figure 1.6). The stroke's popularity was apparent:

> Quite a number of swimmers lay claim to having been the first to use this means of moving through the yielding element. Harry Gurr, the "Pocket Hercules," as he was termed on account of his short stat-

ure, healthy red skin, fair hair and neat physique, and Harry Gardner, now of Woolwich, were the first who, by means of lifting one hand out of the water, carrying it in the air beyond the head, won any races of importance; and these clever exponents of the art deserve every praise for their efforts and perseverance in introducing what was, at one time, looked upon as a style peculiar to, and only used by themselves.

Soon, however, after these swimmers had pulled off several important prizes, it appeared evident to those who adhered to the sidestroke that there was more in the innovation than was first apparent; and, after repeated trials and private rehearsals, those who had at one time laughed at the new movement considered it not beneath their dignity to follow in the wake of the swimmers just named, and adopt the over-hand motions.

W. Woodridge, the swimming-master of the Victoria Park Lake, was, we think, the first teacher of this mode of swimming, and to him is due a large meed of praise for his efforts in this direction. (pp. 51-52)

However, Carlile (1963) attributes the origin of the single overarm sidestroke to an Austra-lian, C.W. Wallis, who had seen it swum by aborigines in the Lane Cove River near Sydney. Carlile claims that Wallis demonstrated the stroke to "Professor" Fred Beckwith during a visit to London in 1855 and that Beckwith used it to become champion of England in 1859. Beckwith then taught it to Gardner, who succeeded Beckwith to the English championship in the following year.

The Development of Double Overarm Swimming

On August 11, 1873, John Trudgen startled spectators by winning the English 160-yard handicap with a most unusual stroke: He remained flat on his chest and alternately swung *each* arm forward over the water, making one breaststroke kick in the horizontal plane with each arm cycle. Trudgen swam with his head high and clear of the water, and his body lifted with each breaststroke kick, causing his progress to be marked by a series of jerky leaps (Carlile, 1963).

It has been said (Thomas, 1904) that this stroke, or one like it, was swum by the Assyrians over 2,000 years ago, although when Trudgen first used it in England he caused quite a stir. According to R.P. Watson, whose memoirs Sachs quotes:

Trudgen made his first appearance in a handicap which was framed by myself, and created quite a sensation. It was then the stroke was fathered on him, but as far back as September 8th, 1859, W. Payton, in a breaststroke race at the Lambeth Baths, swam this stroke and was disqualified. We have seen no man (I am referring of course, to his stroke) in this country equal to Trudgen.

After he won his first handicap at Lambeth and subsequently beat the record for 108 yards at the City of London Baths, Golden Lane (William Cole at the time was 100 yards amateur champion and record holder), I interviewed him with respect to his antecedents and style of swimming. He was surprised on being told that the performance at Lambeth was regarded by good swimmers as somewhat remarkable. Trudgen smiled and remarked, "There are plenty of men can beat me where I've come from" (West Indies). (Sachs, 1912, pp. 144-145)

Figure 1.6 The English overarm sidestroke (Wilson, 1883, p. 53).

Streamlining the Body

Probably as a result of Trudgen's influence, there followed considerable experimentation with double overarm swimming. Many swimmers still wished to remain on their sides, however, because they feared that swimming in a flat position on the chest would cause too much frontal resistance, so they developed a stroke in which they turned from side to side to enable the alternate recovery of each arm.

Up to this stage swimmers had attempted to improve their streamlining mainly by keeping the body on its side and reducing the resistance caused by the leg recovery movement between each propulsive thrust. To eliminate the retarding effect of drawing the legs up preparatory to each sideward kick, they experimented with a variety of kicking methods. A narrower action with legs held straighter gradually evolved from the previously described Jarvis kick. The body was held in a straight line as the kick was made. One side of the face was submerged, and the body was turned slightly on its back so that the mouth and nostrils were free and the top of the head cleaved the water.

Breathing Technique

The breathing technique used in the single overarm sidestroke differed from present methods: The swimmer inhaled through the nostrils while one arm was recovered from the water and exhaled through the mouth while that arm was pulling. The face remained out of the water throughout the action to keep the body on its side.

Up to this time there was no mention of a controlled underwater breathing technique. One can only guess how this important aspect of swimming technique evolved. Perhaps, as often happens, it was by chance; as a double overarm sidestroke swimmer was moving from one side to the other, someone may have noticed bubbles escaping from the mouth while the face was submerged. Of course, the next step would have been to work this into a regular rhythm with face-out-of-water inhalation followed by exhalation as the face submerged.

Double Overarm Sidestroke

The sporadic propulsion of the trudgen stroke, as it came to be called, proved very strenuous, so swimmers sought a modified version of it that would permit them to swim on their sides, and not the chest, if only for part of the stroke

cycle. They replaced the breaststroke kick of the trudgen with a side scissor kick. Because of the constant change in body position and the consequent lack of continuity, the stroke was not very successful. History shows the double overarm sidestroke to have been a cul-de-sac in the development of swimming.

The influence of the dominant leg kick of traditional breaststroke was hard to shake off. As a result, the pioneers were slow to appreciate the potential power of the arms. Sachs (1912) describes how the double overarm stroke was taught:

> The arm strokes remain of secondary value, but they are much more prominent as creators of speed than was formerly the case. The first step towards the double overarm stroke was made in the attempt to lengthen the stretch of the upper arm by bringing the shoulder forward, and the result of doing this was to bring the under arm up, and, not infrequently, this right hand came out of the water when it was forced forward.
>
> It will be noted that the body was first brought over on to the breast to give the left arm full play, and then rolled back on to the side again in order to finish the under-arm stroke and to get in the leg work of the side stroke.
>
> In the double overarm stroke the left arm is brought as far forward as it will go—the head being immersed and even turned slightly on to its left side in order to give the arm full stretch; as the left arm is pulled back towards the body this tendency towards turning on the left side will be increased, and the right arm has thus the opportunity of coming clear of the water. The arm is then stretched ahead as far as possible, and the body rolls back on its right side again. It is necessary to observe here that this roll is very slight indeed, and is confined to the head and shoulders; it is mentioned only to assure those who try this stroke that they cannot do without it even to a modified extent. (pp. 142-143)

This reference to the amount of roll being very slight is significant. The fear of rolling was to be carried right through into the 1950s, when the Australians finally debunked the old theory with their teams of world-record-breaking swimmers, who all used pronounced shoulder *and* body roll. Until then, entire generations of swimmers had swum with shoulder girdle muscles held tense and inhibited as they attempted to follow the prescribed flat body position so rigidly advocated by many authorities.

The Arrival of the Crawl Stroke

The turning point in the development of the crawl stroke came when Dick Cavill, a member of the famous Australian swimming family, realized that the side scissor kick actually *retarded* continuous propulsion. The probable sequence of events, as reconstructed by historians, was as follows: According to Carlile (1963), Fred Cavill, an Englishman, came to Australia in 1879 and started a swimming bath at Lavender Bay in Sydney harbor. Fred Cavill had six sons, three of whom, Syd, Arthur ("Tums"), and Dick, played an important part in the crawl's development. Syd Cavill (cited in Carlile, 1963, p. 133) wrote in the *Sydney Referee* in 1914 that, while on a visit to Apia in Samoa, he raced a woman swimmer who gave him the hardest race of his life. Syd noted with amazement that she swam an overarm stroke but did not kick at all. He watched her intently and then tied his legs to find that he could swim as quickly with his legs tied as he could with his legs free using any other stroke. Then he wrote home and told Tums about it. The rest is history. Sullivan (1927) relates the story:

> The original crawl stroke was evolved in Australia, hence the name Australian crawl stroke. As related by L. de B. Handley, one of America's foremost authorities on swimming, the stroke was originated as follows:
>
> Tums Cavill, a member of the world-famous family of swimmers, was matched to meet Syd Davis over 33 yards, with the legs tied, and beat him, only to be defeated later by the same man at the same distance, after the legs were untied.
>
> Dick Cavill was present and refused to believe what he saw, but a few private time trials convinced him that his brother could really sprint faster without the use of his legs, and this started him to thinking. He reasoned that every ounce of power properly applied must resolve into an increase in speed, so that the "scissors" kick must be radically wrong. The question was to find the right kick.
>
> Then he remembered having seen Alick Wickham, a fast young Rubiana sprinter,

use an odd straight-legged kick, which he had learned from the natives at Colombo, Ceylon, and decided to experiment with it. The result surprised him, as the kick proved speedy from the very first trial.

> Unluckily, the difficulty of finding an arm action that would harmonize bothered him considerably and by the time Dick Cavill found it, the 100 yards championship was only a few days off. He entered, however, anxious to give his find a public trial. Those who followed swimming at the time may remember the race. Starting out at a terrific pace, Cavill reached the 50 yards mark fully five yards ahead of his nearest competitor. But here the imperfectly mastered stroke began to tell upon him and he was passed by the speedy Bishop. Notwithstanding the defeat, this performance gave the coaches an estimate of the value of the new stroke (the peculiar action of which won for it the title of the crawl) and they took it up immediately, forming classes to teach it. Their success was marvellous. Men who had been but indifferent swimmers came to the fore, good men improved, and soon the world was ringing with the news of the "crawlers." Al Wickham at Rubiana swam 50 yards in 24 seconds with it; and then Dick Cavill went his phenomenal 100 yards in 58 seconds. The stroke soon invaded Europe and eventually it reached America, where it was taken up in 1904. (pp. 37-38)

Reactions to the Early Crawl Stroke

It should not be thought that the crawl, the new wonder stroke, was accepted everywhere with acclaim. To the contrary, there were some who thought it inelegant and others who regarded it as very tiring. Few swimmers could use it to complete the 100-yard racing distance. The first swimmers to use the crawl were mainly those who had grown up doing the trudgen stroke. They swam trudgen for most of the distance and switched to the crawl only for a spectacular grandstand finish.

Poor arm-stroke mechanics and ignorance of a breathing technique suited to the welter of rapidly spinning arms caused premature fatigue. The early crawl swimmers bore little resemblance to the polished technicians of modern swimming. They burrowed their heads in the water, mouths shut tight and lungs starved for air, and let their arms fly round and round in a flurry of wild splashing while their feet flailed out of the water.

There were those who regretted that elegance was no longer considered in the development of new swimming strokes (Sachs, 1912). Still others, although acknowledging the new crawl strokes to be much faster than any techniques they had hitherto known, lamented that no sort of success had been obtained in welding speed and elegance.

An important point that the first crawl swimmers were quick to notice was that the stroke was very flexible and open to all sorts of variations.

> The characteristics and powers of thought that individuals draft into the stroke impart the continuous charm of variety, and it is now generally agreed that the best stroke is the one that gets one home first. I read somewhere that it was considered incorrect to splash when executing the proper (it must have been very proper!) sidestroke, and I am wondering what its inventor would say today of the double over-arm and the crawl racers. Elegant?—No. Speedy?—Yes. Personally, I think that the splash and flurry that accompany the man who swims 100 yards in less than a minute are far more exhilarating than the undoubted attractions of a stately and polished sidestroke. (Sachs, 1912, pp. 143-144)

Coaches began to realize the need to increase the efficiency of the crawl so that it could be used for covering longer distances with greater economy of effort. According to Handley (1914), Some eight or nine years ago, Frank Sullivan, one of Chicago's leading instructors, conceived the idea of combining the crawl with some of the features of the trudgen and making it useful for distances greater than 100 yards'' (p. 99). Sullivan's (1927) trudgen-crawl (see Figure 1.7) was

> characterized by the interjection of a small straight legged ''scissors'' kick with a spread of not more than 20 inches on the pull down of the breathing (side) arm, while a comparatively slower up-and-down thresh is maintained between the ''scissors,'' or major drive, and a roll of the body is made as in the double overarm. (p. 40)

Sullivan developed three notable champions who used this style of swimming: Harry Hebner, Perry McGillvray, and Richard Frizelle (Cureton, 1934, p. 98). However, as late as 1926, despite the successes of his swimmers who used this variant of the crawl stroke, Sullivan (1927) did not advocate teaching the crawl as the first stroke to beginners:

> I maintain that the person who is taught the crawl first, becomes a mere navigator or, to be more explicit, one who is able to move from one place to another in the water with no recognized correct form, and remains a navigator longer than the person

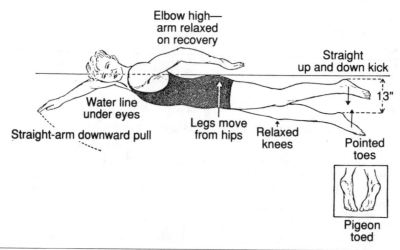

Figure 1.7   The American crawl—the beginnings of stroke analysis (Sullivan, 1927, p. 42).

who progresses in the natural sequence of strokes, i.e., from the underarm side stroke to the single overarm, double overarm and then the crawl. (p. 36).

The Bandwagon Effect. Despite the assertion that the early crawl stroke was a technique open to variations and individual interpretation, what I call "the bandwagon effect" soon took over. The new stroke developed along a precise technique; the crawl was regarded as a "surface stroke in which the feet came out of the water with the main function of maintaining the balance of the body and keeping it well out of the water" (Sachs, 1912, p.146).

Although the crawl action was thought to be very simple, strong emphasis was laid on synchronizing the kick with the arm stroke. Modern swimmers allow their legs to work in a natural cadence, independent of their arms, but in those early years, this forced timing must have limited the success of many a talented swimmer.

Next, perhaps subconsciously inspired by the then-recent invention of the motorized hydroplane, came the idea that by increasing the number of leg beats for each arm cycle, a swimmer could actually "hydroplane" on the water! Hydroplaning becomes possible only when a craft is moving quickly enough to allow the bow wave to come under the boat; nevertheless, the enthusiasm for this brainstorm caused swimmers to try for an ever-increasing number of leg beats to each arm stroke. This era of swimming "development" must have caused many talented swimmers to fall far short of their real potential.

Trial and Error With the Crawl Stroke

Soon after the crawl arrived, swimming entered an era of intense technical analysis and experimentation. During this time, swimming not only proceeded down dead ends but also failed to continue to develop some potentially valuable ideas; the gold was there but thrown away, only to be retrieved by others many years later.

This era also saw the arrival of the synthesist, the person who gathers information, sorts it out, and files it away in neat pigeonholes, ready for future use as needed. A synthesist often will study what has gone before and produce an innovative idea. Fortunately, competitive swimming has had many innovative thinkers.

The Theory Behind the Early Crawl Stroke

One of the first clear descriptions of crawl stroke fundamentals was made by James H. Sterrett, a successful amateur swimming coach in the early 20th century, who is said to have organized the first swimming club in America and was involved in Amateur Athletic Union affairs for many years. Although practically unknown to most people in the modern swimming community, no less a personage than Louis de B. Handley, in the foreword to Sterrett's *How to Swim* (1917), described Sterrett as

among the pioneers of swimming in this country. He was called the "Father of American Swimming" when I entered the field of swimming 20 years ago. Sterrett's prolific pen, too, has done much to spread knowledge of developments. It was in one of his books that I read the first technical discussion of the principles of aquatic progression ever come to my notice, and his numerous articles on all branches of watermanship have ever held interest for me. (p. 3)

In 1917 Sterrett wrote of the crawl stroke:

The crawl stroke is undoubtedly the greatest stroke that has ever been invented or discovered in connection with swimming, and until its adoption and subsequent improvement by experimenting with it until it was brought up to a high point of efficiency, the swimmers of the world had practically reached their limits of speed performances, having perfected the other strokes beyond further improvement, and thus it was that they were eager to take up the new-found method by which it has been discovered that a person can go still faster through the water.

The whole thing is a matter of eliminating resistance, or minimizing the negative parts of the stroke and getting a maximum of positive action; or, in other words, doing the same thing as has been done in many other things to produce greater speed—applying the maximum of power while at the same time reducing resistance to the minimum.

The crawl stroke originated in Australia, and Dick Cavill, one of the members of the famous family of expert swimmers, and one of the best all-around swimmers the author has ever seen, told the writer that his brother ''Tums,'' in an argument with another swimmer as to their relative ability, said he could tie his feet together and then beat the other chap for a length of the pool, and when the contest came off he made good his boast.

''Tums'' Cavill always argued that the legs were not of much use to him in fast swimming, and he believed that they hindered other swimmers when going at top speed, because in drawing them up and separating them they stopped the run on the stroke, and he at once started experimenting on this theory, with the result that a new stroke was developed and launched on the natatorial world and at once became popular, until now it is used by all the fast swimmers of the world. (pp. 20-21)

The Beginnings of Detailed Stroke Analysis

Gradually, the analysts reasoned out improved techniques. The disadvantages under which they worked should be understood. They had to start from scratch to find the best way to apply each phase of the stroke. They had to find answers to the many puzzling questions that confronted them at that early stage of crawl development.

For the first half of the 20th century, swimmers and coaches experimented with all kinds of different notions. Many ideas that initially seemed promising ended in frustration and limited progress. With the benefit of retrospect,

we may smile at these futile efforts, yet we nearly always pass through a phase of confused thinking before we reach enlightenment.

Here are a few examples of abandoned crawl techniques: the dropped elbow entry, the straight arm pull, the wide arm pull, the straight backward arm pull, the overlapping arm stroke with ''downhill swimming'' combined with a quick flip arm recovery and deep ''bicycle pedal'' kick, ''hydroplaning,'' ultraflat body position, the bent knee kick, increased frequency of leg beats, and on and on.

Key Questions on Stroke Fundamentals

Research of the literature shows the following to have been the main questions asked during the development of the swimming strokes:

1. Where and how should the hand(s) enter the water?
2. Should the arm(s) be bent or straight during the pull?
3. What should be the path of the arm(s) during the pull?
4. Should the stroke be long and slow or short and fast?
5. How should the arm(s) be brought forward to start the next stroke?
6. What should be the timing of one arm in relation to the other?
7. What should be the timing of the legs in relation to the arms?

Thanks to trial and error and research in biomechanics, we can now answer these questions with far greater certainty. These are discussed in detail in chapter 2, which deals with the fundamentals of the four styles of swimming. Figure 1.8 shows how these styles developed from the breaststroke.

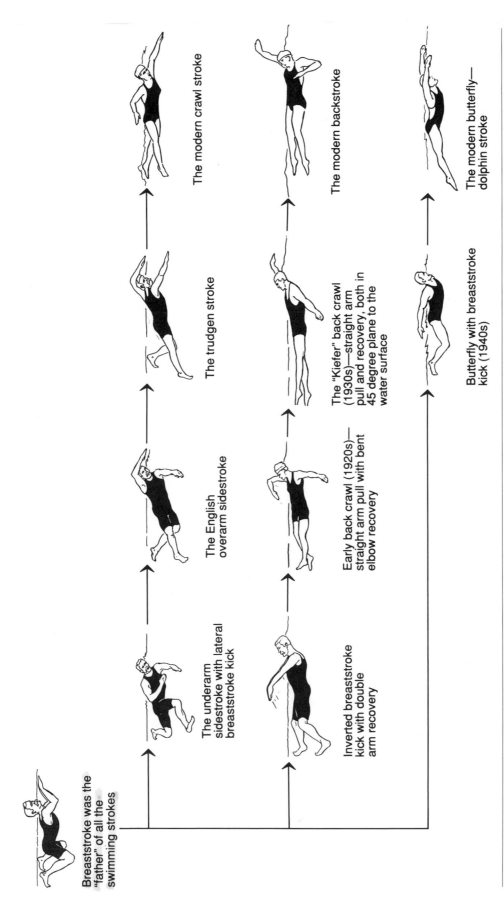

Figure 1.8   The evolution of the swimming strokes.

Chapter 2

Principles of Stroke Mechanics

A swimmer starting a swimming stroke has a *momentum* through the water as a result of a dive or a push-off. It is nevertheless not uncommon for a novice coach to tell a swimmer to enter the hand in the water and pull the body forward, even though the body is already in motion. Most descriptions of swimming strokes fail to note the important aspect of momentum.

The aim of efficient swimming is to keep momentum as constant as possible. The phrase ''as constant as possible'' is used advisedly, for there is no such state as constant momentum in swimming. When a swimmer exerts a *force* on the water, thus causing the body to *accelerate*, the reacting frictional *resistance* of the water very soon causes *deceleration*.

Within each stroke cycle a skilled swimmer applies a series of *force impulses*. The force exerted by each impulse causes the swimmer's *mass* to accelerate, thus increasing its *velocity*. The challenge to the swimmer is to time each application of force so as to avoid extreme fluctuations of velocity.

Throughout a stroke cycle a skilled swimmer continuously adjusts body position to attain optimal streamlining. Precise timing of each propulsive impulse combined with good streamlining will improve a swimmer's propulsion-to-resistance ratio. The greater the momentum, the faster the swimmer; the more efficient the swimmer, the lower the energy demands on the body.

Important Contributions of Research in Biomechanics

So far, there has been little reference to actual stroke technique. The preceding description instead outlines the basic physical principles that apply to efficient swimming. How to apply mechanical principles to swimming became apparent only after years of experimentation. The mechanics of the swimming strokes evolved as a result of trying to translate these principles into efficient technique.

At the end of chapter 1, I listed seven questions continually asked about swimming technique. Finding the answers to these questions wasn't easy, and progress faltered repeatedly until James Counsilman and other researchers inspired by his example started to investigate the many puzzling aspects of swimming technique.

Big advances in knowledge—and consequently in stroke efficiency—resulted from applying the laws of physics to the problems outlined in chapter 1. Biomechanics applies the laws governing all forms of motion to the human body. These laws deal with forces and their resultant motions. The laws concerned with the motion of bodies are commonly divided into two branches: *kinematics* and *kinetics*. Kinematics deals with aspects of the *motions of* bodies, such as speed, velocity, and acceleration, without reference to what causes them.

Kinetics is concerned with the *effects* that forces have on these motions.

At the beginning of this chapter I outlined some of the physical laws affecting swimming propulsion and highlighted their relevant terms. Students of stroke mechanics ought to be acquainted with those terms that enable understanding of research in biomechanics, and coaches ought to know which areas of stroke mechanics can be improved by new knowledge so they can better decide whether any particular biomechanical research has the potential for useful practical application. This chapter contains discussions of significant research in biomechanics and shows how these important findings can be applied by a coach working with a swimmer in the pool.

The Pattern of the Pull

In all the swimming strokes, the correct pulling pattern should follow a curved path across a line describing the body's forward motion (Figure 2.1). For a long time, however, this method was considered a serious defect, a dreaded fault commonly known as "feathering" or "weaving."

Figure 2.1 Correct pulling pattern. The hand follows a curved line across a path describing the body's forward motion.

Swimmers were erroneously taught to move the hand straight backward like a paddle, and the amount of elbow bend was adjusted continuously to achieve this (Figure 2.2a and b). The

pull-through of the arm from start to finish was fairly straight, with only a slight inward direction. The prevailing thought was that any lateral movement inward or outward cut down the efficiency of the backward push against the water, which was believed to be the stroke's power source (Kiphuth, 1942).

The technique, known as the "action-reaction" theory, is based on Newton's third law of motion: "To every action there is an equal and opposite reaction." This method, now known to be inefficient, was probably used for nearly 20 years. Until 1969 there were few coaches not guilty of teaching it. Instead of allowing swimmers to follow their natural inclination to pull in a weaving or curved-line path, they were more often than not coached in the approved straight-line "action-reaction" paddling mode.

The Camera as a Scientific Instrument

The first breakthrough came when Counsilman perfected the use of the camera as a scientific instrument for analyzing swimming techniques. He attached a flashing light to the middle of the swimmer's hand (third fingertip) that flashed 20 times per second. The light was attached to a battery carried in a (money) belt worn around the swimmer's hips. The swimmer swam in complete darkness in front of an underwater window where Counsilman had mounted a still (not motion) camera on a tripod. The camera shutter was left open. At the halfway point during each swim Counsilman flashed a strobe light and made a single picture to see where the swimmer's hand was at a given point. He then extrapolated where the swimmer's hand was at other points. Because the shutter was open during the entire swim, Counsilman obtained a picture of the flashing light before and after the strobe was fired. Counsilman's observations, published in *Swimming World* (Counsilman, 1969), marked an important turning point in the understanding of swimming technique (Figure 2.3a-g).

The Curved Path of the Pull

Counsilman's study showed that, in all the swimming strokes, the pull does not follow a straight line but is composed of short sculling motions, or impulses, that change direction as the hand moves in a *curved path* across the line of the swimmer's forward movement. Nowhere was this curved-line hand movement

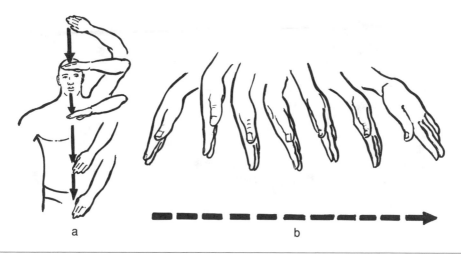

Figure 2.2 Hand incorrectly pulling straight backward like a paddle: (a) underneath view and (b) side view.

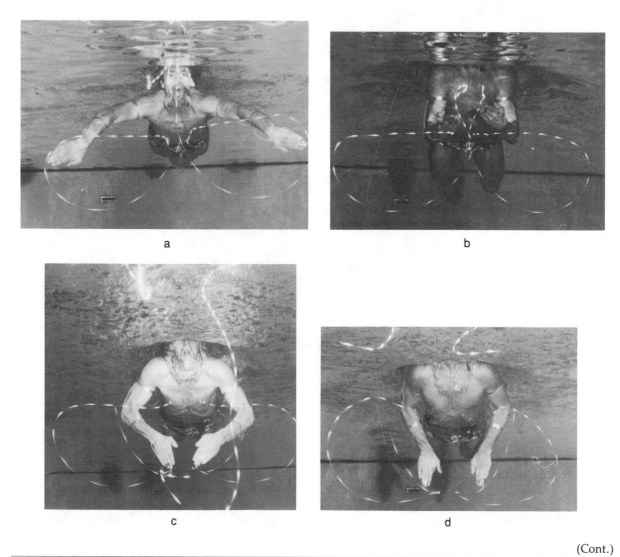

(Cont.)

Figure 2.3 Counsilman's historic strobe light photographs that showed, for the first time, the true nature of human swimming propulsion: (a, b) breaststroke arm pull (front view); (c, d) butterfly arm pull (front view); (e, f) crawl stroke (side view); and (g) two-beat crossover kick. *Note.* Reprinted by permission of James E. Counsilman.

e

f

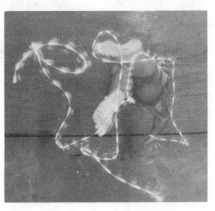

g

Figure 2.3   (Continued)

more obvious than in the typical hourglass pattern of the butterfly stroke. In fact, it was probably observation of this familiar pattern that initially prompted Counsilman to question the validity of the straight-line pull hitherto so fervently recommended (Figure 2.4).

The Role of Lift in Swimming Propulsion

Counsilman's paper on the role of sculling movements in the arm pull showed stroke me-

chanics in a completely new light, but despite the evidence of these unique studies, many authorities were reluctant to discard their notion of the straight-line pull. (It is a sad commentary on human nature that generally we do not accept change gladly.) Most coaches had long taught swimmers to pull straight backward and they continued to do so. Some even claimed that the observed sculling action was the result of trying to keep the propelling surfaces of hand and forearm planing directly backward. Others, of a more open and enquiring mind, thought to ask, ''If the pull is not a straight-

Figure 2.4 The curvilinear path of the hands is very obvious in the typical "hourglass" pulling pattern of the butterfly stroke.

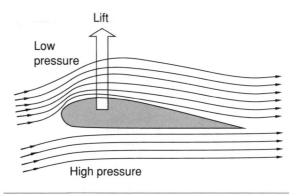

Figure 2.5 The difference in pressure between the low-pressure and high-pressure streams creates a lift force.

line paddling action, how does a swimmer go *forward* by pulling in a *curved* line?''

Counsilman had already discovered the answer to this question, but he bided his time before he presented it. As he told me in 1984, he had wanted the concept of propelling by means of sculling movements to be understood and accepted in practice first, thus laying the foundation for acceptance of his "lift theory" of propulsion as expressed in a paper presented jointly with Ronald M. Brown, "The Role of Lift in Propelling the Swimmer" (Counsilman & Brown, 1970). A year later, at the First International Symposium on the Biomechanics of Swimming, in Brussels, Counsilman elaborated on the theme with his landmark presentation, "The Application of Bernoulli's Principle to Human Propulsion in Water" (Counsilman, 1971).

The Bernoulli Effect

Counsilman's paper showed that efficient swimming relies on a natural law relating the speed at which a fluid moves and the pressure it creates. Formulated by the Swiss mathematician Daniel Bernoulli (1700-1782) over 200 years ago and known as the Bernoulli principle, this law states that as the velocity of a fluid increases, the pressure it exerts decreases.

When a stream of fluid passes around a foil—such as a swimmer's hand—the flow over the convex upper surface has a greater velocity and, following Bernoulli's principle, a lower pressure than that on the under surface; the difference in pressure between the two streams creates a force called "lift" (Figure 2.5).

The Lift Principle

Lift, also known as *side thrust*, always acts in a direction perpendicular to the direction of mo-

tion. In the case of an airplane wing in level flight, lift is directed upward at a right angle to the direction of motion (Figure 2.6).

A propeller is like a wing in that it also generates lift, but the lift, acting at right angles to the blade's motion, is directed forward (Figure 2.7).

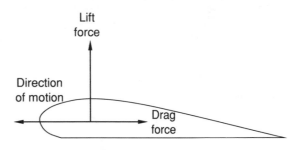

Figure 2.6 Lift always acts in a direction perpendicular to the direction of motion.

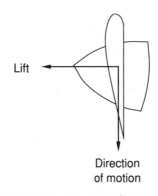

Figure 2.7 A propeller is like a wing and also generates a lift.

Counsilman's presentation revealed for the first time that a swimmer's hand moving in a curved-line path across the line of the body's motion also produces forward lift (Figure 2.8).

Basically, the swimmer uses the resistance provided by the resulting lift to apply thrust.

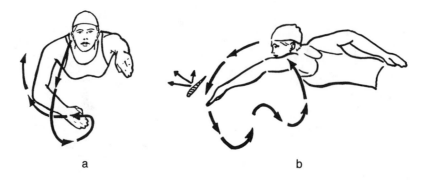

a   b

Figure 2.8 A swimmer's hand moves in a curvilinear path to produce forward lift: (a) front and (b) side views.

The action can be likened to walking up a sandy slope, every step upward pushing the sand downward. Both examples obey Newton's third law of motion.

The action-reaction principle mentioned earlier in the description of the straight-line pull still applies, but in the case of lift propulsion the reaction is created by a different mechanism. Instead of pushing directly backward in a straight line with the *palm* of the hand, the hand moves in a curved path, splitting the water with the *edge* of the hand to create a pressure resistance against which thrust is applied (Figure 2.9).

Figure 2.10 The pitch of the hand is continuously adjusted to achieve maximum lift propulsion.

adjusted to achieve the maximum lift propulsion (Figure 2.10).

The Lift Versus Drag Argument

Counsilman's research was of great significance, causing a complete revision in the previous, comparatively sketchy, thinking on human swimming propulsion. He summarized his findings by pointing out that swimmers have two choices: they can propel by pulling straight backward, using what is known as ''*drag* force'' or by moving the hand backward in a curved-line path to create a *lift* force. Counsilman argued not only that champion swimmers propel mainly by means of lift force but that using lift force is more efficient and economical.

Counsilman's work on sculling and lift-force propulsion marked the first valuable contribution to the infant science of swimming biomechanics. Nevertheless, opinion polarized between the proponents of drag and those who

Figure 2.9 Lift propulsion is created by the hand moving in a curvilinear path (underneath view).

Counsilman's findings established a new approach to swimming efficiency in all the strokes. The hand should not be pulled directly backward in a straight line (paddling) but should follow a curvilinear path (sculling) during which the angle of the hand (pitch) relative to the body's motion should be continuously

advocated the lift theory of propulsion. Particularly in North America, biomechanists and swimming coaches alike were now in disarray. Counsilman's pronouncements had dropped like the proverbial bombshell to shake them from slumber. The supporters of the lift theory of propulsion were in the majority from the start, however, because of the clarity and weight of Counsilman's argument and the extent of his already considerable reputation.

Not all were taken up in the lift versus drag argument, though; as always, there were those who showed no interest at all. To this day, there remain coaches who give little or no thought to the science behind the stroke mechanics they teach. Indeed, there are international coaches who have never heard of the Bernoulli effect or its implications for efficient swimming propulsion.

The Interaction of Lift and Drag Forces

The publication of Counsilman's work on lift propulsion prompted several investigations that sought to analyze the forces produced in human swimming propulsion. Among these, the research findings of Robert Schleihauf (1974, 1977, 1979) were important contributions to the knowledge of swimming propulsion.

Schleihauf, a swimming coach and also a qualified engineer, brought unique skills to the most comprehensive analysis of stroke mechanics to date. The results of his studies show that human swimming propulsion results from neither lift nor drag forces acting in isolation but that there is a constant interaction between the two throughout the changing sequences of a swimming stroke.

Schleihauf set about his research methodically. His first step was to make an exact plastic resin replica of a hand, which he then suspended in a flow channel through which fluid moved at a known speed. The hand was mounted on a rod that measured the total range of forces, both lift and drag, produced by the hand in varying flow conditions and at different angles of pitch.

Lift Coefficient. Schleihauf then compared the lifting characteristics of the hand with the characteristics of a commonly used airfoil of similar profile (N.A.C.A. airfoil 0012). He found that the hand's maximum *lift coefficient* was 20% less than the wing's but attributed this minor difference to the hand's slightly more irregular shape.

The term "lift coefficient" refers to the relationship between the amount of lift on an airfoil and its angle of pitch. The lift component, or amount of lift on an airfoil or human hand, increases or decreases relative to the size of the angle of pitch. According to Schleihauf, the lift coefficient on a swimmer's hand increases up to an angle of pitch (also known as angle of attack) of about 40 degrees and then decreases (Figure 2.11).

Drag Coefficient. Similarly, the term "drag coefficient" refers to the relationship between the drag component on an airfoil or hand and its angle of attack. The drag coefficient also increases or decreases in relation to the size of the angle of attack. Schleihauf's measurements show that the drag coefficient on a swimmer's hand increases as the angle of attack increases to 90 degrees. With a diminishing angle of attack, the drag coefficient decreases.

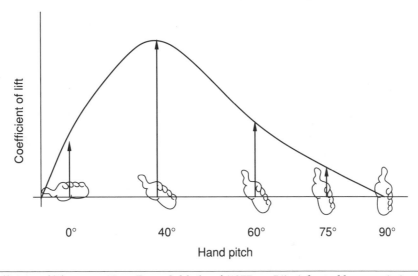

Figure 2.11 Coefficient of lift curve. *Note.* From Schleihauf (1977, p. 51). Adapted by permission.

Schleihauf points out that swimmers propel *at all times* by using a *combination* of lift and drag forces. The type of force developed depends on the hand's angle of attack during any particular phase of the swimming stroke. At an angle of attack less than 45 degrees a swimmer's hand produces predominantly lift-force propulsion; there is an almost equal contribution of lift and drag forces at an angle of approximately 45 degrees; and drag forces predominate when the hand reaches angles greater than 45 degrees (Figure 2.12a-c).

swimming. Schleihauf then combined the data collected from his film studies of leading swimmers with the information obtained in the fluid laboratory.

Schleihauf determined the direction and magnitude of the lift and drag forces created by the hands at key points in the stroke. Using vector analysis on this information he estimated the instantaneous direction and magnitude of the *resultant* propulsive force, that is, the net effect of the interaction between the lift and drag forces. Schleihauf then measured the resultant forces developed during the stroke at selected angles of hand pitch. His work set the scene for the first comprehensive analysis of stroke mechanics (Figure 2.13a-c).

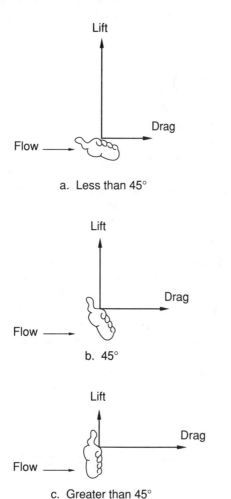

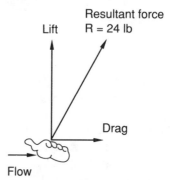

a. Pitch equals 20°, velocity equals 17.0 fps

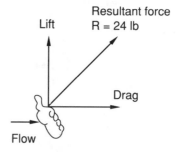

b. Pitch equals 45°, velocity equals 11.2 fps

Figure 2.12 Lift-drag interaction. *Note.* From Schleihauf (1977, p. 53). Adapted by permission.

Determining the Resultant Propulsive Force. The next stage of Schleihauf's studies involved filming champion swimmers from directly below and at right angles to their forward direction. Before doing so he placed four small lights on each hand, which enabled him to determine the hands' paths as well as their changing speeds and angles of attack in all four styles of

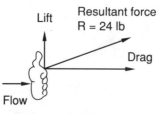

c. Pitch equals 90°, velocity equals 10.0 fps

Figure 2.13 Resultant force production. *Note.* From Schleihauf (1977, p. 53). Adapted by permission.

Counsilman and Schleihauf Revolutionize the Knowledge of Swimming Mechanics

Schleihauf showed that swimmers obtain propulsion from a combination of lift and drag forces and that lift and drag forces each dominate during different phases of the strokes. The angles reached by the hands in the various strokes indicate that lift forces generally dominate drag forces; in fact, in breaststroke swimming lift force predominates throughout the stroke.

Schleihauf's experimental studies (1974, 1977, 1979) provide a reliable method for measuring the propulsive force distributions within a stroke cycle. His conscientious investigations also confirm Counsilman's findings. Within a few years these two men had revolutionized the scientific investigation of swimming mechanics. Swimming knowledge had achieved a sophistication (see Figure 2.14a-c on p. 28) unimaginable to the ''swimming professors'' who once had held sway around the seawater pools of Sydney harbor or to the ''swimming masters'' who had frequented the bath houses of industrial England.

Developing a New Perspective of Stroke Mechanics

Counsilman's discovery and Schleihauf's subsequent painstaking work in expanding on it caused nearly everybody—scientists, coaches, and swimmers—to revise their thinking on practically every aspect of swimming propulsion. Many studies followed supporting Counsilman's papers on the Bernoulli principle and lift-force propulsion in swimming (Barthels, 1979, 1981; Barthels & Adrian, 1975; Hay, 1973; Persyn, 1978; Rackham, 1975; Reischle, 1979; Ungerechts, 1979; Wood, 1979).

Suddenly, the entire perspective had changed. Coaches as well as swimmers now had to consider many new factors involved in efficient propulsion. It soon became apparent that there was a difference in the reference points from which coaches and biomechanists perceived swimming strokes.

Different Reference Points

A biomechanist's camera in a fixed position records a swimmer's torso moving past the arm: *the fixed viewpoint* (Figure 2.15a). A coach standing on the pool deck demonstrates the stroke to a swimmer from a reference point of the arm moving past the torso: *the moving viewpoint* (Figure 2.15b). Both reference points serve a definite need. Although the moving viewpoint has more meaning to a beginner learning the path of the stroke, the fixed viewpoint is of greater procedural value to the biomechanist.

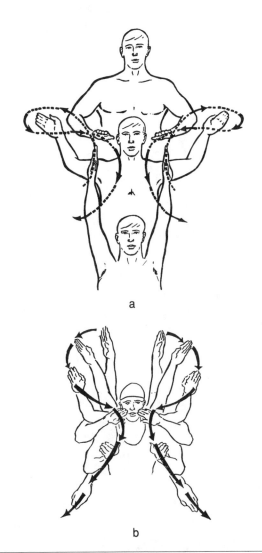

Figure 2.15 (a) The fixed viewpoint (butterfly stroke): torso moving past the arms. (b) The moving viewpoint (butterfly stroke): the arms moving past the torso.

The Three-Dimensional Aspect of the Pull

Further complicating the new perspective was the realization that not only does the hand propel by means of sculling motions in a curvilinear path but this path is also three-dimensional (Figure 2.16). The hand moves simultaneously

An instant in the midportion of the bottom-view pulling data is given (a). The lift (L), drag (D), and resultant (R) hand force vectors are indicated in the illustration. (Magnitude is shown in Newtons.) In addition, the hand speed (V) is shown in meters per second, and the hand pitch (AP) is shown in degrees. Note that three-dimensional force vector data are illustrated, and forces not entirely contained in the plane of the paper appear foreshortened. For example, the L vector is aimed both forward and upward (into the page for a bottom-view illustration), and its length is foreshortened. The hand force produced at a given instant may be compared to the remaining forces produced in the pull by reference to the hand force versus time curve (c). Note that the R force in (a) is shown as the first highlighted bar (marked ''A'') in (c). The hand force curve shows both the total hand force produced, and the effective hand force (RE). For Gaines, the hand force production is small in the beginning and the middle of the pull and greatly increases during the last one third of the pull. The side view of the instant of peak hand force production is also shown (b). Note that the R force is aimed nearly straight forward; thus, the R and RE values are of nearly identical magnitude (c).

The study conducted by the United States biomechanical team on 1984 Olympic swimmers concluded that, in general, the lift-drag ratio index data show that lift force predominates over drag force in breaststroke. In freestyle and butterfly, lift and drag force appear to be about equally important during the most propulsive portions of the stroke. Backstroke swimmers seem to use drag force more than lift force (sculling motions are less important than in breaststroke).

The force distribution index data show that the largest effective propulsive forces occur near the end of the arm pull in freestyle and butterfly. In breaststroke, the largest forces occur about two thirds of the way into the pull (at the midpoint of the inward scull motion; see Schleihauf, 1979). Backstroke in-

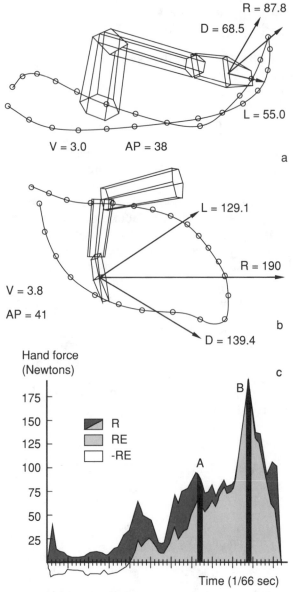

volves large hand-force production just past the midpoint of the arm pull. Unlike freestyle and butterfly, the shoulder roll at the end of the pull in backstroke appears to detract from the hand speed and propulsive force generated on the water during the finish of the stroke.

In each of the four competitive strokes, swimmers employed curvilinear pulling patterns in which diagonal pulling motions played an important role in propulsion.

Figure 2.14 Wire-frame computer model of skilled technique—front crawl stroke of Rowdy Gaines, 1984 Olympic 100m freestyle champion. (a) Bottom view, midstroke; (b) side view, finishing sweep motion; and (c) hand resultant/effective resultant force curves versus time. *Note.* From Schleihauf et al. (1988, pp. 55, 56, 59). Figures and text reprinted by permission.

in three dimensions, namely, the lateral, vertical, and horizontal planes. No longer could a coach merely instruct a swimmer to pull the hand straight back past the body. Although this approach might be used to teach a beginner, the new science showed that this was not what happened in actual practice.

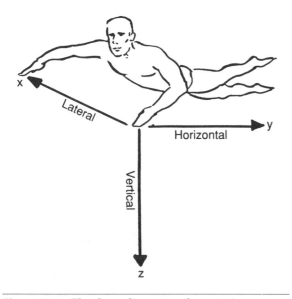

Figure 2.16 The three-dimensional aspect (x, y, z axes) of the pull. *Note.* From Schleihauf (1977, p. 50). Adapted by permission.

Communicating the New Concepts to the Swimmer in the Pool.   While there *is* a definite backward component to all the strokes except breaststroke, the three-dimensional aspect of the pull means that simultaneous movement also happens in the two other planes, the lateral and vertical. The issue became how to coach a swimmer to pull in three movement planes simultaneously. In fact, this proves to be nearly impossible. It is far more practical for swimmers to relate the stroke to their own bodies than attempt to copy the stroke pattern as observed *externally* by the biomechanist. In the practical situation it was found preferable to have a swimmer concentrate on pulling in two planes only (lateral and vertical) and to allow the horizontal (or backward) phase of the stroke simply to happen as a result of applying propulsive force on the water.

Schleihauf showed that skilled swimmers produce their most efficient propulsive motions in the lateral and vertical planes. Barthels and Adrian (1975), in a classic analysis of butterfly swimming, found that acceleration is greatest during inward sculling. Kathie Barthels, who realized the need to translate the new concepts into language understandable to the swimmer, was probably the first person to attempt to simplify the coaching of three-dimensional sculling:

> Verbal and non-verbal teaching/coaching cues often elicit the desired movement response from a swimmer while not conveying the notion of what is actually or should be occurring mechanically. For example, the command ''press the hands backward through the water in an 'S' shape pull'' may convey what the swimmer should *feel*, whereas the body is actually being moved forward relative to the hand, which, in fact, travels backward through the water very little. Such commands serve the immediate purpose, but also do little for the swimmer's understanding of the mechanical process of swimming. (Barthels, 1977, p. 52)

Hand Velocity—A New Dimension of Swimming Skill

Expert swimmers gradually increase their hand speed during the propulsive impulse in each direction. Schleihauf (1974) says that peaks in hand speed should be held only briefly. As a propulsive impulse in a particular direction reaches peak speed, it is important that a change of direction follows, because too much acceleration will cause slippage. He adds that, whereas a stroke pattern defines *where* to pull, velocity curves define *how much* to pull. Pulling either too quickly or too slowly can reduce propulsion.

Schleihauf says that the highest hand velocities occur in the plane perpendicular to the line of forward progress. Because lift forces result from motion in this plane and the magnitude of lift force increases with hand velocity, this is convincing evidence that lift forces dominate swimming propulsion.

According to Schleihauf, the hand velocity curves that occur in each of the three reference planes of a swimming stroke identify an abstract quantity of motion and a new dimension of swimming skill. The variety of emphasis placed on each part of the stroke separates the champion from the less-skilled performer.

Counsilman and Wasilak (1982) studied hand

speed and hand acceleration patterns in swimming strokes. They found that the hand follows a velocity pattern in which the three-dimensional speed continuously increases except for a deceleration point in midstroke, a finding that confirms Schleihauf's (1974). They claim that a continuously increasing forward thrust can be achieved from a hand movement that fluctuates in its speed pattern.

Individual Stroke Characteristics

Ernest Maglischo (1982) recommends ideal patterns for directional "sweeps" by the hands to develop the most effective resultant forces.

In a biomechanical analysis of the crawl stroke mechanics of six members of the 1984 U.S. Olympic team, Maglischo et al. (1986) suggest that the swimmers favored either lateral or vertical stroking motions. Some had more effective stroke mechanics while moving their hands in the vertical plane but were less effective when using lateral motions. Those who were more effective when using lateral motions were less effective when moving their hands vertically. One conclusion is that perhaps swimmers make best use of energy output by putting their greatest effort into the movement planes most effective to their individual stroke patterns.

It is unlikely, however, that any swimmer *consciously* emphasizes either the lateral or vertical component of the swimming stroke. Moreover, it is possible that a swimmer's stroke may alternate in effectiveness between one movement plane and another depending on such factors as speed, the style of swimming used, muscle fatigue resulting from weight training, and perhaps even a subconscious change in day-to-day preference.

Familiarization Exercises. Swimmers should be made aware of the vertical and lateral components of their strokes. A useful drill is to swim three lengths of the pool as follows: on the first length the swimmer concentrates on the lateral phases of the stroke, on the next length the emphasis is on the vertical phases, and on the third length the swimmer tries to be aware of both lateral and vertical components simultaneously.

This drill should neither be done too often nor be prolonged on those occasions when it is used; otherwise, it could easily interfere with a swimmer's natural style. Its main purpose is merely to familiarize a swimmer with the feel of the lateral and vertical components of the stroke.

Simple Communication of the New Perspective

Biomechanical analysis has revealed a new perspective of stroke mechanics, namely, the moving and the fixed reference points, as well as the three-dimensional aspect of the pull. This new knowledge should be applied in the simplest possible terms, or else a swimmer may suffer "paralysis by analysis."

Stroke mechanics should be related to the flow reactions of the water. This new approach greatly simplifies the application of biomechanical and fluid dynamic principles and is discussed in chapter 5, "Coaching the Feel of the Water."

Developing a New Perspective of Foot Propulsion

The feet propel in the various strokes by means of predominant lift propulsion. Studies of the crawl kick and the dolphin leg action show curvilinear patterns similar to those produced by the hands in the swimming stroke (Counsilman, 1977; Hoeke & Gründler, 1975; Reischle, 1982; Figure 2.17a and b).

The degree of ankle flexibility is a factor in the efficiency of the foot action. According to Schleihauf (1986), flexible ankles permit a high lift:drag ratio to develop because of the more acute pitch angles presented by the feet. Less force is wasted in the oscillating motions of the feet, and the net propulsion is directed more forward as a result of a relatively large lift-force component.

Unorthodox Lift-Producing Mechanisms

I believe that lift propulsion in swimming is not always produced by means of orthodox airfoil-type lift. There are other mechanisms that also produce lift, but unlike an airfoil they do not depend on the existence of ideal angles of attack.

Flow reactions in the water show that a variety of lift-producing mechanisms operate in foot propulsion during the different strokes. For example, there appears to be a difference between the lift-producing mechanisms present in a six-beat crawl kick and in a two-beat

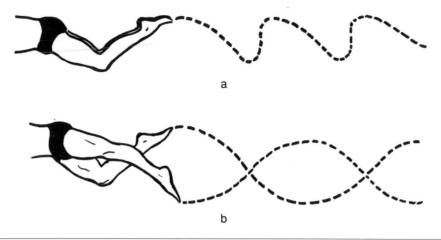

Figure 2.17   Curvilinear patterns produced by (a) the dolphin leg action and (b) the crawl kick.

kick. Similarly, lift is produced differently in the subdued dolphin kick used by many swimmers in the 200-meter butterfly event (commonly known as the *soft-kick* technique) and the *power kick* used in the 100-meter race. These mechanisms are described in chapter 4, "A New Look at the Propulsive Mechanisms of Swimming."

Understanding and Minimizing the Resistance of the Water

The following are the main impediments to a swimmer's forward motion.

1. *Frontal resistance* is caused by wave-making drag. The swimmer's forward momentum causes a buildup of moving pressure disturbances in the water in front of the body, which results in frontal resistance. These disturbances occur where the body presents curvature changes around such areas as the head, shoulders, and hips. Each pressure disturbance makes a traveling wave system at the surface. Most of the flow resulting from pressure disturbance, however, travels backward under the body rather than around the sides. Lifting the head and shoulders too far from the horizontal plane will lower the hips and legs to set up increased frontal resistance.

In freestyle and backstroke, the strokes in which the body rolls or rotates on its long axis, the use of gradually curved surfaces along the general paths followed by the water flow will minimize resistance. By rotating the body to each side within the natural rhythm of the stroke, smaller changes in the curvature of the flow lines will result. This rotating action also enables a swimmer to use the large trunk muscles with increased effect.

2. *Form drag* (or "skin friction") is caused by water resistance on the swimmer's skin. This type of resistance is generally considered to have little negative effect on propulsion. The practice of shaving body hair ("shaving down"), however, *has* been shown to enhance swimming speed. Its benefit was once thought to be only psychological, stemming from heightened sensitivity to the flow of the water, which made swimmers believe they were swimming faster. However, Sharp and Costill (1989) showed that shaving down also provides physiological advantages.

3. *Eddy resistance*, or *separation* (also known as "tail suction"), is caused by water pressure at a given region insufficient to force the water laterally inward and make it follow closely along the body, especially toward the body's tapering "aft-end." Water is dragged in from behind the swimmer to fill the gap left because the flow has not closed in from the sides. Resistance is generated by the forward acceleration of water that otherwise would flow backward and be left behind. The pressure differential causes the water to suck backward on the swimmer in the form of retarding eddies.

Eddy resistance can also be caused by poor horizontal and lateral body alignments, which cause separation of the flow of water past the body.

Prolonged Momentum

Some swimmers naturally prolong their momentum past the point where it would normally start to diminish. A stroke cycle that is well coordinated with each propulsive impulse occurring in ideal sequence can avoid extreme fluctuations of acceleration and deceleration. The more constant the momentum, the better the index of efficient technique (Colwin, 1984b).

The ability to prolong momentum allows a swimmer to take fewer strokes to cover a set distance, which is an indication of proficiency. Measurement against a grid shows that a skilled crawl swimmer is able to complete a swimming stroke with the hand leaving the water ahead of the point at which it entered (Schleihauf, 1977). At first, this phenomenon was thought to result from lift force causing the hand to move forward as it stroked, but the real reason is that, while the hand is entering, the body is being propelled forward by the other hand. In Figure 2.18a-e, the right arm enters in a streamlined posture that permits water to flow under the arm and torso, enabling the body to prolong the momentum developed by the left arm as it accelerates through its pull.

Other factors also result in prolonged momentum, such as having a streamlined and buoyant body and the ability to accelerate the arm stroke to overcome resistance drag. Although these are important contributing factors, kinetic streamlining is another aspect of technique that warrants consideration (Colwin, 1984b).

Kinetic Streamlining

Kinetic streamlining refers to the synchronization of body and limb alignments aimed at reducing drag during the impulses of force and the resulting propulsion (Colwin, 1984b). Most competent swimmers naturally assume streamlined body alignments. However, the presence of bilateral body alignments in the crawl and backstroke, for example, will not necessarily result in prolonged momentum. The *timing* of the changing alignment sequences is the key factor.

Improved knowledge of the time increments of acceleration and force application now makes it possible to better guide swimmers on how to change their body alignments smoothly with each new application of force. Kinetic streamlining implies *streamlining within the mechanics of the stroke*.

Kinetic streamlining should be viewed mainly as a natural process and not as a pretext for analyzing the angular distances between the limbs with a micrometer. It is vital that the stroke not become stilted by too much analysis.

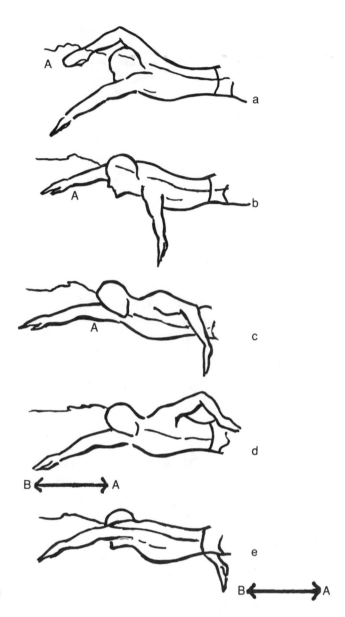

Figure 2.18 Prolonged momentum in the crawl stroke. The right arm enters the water in a streamlined posture that permits water to flow under the arm and torso and enables the body to prolong the momentum developed by the left arm as it accelerates through its pull. (a) The right hand enters at point A. Note that the swimmer moves past point A (b-d) before right hand starts to pull at point B (d). (e) When the right hand finishes its pull (several frames have been omitted here), it is still at point B, showing that there has been no ''slip'' in the stroke. The distance from points A to B indicates the swimmer's ability to prolong momentum.

Again, the aim of kinetic streamlining is to streamline interchanging body postures and configurations to reduce drag and to prolong momentum. Each change of body configuration forms a new *envelope* of streamline patterns about the body. This happens because streamlines are instantaneous and vary from moment to moment. In general, streamlines converge or diverge as they curve because the velocity usually varies in magnitude and direction from point to point.

Toward a Unified Concept of Kinetic Streamlining

Low wave crests and shallow troughs around a swimmer at speed indicate good streamlining. Poor swimming is characterized by wasteful activity, forceful motion, and a confused, eddying mass of water.

A unified concept of kinetic streamlining involves implementing techniques that reduce both frontal resistance and the retarding effects of eddy formation. Generally, instruction in kinetic streamlining improves skill. A swimmer should be made aware of the body's interaction with the water through each change of alignment.

When the body rotates on its long axis in freestyle and backstroke the water flows smoothly around the body with smaller changes to the curvature of the flow lines. This reduces resistance because the rotating action results in a smaller surface area of the body being presented to the water. To maximize this effect in crawl and backstroke a skilled swimmer spends most of the stroke cycle with the body tipped equally to one side or the other rather than in the flat, central posture that produces increased resistance.

Transitional Phases of the Swimming Strokes. The body roll on its long axis in freestyle and backstroke results from the rotation of the arms as they alternately pull and recover over the water. The entire body rotates at once: shoulders, hips, and legs. The total amount of roll varies from 70 degrees to 90 degrees or 35 degrees to 45 degrees on each side of the body's long axis in both the freestyle and backstroke.

The direction and speed of the body's rotation is controlled by the arms throughout the stroke cycle. During each arm recovery, the shifting mass of the shoulder and upper arm causes the body to roll gradually to the other side. The directional change of the body roll is synchronized with the other arm as it starts its pull. This transition from the end of one stroke to the start of the next is critical. It requires smooth streamlining of the changing alignments and split-second arm coordination to ensure the body's prolonged momentum.

As the body rolls through the flat, central position, the recovery arm enters and extends forward in a streamlined posture. The opposite arm accelerates to the end of its pull as the body continues its roll to the other side. The cycle is repeated in smooth sequence.

Individual Rolling Time. Some swimmers, because of their physical characteristics, are unable to roll quickly enough to synchronize the body rotation with the arm action. It is likely that each swimmer has an individual "rolling time"—the time taken for the total amount of roll from one side to the other. This could be related to height, the average width of the body, buoyancy, and so on.

Usually, swimmers who are broad and stocky seem to have a slow rolling time from one side to the other. They encounter more frontal resistance because of their less-streamlined physiques and because they take longer to roll through the flat, central position. Conversely, tall, light-boned, and buoyant female swimmers are able to roll quickly, thus avoiding excessive resistance by not staying too long in the central position.

Timing Body Rotation With Postural Alignments of the Limbs. In freestyle and backstroke, the ideal streamlined body alignments should coincide with peak hand acceleration to reduce drag and increase momentum. As each pulling hand passes its respective shoulder there is a marked acceleration (Colwin, 1969).

The arm pull and the body roll are smoothly synchronized to preserve steady flow about the body. In fact, the speed of the roll at any given moment appears to be commensurate with the speed of each arm stroke. Relative to the body, the hand reaches maximum speed when the arm pull is about 65% to 80% complete (Counsilman, 1980). Careful study of underwater motion films of skilled swimmers, when traced and reproduced on a grid, seems to indicate that maximum body rotation in a particular direction is reached during peak hand acceleration.

Another streamlining effect results from the downward beat of the leg on the same side as the hand that is completing its pull. This timing prevents any tendency by the finishing arm to pull the swimmer down in the water. The downward beat of the leg during the end of the arm stroke happens irrespective of the type of kicking rhythm a swimmer uses: six-beat, straight two-beat, or two-beat crossover (Counsilman, 1977).

The completion of the stroke at the same time as the maximum body rotation and the stabilizing downward leg thrust are key streamlining factors in freestyle and backstroke. Indeed, these aspects of bilateral body alignments are fundamental to these two strokes; as such they should be viewed as natural movements not normally requiring specific attention.

The Importance of Accurate Timing. The next stage of the stroke cycle is critical: the *transition* from the end of one stroke to the start of the next. A smooth interchange of body alignment and split-second stroke coordination are essential to ensure a minimum of interference with the body's momentum. During this time a swimmer must preserve the water's steady flow down the length of the body, including the legs, by carefully managing the body's rotation to the other side. The posture and speed of the recovering arm should be carefully controlled to keep the body rotation as smooth and as gradual as possible.

The posture of the arm at entry in crawl, and to some extent in backstroke, plays an important role as a streamlining agent. In crawl, almost throughout the stroke cycle, one arm or the other is extending forward at the entry to intercept and smoothly channel the oncoming flow of water around the side of the body in much the same manner as the prow of a ship. Unnecessary frontal resistance is thus reduced by diverting the water from the swimmer's head and shoulders. This action is discussed in detail in chapter 4, ''A New Look at the Propulsive Mechanisms of Swimming,'' and in chapter 5, ''Coaching the Feel of the Water.''

Unfortunately, in butterfly and breaststroke, because the arms stroke simultaneously, it is not possible to constantly intercept the oncoming flow at the entry. Moreover, the lifting of the head and shoulders presents considerable frontal resistance to the water during periods of peak acceleration. Many skilled butterfly and breaststroke swimmers partially offset these negative effects by completely submerging the body for brief periods during each stroke cycle. The submerging action takes the swimmer under the disturbed surface water and thereby reduces resistance, if only for a brief period in every stroke. (Note: The breaststroke law now permits a swimmer to submerge completely, provided part of the swimmer's head becomes visible above the surface once during each arm cycle.)

The Relationship Between Stroke Length (Distance per Stroke) and Stroke Frequency (Stroke Rate)

Stroke length (SL) and stroke frequency (SF) govern a swimmer's average speed (S). Should a swimmer use long, slow strokes or short, fast strokes? Actually, skilled swimmers tend to use long, fast strokes. When they increase their speed, better swimmers usually try to take even longer strokes and turn the longer stroke over more quickly.

Though the concept of taking long strokes is not a recent one, it took hold only gradually. Most competitors in the early years of the sport thought speed was to be achieved by fast and furious stroking, but Louis de B. Handley (1928), one of the pioneers of women's competitive swimming and a prolific writer on aquatic subjects, observed that a swift stroke is not conducive to fast swimming and that, though contestants were inclined to think wild action necessary to attain great speed, this is not the case. Handley added that slow arm movements with a vigorous drive and a restful recovery give the best results.

Over 50 years ago the great John Weissmuller took fewer strokes than his rivals (Weissmuller, 1930). Weissmuller's coach, William Bachrach, believed that slower stroking enabled firmer purchase on the water. Weissmuller said that the secret of taking fewer strokes was to start the stroke slowly, then gradually increase the force as one started to feel the purchase on the water. In this way, one would not attain the full force of the arm stroke until the arm was nearly halfway through its sweep. (It is interesting to note Weissmuller's use of the word ''sweep,'' a swimming term resurrected by Ernest Maglischo in his book *Swimming Faster* [1982].)

Distance per Stroke

Jack Nelson (1973) believes ''sprinting'' to be an inappropriate term because of its connotation that to swim quickly one must change something: stroke rate, stroke coordination, or timing. Nelson introduced the concept of DPS—distance per stroke—and his swimmers practiced drills designed to increase stroke length.

Basically, these drills enable a swimmer to improve efficiency by feeling what one arm does by itself. Nelson also developed another exercise in which the swimmer repeats 100-meter swims keeping a 24 full stroke count for each 100 meters. Swimmers who cannot maintain this rating are allowed to do a set number of strokes more suited to their individual ability.

Tempo Awareness

Ron Johnson (1982) delivered an address on "Tempo Awareness Training" at the World Clinic convened by the American Swimming Coaches' Association. He mentioned that he had seen the famed Hawaiian coach, Soichi Sakamoto, counting tempo to his swimmers as far back as the 1941 American Championships in St. Louis, Missouri. Johnson maintained that, whereas there had been much emphasis on reducing the number of strokes per length, there had been little development of what he termed "tempo awareness." Johnson was convinced that only two factors made a real difference to swimming speed, distance per stroke and stroke speed.

Johnson outlined methods for measuring tempo as either the time taken for one complete stroke cycle or, for more accurate measurement in long-course swimming, the time taken to complete 2, 5, or even 10 arm cycles.

Johnson introduced methods for timing stroke tempo with a 1/100-second stopwatch or a computer that depended on the stroke being swum. For freestyle, Johnson timed the stroke from the right-hand entry through at least two stroke cycles to the next right-hand entry, obtaining the tempo by halving the time for two cycles. Johnson said that in freestyle a typical tempo for a middle-distance collegiate swimmer is around 1.30-1.35 seconds. For a good college male sprinter a typical tempo is around .95 second, and female swimmers at the elite level are approximately .05 second faster than men per stroke cycle.

Backstroke tempo, on the other hand, is slower than freestyle by about .2 to .3 second per stroke revolution. Johnson said that backstrokers take about the same number of strokes per length as a freestyler, but because of the more limited mechanics of the stroke, they simply cannot stroke as quickly.

Johnson suggested two ways for measuring breaststroke tempo: first, measuring from the time the feet close until they close again in one stroke cycle; and second, from when the chin breaks the surface as the swimmer breathes until the next time the chin breaks the water. He said that breaststroke swimmers on average stroke about .10 to .15 second faster than freestylers of similar expertise.

In butterfly, the stroke is measured from the time the hands enter the water until they enter again for the next stroke. Johnson said that the stroke revolutions in butterfly are similar to freestyle. A good collegiate male 100-yard butterfly swimmer is typically in the 1.05 to 1.15 seconds range, whereas females in the same category vary between 1.00 and 1.05 seconds.

The Relationship Between Stroke Length and Stroke Frequency

With the exception of those swimming the butterfly stroke, skilled swimmers usually increase their stroke length as the distance of the race increases. However, probably because of the accumulative effects of fatigue, a swimmer's stroke frequency may decrease and so will average speed (Pai, Hay, & Wilson, 1984; Craig & Pendergast, 1979; Craig, Skeehan, Pawelczyk, & Boomer, 1985).

Researchers report no consistent pattern with regard to stroke frequency during a swimming race. Stroke frequency may often remain constant throughout a race or it may either decrease or increase (Craig et al., 1985; Curry, 1975; Hay, Guimaraes, & Grimston, 1983; Pai et al., 1984).

Researchers agree, however, that stroke length rather than stroke frequency is the determining factor in a swimmer's average speed. They also agree that in freestyle, butterfly, and breaststroke, stroke frequency is very similar. Backstroke, however, probably because of the mechanical disadvantage of the body in the dorsal position, has a much slower stroke frequency and greater stroke length than the other strokes.

Male swimmers attain greater speed than female swimmers because they swim with a greater stroke length. However, the two sexes have very similar stroke frequencies (Craig & Pendergast, 1979; East, 1970; Pai et al., 1984).

Practical Effects of Training on Stroke Length and Stroke Frequency

Researchers have not devoted much attention to the effects of training on the ratio of stroke length to stroke frequency. James G. Hay, director of the Biomechanics Laboratory at the University of Iowa, conducted the only study to date on this topic (Hay et al., 1983). Based on a season of observation of the four racing strokes in the 200-yard events, the study showed, except for the backstroke, a marked correlation between average speed and stroke length. The study found no significant correlations between average speed and stroke frequency. The researchers mention that the method used in the study has a number of limitations and for this reason the study needs to be replicated. The early indication, however, was that swimmers should concentrate on increasing their stroke length while maintaining a constant stroke frequency.

Hay mentions that few procedures had been developed to enable coaches, during practice and competition, to easily determine stroke length, stroke frequency, and average speed. Hay describes a simple analog watch to help alleviate this lack (Figure 2.19). Now (as with everything in the computer age) an electronic solution has been developed: the Chronostroke watch (see Figure 2.20).

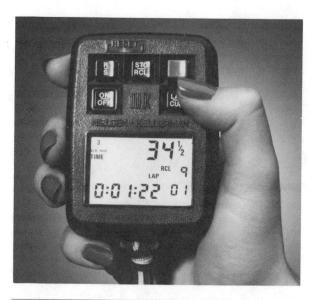

Figure 2.20 The Chronostroke™, a crystal-controlled microcomputer, is a rating watch/memory timer that quickly and accurately measures stroke rate (turnover). The large key is pressed in time with the swimmer's stroke. *Note.* Reprinted by permission of the Nielsen-Kellerman Company of Marcus Hook, PA.

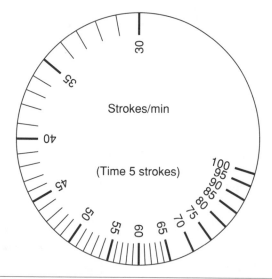

Figure 2.19 Hay's specially designed watch face for measuring stroke rate. The watch hand completes one full sweep in 10 seconds. The watch is started at hand entry, or at another convenient point in the stroke cycle, and stopped at this same point five strokes later. The stroke frequency, in strokes per minute, is then read directly from the watch. *Note.* From Hay (1986, p. 80). Reprinted by permission.

The Dominance of One Arm Over the Other

Earlier in this chapter, when I discussed the topic of *prolonged momentum*, I described a

method for measuring the respective entry and exit points of crawl stroke swimmers' hands. Some years ago, I noted significant differences in some swimmers in the distances between their right- and left-hand entry and exit points. The obvious implication is that these individual swimmers showed a dominance of one arm over the other, which was probably also related to differences in strength between the two arms.

Rather than advise these swimmers to try to balance their stroking equally on both sides of the long axis of the body, I encouraged them to roll *slightly* more toward the dominant arm as it pulled. This action was to be accompanied by turning the head slightly toward the side of the body opposite the stroking arm to enable the shoulder of the stroking arm to get a little deeper into the stroke. At the same time, I told the swimmers to avoid a lopsided stroke but to find just the right amount of adjustment to ensure smooth propulsion. Although this was typical "seat of the pants" coaching, most of the swimmers involved reported favorably on the effects of this minor stroke adjustment.

I mention these observations because the question of hand or foot dominance in competitive swimming does not appear to have been the subject of scientific study. The measurement of different stroke patterns, velocities, and forces between one arm and the other could produce valuable information for improving stroke efficiency, especially in those swimmers who show marked strength differences between their left and right arms. This information could also prove to be important during the developmental stages of young swimmers, because the consistency with which children use one hand in preference to the other increases with age, at least through preschool years and probably longer. An often overlooked fact is that most people also have a dominant foot, which may partially explain why some swimmers are unable to achieve symmetry in the breaststroke and dolphin kick.

The Individuality of a Swimmer's Stroke

Variations exist between individuals in the way they swim. Swimmers often look different even though they are observing the same fundamentals. Detecting and evaluating individual stroke characteristics is an essential part of coaching. A coach should learn to distinguish between idiosyncracy and faulty mechanics; this is when coaching becomes art and not science.

Two all-time great coaches of American swimming, Matt Mann (University of Michigan) and Bob Kiphuth (Yale University), both made pertinent comments on this topic in their time.

Kiphuth said that individuals possess a certain neuromuscular system at birth, and because of this, try as one will, there is not much that can be done to change a swimmer's *basic* movement pattern. Matt Mann said that the very first point of technique a university coach tries to correct at the start of a swimmer's college career will be the very last thing a coach will be trying to correct at the end of the swimmer's career.

Although most coaches recognize the individuality of each swimmer's basic stroke technique, not much thought has been given to the reasons for these differences among individuals. A swimmer's style is as individual as a signature. It is a mysterious physiological fact that whenever one makes the appropriate volitional effort to sign one's name on a piece of paper it always comes out the same, or similar enough to be recognizable and different from what is produced by anyone else trying to write the same name.

Something more is learned about this puzzling mechanism when one chalks one's name in large letters on a blackboard. Again, it comes out the same. Although the muscles used are different—writing on paper with a pen mainly uses finger and hand muscles, whereas large writing on a blackboard involves the predominant use of arm muscles—the signature remains constant.

This observation teaches us something about the motor system, namely, that although movement patterns are stored in the pyramidal cortex of the brain, there are also sensory mechanisms in the muscles that affect motor function in a *specific* way. Moreover, it appears that similar, if not identical, sensory perceptions probably determine the "individualized" stroke patterns that are characteristic of each swimmer.

Psychophysics and Stroke Individuality

This relationship between conscious mental and physical events is the subject of in-depth research in a branch of experimental science known as *psychophysics*. There are two branches of psychophysics: *sensory psychophysics* and *motor psychophysics*. Sensory psychophysics refers to the relationship between a physical stimulus and the resulting sensation experienced by the subject. Motor psychophysics deals with the reciprocal problem, the relationship between a conscious effort of will and the resulting physical movement of the body.

Sensory psychophysics is an old and highly respected subject that has contributed much information about vision, hearing, and the other senses. Thomas Young's (1773-1829) three-color theory of color vision is based on psychophysical evidence and provides the fundamentals of color television and color photography. Sensory psychophysics attempts to draw inferences about what happens inside a sense organ, a nerve, or the brain by understanding the physiological mechanisms that lie between the stimulus and the sensation. Examples of sensory-psychophysical observations are the experiments that have been used to measure tactile, visual, auditory, and other sensory thresholds.

Motor psychophysics is concerned with the movements we produce as a result of conscious will, or volition. The individuality of handwriting and swimming stroke patterns are examples of motor-psychophysical mechanisms. Unfortunately, compared to our knowledge of sensory psychophysics, very little has been learned about voluntary movements and the physiological mechanisms that make our muscles do what we expect of them. Nevertheless, a few definite phenomena have been described that may assist coaches to distinguish more easily between an individual swimmer's characteristic movement pattern and any fundamental technical errors that may exist within this pattern.

Subtle Differences Between Individual Swimmers

A skilled coach knows what to teach, what to correct, and what to leave alone; how to distinguish between faulty technique and idiosyncracy; and how to mold technique around the individual and not vice versa. Humans come in all shapes and sizes. They have different neuromuscular patterns that cause them to move differently. Some float easily whereas some do not; some are streamlined as well as buoyant and are able to slip through water easily with a ghostlike glide; some form concepts quickly and have a highly developed tactile sense; and some are flexible and move with ease and skill, whereas others are not so well endowed. A skilled coach, therefore, will assess individual characteristics carefully before deciding what assistance, if any, a swimmer may need to shape the stroke for utmost effectiveness.

THE TECHNIQUE OF THE CRAWL STROKE

The 20th century saw the invention of a completely new form of human locomotion in the development of the crawl stroke. The smooth, flowing action of the crawl is a far cry from the almost painful efforts of early swimming pioneers and a tribute to human ingenuity. The style is characterized by split-second timing of the arms and smooth transitions from one phase of the stroke to the next. Throughout the changing sequences of the stroke, the body assumes streamlined alignments that reduce resistance and prolong the momentum developed by each successive stroke.

KEY POINTS IN TECHNIQUE

The Pattern of the Stroke

The dotted line shows the S pattern the hand makes as it moves through the stroke. The stroke consists of three short sculling motions. The hand sculls slightly outward from the shoulder line after entering the water. It then changes direction inward to cross over the body's center line in midstroke. The hand rounds out past the hips as the stroke ends. The inward and outward sculling motions under the trunk produce two pronounced force impulses. Although the overall hand speed accelerates throughout the stroke, there is a noticeable dip in the hand-speed curve as the first impulse ends and the second impulse begins.

CRAWL STROKE SIDE VIEW

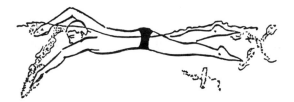

1. Split-second timing is shown; as the right arm starts to enter the water, the left arm begins the power phase of its stroke. Note the high elbow posture of both arms.

2. The right arm has completely entered the water as the left arm is halfway through its stroke. Note the marked acceleration of the left hand in comparison to the slower right hand.

3. The face turns for inhalation in time with the backward thrust of the left hand. The left leg kicks downward to counterbalance the upward motion of the left hand.

4. The left arm starts to recover as the head returns to a face-forward position. The right arm starts the power phase of its stroke. The body has reached maximum roll to the left.

5. As the left hand starts to enter the water, the split-second timing of the arms is repeated, giving the stroke perfect symmetry (compare to the beginning frame of this sequence).

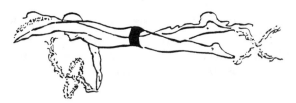

6. The left arm has completely entered the water and the head is centered in line with the long axis of the body. This is a fundamental aspect of the stroke—the face is forward as each hand enters the water. Note the right-angle timing of the arms in relation to each other.

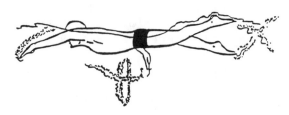

7. The right hand shows marked acceleration in comparison to the slower movement of the left hand.

8. The trailing vortex in the flow reaction to the left-hand pull indicates the existence of a lift-producing pressure differential in the flow around the hand. The right hand has shed a ring vortex, indicating its completion of a force impulse at the end of the stroke. (See chapters 3 and 4.)

CRAWL STROKE FRONT VIEW

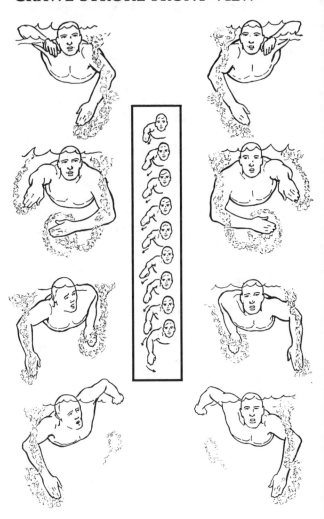

The hand moves slower at the entry than at any other phase of the stroke. The hand speed at entry is approximately the same as the speed of the body moving forward. Too rapid an entry reduces the forward speed of the body.

During the entry and early part of the stroke, the elbow is kept higher than the hand. The elbow-up posture provides strong leverage and gives the arm a cambered, foil-type shape that probably assists a high body position. The high elbow is only a fleeting phase of the stroke and should not be held too long because doing so causes a stilted action. In midstroke the elbow should reach a maximum bend of approximately 90 degrees.

After the entry, the hand performs a short downward and outward sculling motion to just wide of the shoulder line until it reaches a point where its direction changes from downward to backward. From here the hand accelerates through its curvilinear path to the end of the stroke. Effective hand acceleration causes a power surge and helps the swimmer cover greater distance with each stroke.

While the accelerating arm is producing its power surge, the forward arm is sliding into the entry at considerably slower speed as it channels and directs the oncoming flow of water in preparation for the next stroke. The entry is slow; otherwise, the momentum developed by the propelling arm would be offset. The subtle timing between the arms results in two ''different'' swimming strokes—a slow stroke by the entering arm and a rapidly accelerating stroke by the pulling arm.

The body is allowed to roll evenly on its long axis. The roll is a natural action that streamlines the body in the water and allows the arms to rotate evenly and brings the large trunk muscles powerfully into the stroke. Timing the arm stroke with the body roll is accomplished by starting the pull as the body rolls toward the for-

ward arm, and timing the end of the stroke with the roll of the body away from the stroking arm.

The arm relaxes as it recovers from the water with elbow up, and the forearm swings slowly forward in a controlled semicircular action until the hand is a few inches in front of the face. From here the hand slides into the water on an imaginary line forward of the armpit. The elbow is bent and set slightly higher than the wrist. As the arm extends slowly forward into the water, the swimmer allows the body to continue its run, using the momentum developed by the pull of the opposite arm.

The arm recovery is carefully controlled because it affects streamlining and body balance. The initial semicircular phase of the recovery keeps the body balanced over the opposite arm as it starts its stroke. The second phase of the recovery, as the hand moves forward into the water from a position in front of the face, helps the body roll smoothly to the opposite side, thus completing a subtle transition from the end of one stroke to the beginning of the next.

THE TECHNIQUE OF THE BACK CRAWL STROKE

The fundamentals of the back crawl stroke are similar to those of the front crawl, with two significant exceptions: The face is not submerged in the back crawl, so there is no need for head-turning mechanics, and the back crawl stroke is performed with the arms out to the side of the body. This arm position results in the back crawl being less efficient than the crawl stroke; structural limitations place the arms at a mechanical disadvantage because they cannot pull directly under the body and thus develop their full potential power. This also inhibits ideal stroke frequency.

KEY POINTS IN TECHNIQUE

The Pattern of the Stroke

The dotted line shows the curvilinear pattern the hand makes as it moves through the stroke in a "down-up-down" path that produces three pronounced force impulses. Adroit adjustment of hand posture is required as each directional change occurs. These adjustments are accompanied by a gradual acceleration of hand speed throughout the stroke.

The arm is straight as it enters the water. Then the elbow gradually bends until a maximum bend of approximately 90 degrees is reached as the hand passes a line with the shoulder. From here, the forearm extends and the hand finishes the stroke with a rounded backward and downward thrust to a point below the hips.

BACK CRAWL STROKE SIDE VIEW

1. The right arm has entered the water a split-second before the left arm has completed its stroke; this ensures continuous propulsion.

2. The right elbow bends as the arm starts to pull. The roll of the body toward the pulling arm brings the powerful large trunk muscles into the action. The left arm, with shoulder leading, is about to leave the water.

3. The right elbow bend increases as the right hand moves upward. The left arm recovers in the vertical plane. The head is centered in the long axis of the body to ensure perfect balance and prevent excessive sideways movement of the body.

4. The right elbow reaches maximum bend, causing the hand to come very close to the surface; however, the roll of the body to that side prevents the hand from breaking out of the water. Note excessive vortex shedding from the right hand. (This is typical even in skilled performers.) The left hand moves slightly faster than the right, ensuring the necessary slight overlap in the timing of the arms.

5. The left arm enters the water and the split-second timing of the arms is repeated, giving the stroke perfect symmetry (compare to the first frame of this sequence). The left arm enters deep below the surface in line with the back. The hips are kept high to reduce resistance. The right hand sheds a ring vortex denoting the end of the propulsive impulse as the hand completes its stroke below the hips.

6. With the shoulder leading, the right arm moves smoothly into the recovery without waiting at the hips.

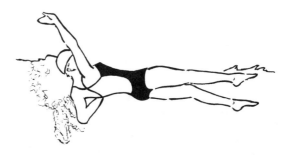

7. The body roll allows the swimmer to synchronize the pull of the left arm with the vertical recovery of the right arm.

8. The right arm, still recovering vertically, moves to the entry slightly faster than the left hand, which is completing its stroke. Note the high position of the hips.

BACK CRAWL STROKE FRONT VIEW

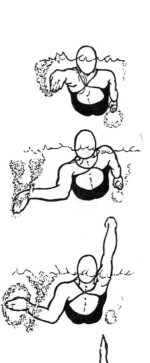

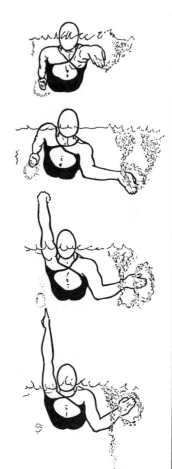

The arm enters the water behind the shoulder, elbow straight, little finger first. The opposite arm, palm down, completes its pull with a vigorous thrust below the hips. For a brief moment both arms are completely submerged, thus ensuring continuous propulsion.

Without pausing, the entry arm presses down deep to a line with the back. Then the elbow starts to bend and the body rolls toward the pulling arm. The opposite arm, with the shoulder leading, leaves the water.

The recovery arm, with the elbow straight, recovers in the vertical plane in a trajectory aimed directly over the shoulder. The body roll starts to reverse direction. The elbow of the pulling arm continues to bend.

The recovery arm, without deviation from the vertical, accelerates slightly as it passes back over the shoulder. This acceleration will cause a slight overlap in the stroke as the arm enters the water. The pulling arm reaches maximum elbow bend of approximately 90 degrees and is now set to press downward to the end of the stroke.

THE TECHNIQUE OF THE BUTTERFLY STROKE

An efficient butterfly stroke depends on accurate timing of the head movement, arm stroke, and the accompanying two-beat leg action to ensure that the hips always ride high in the water. Without this ideal body position, butterfly can become a very difficult stroke to perform.

There are two downward leg beats for each arm stroke. The first downward beat occurs as the arms enter the water and the second downward beat is timed as the hands push backward to end the stroke.

The head action is critical to good body position; the face must come out of the water before the hands, and enter the water before the hands.

KEY POINTS IN TECHNIQUE

The Pattern of the Stroke

The dotted line shows the typical "keyhole" pattern made by the hands during the pull. The stroke consists of three sculling motions as the hands pitch outward, inward, and then outward again.

The arms are almost completely extended as they enter the water slightly wide of their respective shoulders. From here, the hands sweep out, round, and together to form the upper part of the "keyhole" pattern. As the hands come close together under the body, a maximum elbow bend of approximately 90 degrees is reached. Then the hands push round and out past the hips as the stroke ends.

BUTTERFLY STROKE SIDE VIEW

1. The face is submerged as the arms approach the entry and the first downward leg beat begins.

2. The arms, almost straight, enter the water as the hips push upward. The first downward beat of the legs keeps the stroke continuous and is the key to butterfly timing. The downward beat does not result from conscious effort, but is a reaction to the deliberate upward push of the hips as the arms enter the water.

3. The hands spread outward from the shoulder line as the elbows bend. The head lifts immediately to prevent the body from sinking too low. The hips reach their highest point as the downward leg beat ends. The feet shed a large ring vortex in the vertical plane, showing that a large mass of water has been acted upon and driven directly backward.

4. The high elbow position provides good leverage and effective functional shaping of the arms. The large rounded action of the hands gives the feet time to recover in preparation for their second downward beat.

5. The hands join under the body in preparation for their final round-and-outward backward thrust. Two large vortices are shed as the hands each end a propulsive impulse. Unlike the first downward leg beat, the second downward beat *will* be consciously directed by the swimmer.

6. The hands push round and back in an accelerated motion. The mouth clears the water just before the hands emerge. The feet separate the air-water boundary at the surface and carry a bound vortex as they begin their second downward beat.

7. The swimmer inhales as the arms recover and the second downward leg beat ends. Note how the leg beat keeps the hips high as the arms recover.

8. The body is in the high "sailing" position that results from correct timing. The hips are high and the legs extended. The arms rotate in the shoulder joints as they recover laterally over the water.

9. The arms are about to pass a line with the shoulders. At this point the head will begin to submerge so that it is down as the arms enter the water (as in the first frame of this sequence). Careful control of the head position throughout the stroke is vital to maintaining good body position.

10. The face has submerged a split second before the hands enter the water. The soles of the feet separate the air-water boundary (surface) as the feet start downward.

BUTTERFLY STROKE FRONT VIEW

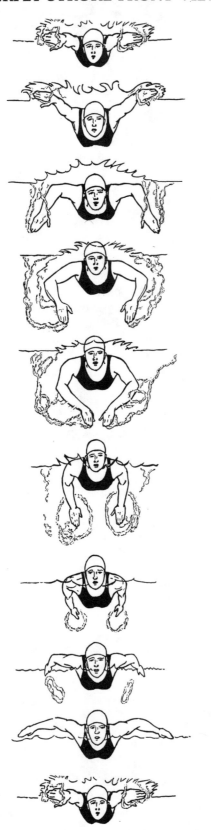

The arms are almost straight as they enter the water just wide of their respective shoulders. The inital outward scull is performed as the arms spread outward and downward. As the elbows bend, the hands cut inward in a rounded action that brings the hands close together under the body until they are almost touching. The stroke ends as the hands round out past the hips. Note how the chin is gradually eased forward as the stroke progresses until the mouth clears the surface for inhalation just as the hands complete their backward thrust. Note also how the head submerges before the arms completely enter the water and then leaves the water again before the hands clear the surface in recovery.

THE TECHNIQUE OF THE BREASTSTROKE

Since its inception as a racing stroke, the breaststroke has undergone technical changes too numerous to mention. Continuous rule changes saw the advent of many variations of breaststroke swimming: butterfly-breaststroke, underwater swimming of various permitted durations, and on and on. For years, progress in breaststroke technique was hindered by restrictive laws set by traditionalist administrators that, to great extent, limited progress and, in some instances, ended the careers of reigning champions who could not adapt their techniques to meet the requirements of new legislation.

However, more progressive laws now permit a swimmer to submerge completely for part of each stroke cycle, an improvement that appears to have resulted in a more free-flowing overall action. The experimental process continues, particularly with reference to techniques such as "wave-action"; hip undulation; and above-surface, forward extension of the arms.

KEY POINTS IN TECHNIQUE

The Pattern of the Stroke

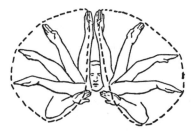

The dotted line shows the typical heart-shaped pattern of the pull and subsequent forward reach of the hands. This is the stroke pattern as seen from the *moving* viewpoint of the hands moving past the swimmer. However, seen from the *fixed* viewpoint of the torso moving past the arms (not shown here), the breaststroke pull consists of an outward and inward sculling motion of the hands that follows almost the same line, with only a small backward component to the action.

BREASTSTROKE SIDE VIEW

1. The body is streamlined and submerged with the head facing straight down. The continuing hip undulation maintains the momentum of the preceding kick and also prevents the legs from sinking (compare to the last frame of this sequence).

2. The thighs move upward to lift the legs. The hands scull laterally to a point wide of the shoulders. The head and shoulders, in unison, lift gradually.

3. The trunk rises as the elbows bend sharply and the hands change direction inward before there can be any tendency to pull backward. The hands move inward almost on the same line as the preceding outward scull. The leg recovery starts as the knees bend.

4. The bent arms are drawn vigorously inward as the pull ends. The hands continue forward without hesitation. The face clears the water as the trunk is elevated. The hips push downward, causing the legs and feet to lift.

5. The shoulders and upper back are clear of the water and the swimmer inhales without needing to consciously lift the head. The deep knee flexion brings the heels close to the buttocks with the feet remaining just below the surface of the water. In contrast to the angle of the knee bend, the angle between the thighs and the trunk is about 130 degrees.

6. The arms extend forward with shoulders following to enable the swimmer to obtain a long reach, an action that will help to involve the powerful shoulder girdle muscles in the subsequent pull. The feet are dorsi-flexed as the kick starts. The head submerges quickly.

7. The hips extend, causing thighs and buttocks to lift in reaction. The leg drive nears completion; the feet accelerate through this most powerful phase of the kick.

8. The body is streamlined and completely submerged during a short glide that takes it beneath the turbulent surface water. Note the raised hips and the start of a slight undulating motion that will prevent undue deceleration.

BREASTSTROKE FRONT VIEW

1. The body is outstretched and streamlined with head submerged as the arms begin the pull.

2. The pull begins with the hands sculling sideways and downward. The start of the pull causes the trunk to lift.

3. The hands reach the widest point of their lateral sculling action. Note the increasing elbow bend.

4. The elbow bend continues to increase as the hands scull inward. The knees bend as the feet begin to recover.

5. The hands join in front of the chest as the inward scull ends. The swimmer inhales as the body reaches its highest point in the stroke. The heels have recovered close to the buttocks. At this phase of the stroke some swimmers lift higher in the water than shown here, even to the point where the front chest clears the surface.

8. The shoulders follow the forward reach of the arms. The feet close together in a pressing action, soles facing, as the kick ends.

6. The head submerges rapidly. The kick starts as the hands are pushed vigorously forward.

9. The body, head completely submerged, is outstretched during a brief subsurface glide. Note that the new breaststroke laws permit the head to be completely submerged, as long as it clears the water at some stage of each stroke cycle.

7. The arms extend forward as the kick accelerates into its final phase.

Chapter 3

The Fluid Dynamics of Swimming Propulsion

A moving fluid has very different properties from a static fluid, for as soon as a swimmer's hand and the water start moving in relation to each other, another force begins to exert its influence. This force is so familiar that we accept it without second thought, yet all propulsion through a fluid, whether mechanical or natural, depends on it. The force in question is *resistance*, or more precisely, the fluid's resistance to motion.

It is a curious fact that stroke mechanics rarely have been analyzed with reference to the resistance of the water and its resultant flow reactions. Most biomechanical studies have been based on the convenient assumption of "essentially still water," but this treatment is incomplete because it assumes that swimmers perform their strokes in "negative space" or "dry water." Because water *does* move under the action of forces, however, we need to understand the relative velocities of the hand and water during swimming. Ideally, the effectiveness of swimming strokes should be analyzed from both the biomechanical and fluid dynamic perspectives.

Applying Fluid Dynamic Principles to Swimming

I have conducted a number of studies aimed at explaining what happens to the water during the swimming action. In the course of these studies I observed the flow reactions produced by the stroke mechanics of world-class swimmers and applied fluid dynamic principles to a methodical analysis of underwater movies, video, and still photographs. The flow reactions in the water produced remarkably similar patterns, and it was soon evident that fluid dynamic principles could provide a new basis for analyzing stroke efficiency (Colwin, 1984a).

Understanding fluid dynamics as applied to swimming yields three practical benefits:

1. *Understanding propulsion*—learning how water reacts to the forces developed by different propulsive mechanisms, for example, pulling straight backward versus pulling in a curved-line path. Each mechanism produces its own distinctive pattern of flow reactions in the water (Colwin, 1985b).

2. *Analyzing propulsion*—learning to observe and analyze the flow reactions caused by the swimming stroke. An observer can relate flow reactions to the efficiency of the actual stroke mechanics by assessing the *size*, *shape*, and *placement* of the vortex patterns (rotating flows) left in the flow field; when the flow reactions are clearly visible, the trained observer can analyze the net effect of an entire stroke almost at a glance (Colwin, 1985a). It is not yet possible, however, to provide detailed and accurate measurements of the flow reactions to the swimming stroke, as fluid dynamicists do when analyzing the flows around ships and airplanes, because we lack a safe and reliable method of making the flow visible.

3. *Improving propulsion*—learning to recognize through the sense of touch the ideal flow reactions necessary to produce efficient propulsion. This involves a new and unique method

of coaching stroke mechanics by having a swimmer associate the feel of the moving water with key phases of the swimming stroke (Colwin, 1987). This method is described in depth in chapter 5, "Coaching the Feel of the Water."

Understanding Basic Concepts

The preliminary explanations in this chapter are essential to an understanding of the propulsive mechanisms used in swimming. They outline in simple terms the ideas that lie behind the mathematical theory of fluid dynamics, the branch of science dealing with the application of propulsive forces in fluids. Indeed, a first requirement for understanding the following account is familiarity with the basic concepts and terms used in fluid dynamics.

It will be necessary, for example, for the reader to know how streamlines are used to form the patterns that show the *direction, velocity*, and *pressure differences* in the flow. These three factors always have an important effect on propulsion. In particular, a flow pattern will reveal whether propulsion is taking place in *steady* or *unsteady* flow, a distinction I will explain later. I will also explain why airfoil-type lift propulsion cannot occur in unsteady flow. When we combine this knowledge with the fact that human swimming propulsion takes place mostly in *unsteady* flow, it becomes apparent that top exponents must use a propulsive mechanism other than the airfoil-type method previously thought to predominate.

Flow patterns show us that skilled human swimmers develop predominant lift propulsion in unsteady flow conditions via a comparatively unorthodox mechanism that does *not* require the hand to be presented at all times at an "ideal" angle of attack for lift-force propulsion to occur. In fact, propulsion in an unsteady flow is a common aspect of fluid dynamic propulsion in nature and is dependent upon establishing a *flow circulation* around a propelling surface before lift propulsion can occur. I will later explain in detail this important principle of *circulation* as it applies under various sets of circumstances.

It is necessary, then, to proceed step by step through a sequence of simple explanations of important fluid dynamic principles, whose significance to human swimming, especially in developing new teaching and coaching methods, will gradually become apparent. (Refer also to chapter 5: "Coaching the Feel of the Water.")

Using Streamlines to Judge How Water Reacts Under the Action of Forces

Like all fluids, water changes shape under the action of forces. These changes are known as *deformation* and appear as *flow* and *elasticity* (caused by *viscosity*). Flow increases continuously without limit under the action of forces, however small. A given force produces elasticity, which vanishes if the force is removed. Flow and elasticity are the two characteristic qualities of moving water that a skilled swimmer feels and recognizes.

Direction of the Flow

Streamlines indicate the direction and velocity of the flow. Fluid dynamics makes considerable use of the concept of *streamlines*, or lines imagined drawn in the fluid to indicate the *direction* of flow at any point. A streamline is defined as a curve that is always tangential to the flow, so that fluid cannot cross a streamline but only flow along it. We can thus imagine adjacent streamlines to form a series of tubes through which the flow is passing.

Velocity of the Flow

The picture of flow given by the pattern of streamlines is, however, much more than a chart of flow direction—it is at the same time a map of the *velocity* field, one that is quite easily read because of the simple rule that fluid velocity is high where streamlines are close together and low where they are widely separated. This is exactly what would be expected if the streamlines indicated the position of real tubes, because in a fluid of constant density, wherever a tube narrows, the velocity must increase if the same mass of fluid is to pass in a given time.

Steady and Unsteady Flow

When streamlines retain the same shape at all times the flow is said to be *steady*. It is far simpler to analyze a pattern of steady flow than *unsteady* flow because the appearance and velocity of an unsteady flow at any fixed point vary from instant to instant.

Flow Patterns

The pattern of flow around a submerged object can be represented on a diagram by means of a selection of streamlines. When the fluid velocity at a given point depends not only on the position of the point but also on the time, the streamlines will alter from instant to instant. The aggregate of all the streamlines at a given instant constitutes the *flow pattern* at that instant.

A flow pattern can be indicated by selecting streamlines that show the direction of flow at various points in the pattern. Of the infinite number of possible streamlines, a few are chosen, usually from 5 to 10, in such a way as to divide the flow into a number of "channels," all carrying the same quantity of water per second. Given that a reduction in width corresponds to an increase in velocity, a flow pattern can be used to give not only the direction of flow but, from the spacing of the streamlines, the velocity of flow at any point (Figure 3.1). With a knowledge of the velocities, fluid dynamicists are able to use a flow pattern to estimate the pressure forces on the boundaries of the flow.

"Ideal Fluid"

When, in the 18th century, Euler and Bernoulli applied calculus to problems of fluid motion they founded the school of classical hydrodynamics that deals with motion in a hypothetical medium called an *ideal fluid*. Classical hydrodynamics became a subject immensely attractive to mathematicians, who made it so abstract as almost to deserve the name of "pure" mathematics.

In the real world, however, water reacts in ways not predicted by mathematics; for this reason, classical hydrodynamics has had considerably less appeal to engineers, who find its results either unintelligible or completely at variance with the behavior of real fluids. This largely academic study has made little effective contribution to solving practical problems because its ideal fluid is in one important respect unreal: It has no viscosity.

Problems in Predicting Resistance

Classical hydrodynamic theory, based on an ideal, nonviscous fluid, cannot predict resistance, even though prior to its construction Isaac Newton had explained the existence and the importance of viscosity and its effect in creating a resistance to the motion of bodies, even in such seemingly innocuous fluids as water and air. The lines of the classical hydrodynamicists' flow pattern diagrams are regular and constant and fail to explain those phenomena in which viscosity plays a significant part (Figure 3.2).

Figure 3.2 shows how classical hydrodynamics yields a flow pattern that is exactly the same at the front as at the rear, so that the velocity and pressure distributions fore and aft are the same. This diagram is remarkable in that if the arrows indicating the direction of flow were removed, it would be impossible to ascertain the stream's direction because the flow and pressure patterns are completely symmetrical. In addition, according to the ideal flow theory, the fluid slides past the body without sticking to it and forming a boundary layer. The symmetry of the flow pattern and the absence of a layer

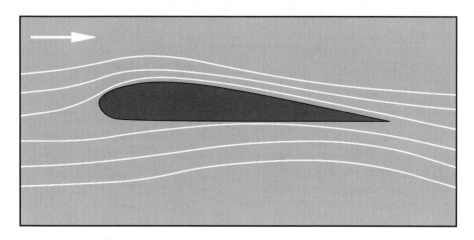

Figure 3.1 Flow pattern around airfoil showing the direction and velocity of the flow. Smaller spaces between streamlines show where velocity of the flow is highest.

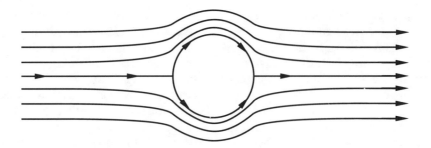

Figure 3.2 The classical hydrodynamicists drew beautiful patterns of "ideal" flow but made no allowance for the viscosity of a fluid. This figure, derived mathematically, depicts a nonviscous fluid's pattern of flow past a cylindrical obstacle.

of retarded fluid in this ideal nonviscous fluid mean that there is no drag force on the cylinder.

Similarly, in the illustrations accompanying texts on swimming, swimmers are often depicted in an ideal flow composed of neat, orderly, and predictable lines or, in other illustrations, shown suspended in "white" negative space as though the water did not exist.

Prediction of Flow Past a Solid

Because the viscosities of water and air are rather small—at least in comparison to obviously viscous fluids such as oil or honey—one might expect the ideal fluid theory to apply to flows of water and air with reasonable accuracy. In some types of problems this is so, but in the prediction of flow past a solid it gives significantly erroneous answers.

Water and air obviously exert drag, as can be observed readily by holding a tube out a car window or over the side of a boat. Their viscosities, small as they are, cannot be neglected in any theory for the prediction of drag. What actually happens is shown in Figure 3.3a and b.

The thin lines in this figure represent the average flow paths with the turbulent fluctuations removed. (This is a justifiable simplification of the actual flow pattern.) There is a boundary layer of retarded fluid around the front half of the cylinder, shown shaded, in which the fluid elements in contact with the body stick to it and, by viscous effects, slow down the motion of their outer neighbors.

Seen in another way, these moving neighbors, in resisting the retarding forces, exert a drag in the downstream direction on the sticking elements, which transmit it to the body as surface drag or skin friction. A drag between the wall and the fluid is thus always associated with the boundary layer. We can think of it in two ways, either as the fluid tending to drag the boundary downstream or as the boundary tending to retard the fluid.

Viscosity

Water does not accelerate to infinite speed because it has viscosity, or more simply, a "stickiness" or "elasticity." If water had no viscosity, the world's rivers, moving down valleys under the action of gravity, would flow with ever-increasing speed, reaching hundreds of miles per hour with disastrous results. A swimmer is able to "grip" the water only because viscosity pro-

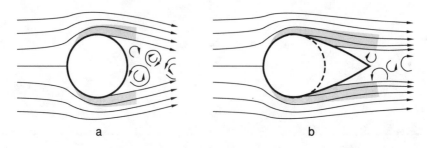

a   b

Figure 3.3 Turbulent flow past submerged bodies: (a) cylindrical body and (b) streamlined body. The boundary layers of retarded fluid are shaded.

duces separation of the flow. Flow separation causes a difference in the pattern of pressure around the hand. Under certain conditions, this pressure differential provides the resistance against which propulsion can be applied (Counsilman, 1971).

Paradoxically, although it helps a swimmer propel, viscosity also results in the form drag that resists the body's forward motion. Because of viscosity, when a body moves through a fluid the elements of that fluid in contact with the solid boundary stick to it. They do not slide along it, as one might expect. The elements close to the boundary move past their clinging neighbors. This relative movement brings into play viscous drag forces that oppose motion and cause friction or shearing. The reader can easily detect this viscous drag force by pulling a spoon out of a jar of honey. Part of the honey clings to the side of the jar and the intermediate honey suffers a distorting motion to which it objects and so resists. The faster the motion, the greater the resistance.

When a piece of rubber is bent or compressed it exerts a resisting force that disappears only when the rubber is allowed to return to its undistorted shape. In the case of honey, however, the resistance is to the distorting motion, not to the distortion itself, for when the motion ceases, the viscous drag force disappears—the spoon is not pulled back into the jar, as it would be if the honey behaved like rubber. In this sense, viscous resistance is quite different from elastic resistance.

Viscous drag effects are always present in the movement of air or water past solid boundaries, though they are less pronounced than those produced by thicker, stickier honey. Again, you can readily detect them by holding your hand out the window of a moving automobile or trailing it in the water over the side of a speedboat.

Viscosity plays a leading role in any state of fluid motion and is of particular importance in the process of fluid deformation. Fluids do not simply slip over solid surfaces, whether they are rough or smooth or, in the case of a swimmer, shaven or unshaven. In fact, right at the solid's surface, velocity is zero.

The Boundary Layer

It was the German mathematician Ludwig Prandtl who gave to the world the term "boundary layer" (*Grenzschicht*) and thereby introduced a concept now so familiar that it would be difficult to find many papers on fluid dynamics in which the term does not occur.

The major part of a viscous deformation is confined to what is known as the boundary layer, a relatively thin zone immediately adjoining the surface of a body moving through a fluid, such as air or water. The boundary layer, which is actually composed of a number of very thin layers, always holds a *velocity gradient*; this means that each successive layer moves at a greater speed than the previous one. At the surface, velocity is zero, because the first layer sticks to the skin, and each successive layer flows a little more easily until free flow results (Figure 3.4a and b).

Whenever a fluid flows past a stationary obstacle or a solid body moves through a fluid, molecular attraction prevents any relative motion

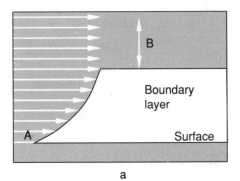

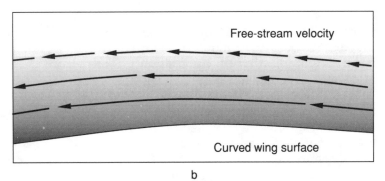

a   b

Figure 3.4 Velocity gradient at the boundary layer. (a) Viscosity at the boundary layer causes a velocity gradient in the passing flow. Flow decreases speed toward the surface. At A the flow is static and at B it is moving at full speed. (b) The nature of flow over a foil is the result of viscosity (or "stickiness") of the fluid. The first layer actually sticks to the foil surface, not moving at all, but each successive tier of the flow moves a little faster and gradually builds up to free-stream velocity.

between the fluid and the body at the surface itself. Thus, no matter how rapidly a fluid is forced through a pipe or a flow channel, its speed is exactly zero at the wall. When an aircraft or an artillery shell rushes through the atmosphere, the velocity of the air immediately adjacent to the surface of the body is, at any instant, exactly equal to that of the moving body, although a fraction of an inch away, outside the boundary layer, it is quite different.

A Fluid's Resistance to an Object Moving Through It Appears as Drag or Lift

Both air and water are fluids. Fluid mechanical principles apply to any propulsion through a fluid whether by natural or mechanical means. All propulsion through a fluid, whether by airscrews, propellers, birds, flying insects, fish, or human swimmers, employs the same physical laws but not always in quite identical fashion. Where appropriate, I will compare swimming propulsion to these other mechanisms.

Propulsion results from the application of force against a fluid's resistance to the motion. A fluid can manifest its resistance to an object moving through it in two ways: as drag acting in the direction opposing that of the motion, or as lift, also known as *side thrust*, acting perpendicular to the direction of motion.

Unless there is some obstruction, a flowstream will take the shortest route from one point to another of lower pressure. Any obstacle in the flowstream will force the fluid to deviate from its normally straight path, producing a reaction on the obstacle in the form of resistance. The greater the deviation inflicted on the fluid, the greater the resistance. Therefore, the shape of the body in relation to the flowstream has a significant effect on the resistance. The best way to illustrate this is by drawing streamlines to indicate both the direction and speed of the flowstream at given points.

A thin plate held with its edge toward the flowstream offers minimum resistance because it causes minimum deviation in the path of the fluid, which follows a steady smooth route (Figure 3.5).

Holding the same plate at right angles to the flowstream will increase the fluid resistance, or drag, several hundred times (Figure 3.6). In this position, the fluid in front must change direction drastically, while behind the plate the flow-

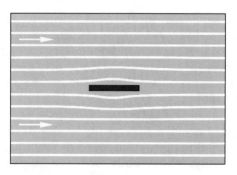

Figure 3.5 Thin plate held edge-on to the flowstream.

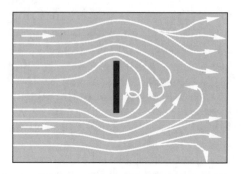

Figure 3.6 Thin plate held perpendicular to the flowstream.

stream is broken into turbulent eddies—the greater the turbulence, the greater the drag.

The Angle of Attack

The angle at which a body meets the flowstream, or angle of attack, is a crucial factor. The angle of attack has nothing to do with the horizontal (parallel to the ground) but is instead the angle at which the object meets the flowstream. In the example of the thin plate, we know that there is minimum flow resistance when the plate is held with its edge to the stream and maximum drag when held at a right angle, but what happens when the leading

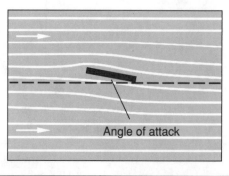

Angle of attack

Figure 3.7 Thin plate inclined to the flowstream to form an angle of attack.

edge is inclined at a slight angle? (See Figure 3.7.)

The fluid pressure is now greater underneath the plate than on the top surface, producing a lifting force, or side thrust, acting at right angles to the oncoming flowstream. But whenever lift is generated, drag is also created. Drag acts in the direction opposite to the motion of the object. Whereas lift acts at right angles to the flowstream, drag acts parallel to it. The net result is that the total force on the plate will be backward as well as upward (Figure 3.8).

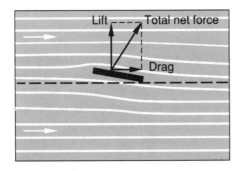

Figure 3.8   Lift and drag forces act upon a thin plate inclined at an angle of attack.

The Role of Airfoils in Creating Lift

Heavier-than-air flight is a frequently cited example of lift. Lift, or the force that pushes a wing upward, results from a difference in pressure between the wing's top and bottom surfaces. Although it is possible for a flat object to function as a simple wing—for example, the thin, balsa wood wings of toy gliders—shaping and streamlining a wing in a certain way can dramatically improve its aerodynamic and lifting qualities.

An airfoil is a body (in this case, a wing) designed to present a surface rounded and angled to the flowstream, creating maximum downwash and lift with minimum turbulence and drag. The gradual curvature of the airfoil produces a faster flow over its more rounded upper surface that does not break away and form eddies.

The wing's shape—slightly cambered, with a blunt leading edge and a sharp trailing edge—causes faster air flow over the top than across the bottom. This creates a lower average air pressure on top, producing enough lift to keep aloft an airplane or, for that matter, a bird.

This is how the airfoil scores over a flatter wing: Unlike a flat plate, an airfoil, with its humped upper surface, will produce lift even when the angle of attack is zero degrees. Further lift is gained by increasing the angle of attack so that the air meets the under surface at a steeper angle.

A propeller works exactly as a wing does, by making use of the lift-producing property of an airfoil, but with this exception: An airfoil used as a wing should produce the maximum force at right angles to the direction of motion, but one used as a propeller should deliver a maximum force in the direction of motion.

The Principle of the Propeller in Nature

The thrust of the propeller is obtained by giving a backward velocity to the fluid with which it comes in contact; to do this effectively, the propeller blades are given first an airfoil shape and then a twist. The airfoil contour combined with a twist is a shape common in nature, and in fact, these shapes originally were borrowed from nature. Unlike the mechanical propeller, however, birds and fish can change the shapes of their propelling surfaces according to the needs of propulsion: high-speed bursts, cruising, soaring, and so on.

Implications for Human Swimming Propulsion

The motion of an airplane propeller through a fluid is composed of a rotation about its axis together with the forward motion of the aircraft, so that the blades move forward on spirals. This *spiral*, or *helicoidal*, path is common in locomotion in nature. This spiral-like action may have a distinct application to improving the efficiency of human swimming propulsion, especially during those transitional phases of the stroke when the hand changes its direction.

Reference has been made to the unique qualities of the airfoil, a version of which is the propeller, but what is its application to swimming? James Counsilman (1971) cites the Bernoulli principle to show that swimmers propel by using their hands and feet as foils to produce lift. Counsilman's landmark presentation was followed by numerous papers by other observers contending that lift is produced by using hands and feet like propellers.

Fluid dynamic principles suggest, however, that although human swimmers do use foil-like actions to produce predominant lift propulsion, it is unlikely that the mechanism used is exactly like that of a mechanical propeller or any other form of conventional airfoil. Studies of the flow reactions produced by skilled swimmers indicate instead the use of ''unconventional'' lift-producing mechanisms that, albeit to a limited and modest extent, are basically similar in principle to those observed in nature. Before I develop this argument, however, the reader must understand the role of *flow circulation* and why it is necessary to produce lift.

The Role of Flow Circulation in Lift Propulsion

How Different Pressures Cause Lift to Occur

When a stream of fluid passes around a foil, the flow over the convex upper surface has a greater velocity and, following the Bernoulli principle, a lower pressure than that on the under surface; the difference in pressure between the two creates lift (Figure 3.9).

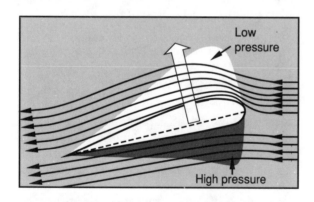

Figure 3.9   Differences in flow pressure around a foil create a lift force.

The Bernoulli principle can be demonstrated quite simply by creasing two pieces of paper at an obtuse angle, holding them an inch or two apart, and blowing between them. Instead of opening up, the space between the two sheets narrows. Because the air is incompressible, it must accelerate to pass through the constriction, thereby reducing the pressure inside, and the higher pressure on the outside surfaces forces the two sheets together (Figure 3.10). Another experiment demonstrating Bernoulli's principle is to lightly dangle a tablespoon be-

Figure 3.10   Simple demonstration of the Bernoulli principle.

tween finger and thumb and direct a jet of tap water along its convex surface. Instead of pushing the spoon away, the water will draw it into the jet (Figure 3.11).

Figure 3.11   Instead of pushing the spoon away, the jet of water sucks the spoon inward.

Both experiments illustrate the drop in pressure that occurs when the speed of air or water increases. The shape of the spoon shows a marked similarity to the wing of a bird or airplane, and in fact, all three behave like foils.

Understanding Circulation

Circulation is a fundamental concept in fluid dynamics. Even a stone thrown through the air has a circulation associated with it. Circulation in the form of a *bound vortex* around a propelling member must exist before lift propulsion can take place. The principle of circulation is not only the basis of airfoil design, but is valid for bodies other than airfoils and applies to fish propulsion, bird flight, and human swimming propulsion. In the case of a human swimmer, a bound vortex appears as a rotating flow in circulation around a hand, foot, or limb (Colwin, 1984a).

The Magnus Effect

The *Magnus effect* is the example commonly used in fluid dynamics of how lift is created when circulation exists around a rotating body in a uniform flowstream. If we could see a stream of fluid (air or water) flowing past a lifting foil, it would appear as if the fluid were actually circulating around it. Consider, for example, a horizontal revolving cylinder. When the cylinder is immersed in a fluid and spun anticlockwise around its axis, the surrounding fluid is set in motion and rotates with the cylinder. This is called a *bound vortex* (Figure 3.12).

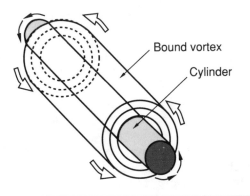

Figure 3.12 Bound vortex forms around a rotating cylinder in a still fluid.

If a horizontal flow were now to stream from right to left, the combination of the anticlockwise rotating fluid of the bound vortex and the horizontal flow would cause an increase in the speed of the fluid above and a decrease below. The net result would be a decrease in pressure above and an increase below—the usual Bernoulli effect—together with an upwash in front and a downwash behind. *In effect, the spinning cylinder would be subjected to lift in the same way as an airfoil* (Figure 3.13). This phenomenon is known as the Magnus effect. The resulting pressure differential causes the cylinder to

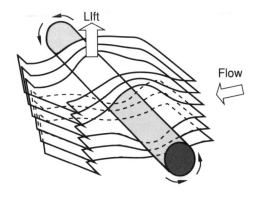

Figure 3.13 Lift generated by a rotating cylinder in horizontally moving flow.

move upward. It is important to understand that without the rotational flow of fluid (bound vortex) and its superimposition on the flowstream there would be no lifting force. A difference in pressure transverse to the direction of motion always exists, as we have seen, when a cylinder or sphere rotates in a flow and so introduces circulation into a uniform stream. The Magnus effect also explains the flight of a "cut" tennis ball or the swerving flight of a golf ball.

Flow Circulation and the Human Swimmer

Although human limbs cannot develop lift propulsion in exactly the same manner as a revolving cylinder, this basic example of the Magnus effect shows that lift depends on the presence of a bound vortex around a propelling member that is superimposed on a flow.

Later in this chapter I will show how human swimmers generate predominant lift-force propulsion. The necessary flow circulation is developed mainly by directional changes of the foil-shaped hand aided by a significant degree of hand-forearm rotation. However, it is first necessary to enlarge on the subject of circulation with specific reference to the profile of the propelling member.

Joukowski Airfoils or Profiles

The Russian scientist N.E. Joukowski developed a mathematical process (Kutta-Joukowski Theorem, 1905) for changing the *profile* of a circle into an airfoil profile. The same process can be used in developing a profile of the hand of a human swimmer. The ability to use this information to determine the flow circulation around a swimmer's hand, especially when superimposed on the general flow, has obvious implications.

The example of a revolving cylinder in a flow-stream cited in connection with the Magnus effect frequently forms a most convenient starting point for discussions on the lift principle because of the symmetry of the cylinder and the simplicity of the resulting flow. Joukowski saw that it would be a great advance if some way could be found to deduce the flow around a body of more difficult shape, such as an airfoil, from the flow around a cylinder. He devised a method of doing just that which also provided a means of producing airfoil shapes by a purely mathematical, almost mechanical, process.

Conformal Transformation. Joukowski's method is based on what mathematicians call *conformal transformation*, essentially the same method used to make a flat map of the earth's surface, which is known as a Mercator projection. This is simply a two-dimensional map of the earth's curved, three-dimensional surface in which the meridians and parallels of latitude on the sphere correspond to straight lines parallel to the axes on the flat map. Like all conformal maps, it leaves angles unaltered, but lengths become distorted. In a Mercator projection the distortion is greatest near the poles and least in the center of the map.

In the aerodynamic problem, Joukowski's task was very different from the mapmaker's. He wanted the circle representing the cross-section of the original cylinder to occupy the center of the original picture, but in the center of the map he wanted not a circle but a shape bearing a close resemblance to an airfoil. That is, the distortion must be severe in the center of the map but negligible at points remote from the center, so that he could retain the same undisturbed flow in both the original and the map.

Joukowski developed a simple mathematical formula that had exactly these properties: He found how to transform a circle into an airfoil shape, with the streamlines of the flow around the circle transforming into those around the airfoil, leaving the flow unchanged at points far away from the body.

Figure 3.14 shows examples of some of these transformations. In the first of these, the original circle lies with its center at the origin of coordinates, and as would be expected, the map

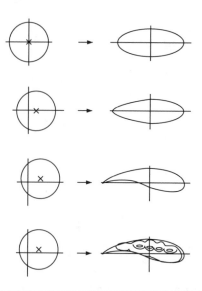

Figure 3.14 Conformal transformation: Joukowski's mathematical process for changing the profile of a circle into an airfoil profile. It is possible that the same principle could be used to develop a profile of the hand of a human swimmer, proving its use as a foil.

shows a symmetrical figure (actually an ellipse), so that the flow would be around a new shape more streamlined than a circle. The second example introduces a certain amount of asymmetry by placing the center of the circle to the left of the origin; the map shows what may be regarded as a distorted ellipse, a curve with a blunt, rounded nose and a sharp tail, having symmetry around a center line. Such a shape is suitable for a rudder or strut and is a closer approximation to a true streamlined shape than is the ellipse.

Finally, when symmetry is destroyed in both directions by displacing the center of the circle both to the right and upward, the map produced shows an asymmetrical closed curve of the desired airfoil type, with a rounded nose leading to a well-arched upper surface and a sharp tail. The flow around a body of this type should approximate that around a real wing. The last diagram shows that a hand resembles this final transformation.

Such outlines are called *profiles*, and it is possible to obtain almost any airfoil shape by using the method just described. The basic idea underlying the use of conformal transformation in aerodynamics is that the overwhelmingly difficult problem of finding the flow around a given airfoil profile can be solved by starting with the known flow around a body of very simple shape, and deducing from it the flow around another body that looks very much like an airfoil. Profiles that have been developed by purely mathematical methods from circles have certain definite advantages, including the fact that lift can be calculated in advance.

Lanchester's Theory of Circulation

In the case of an airfoil, there is no source of mechanical rotation, so it is not obvious at first sight how it develops lift by creating circulation. F.W. Lanchester (1907), with what later proved to have been amazing insight, took the bold step of assuming that an airfoil's lift is associated with circulation despite the fact that the airfoil does not rotate.

This must have seemed a very dubious assertion at the time, but it is now known that any kind of body must have circulation around it to develop lift in a flowstream. Unless the body is specially shaped, however, the circulation is very feeble, and there is virtually no lift. As mentioned earlier, an airfoil has a specially designed shape that, when the airfoil is propelled through a fluid, generates a strong circulation without causing a large drag, and it is just this property that enables propulsion without rotating surfaces to create lift.

How an Airfoil Creates Circulation. We can now study airfoils as specially designed devices that do not need to rotate but are still able to create and maintain circulation. If we could move with an undisturbed flowstream and watch the fluid moving over an airfoil, the fluid would seem to circulate. The fluid moving upward and over the top of the airfoil flows more quickly then the main flowstream, whereas the fluid underneath flows more slowly; relatively speaking, the flow appears to move in a circle.

The idea of relative flow around an airfoil is a different perception of circulation; in this case, the *bound vortex* is a mathematical concept represented by the surface of the airfoil itself and not actually visible (see ''Joukowski Airfoils or Profiles,'' page 59). The bound vortex around an airfoil is usually denoted as shown in Figure 3.15.

How a Starting Vortex Creates Circulation in the Form of a Bound Vortex

To see what happens when a foil starts to move through a stationary fluid, hold a piece of inclined cardboard in smoke and move it from rest: You will see an eddy shed from its trailing edge (Figure 3.16). This is called a *starting vortex*; it is generated every time a foil starts its movement. A starting vortex is also generated when the hand or foot of a skilled swimmer starts a propulsive impulse in a particular direction.

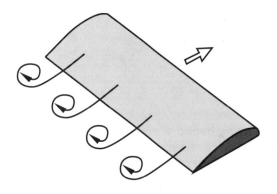

Figure 3.16 Eddies shed from the trailing edge of a moving foil.

One of the rules of fluid dynamics is that a vortex cannot be created without the production of a countervortex of equal strength circulating in the opposite direction (the principle of conservation of angular momentum). In the case of an airfoil, the countervortex is in fact the bound vortex, which is responsible for circulation and the production of lift, and it owes its continuing existence to the shearing forces over the surfaces of the foil (Figure 3.17).

Experiments with a revolving cylinder in a flow channel show the reappearance of the starting vortex once the flow is switched off and circulation has ceased. Right at the end, the starting vortex appears, almost like a movie played in reverse. In the strict technical sense, however, this vortex is known as the *finishing,* or *shed, vortex.*

It is provable mathematically that because a

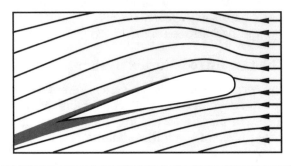

Figure 3.15 A bound vortex around an airfoil is a mathematical concept represented by the profile of the airfoil itself and is not actually visible.

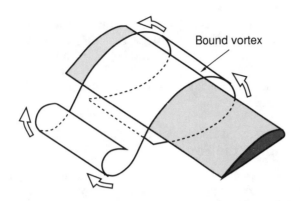

Figure 3.17 Starting vortex and the production of its countervortex, the bound vortex.

flow does not contain a circulation at the start of a movement through it, it cannot contain a circulation at the end of the movement. This principle applies to lift propulsion in human swimming: The shed vortex at the end of each propulsive impulse within a swimming stroke indicates that the propulsive effort in that particular direction has ended.

From the preceding it can be seen that any lift-producing mechanism comprises the following three phases of vortex action:

1. The starting vortex
2. The bound vortex
3. The finishing vortex (also termed the shed, or free, vortex)

Tip or Trailing Vortex

As well as providing lift, the difference in pressure between the lower and upper surfaces of a foil causes a related effect known as *tip vortex* or *trailing vortex*. Explained simply, tip vortex results from the tendency of any fluid to flow from high to low pressure. As there is no barrier

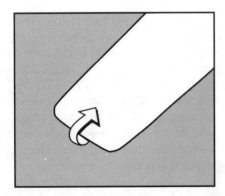

Figure 3.18 As there is no barrier at the foil tips, the fluid leaks from the high-pressure area beneath the foil to the low-pressure area on the top surface.

at the foil tips separating the high from the low pressure areas, the fluid leaks from underneath the foil to the top surface (Figure 3.18). This flow, or leakage, deflects the fluid on the top surface slightly inward and that on the bottom surface outward, introducing a third dimension to the flow around the foil (Figure 3.19).

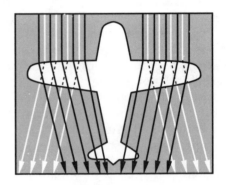

Low-pressure air = black

High-pressure air = white

Figure 3.19 Foil tip leakage introduces a third dimension to the flow around the foil.

The streams meeting at the foil's trailing edges cross one another to form a series of small trailing vortices that join into one large vortex at each foil tip. The energy utilized in the formation of the *vortex trail* appears as the *induced drag*. Obviously, to increase speed, extra thrust is needed to overcome the resistance caused by induced drag (Figure 3.20). Even on a foil of finite span in steady motion, however, induced drag cannot be eliminated, for it is a necessary adjunct of lift. Similarly, a swimmer propelling with lift force predominating will always produce induced drag. Accidental flow aeration (entrapment of air in the water) often produces visible evidence of trailing vortices on a swimmer's hands in the early stages of crawl, butterfly, and backstroke (Figure 3.21).

The Organized Vortex System

The term *organized vortex system* refers to propulsion developed by foil-type lift with a bound vortex in place and trailing vortices springing from the tip of the foil. As mentioned earlier, a propeller is a rotating foil or wing, and when lift is uniformly distributed along its blade span, an *organized vortex system* will exist. When swimmers use the hand like an airfoil, an *organized vortex system* will exist.

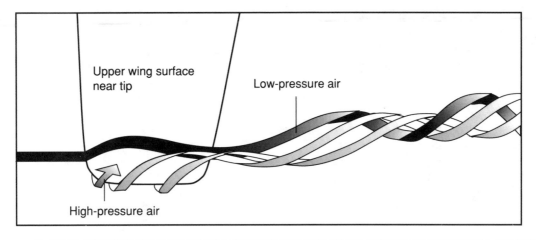

Figure 3.20 High- and low-pressure streams meet to form a vortex trail.

Figure 3.21 Trailing (tip) vortices are often shed from a swimmer's hands in the early stages of the crawl, butterfly, and backstroke pull. In these instances it is certain that lift is the predominant force acting upon the swimmer's hand at the start of the stroke. However, if a swimmer's hand enters the water and immediately pulls directly backward, a predominant drag force will be created and, instead of tip vortices, a typical loop (elongated) vortex will be shed from the hand early in the stroke.

Foil-Type Propulsion in Steady Flow Conditions

The use of foil-type lift propulsion, in the strictest sense of the term, is limited to steady flow conditions, in which the flow pattern does not change over time; such is the case for a conventional airfoil lift-producing mechanism. This means that the foil must be positioned at an angle of attack that results in a steady circulating flow over its surface. If the foil's angle of attack becomes too large, the flow will detach from it, break up, and become unsteady, causing a loss of the vortex circulation necessary for creating lift. This phenomenon is called "stall."

Airfoils are designed specifically to create the steady flow circulation that causes constant lift propulsion. *Lift may be generated in any direction.* A swimmer's arm can be used as a swimming foil, if angled properly (Figure 3.22); for example, as a crawl swimmer's arm enters the water with the elbow set higher than the wrist, its cambered upper surface causes the oncoming

flow to move more quickly over the upper surface of the arm and more slowly along the lower surface. The different flow velocities over the upper and lower arm produce the pressure differential necessary for lift. In this case, the lift is upward, causing a high position of the upper body in the water but not contributing directly to propulsion.

As the hand moves further into the stroke it assumes an angle favorable to producing forward-inclined lift. This position lasts only a

Figure 3.22 Different flow velocities over the upper and lower arm produce a pressure differential.

short while, however. Most skilled swimmers establish steady flow propulsion (with an organized vortex system) at the beginning of the stroke. But subsequent directional changes of hand and limb cause increased angles of attack that quickly lead to quasisteady, then nonsteady, flow. In crawl, butterfly, and backstroke it soon becomes difficult to continue developing lift circulation by means of the conventional airfoil lift-producing mechanism because the changing postures of the hand cause too large an angle of attack.

The hand and forearm action in swimming propulsion has been likened to that of a propeller blade. But the 360-degree rotation around an axis of a mechanical propeller is anatomically impossible for a hand. An airfoil can maintain an angle of attack which produces continuous steady flow circulation. But photographs taken in a wind tunnel show what happens to the flow reaction around a cranked plate (a type of foil) as the angle of attack is changed (Figure 3.23): the flow changes from steady to quasisteady and then to unsteady. Under unsteady flow conditions ideal foil-type lift becomes impossible.

The onset of unsteady flow conditions is marked by the tendency of the vortex trail to swell and start to burst. If the foil's angle of attack continues to increase, the vortex trail will detach from the foil, indicating that circulation has been lost and that an organized vortex system is no longer in place. Foil-type propulsion, in its accepted sense, has terminated. Similarly,

when a swimmer's hand approaches too large an angle of attack, conventional foil-type propulsion is no longer possible.

The illustrations of an Olympic butterfly champion show reactions similar to those around a cranked plate in the wind tunnel (Figure 3.24). This is not a unique observation, for

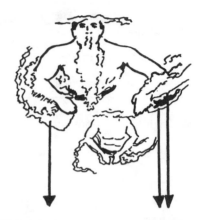

Right hand is pitched at too large an angle of attack, causing trailing vortex to swell and start to burst. Trailing vortex is about to detach from hand, indicating foil-type lift is ending (see inset figure).

Left hand is pitched at ideal angle of attack. Thin trailing vortices are characteristic of steady flow. Vortex sheet is seen as dark area between trailing vortices.

Figure 3.24 Butterfly stroke: quasi-steady flow (right hand) and steady flow (left hand). Adapted from photos courtesy of James E. Counsilman.

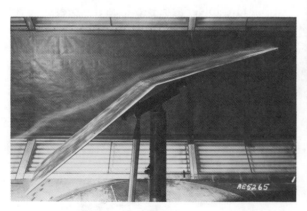

a   b

Figure 3.23 The changing flow reaction around a cranked plate at different angles of attack. (a) A steady flow over a cranked plate at the angle of attack. (b) As the angle of attack becomes too large, a quasi-steady flow results and the trailing vortex is about to burst. These smoke flow visualizations were created in a 6 × 9 foot tunnel. This effect has also been reproduced in a 13 × 10 inch water tunnel using the hydrogen bubble technique. *Note.* Reprinted by permission of National Research Council, Ottawa, Canada.

the flow reactions produced by skilled swimmers consistently indicate that human swimming propulsion takes place in conditions of unsteady flow.

Propulsion in Nonsteady Flow

The essential problem, hitherto ignored in analytical studies of human swimming, is that swimming propulsion occurs mainly in unsteady flow. There can be no doubt about this; the stroke mechanics of even the most skilled swimmers consistently produce unsteady flow reactions, because a swimmer's hand, as it travels through a wide range of movement, quickly assumes too large an angle of attack for steady flow to continue. Whereas an airfoil, which is specifically designed for the purpose, can maintain the ideal angle of attack to produce the steady flow necessary for constant lift propulsion, a swimmer cannot use the hand like a conventional foil throughout a swimming stroke. The action of the hand in the swimming strokes simply cannot be described with steady state aerodynamics.

Another important reason why the hand does not operate as a conventional airfoil is that at the start of an airfoil's movement (for example, an airplane at takeoff), the net lift around the airfoil is very small. The smooth characteristics and lift of steady flow are established only after the airfoil has moved about ten chords (a chord is the width of the foil from leading edge to trailing edge) from its starting point. The interaction between opposing currents of air (or fluid) that delays the creation of steady lift is called the *Wagner effect* and contributes an unavoidable nonsteady phase in the action of normal airfoils. A swimmer's hand is not in the water at an ideal angle of attack long enough to obtain constant lift in the manner of an airfoil.

The question, then, is whether predominant lift-force propulsion can be developed in unsteady flow conditions. It can, but the lift-producing mechanism is an unconventional one that does not require the propelling member to be placed at an ideal angle of attack.

The lift force generated by a foil is directly proportional to the foil's surface area and the density of the fluid in which it is moving. Given that the density of water is 800 times the density of air, the human hand moving in water generates a force equal to that generated by a surface 800 times its size moving in air at the same speed. Because the lift force generated by a foil is directly proportional to the square of its speed through the fluid, a 40% increase in the speed of the hand when employed as a foil can almost double the propulsive force generated.

In swimming, lift-force propulsion is developed in unsteady flow primarily by the directional changes of the foil-shaped hand as it moves through the stroke. The gradual rotation of the hand and forearm as a unit as the stroke progresses is an important part of this lift-producing mechanism. In all the styles of swimming, the stroke commences with the palm facing outward (to lesser or greater degrees, depending on the flexibility of the individual swimmer). As the arm reaches midstroke, the elbow reaches maximum flexion at plus or minus 90 degrees, thus indicating a considerable amount of hand-forearm rotation since the stroke commenced.

As stated, it is the rotating hand-forearm unit, moving laterally, or transversely across the line of the body's forward movement, that generates the lift. This action causes a pressure differential in the flow, which in turn sets up the flow circulation around the hand and forearm necessary for lift to occur. As the arm bends and the hand and forearm gradually rotate, the flow is *swirled* or *wrapped* around the hand and forearm. This swirling flow constitutes the bound vortex, or circulation, whose superimposition on the general flow is necessary for lift. As the arm extends again and the final propelling thrust of the stroke is applied, this circulating flow is gradually *unswirled* or *unwrapped* from the arm in the form of a shed vortex.

It can be seen that propulsion is created by means of force impulses applied against the water. These force impulses are associated with sculling actions produced by directional changes of the hand as it follows its curved-line path through the swimming stroke. Depending on the style of swimming, skilled swimmers usually create two or three impulses within each swimming stroke when swimming at speed and only one impulse when swimming more slowly. Some "long-geared" swimmers, however, with classic long-flowing strokes, perform only one impulse within the stroke even when moving at speed, but these "one-impulse" swimmers usually have difficulty accelerating when they need to because of their inability to "gear up" the action.

As already explained, directional changes of the hand combine with a significant range of hand-forearm rotation to set up the mechanism necessary for creating flow circulation. These flows are readily visible in shadowgram tests conducted at low speeds, when the flow is not too compressed to be easily seen.

You may conduct similar tests by simply moving a spoon or any other suitable foil-shaped object through the appropriate directions in a container of water. If you have a strong overhead light and the bottom of the tank is white, you will see the shadow cast by the resulting vortex on the bottom of the tank and be able to note the different flow reactions produced by rectilinear and curvilinear movements. This simple test shows distinct differences between the flow reactions set up by

1. drag propulsion (pulling directly backward),
2. the conventional airfoil mechanism, and
3. a curvilinear pulling pattern (Figure 3.25a-c).

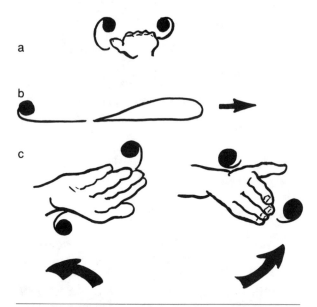

Figure 3.25 Typical flow reactions: (a) drag propulsion (pulling directly backward); (b) conventional airfoil method; and (c) outward and inward sculling—curvilinear pulling pattern. In both the inward and outward scull there are always leading edge and trailing edge vortices around the hand.

Vortex Reactions in Producing Lift

Essentially, fluid dynamics as applied to lift-force propulsion in swimming comprises a three-fold sequence of events:

1. At the start of a propulsive impulse, a starting vortex produces a bound vortex around a hand, foot, or limb.

2. The bound vortex is then manipulated in such a way as to enable lift force to be applied.
3. When circulation (in the form of a bound vortex) can no longer be produced and maintained, a vortex is shed, indicating that the propulsive impulse has ended.

The Significance of the Shed Vortex

A vortex is shed whenever a propulsive impulse ends. The analysis of these vortex patterns produced by each swimming stroke provides a new perspective from which to view swimming efficiency. The pattern of shed vortices a swimmer leaves in the water provides an instant history of the swimming stroke, because each propulsive impulse within the overall stroke produces a distinctive type of vortex as its signature.

Recognizable patterns reveal how individual swimmers apply their power. By its size, shape, direction, velocity, and placement in the flow field in relation to the swimming stroke, the shed vortex reveals

1. the type of propulsive mechanism the swimmer has used and
2. the net effectiveness of the propulsive impulse just completed.

Kinetic Energy

A shed vortex represents a form of *kinetic energy*, or in other words, the energy of motion. We know that energy cannot be created or destroyed, but it can be transferred from one type to another. Energy is transferred from the swimmer to the water in the form of kinetic energy whenever a vortex is shed. (In fact, energy is being changed from one form into another whenever work is done or energy expended.) Vortices shed at random and not at the end of a propulsive impulse indicate wasted energy that a swimmer is not applying to the water in the most effective manner.

Studying Flow Reactions to the Swimming Stroke

I conducted a study that sought to identify flow reactions common to the stroke mechanics of world-class swimmers. A methodical analysis of underwater movies, slides, and photographs consistently revealed similar patterns of vorticity (Colwin, 1984a).

By correlating commonly observed flow reactions with established fluid dynamic principles—particularly those concerning lift propulsion—I attempted to establish a basis for further study. The flow visibility was not always complete because observation depended largely on accidental air entrapment (aeration) in the swimming stroke; nevertheless, it was possible to form a synthesis of the flow reactions that could be anticipated during key phases of propulsion. (More recently, I have noted the advantages of underwater video recordings of swimmers during actual competition races using the ''Coachscope'' apparatus invented by Albert Stephens. When swimming at speed most swimmers accidentally entrap enough air into the water to make the flow reactions almost continuously visible.)

I systematically compared these observations with aerodynamic theory as well as with the theory that relates to lift-propulsion in nature. I was especially interested in seeking reasons for what initially appeared to be unusual vortex formations that indicated propulsion was taking place in unsteady flow.

Although airfoils are designed to develop steady flow, human swimming propulsion, because of anatomical restrictions, must employ directional changes of the limbs that cause unsteady flow. I believe that skilled human swimmers, like birds, fish, and certain flying insects, are able to turn unsteady flow to advantage by using dexterous movements that establish the necessary flow circulation through the rapid generation and shedding of vortices.

Chapter 4

A New Look at the Propulsive Mechanisms of Swimming

The dynamics of all the swimming strokes cause fluctuating flow conditions because the continual directional changes of the hands are not conducive to maintaining steady flow. Although most skilled swimmers establish steady state propulsion with organized vortex systems at the beginning of a stroke, subsequent hand and limb directional changes quickly lead to a sequence of quasisteady to nonsteady periods. These directional changes are often difficult for some swimmers to accomplish without losing propulsion. However, underwater photography of skilled swimmers indicates the shedding of large separate vortices approximate to the time of the hand's directional change.

The Hand as a Swim Foil

A shed vortex indicates that a propulsive impulse in a particular direction has ended. World-ranked swimmers are invariably observed to shed a large vortex during a change of hand direction; these great athletes may be showing the ideal way to propel. Acceleration to top swimming speed requires sharp directional changes of the hand instead of the smooth, rounded transitions seen at slower speeds. However, vortex shedding *before* a propulsive impulse has ended is often a sign of inefficient technique. Common causes of prematurely shed vortices are holding the hand too

rigidly on the wrist or too sudden a directional change combined with excessive acceleration and application of force.

In high-speed swimming every stroke consists of *distinct* impulses that accelerate with each change of hand direction. After a vortex is shed at the end of an impulse, a new vortex is quickly generated around the hand as it changes direction. Proof of this can often be seen in the subsequent shedding of the "new" vortex—albeit a somewhat smaller one—at the end of the stroke.

An Alternative Lift-Generating Mechanism

The quick generating and shedding of vortices just described is a propulsive mechanism prevalent in nature. This alternative lift-generating mechanism, unlike that of the conventional airfoil, is independent of foil shape and the existence of an ideal angle of attack. Instead, lift is established by creating a circulation (bound vortex) around the propelling member and superimposing this circulation on the general flow. (The role of flow circulation in lift propulsion is discussed extensively in chapter 3, "The Fluid Dynamics of Swimming Propulsion.")

Careful study reveals different types of vortex patterns in the flow field (Figure 4.1). The vortex pattern developed depends on the aptitude of the individual swimmer and the speed at which a distance is to be covered. As mentioned, high-speed swimming requires sharp

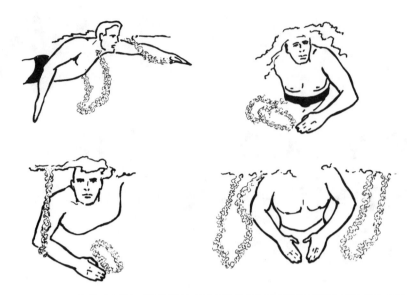

Figure 4.1 Different vortex patterns.

changes of hand direction that cause rapid shedding of large separate vortices at the end of each propulsive impulse. Conversely, longer distances may be covered more economically by steady acceleration of the hand with smoother and more rounded directional changes that result in a single propulsive impulse within each stroke. Drawings adapted from films confirm that an organized vortex system is maintained longer at slower swimming speeds (Figure 4.2a-c).

The Dual Function of the Hand

Although the literature contains frequent discussions of the elbow's changing posture during the swimming stroke, little reference is made to the articulation of the hand on the wrist. A swimmer who possesses a natural "feel of the water" uses the hand to perform a dual function by *directing* and *channeling* the flow circulation while also *applying propulsive thrust*. In fact, the dexterous functioning of the entire arm in an undulating fashion, almost in the manner of an elongated flipper, is quite noticeable. Talented swimmers show unusual dexterity, particularly during transitional phases of the stroke, and create remarkably consistent vortex patterns in the flow field.

Comparisons are appropriate between human swimming and fluid dynamic propulsion in nature. This is because there are similar difficulties in coping with nonsteady flow. In fact, the similarities observed among the most diverse phenomena of fluid motion are not acci-

dental. They constitute, rather, a universal law of nature. It is therefore logical to compare examples from nature with human swimming propulsion.

Comparisons With Bird Flight

Lift-force propulsion is based on aerodynamic principles that in turn originated from Lilienthal's (1889) intensive observations of bird flight. Similarly, it is highly probable that skilled swimmers use methods of developing lift during nonsteady periods of propulsion which resemble those found in nature. I will discuss some of these unconventional mechanisms presently.

Aircraft and the majority of flying creatures fly in what might be called a standard way, using well-understood aerodynamic principles. But small birds and flying insects are able to perform in a manner that cannot be explained in simple aerodynamic terms. We know that aircraft depend on airfoils that move through the air steadily. Nonsteady flows around aircraft wings have to be minimized because they reduce flight efficiency. In contrast, nonsteady aerodynamics are an inherent feature of natural flapping flight.

The subtleties of oscillating, or flapping, wing movement are still not fully understood, but bird flight in its simplest form—gliding or soaring—does not require flapping or the consumption of muscle power. Simply by stretching out the wing, the outer part merges with

High-speed swimming may cause sharp changes in hand direction with shedding of ring vortices at the end of each propulsive impulse (a). A large ring vortex is shed as the hand changes direction in midstroke. The trailing vortices detach from the hand, indicating that the organized vortex system has ceased and that propulsion is no longer by foil-type lift. The remaining vorticity in circulation around the hand is shed at the end of the stroke by the fling-ring mechanism.

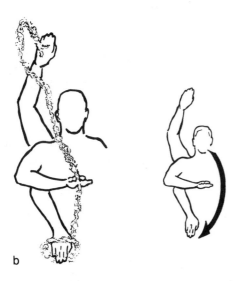

Smoother and rounder directional changes are achieved more easily at submaximal hand speed (b). Single-impulse propulsion and smooth hand acceleration help maintain an organized vortex system for most of the stroke. In the final stage of the stroke the vortex trail becomes unsteady and starts to burst as a single vortex ring is shed by the fling-ring mechanism.

By applying excessive power and/or accelerating the hand too rapidly, even top swimmers may shed random vortices (c). Spasmodic vortex shedding represents kinetic energy lost to the water and is also characteristic of poor directional control of the hand. Excessive vortex shedding is common; this suggests that overapplying propulsive force and failing to accelerate the hand smoothly are more prevalent faults than generally recognized. These habits may account for subpar performance even when an athlete feels strong and powerful.

Figure 4.2   Vortex shedding reveals the effects of different stroke patterns.

the arm section to form a continuous plane, so that the bird flies in a manner similar to a fixed-wing aircraft. This use of steady flow is similar to the way in which a swimmer "spreads" the arms sideways during the beginning phase of the butterfly and breaststroke arm actions.

This is one of the most economical movements in swimming, particularly in the butterfly stroke. It is also a remarkable simulation of natural flight. In fact, I like to instruct young swimmers to imagine they are giant condors with wings outstretched launching themselves from a high cliff into an oncoming sea breeze. When the start of the butterfly arm stroke is properly timed, this form of "subaqueous flying" (a term sometimes used to describe sea-lion propulsion) develops high body velocity and is aided by the momentum developed a split-second earlier from the downward thrust of the dolphin kick, another derivation from nature.

This steady flow phase of the arm action is present at the beginning of all four swimming styles. During this phase, an organized vortex system is in place, as shown by the presence of tip vortices coming off the hands. As the stroke changes direction, however, it becomes difficult to maintain steady flow and to continue to use the hand in an airfoil fashion. This is also true of the flapping (oscillating) wing. Because of anatomical structure, birds and insects are unable to maintain a constant production of lift.

Until quite recently, standard aerodynamics had failed to explain how birds and insects overcome these handicaps. But, thanks to the evidence of high-speed photography, the mystery is now near a solution.

The Rapid Generating and Shedding of Vortices

Birds and insects apparently employ mechanisms that swiftly establish air circulation around their wings, entailing the rapid generating and shedding of vortices. By so doing, they are able to generate lift more quickly than would be possible in steady airflow. This discovery cast an entirely new light on the problems that had long perplexed observers of bird and insect flight. The examples of aerodynamic propulsion in nature provide valid comparisons with human swimming propulsion, which also

has to cope with the problem of propelling in nonsteady flow.

Comparison Between an Oscillating Wing and a Propeller

In an important study von Holst and Kuchemann (1942) compared an oscillating wing with a simplified propeller. The study indicated that the propulsive efficiency of an oscillating wing is no less than that of a propeller. In fact, a propeller has the disadvantage of the induced drag caused by the trailing vortex system.

Most of our present knowledge of the flying characteristics of birds and insects has been gained by direct observation, sometimes aided by slow-motion movies or other means. This has been supplemented by model tests, either on actual flying models (ornithopters) or on ordinary wind-tunnel models. Von Holst and Kuchemann developed a great variety of models, each representing a certain type of flight. Special emphasis was placed on studying how to produce lifting and propulsive forces simultaneously.

Unsteady Flow in Nature. The flexible wing of the flying models uses a transverse oscillation as well as a rotating, or pitching, oscillation. Their motion bears an interesting comparison to the human swimming stroke with its constant directional changes of the hand in a path transverse to the swimmer's forward direction. The swimming action is accompanied by a significant degree of hand-forearm rotation combined with a continual adjustment of the degree of elbow bend. It is probable that this mechanism produces the necessary flow circulation for predominant lift-force propulsion to occur (Figure 4.3). When observing propulsion in unsteady flow in nature, it is important to note that the necessary bound vortex is created by mechanisms that operate *intermittently* in timing with the changing directions of the oscillating wing. As each propulsive impulse ends, a vortex is shed.

An expert swimmer propels by means of directional changes of the hands, which cause the rapid generating and shedding of vortices. This mechanism is probably similar in principle to the oscillating wing but only to the extent that the quick changes of hand direction generate the flow circulation necessary to produce lift-force propulsion. But, there the similarity to bird flight ends. Apart from possessing a basi-

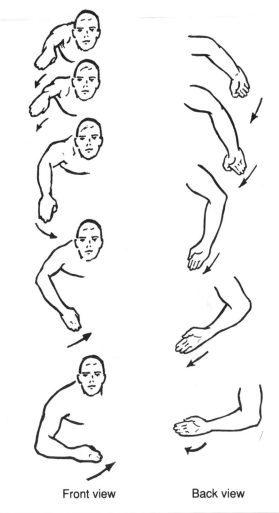

Front view   Back view

Figure 4.3 The crawl stroke arm action, from entry to midstroke. The directional changes of the hand, the bending of the elbow, and a significant degree of hand-forearm rotation set up the flow circulation necessary for predominant lift force propulsion to occur.

cally similar skeletal structure, the human arm bears not even a remote resemblance to a bird's wing nor does it flap while it propels.

Comparisons With Propulsion of Marine Animals

Marine animals, fishes, and birds are highly specialized for propulsion in their respective fluid mediums. At the outset, we may find it difficult to imagine how the human swimmer could possibly adopt any examples at all from nature, yet the classic example is the dolphin kick used in the butterfly stroke, which was developed in 1933 by Henry Myers, a swimmer at

the Dragon Swimming Club, Brooklyn (Kiphuth, 1942).

Based on the movement of the dolphin's tail, the dolphin kick represents the most effective attempt so far by humans to adopt a swimming technique from nature. Yet, despite the natural ease with which the dolphin kick fits in with the butterfly arm action, certain limitations in the human physique prevent the butterfly swimmer from completely emulating the harmonious locomotion displayed by the dolphin.

The main difference between the natural action of the dolphin and the acquired dolphin kick of the human swimmer is that the dolphin can perform the upbeat of its fluke, or tail, more quickly than the downbeat. The upbeat of the dolphin fluke is also faster than the upbeat of a swimmer's feet at equal movement frequencies. This is because the dolphin's musculature is more suited to producing a stronger movement on the upstroke of its fluke. The traces of the dolphin's fluke appear to be more symmetrical than those of human swimmers (Ungerechts, 1983).

Comparisons With Flipper Propulsion

We have seen how human swimmers use propulsive mechanisms based on the foil-type motions of bird flight and dolphin propulsion, despite the fact that our arms have not the slightest resemblance to wings or our legs to dolphin flukes. Are there other examples from nature that may also have relevance to human swimming? When we examine some of the principles of vertebrate locomotion in water, more similarities become apparent.

Vertebrates propel in water either by body undulations or movements of the limbs. There are two sorts of limb movements used by mammals and birds while swimming. One employs a directly backward thrust against the water, as in the paddling motion used by surface swimming birds and land animals. This motion is inefficient. This was the method used by human swimmers before biomechanical studies showed that talented athletes pull in a curved-line path.

The other method of limb propulsion employs an oblique thrust as in sculling with a single oar. This is a much more efficient method and is used by the forelimbs, or foreflippers, of sea lions, and the hind limbs of hair seals and walruses—and by the arms of skilled human swimmers.

The foreflipper action of the sea lion is of special interest because the sea lion is the only marine mammal that habitually uses its pectoral appendages for swimming. Sea lion foreflippers are exceptionally versatile in that the sea lion uses them to produce effective thrust on both land and in the water. In fact, the sea lion can fly clear of the water when it works up to high speed (English, 1976).

With its fusiform, or cigar-shaped, body (Figure 4.4), the relatively large surface area of its

Figure 4.4   The sea lion has a streamlined, cigar-shaped body. Its foreflippers have a relatively large surface area. *Note*. From Feldkamp (1987, p. 44). Reprinted by permission.

broad foreflippers, and center of gravity forward of the middle, the sea lion is highly adapted to swimming and altogether far better equipped than the human swimmer. Of special interest is the fact that its foreflipper is shaped not unlike the cantilevered strut of a hydrofoil. Apart from its hydrofoil shape, a sea lion's flipper is relatively long and narrow, with an aspect ratio (span over chord) of 7.9 (Feldkamp, 1985). A long flipper also produces thrust more efficiently (Alexander, 1983) (Figure 4.5).

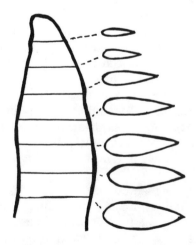

Figure 4.5   The streamlined cross section of the sea lion's foreflipper. *Note*. From Feldkamp (1987, p. 43). Reprinted by permission.

Does the swimming human arm work like a flipper? A skilled swimmer employs oblique sculling motions that produce a flipperlike three-dimensional undulation of the entire arm. Although the arm does act like an elongated flipper, a study of sea lion propulsion quickly shows the human arm to be severely limited by comparison. The human arm is much longer and narrower than a sea lion's foreflipper. Apart from the foil-shaped cross-section of the hand, the arm itself is of a more oblong shape, presenting less than ideal lifting surfaces (Figure 4.6a and b).

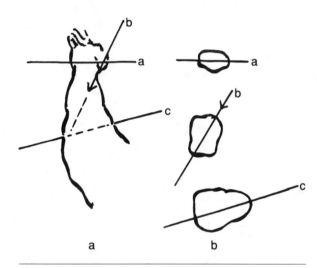

Figure 4.6   (a) Top view and (b) cross section of the human arm.

Something significant happens, however, when the arm is held in an elbow-up posture at the beginning phase of a swimming stroke: It assumes the typical cambered shape of a lift-producing foil, and, particularly in butterfly, with the hands set out from the wrists (ulnar-flexion), the arms resemble rudimentary hydrofoils. Acting like submerged hydrofoils, this assumed posture of the arms, shortly after the

Figure 4.7   Foil-like shape of arms in the butterfly stroke. *Note*. Drawn from photographs of Olympic swimmer Gary Hall (Counsilman, 1977, p. 183). Adapted by permission.

entry, seems to keep the body from sinking and in a level position so that straight forward propulsion can be applied effectively (Figure 4.7).

Transitional Phases of Sea Lion Propulsion.
Specialization for an amphibious lifestyle has produced increased mobility of the sea lion's shoulder joints, which permits large ranges of abduction and adduction (English, 1977). The range of motion permitted by these adaptations enables the sea lion to use its foreflippers effectively as hydrofoils (Feldkamp, 1987) (Figure 4.8).

An important feature of sea lion propulsion is that it avoids building up drag during transitional phases of its flipper action. It largely avoids the cyclic interruption of propulsive force by rotating the flipper to a positive angle of attack and raising it dorsally, thereby using its hydrofoil properties to create lift and thrust during recovery. Except for brief transitions between phases, it produces forward thrust throughout the entire propulsive cycle (Blake, 1980; Fish, 1984) (Figure 4.9a-c).

Here again, without the same shoulder joint mobility, the human swimmer is at a distinct

disadvantage. Neither is it possible for the human swimmer to produce thrust during recovery phases of the stroke. In midstroke, however, where there is often a dip in acceleration as the hand changes direction (Counsilman & Wasilak, 1982; Schleihauf, 1974), it may be possible to make this transition with less drag by experimenting with some of the maneuvering shapes used in fish propulsion. This topic is discussed later in this chapter.

Stroke Length and Stroke Frequency in Sea Lion Swimming. The California sea lion generates propulsion solely through the use of its foreflippers, with no apparent contribution from its body or hind flippers. It changes swimming speed by varying the amount of thrust generated per unit time, either altering stroke frequency or adjusting the angle of attack and amplitude of the flippers during a stroke.

The sea lion is intermediate between birds and fishes in the method it uses to modulate swimming speed. Unlike most, if not all, human swimmers, at higher speeds the sea lion increases *both* stroke frequency and the distance traveled per stroke. It seems that sea

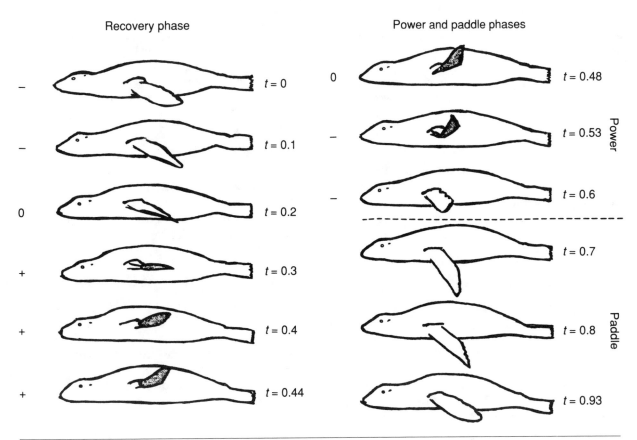

Figure 4.8 Sea lion propulsion. *Note.* From Feldkamp (1987, p. 54). Reprinted by permission.

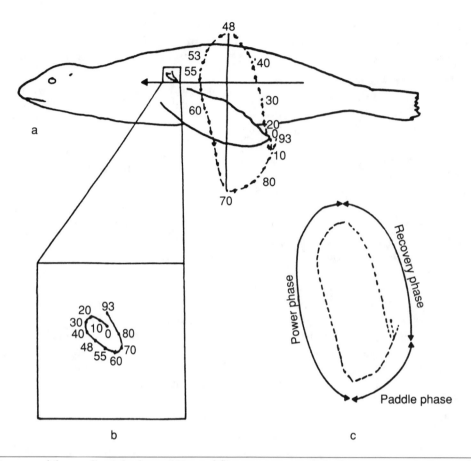

Figure 4.9 Diagram of the sea lion's body position and flipper movements during a representative stroke, relative to an observer moving at the same speed as the animal. This figure was composed from tracings of 16 mm cine film shot at a flume speed of 1.3 m · sec⁻¹. (a) Flipper path over the course of a stroke. Numbers refer to the frame each image was traced from. Each frame equals 1/100 of a second. (b) Expanded view of the body's motion during the stroke. (c) Breakdown of the various stroke phases. *Note.* From Feldkamp (1987, p. 56). Reprinted by permission.

lions, like birds, can change the distance traveled per stroke through the degree of thrust produced per beat and, like fishes, increase the frequency of stroking—but probably in neither case as well as these counterparts (Feldkamp, 1987).

Comparisons With the Flight of Flying Insects

The most fascinating aerodynamic discovery of recent times has a counterpart in nonsteady swimming propulsion. It concerns the novel lift-generating mechanism used by some flying insects (Lighthill, 1973). Aerodynamic calculations have shown that some insects are unable to generate enough foil-type lift to remain airborne. Their unique lift-generating mechanisms instead depend on means different from

those of ordinary foils; the actual shape of the foil is of little importance. What is needed is an elongated body that carries a bound vortex and is moved relative to the stationary fluid. It does not involve refined adjustments of the angle of attack but does require rapid control of the flow over the tip of the foil.

The Clap-Fling-Ring Mechanism

Some flying insects use a *clap-fling-ring* action of their wings, which circulates air to form a vortex on each wing tip (Figure 4.10). At the end of the downstroke these two vortices are shed in a flinging action and combine to form one large vortex ring directly beneath the insect. The force needed to create the ring sustains the insect's weight.

The difference between a normal airfoil and the nonsteady fling-ring mechanism is that the vortex patterns leading to circulation are cre-

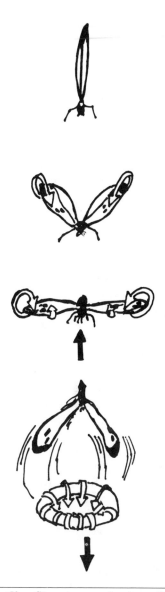

The Power Dolphin Kick.   The power dolphin kick requires a rapidly established vortex circulation—in this case, around the feet prior to commencing the propulsive impulse. This is accomplished in a manner slightly different from the clap-fling-ring mechanism used by some flying insects.

In the absence of the preliminary clap phase of the mechanism, the soles of the feet set up the necessary preliminary circulation as they touch the surface of the water prior to the feet starting downward. The contact by the soles with the surface water sets up a *surface tension* caused by molecular attraction between the two fluids, water and air. As the feet thrust downward a bound vortex forms around each foot. These vortices combine to form one large vortex ring that is shed in the vertical plane as the feet complete a powerful downward thrust (Figure 4.11). The large size of the ring indicates that a large mass of water has been acted on whereas the velocity of the water has remained relatively low. One indication of the kick's effectiveness is the distance between the regularly spaced vortices: The greater the distance between each shed vortex ring, the more effective the kick. I have often asked butterfly swimmers to swim a few strokes and then stop and look back underwater at their own still-visible vortex trails. They were fascinated that they could actually *see* the result of their own propulsion.

Sometimes, when a swimmer's feet have spread too far apart during the downward

Figure 4.10   Clap-fling-ring mechanism of butterfly flight.

ated *prior to* and *independently of* the movement of the foil through the fluid (Weis-Fogh, 1973).

The Fling-Ring Mechanism in the Dolphin Kick

Although it is obviously impossible for human swimmers to perform the "clap" phase that precedes the fling-ring mechanism, they may use similar mechanisms during nonsteady swimming propulsion. A typical example can be seen in the "power" dolphin kick *when used at maximum effort.* (The kick in the following description should not be confused with the gentler action of the "soft" dolphin kick, often used in the 200-meter event, which is more similar to a foil operating in steady flow.)

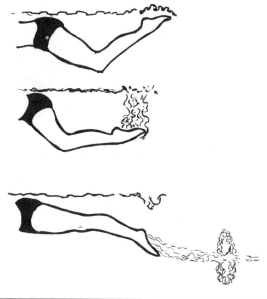

Figure 4.11   The fling-ring propulsive mechanism in the power dolphin kick.

thrust, two smaller vortices, one from each foot, will be shed. The effectiveness of this action is not as great as when a large single vortex is shed.

The use of the fling-ring lift effect in the power dolphin kick depends to a large extent on a swimmer's ability to hyperextend the ankles and feet quickly to establish surface tension. Circulation results from the impulsive force created by the feet as they separate the air-water boundary.

The Fling-Ring Mechanism in the Two-Beat Crawl Kick

Crawl swimmers using a power-producing two-beat kick also employ the fling-ring mechanism. Shed vortices of a smaller size often can be observed in the vertical plane behind each foot as it completes its downward thrust. For instance, this effect can be seen in the women's 1500-meter event, in which the use of the two-beat kick usually predominates. Each swimmer in the race often leaves a "ladder" of small separate vortices trailing in the lane behind her.

The Fling-Ring Mechanism in the Breaststroke Kick

Underwater movies of breaststroke swimmers show that the *essential preliminary flow circulation* is set up by the dorsi-flexion of the feet combined with their change of direction as they move from recovery into the propulsive phase. That the breaststroke kick uses the *fling-ring* lift mechanism can be seen when a breaststroke swimmer misjudges the depth of a push-off from a turn and inadvertently introduces air into the kick. The resultant aeration of the flow reveals vortex rings behind each foot as the first kick off the wall is completed, a clear demonstration that the kick uses the fling-ring mechanism.

Discussion: Practical Application of Flow Analysis as a Coaching Tool

The following discussion is couched in question and answer format. (I am frequently asked these questions in conversation and correspondence.)

What Is a Vortex?   A vortex is a mass of fluid that rotates about an axis. The axis of the vortex

may be in almost any plane from vertical to horizontal.

What Causes a Vortex to Be Shed at the End of a Propulsive Impulse?   As already shown, the presence of a bound vortex is essential for lift to occur. When a starting vortex is formed, it causes a bound vortex to be closed around a foil. Because a flow does not contain any circulation at the beginning of a stroke, it must not contain any circulation at the *end* of a stroke.

For example, experiments with a rotating cylinder in a flow channel show the reappearance of the starting vortex, now rotating in the opposite direction, once the flow is switched off and circulation has ceased. Right at the end, the starting vortex reappears, almost like a movie film played in reverse.

Similarly, it can be seen that a vortex must be shed if the hand is brought to a complete stop with respect to the local flow, because there is no longer a mechanism producing and maintaining circulation. Therefore, during a swimming stroke, when the hand stops or completes a propulsive impulse in a certain direction, whatever circulation is bound on it is shed to form a vortex ring.

The reader can easily demonstrate these phenomena. Stand in shallow water, dip a hand into it, and move it: The rapidly formed starting vortex will appear. Now end the movement by stopping the hand suddenly. This will cause a shed vortex visibly whirling away very rapidly from the hand.

What Should Be the Ideal Shape of a Shed Vortex?   A shed vortex should be circular rather than elongated because a circular vortex acts on a larger area or mass of fluid. Its velocity is slower than that of an elongated vortex, which acts on a smaller area and a smaller mass. Although an elongated vortex (long loop) will produce a flow causing forward thrust, this is *not* the most efficient mode of propulsion for the reason just stated. The elongated vortex usually results from predominant drag propulsion when the hand is pulled straight backward like a paddle instead of in a curved path like a foil (Figure 4.12a and b). The vortex is shed from both sides of the hand and arm and appears early in the stroke. This flow reaction is frequently produced by the techniques of male butterfly swimmers and 50-meter freestylers.

According to propeller theory, it is much better for a propeller to act over a large mass and accelerate it relatively slowly than to act on a

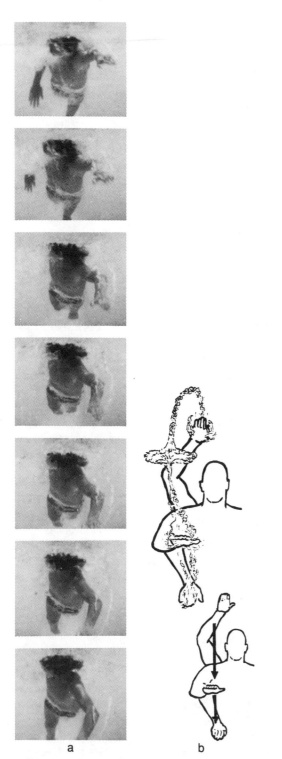

a   b

Figure 4.12 Predominant drag propulsion: flow reactions. (a) The flow reaction shows drag force propulsion resulting from pulling directly backward. All organized vorticity is shed very early in the stroke. (b) The typical "lasso-type" vortex consists of a short vortex tail attached to a large ring. The stroke is completed with wake turbulence behind the hand. Sometimes this fault is shown by early detachment of the trailing vortex without the presence of a ring.

small mass and accelerate it quickly. This is what happens when a swimmer sheds a circular vortex rather than an elongated one.

What Should Be the Ideal Plane of a Shed Vortex? Refer to the example of the circular vortex and assume, for the time being, that we have a swimmer who can produce this perfectly shaped circular vortex. Again, a vortex is a mass of fluid rotating about an axis that may be in almost any plane. Let us orient the plane of this circular vortex at different angles, from vertical to horizontal.

When the plane of this circular vortex is vertical and its axis is horizontal, all the fluid particles the vortex acts on will be moved in the stream direction (the horizontal direction). This will result in ideal direct forward propulsion. When the plane of the vortex is horizontal, or lying parallel to the surface of the water, all the fluid particles that this vortex acts on will be directed downward, meaning that the net force created by the swimmer is upward rather than forward.

Conclusion: If a swimmer's stroke is efficient, the plane of the shed vortex will tend to be vertical or nearly so. The more vertical the vortex plane, the more likely that the propulsive impulse has generated near maximum forward thrust.

What Do Different Sized Vortices in the Flow Field Tell Us? Counsilman (1971) states that it is better to move a large mass of water a short distance than to move a small mass of water a long way. In terms of propeller theory, it could be expressed as "it is better to move a large mass of water *slowly* than to move a small mass quickly." Stated thus, the principles of propeller theory apply directly to swimming propulsion.

In another of his prominent studies, Counsilman (1980) showed that skilled swimmers produce marked hand acceleration in the latter phase of the crawl stroke, a finding borne out by analysis of the flow reaction. A smaller vortex appears after the end of the stroke whereas a larger vortex appears during the stroke, when the first propulsive impulse of the stroke is completed (as the elbow reaches maximum flexion). The smaller vortex at the end of the stroke shows an increase in the flow velocity caused by the hand's acceleration.

It may be that the first, larger vortex creates a new flow direction, and the hand may have to move faster to make maximum use of the new flow velocity. The skilled swimmer may actually be aware of this—albeit subconsciously—and adjust the hand accordingly.

What Does the Presence of Excessive Vorticity Mean? A coach can learn a great deal from a swimmer's subjective comments, especially immediately after a race. Sometimes, when a swimmer has turned in a particularly fine performance, the swimmer may say, ''I felt so good that I could have gone faster,'' or, conversely, a swimmer may express disappointment at a recorded time by saying, ''I felt so strong and powerful—I can't understand why my time wasn't faster.''

As has been observed underwater, very powerful swimmers often shed vortices in the middle of a propulsive impulse. This shows that they are exerting more power than necessary. In contrast, the swimmer who finishes with power in reserve, feeling that it was possible to go faster, perhaps instinctively has not overapplied power.

There could be another reason for excessive vortex shedding, however. As the hand exceeds the ideal angle of attack (in terms of the conventional airfoil mechanism), the flow separates, destroying the circulation. At this stage a swimmer will start to use unconventional propulsive mechanisms to propel in the resultant unsteady flow. One reason for excessive vortex activity, then, could be that the swimmer is no longer able to adjust the hand incidence so as to maintain airfoil-type propulsion and, therefore, has to shed the existing flow circulation to establish a new flow around the hand.

Why Is It Not Always Possible to See the Swimmer's Flow Reactions in the Water? The presence of *visible* flow reactions depends on accidental air entrapment. Aeration is a recognized visualization technique used by fluid dynamicists. Although most swimmers produce a visible flow reaction when swimming at speed, there is no procedure that will ensure regular visualization of the surrounding flow field. There are a number of flow visualization methods used to analyze the flow around models in flow channels and wind tunnels, but the use of dyes, lasers, smoke, and so on could pose a safety hazard for swimmers. Up to now, photography, especially shadow photography, has provided promising results.

The flow patterns of great swimmers at key phases of propulsion are remarkably predictable. When observing these top performers it is not difficult to form a synthesis of the flow patterns that can be anticipated. Nevertheless, we lack a sophisticated method of flow visualization that will enable vortex reactions to be measured accurately against a grid. Ideally, such a method would require both front- and side-view photography of swimmers at racing speed. The side views should be photographed by an underwater camera moving on a track and kept constantly abreast of the swimmer; where access to a swimming flume is available the swimmer could be filmed while tethered in an oncoming flow. Comparing the results produced by the two approaches would add another dimension to flow analysis.

Should Swimmers Be Told to Entrap Air Into Their Strokes To Make the Flow Reactions Visible? Intentional aeration is not a good idea because, under certain conditions, air entrapment can cause bursting bubbles that may increase drag. Although air entrapment should *not* be encouraged, the introduction of a bubble can *improve* efficiency sometimes, when a bubble attaches to the upper surface of a foil, causing a modified contour that prevents massive separation of the flow from taking place.

Shaping the Flow

Little is known about the effects of body shape on a swimmer's efficiency. In the late 20th century, the bulky, squat body type has not been as prevalent in competitive swimming as before, and most of the leading swimmers, irrespective of their events, have possessed a tall, lithe, lean physique similar to a basketball player's; the muscles have tended to be long rather than short and heavy like a weightlifter's. The effects of a swimmer's shape and physical proportions on speed and efficiency are governed by certain factors. The ratio of height to bulk is probably the most important single factor in reducing resistance. The more slender the swimmer, the less the underwater volume compared to the swimmer's height, or length, in the water. If a swimmer has a gradually tapering physique, the water will be able to flow past more easily. (Other variables include buoyancy, body composition, flexibility, neuromuscular patterns, and individual aptitude.)

However, the shapes of certain human body types (also known as *somatotypes*) are at a distinct disadvantage in speed swimming. Observation of the water's flow reactions around individual swimmers confirms this.

Controlling the Oncoming Flow

Some swimmers have extreme difficulty controlling the oncoming flow of water along the entering arm(s) with sufficient continuity to obtain the best timing of the stroke. The more successful swimmers appear to be favorably endowed by nature with streamlined body profiles and functional limb shapes that enable them to continuously control the oncoming flow between one stroke and the next.

In all four styles of swimming, the arms at the start of the stroke should act much like the bow of a ship, channeling the oncoming flow along each arm and around the body.

The crawl permits a skilled swimmer to smoothly control the oncoming flow as one stroke ends and the next one commences. The overlapping arm action of the crawl stroke allows a swimmer to feel the oncoming flow of water advance along the entry arm at the same time as the opposite arm is unswirling the flow from the hand and forearm at the finish of its stroke. The expert crawl swimmer is thus able to control simultaneously two separate flow reactions during this fleeting but critical timing phase of the arm stroke.

Compared to the crawl, the other three swimming styles—backstroke, butterfly, and breaststroke—produce oncoming flows a swimmer cannot so easily intercept and translate into smooth continuous propulsion.

In the back crawl, the arms remain almost the same distance from each other during the complete stroke cycle and they do not overlap as much as in the crawl stroke. Therefore, unless a backstroke swimmer has a tall, lean body and an arm reach long enough to control the oncoming flow efficiently at entry, accurate timing between the entry arm and the finishing arm is more difficult than in the crawl.

In efficient crawl and backstroke swimming, the alternating action of the arms ensures that at nearly every stage of the stroke cycle one arm is extending forward at entry to intercept and smoothly channel the oncoming flow while the other arm is completing its stroke. In butterfly and breaststroke, however, because the arms move simultaneously, such nearly constant interception of the oncoming flow at entry is not possible.

Moreover, some butterfly and breaststroke swimmers have difficulty controlling the on-coming flow around the arms at the beginning of each stroke because the momentum necessary to produce this oncoming flow depends on accurate timing between the arm and leg actions.

Exploiting Examples From Nature

I have described how humans developed their admittedly limited swimming ability. Through considerable invention and the gradual acquisition of increasing skill, we learned to adapt our comparatively awkward land-type bodies for efficient use in water.

Earlier, I made a comparison between human swimming and similar propulsive mechanisms in nature. Is it possible to improve the efficiency of human swimming by seeking out and adopting further examples from nature? Can we learn to use propulsive mechanisms and postural shapes derived from nature to provide a more facile, dexterous, and efficient mode of swimming?

Although probably no further adaptation from nature will have the same dramatic effect on the sport as the development of the dolphin kick, we can learn much by studying fishes and birds—both their *natural shapes* and the *changing shapes* they adopt during various phases of propulsion. Much of their efficiency can be attributed to their skill in making smooth transitions from the end of one propulsive impulse to the start of the next. The subject of *transitional phases* of the stroke in human swimming unfortunately has not been studied.

Ideal Postures and Shapes

The literature contains little mention about the possibility of ideal postures or shapes of the hand in relation to the wrist as the arm moves through the changing phases of a swimming stroke.

A better understanding of how to shape the hand-wrist posture during the arm stroke could improve swimming efficiency. This applies to the postures assumed by the hand and wrist in relation to each other

1. during the propulsive impulse,
2. at the end of the propulsive impulse, and
3. during the transitional phase between the end of one propulsive impulse and the start of another.

Birds and fishes exhibit shapes adapted to their function, and they are able to change their body forms somewhat to alter the flow reactions around their bodies. A study of the shapes and changing forms adopted by fishes and birds may have beneficial applications for human swimming.

Careful study of the arm posture of an expert butterfly swimmer during the inward sweep of the stroke (Figure 4.13) indicates that the swimmer, probably without knowing, has adopted two characteristic shapes commonly seen in nature:

1. The projecting thumbs each act like an *alula*, or small "extra" wing.
2. The hand and forearm, from the tip of the little finger to the point of the elbow, assume a lunate, or crescent-shaped, configuration.

Both shapes are concerned with lift enhancement in that they help keep the flow attached to the hands and forearms. Some butterfly swimmers who keep their thumbs pressed in and their hands in a straight line with their forearms encounter flow separation very early in the stroke. The vortex patterns set up by the swimmer in Figure 4.13 show that she has kept the flow attached to her hands and forearms even though her hands have already changed direction from their initial outward sweep and are well into the inward phase of the stroke. The only visible signs of pending flow separation are slight swellings in the vortex trails near the fingertips.

The Alula Effect in Smoothing Out the Flow. In bird flight, the alula, sometimes referred to as the bastard wing, is an interesting refinement that acts as a subsidiary airfoil in front of the leading edge of the main wing. Under normal flight conditions the alula is folded back, out of the way; as the bird approaches stalling speed, however, and the airflow over the upper wing surface becomes turbulent, the alula is spread forward to form a slot through which air rushes, restoring a smooth, fast airstream and curtailing stall (Figure 4.14a-d). In similar fashion, when a swimmer's hand is inclined at too large an angle of attack to keep the flow attached to the hand, the thumb, when held away from the hand, forms a narrows through which the speed of the flow increases, creating a low-pressure area on the knuckle side of the hand that produces more lift and a smoother flow around the hand.

Figure 4.13 Arm posture of expert butterfly swimmer.

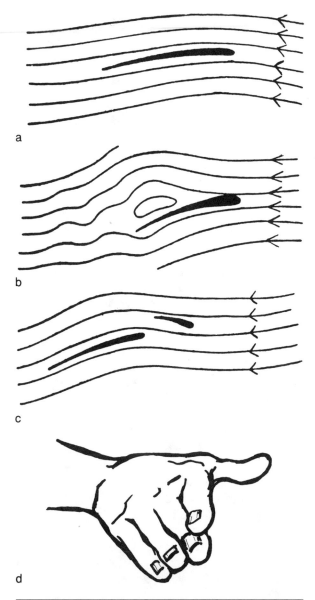

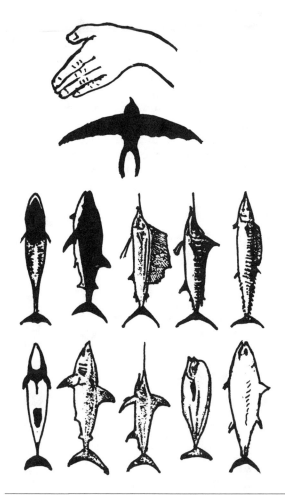

Figure 4.15 The ulnar-flexion of the wrist in the human swimmer resembles various lunate shapes in nature.

Figure 4.14 Use of alula mechanism to create steady flow. (a) Foil in steady flow. (b) Steep angle of attack produces unsteady flow. (c) Alula restores steady flow. (d) The thumb used as an alula.

The Efficiency of Lunate or Crescent-Shaped Contours. The wings of such seagoing birds as shearwaters and albatrosses, which spend an enormous amount of time in the air, are swept backward. Even the limbs of species adapted to propulsion through water (a fluid, just as air is, and thus subject to many of the same physical laws) show the same crescent shape, in particular, the tail fins of marlin and tuna (fish) and dolphins and whales (marine mammals) (van Dam, 1988) (Figure 4.15).

Does the crescent shape bestow some special advantage? Only recently, with the develop-

ment of computerized modeling techniques that faithfully represent the dynamics of vortex wakes, was it discovered that the most aerodynamically efficient shape is not the conventional flattened ellipse. A half-moon planform, like that of a whale's tail, with a curved leading edge and a straight trailing edge is superior; and a crescent planform, in which both edges curve backward like a swift's wing, is more effective still.

These shapes enhance performance because the vortices that form at the trailing edge of the inboard section of a curved wing or fin wash downward (sideways for a fin) ahead of those further along the limb, producing updrafts and sidedrafts that, like miniature hurricanes, agitate nearby fluid particles.

The tip of a wing or fin acts in turn as a sail, converting some of the kinetic energy of these spiraling streams into forward thrust. In this manner, a crescent planform generates at least

10% less induced drag than an elliptical one—a reduction that grows in significance as the time an animal spends flying or swimming increases.

In the human swimmer, the ulnar-flexion of the wrist in relation to the forearm creates a crescent-shaped contour that keeps the flow attached around the hand and forearm. This is important because if the flow were to separate from forearm and hand, drag would increase. In fact, some swimmers who changed to an ulnar-flexion of the wrist during the inward sweep of the arm reported increased ease in this phase of the stroke without experiencing loss of propulsion (Figure 4.16).

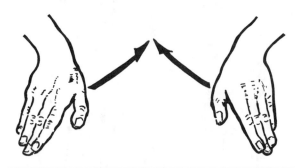

Figure 4.16 Ulnar wrist flexion on inward sweep of the hand.

The discussion so far has centered on the effect of ulnar wrist flexion during the inward sweep of a swimming stroke, but what are we to make of the ulnar wrist flexion sometimes seen during the *outward* sweep of a swimming stroke? In addition to assuming the crescent-shaped contour of the lower arm, some swimmers also incline the hand slightly upward during the outward sweep so that the fingertips appear to be the highest part of the entire arm.

The outward arm sweep of champion butterfly swimmer Mary T. Meagher is a good example of this action (Figure 4.17). The slight upward tilt of her hands is not unlike that of a large soaring bird turning up its wingtip primary feathers to reduce drag induction. In other swimmers, such as Gary Hall (see Figure 4.7), the elbows are pronouncedly higher than the hands, which in turn are set at a sharp angle from the wrists to shape the whole arm remarkably like a cantilevered hydrofoil. (Gary Hall's action can be seen clearly in Counsilman's [1977] *Competitive Swimming Manual*, page 183.) By making models of the functional arm shapes of such talented swimmers and testing them in flow channels, it should be possible to analyze the exact effects these shaping techniques have

Figure 4.17 Outward arm sweep of champion butterfly swimmer Mary T. Meagher. The fingertips appear to be the highest point of the entire arm. *Note.* Adapted from instructional film by Maglischo and Gambril, produced by First Essex Productions. Used by permission of Mary T. Meagher and First Essex Productions.

on the surrounding flow field. It would also be possible to measure at what angles of attack flow separation (and consequent vortex shedding) takes place.

Transitional Shaping During the Swimming Stroke

Even at topflight swimming meets it is still commonplace to see swimmers whose techniques are based too much on tugging, pulling, and pushing, which are essentially land-type concepts. Many swimmers try to pull directly through the "hard" part of the stroke instead of adopting transitional postures of the hand that would enable them to more easily control the oncoming flow.

Midstroke Transitions. We might possibly learn something from observing the transitional shapes adopted by certain reef fishes when maneuvering. Their fins move through a very flat angle as they "fan" around to a new posture in a helicoidal path. Fish do not waste energy by trying to overcome a developing or increasing resistance such as that encountered by a human swimmer as the elbow reaches maximum bend in midstroke and the hand reaches an angle almost perpendicular to the line of forward progression. The spiraling fin of the reef fish simply "goes around" the obstacle of increased resistance.

Perhaps the human swimmer could copy this action, when swimming crawl, for example. In midstroke the forearm is medially rotated so that the hand is turned slightly, as shown in

rectly backward instead of in a curvilinear path, they were also told to keep their hands flat and not to cup them because this action could cause the water to spill off the hand. Given that a curved-line path is the most efficient pulling pattern, however, a slight cupping of the hand may actually add to the amount of lift created, because the convex shape of the cupped hand provides a more efficient foil.

The Variable Camber Approach to Hand Shaping

Designers of military aircraft have developed a variable camber wing that is digitally controlled through a flight computer (Figure 4.20a-c). This digital flight control allows continuous adjustment of the sweep (analogous to the swimmer's ulnar wrist flexion) and camber (analogous to the swimmer's amount of hand cupping) to create optimum lift and drag for cruise, maneuver, and other flight functions.

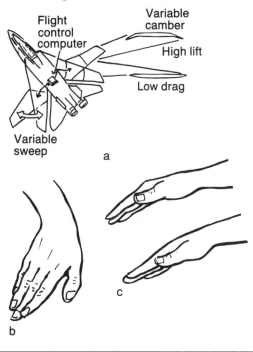

Figure 4.20 Camber and sweep in airplanes and swimmers: (a) airplane; (b) ulnar wrist flexion, or *sweep*; and (c) amount of hand-cupping, or *camber*.

A swimmer perhaps should experiment with how much cupping, or cambering, of the hand is needed, especially when fatigued. A fatigued swimmer may actually develop more lift force by slightly increasing the amount of hand cupping, even though the tired muscles may not be able to develop more power.

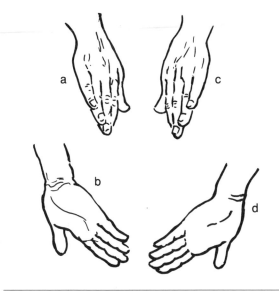

Figure 4.18 Midstroke transition showing four views of medially rotated hands in crawl stroke: (a) top right view, (b) bottom right view, (c) top left view, and (d) bottom left view.

Figure 4.18a-d. The transition is made with a quick, deft movement. The palm of the hand is turned to face slightly forward, almost like turning a vertical slat in a venetian blind. The motion quickly presents the hand at a more acute angle with less drag as the hand and forearm round out to finish the stroke with a fanlike action (Figure 4.19). A biomechanical study of this suggested midstroke transitional maneuver, performed by a skilled swimmer, could prove interesting and enlightening.

Functional Shaping of the Hand

In the past, when swimmers were still being incorrectly instructed to pull their hands di-

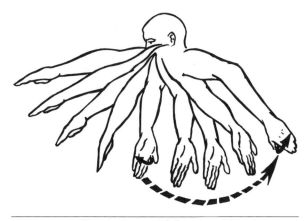

Figure 4.19 Fanning to avoid drag in midstroke transition—side view.

Underwater photography shows that talented swimmers use a variety of hand, finger, and thumb configurations during the changing phases of a swimming stroke (Figure 4.21). It is highly unlikely that any one swimmer could incorporate all these principles within an individual stroke pattern nor is it recommended that a swimmer attempt to do so. How should a coach approach teaching the various shaping techniques such as the alula effect, the ulnar wrist flexion, hand cupping, and so on? Each person should experiment to find which of these techniques can be *comfortably* used within his or her own personal swimming style. For example, whereas one swimmer may feel an advantage is gained by assuming a lunate shape between hand and forearm, another swimmer may feel more comfortable keeping the hand aligned with the forearm. The coach's role will not be to enforce these finer embellishments on a swimmer but merely to recognize their value and not intervene when a swimmer uses them naturally.

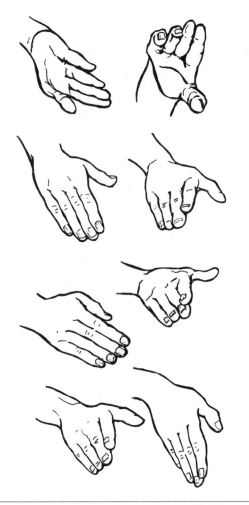

Figure 4.21 Various hand-digit postures used by talented swimmers.

Functional Shaping as a New Approach to Stroke Technique

The purpose of this chapter has not been to recommend dramatic new changes in technique but rather to show how efficient propulsion depends on adroit manipulation of the reacting flow. A good example of functional shaping and dexterous flow control is shown in the outstanding technique of champion swimmer Mary T. Meagher (Figure 4.22a-i).

Traditional coaching methods have focused on establishing desired stroke patterns but have neglected to provide the swimmer with adequate feedback on the efficiency of performance. Children should be taught flow recognition and manipulation from an early age. They should be made aware of functional shaping of the hand and arm as important aspects of technique. Learning to create, feel, and recognize the ideal reacting flow of the water will give swimmers instant feedback on the efficiency of their swimming strokes.

The cambered shape of Meagher's arms is a remarkable simulation of soaring flight (a). The hips are raised in an undulating dolphin motion. The completion of the downward leg beat sheds a large ring vortex, using the fling-ring propulsive mechanism.

The soaring arm action continues as the arms spread laterally and downward (b and c). The vortex trails visible above the arms indicate conventional foil-type propulsion at this stage of the stroke.

The arms assume the typical hydrofoil posture common to skilled butterfly exponents (d). (See Figures 4.7 and 4.13.) The projecting thumbs and ulnar wrist flexions show the use of the alula and lunate sweep-shaping mechanisms that smooth the reacting flow. The outward motion of the arms is ending and a large ring vortex is about to be shed from each arm. The size and shape of each vortex indicate that the impulse has acted on a large mass of water.

The hands sweep inward under her body (e). The legs have recovered from their first downward beat and assume a preparatory position for their next downward beat, which will be timed with the completion of the arm stroke. The feet have separated the air-water boundary at the surface and, as a result, carry a bound vortex that will be shed as the downward beat is completed.

The hands will now thrust backward and outward in a rounded motion to complete the stroke (f-i). The arm stroke ends in time with the second downward beat of the legs.

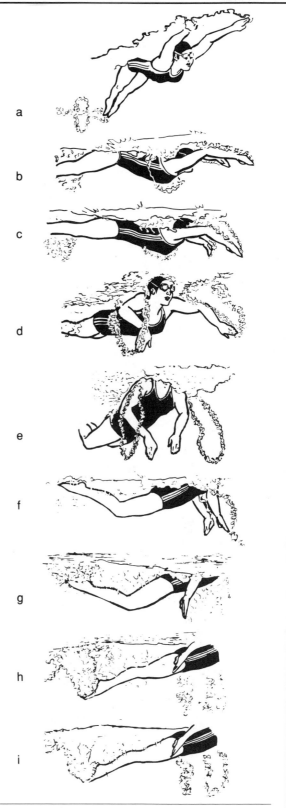

Figure 4.22   Mary T. Meagher of the U.S.A., the greatest female butterfly swimmer in history, has the world's 10 fastest times for the 200-meter butterfly. Her outstanding stroke technique reveals several examples of propulsive mechanisms common to nature, such as her overall arm reaction, which resembles a bird's wings oscillating in flight. *Note.* Adapted from instructional film by Maglischo and Gambril, produced by First Essex Productions. Used by permission of Mary T. Meagher and First Essex Productions.

Chapter 5

Coaching the Feel of the Water

The "feel of the water" refers to a swimmer's intuitive ability to feel and effectively handle the water. It is generally believed that feel of the water is an elusive quality unique to the talented athlete: Swimmers of only average ability cannot hope to emulate the acute sensory perception of the talented motor genius. Nevertheless, I intend to show that by heightening the sense of touch and learning how to interpret sensations of moving pressure, swimmers of average ability can acquire the subtleties of advanced stroke technique. Talented swimmers coached in this method will likewise achieve greater expertise.

A more apt title to this chapter may well be "Coaching the Feel of the *Flow*." Water flows when a force acts on it; a swimmer's hand always propels against the pressure of moving water. The force exerted by a skilled swimming stroke causes the water to flow in a distinct pattern (Colwin, 1984a). The method in this chapter shows swimmers how to feel for the ideal flow reaction to their stroke mechanics and thus receive instant feedback on their efficiency.

Basics of the Method

This new approach teaches swimmers to anticipate, control, and manipulate the flow of the water. They learn that the arm functions not only as a propelling instrument but also as a skilled and sensitive "shaper of the flow."

Ideal Flow Reactions

The first step is to explain how the flow behaves during each phase of an efficient swimming stroke. The flow directions that can be anticipated in the different swimming strokes can be described simply. The oncoming flow, which in the crawl stroke hand entry moves from the fingertips to the wrist and along the arm, is known as *distal* in its direction.

A flow that moves toward the radial bone (or from thumb to little finger) is termed *radial*. Example: the flow produced when the elbows bend to bring the hands under the body in the crawl, butterfly, and breaststroke.

An *ulnar* flow moves toward the ulnar bone or from little finger to thumb, for example, the flow produced as the arms extend and the stroke "rounds out" to the hips in the crawl and butterfly.

A flow is *proximal* when it moves from wrist toward the fingertips, as happens in the backstroke as the arm straightens at the end of the stroke (Schleihauf, 1979).

The Importance of Hand-Forearm Rotation

The swimmers are shown how the behavior of the flow is related to an important aspect of stroke mechanics: emphasizing hand-forearm rotation within comfortable limits for each individual swimmer. This is the mechanism that

89

sets up the ideal flow around the hand and forearm in all the swimming strokes. The practical application of this mechanism for swimmers in *all* the strokes is quite simple: Start the stroke with the palm(s) facing outward and gradually rotate your hand-forearm unit throughout the stroke with particular emphasis on achieving the maximum amount of elbow bend in mid-stroke that is comfortable for you. Find the amount of hand-forearm rotation and elbow bend that develops the strongest pressure on the moving flow and yet still feels comfortable.

New Terminology Related to Feedback on Flow Reactions

Introduce a new terminology. Short descriptive phrases such as "trap, wrap, unwrap" tell a swimmer how to handle the flow correctly during the split-second action of a swimming stroke. This differs from previous methods that describe only the mechanics of the stroke. In addition, the new terminology relates to obtaining feedback by feeling the flow on the hand and forearm.

These verbal cues are important to the effectiveness of the method and are valuable as rehearsal techniques to enhance subsequent performance. Later in the chapter I will discuss appropriate descriptions of what pressure sensations a swimmer should feel.

Flow-Shaping Skills

The swimmers are taught flow-shaping skills by which they create and detect specific flows in the water. These "flow shapers," as they are called, have a beneficial two-way effect in that a swimmer's efforts to shape the flow cause a reciprocal shaping effect on the limb itself. The feedback received from the flow reaction causes the proprioceptors in the muscles to respond by adjusting the posture and attitude of the propelling arm.

Flow shapers produce positive and even exciting results because they instantly "groove" the hand and arm in accurate stroke patterns. Even the skeptics become convinced that this is a unique and effective way to teach efficient stroke mechanics. The essence of the method is: The feel of the flow shows a swimmer exactly where to place each moving sequence of the swimming stroke.

Sensitizing Procedures

Special sensitizing procedures are introduced to sensitize the sensory nerve endings to the moving pressure of the water (or, more precisely, transient pressure induced by motion). The propelling surfaces of the hands and forearms are also sensitized to simulate specific flow reactions. The method is simple. Sensitivity to the flow increases at once. Swimmers of average ability learn to regulate a smooth and efficient stroke.

Although these techniques quickly stimulate the sensory nerve endings, this is of little value unless the swimmer makes an association between the feel of the moving water and the particular phase of the swimming stroke. Only then can meaning be given to the sense of touch and an intelligent concept formed of the desired stroke mechanics.

Connecting Sensory Information With Stroke Effectiveness

The method "short circuits" the motor-learning process and renders the complex more simple. The deliberate intention is to cause an immediate connection between sensory information and stroke effectiveness. By giving instant meaning to the sense of touch, the procedure adds a new perspective to traditional methods. So it is used even in the early stages of learning. Young swimmers quite rapidly improve their ability to seek out and recognize ideal flow reactions.

It is unnecessary to burden a swimmer with such academic considerations, valid though they may be, as lift, drag, ideal angles of attack, and which movement planes to emphasize. Talented swimmers, when exposed to the method, develop unusual dexterity in directing and channeling the flow efficiently. Even accomplished swimmers improve their techniques when made aware of the exact flow reactions they can anticipate; in fact, they become enthusiastic and keen to learn more about the process.

The Goal of the Method

The goal of this method is to coach the feel of the water by showing swimmers how to use the sense of touch to interpret and improve stroke effectiveness. The method encompasses the following tasks:

1. *Describe* and *explain* the flow reactions that can be anticipated during each phase of a skilled swimming stroke.

2. *Demonstrate* and *explain* hand-forearm rotation and elbow bending and how these mechanisms set up the ideal flow around the hand and forearm in all the swimming strokes.

3. *Demonstrate* flow shaper skills and *explain* how they shape ideal stroke patterns for the individual swimmer.

4. *Demonstrate* sensitizing procedures and *explain* how they can be used to simulate specific flow reactions.

5. *Emphasize* the importance of regular practice. *Ensure constant repetition* by swimmers of all the procedures outlined in the preceding tasks.

The Use of Appropriate Descriptions

What sensations of touch should a swimmer experience when manipulating water efficiently? How should they be described? Little thought has been given to this aspect of coaching, which is not surprising when even acknowledged stroke technicians have used such descriptions of water as ''fickle substance.'' We have all been guilty of inadequately describing how the water should feel to a correctly stroking swimmer.

For years, one of my favorite descriptions was ''Enter your hand and feel the pressure of the water on your palm. Try to make the pressure progressively harder as you drive through.'' Although this may have been as good a description as possible at the time, it does not describe the desired feel accurately enough in the context of existing knowledge.

A once popular and comparatively apt description of the feel of the water likened it to the feeling of pulling through soft mud. More recently, however, a ''fixed point of resistance'' description has become popular. (This probably resulted from biomechanical studies based on the convenient assumption of essentially still water.) To convey the concept of a force acting on a mass of water, the act of propulsion has been variously described as feeling for undisturbed water, anchoring the hand on a fixed spot in the water and pulling the body past it, pulling along an imaginary knotted rope, and other similar descriptions.

These descriptions, strictly speaking, are inappropriate because the propulsive force is not applied against a solid or rigid resistance. Coaches should use carefully chosen words when instructing a swimmer. Many of our well-worn coaching terms may not produce the reactions we desire.

The Concept of a Relative Flow

A good example of a potentially misleading term is the word ''catch,'' which has been used since the early days of swimming to describe how a swimming stroke should begin. The old idea of feeling for the ''catch-point'' is incorrect, however. Fluid dynamic principles contradict the popular notion that the hand attaches to a ''fixed point'' in the water and levers the body past it. Instead, one should feel the oncoming, or relative, flow advance over the palm of the hand and along the forearm. The hand always encounters an oncoming flow of water.

The instant the fingertips enter the water there is a reacting flow that continues throughout the stroke. Like all fluids, water responds immediately to any movement through it; like all fluids, water changes shape under the action of forces. These changes are known as deformation and appear as elasticity and flow. When a swimmer propels efficiently, the flow and the elasticity of the water will be felt as a stretching effect.

Correct Manipulation of the Hand

Swimming skill is dramatically increased by learning the simple act of splitting the flow with the fingers and hand throughout the stroke. Flow separation causes different patterns of pressure to form around the hand. There is always flow from an area of high pressure to one of lower pressure in a correctly performed stroke. This causes a bound circulation of water around the hand that generates the propulsive force. All one needs to do is to continue splitting the flow to maintain this propulsive force.

The contour of the hand and the angle at which it is held while splitting the flow will affect the amount of propulsive pressure produced. This is based on sound principles of fluid dynamics. It is more efficient to split the flow with the edges (either the fingertips or sides) of the hand than to use the hand like a paddle and pull with the palm of the hand flat against the pressure resistance of the water.

When the edges of the hand are used to split or separate the flow, the hand is used as a foil, causing a fine, thin, shearing separation at the trailing edge rather than the broad, blunt, excessively turbulent separation that results from the straight backward paddle action.

To avoid pulling straight backward the hand is moved in a curved path across the line of forward progress (Counsilman, 1971). Another way of describing this action is to say that the hand is moved in the lateral, or transverse, plane. (Of course, the path of the hand actually moves in three planes simultaneously, namely, the lateral, vertical, and horizontal.) By moving the hand along a curved path a swimmer will be able to tilt its leading edge slightly upward, thus creating a foil-like effect that will increase the pressure resistance on the palm of the hand. In this manner, a swimmer can feel the pressure of the flow on the palm of the hand *without* pulling directly backward.

Pressure Sensations Caused by Different Propulsive Mechanisms

The obvious question at this point is what the differences in the "feel" of the water are between using the hand as a foil and using it as a paddle. When the hand is used as a foil, pressure resistance is felt on the palm of the hand and the flow is felt on the backs of the hands and fingers, particularly on the skin over the knuckles. The water is also flowing over the palm of the hand, but its presence is felt as pressure resistance, not flow, because the water flows more slowly over the palm of the hand than over the knuckle side, thus creating an area of higher pressure. The swimmer feels this pressure instead of the flow.

When the hand is used as a paddle, the pressure resistance is also felt on the palm of the hand, but there is no sensation at all on the knuckle side because the flow separates around *both* edges of the hand, not one edge only (the trailing edge) as in the foil-type method. Pulling the hand like a paddle causes excessive drag turbulence on the hand and results in wasted energy when compared with the more efficient foil-type method. Obviously, the previously cited descriptions are inadequate to convey the tactile sensations ("feel") of modern stroke mechanics.

Terminology Describes Each Phase of Flow Manipulation

Assuming a swimmer has been taught the function of hand-forearm rotation and elbow bending in manipulating the flow, the swimming stroke should be taught as a working sequence of "trap, wrap, and unwrap the flow." This helps relate each important phase of the stroke with the relative flow reaction. In the crawl stroke this sequence works as follows: The trap occurs as the arm enters the water with elbow up and hand pitched diagonally outward. The swimmer feels an oncoming flow of water advance along the entire under surface of the arm from the palm of the hand to the armpit. At this point the flow is considered to be trapped under the arm.

The wrap occurs as the flow is wrapped around the hand and forearm as they rotate inward after a short downward press. The wrap is completed when the elbow reaches maximum bend (approximately 90 degrees) and the hand has moved across under the body.

The unwrap occurs as the elbow extends and the arm straightens. At the end of the stroke the flow is finally unwrapped from the forearm and hand as the stroke rounds out past the hip joint.

The entire sequence of trap, wrap, and unwrap occurs within a fraction of a second. The swimmer is taught to think of the sequence as a very quick passage of events. Each successive phase happens with increasing speed to produce the desired stroke acceleration (Counsilman & Wasilak, 1982). The precise application of the trap, wrap, unwrap concept of flow manipulation varies with each swimming stroke.

Manipulating the Flow at the Hand Entry

The way a swimmer controls the hand at entry is usually a first indication of talent. The hand entry of a talented swimmer often seems almost leisurely. The swimmer feels for the moving pressure of the oncoming flow and gradually starts to apply force against it. The hand of the talented swimmer possesses a complex sensitivity (or, more accurately, a sensibility) that almost seems to give it sight.

The talented swimmer appears to possess an innate awareness of not only the exact speed at which to enter the hand but also how to time the start of the stroke effectively. The hand neither slows to a stop out in front of the swimmer nor starts the stroke too soon, before the oncoming flow has been accepted and trapped under the arm.

The hand's first contact with the water at entry is critically important. Coaches often correct the "middle" part of a stroke before checking to see whether the entry has been made efficiently. If the oncoming flow has not been engaged initially, there is no sense in correcting a subsequent phase of the stroke.

Anticipating the Oncoming Flow

Most faulty handling of the flow originates from incorrect technique at entry. The entry hand's forward motion into the water produces an oncoming flow. If this flow is broken up or disturbed at entry, the swimmer will have difficulty manipulating the water during the later phases of the stroke. A swimmer should know in advance the nature of the pressure sensation that will be experienced when the hand enters. In this way a swimmer will be able to anticipate the oncoming flow and handle it effectively. The aim is to insert the hand smoothly into the oncoming flow and immediately feel the flow move along the palm and under the forearm and upper arm.

As mentioned earlier, the arm enters the water with elbow up and hand pitched diagonally outward. It is easy to imagine the hand and arm in this position as being shaped similarly to the side of a ship, which gradually slopes backward from the bow and bulges at the waist. By imagining this portion of a ship moving forward under the water, cutting the water sharply at the bow and channeling it backward around and slightly under the hull, a swimmer will form a good concept of the function of the hand at entry: The hand, *pitched diagonally outward* as it enters, performs much the same function as the bow of a ship.

As stated before, the entry is the preliminary phase of the stroke—the trap phase—during which the flow is allowed to advance along the under surface of the arm as the swimmer maneuvers it into position for the wrap phase.

Entry Errors

Unfortunately, there are several errors a swimmer can easily commit at the hand entry that can not only diminish the efficiency of the stroke but also cause a swimmer to "muscle" through the water in a futile attempt to gain purchase on it. Probably the most harmful error is to crash the hand into the entry, attempting to start the stroke before subtly accepting the oncoming flow.

The effect of this error can be understood by imagining a fast naval destroyer equipped with a guillotine-like device fixed to the bow at a right angle to the oncoming flow. At intervals, this guillotine suddenly drops into the water and disturbs the flow. The effect is to continually interrupt the vessel's forward momentum.

A similar effect, surprisingly enough, can frequently be seen in competitive swimmers, even talented world-class ones—particularly distance swimmers using an "inertial" type of stroke. As the stroke starts with what used to be called a "dig-pull" or "chop-catch," the bow wave drops, or "splutters," indicating sudden interference with the body's momentum.

The rationale behind the inertial type of hand entry may be based on a technique used in athletics and rowing. At the start of a stride, a runner's foot is already moving backward to maintain the runner's momentum and to prevent jarring the foot on the ground. Similarly, a rower's blade travels backward before it enters the water.

If the dig-pull is based on this principle, it should be understood that it cannot be applied successfully to swimming: The body is not favorably positioned in the water to perform such a technique; moreover, a swimmer cannot generate sufficient speed to achieve this effect.

Detecting the Stretching Effect in the Oncoming Flow

Great emphasis and attention should be given to adequate coaching of the entry phase of the stroke. Engaging the water correctly at entry is crucial to an effective stroke. The "ship" drill, which will be explained presently, is designed specifically to simulate the posture of the hand and arm at entry and to teach a swimmer to feel the moving pressure sensation of the oncoming flow.

The ship drill is perhaps the most valuable drill I have ever used in coaching. It is extremely effective in helping a swimmer form a concept of the entry phase of the stroke. As proficiency in discerning the sensation of moving pressure increases, it becomes possible for a swimmer to detect the "stretching" effect in the oncoming flow. A swimmer learns to relate the amount of stretch in the flow with swimming speed and correct timing of the arms.

The Role of the Sense of Touch in Motor Learning

Skilled swimmers create a fast output of high-quality movements. Yet, even when swimming at high speed they frequently give the impression of being unhurried. The expert seems to have all the time in the world when compared with the novice, whose forward progress is more like a series of emergencies. In skilled performance there are no surprises. The swimmer is always ready for each changing sequence of the stroke.

Exact timing is an obvious element of skill, which in large part involves the predictable repetition of many successive movements in accurate and precise patterns. How are the components of each sequence coordinated and organized? We tend to think of skill mainly in terms of movement. In describing a swimming stroke we tend to concentrate on what is *done*. The analysis usually breaks down the action into detailed "units" of movement. This represents the swimmer's *output*, but we tend to ignore the *input*, partly because it is taken for granted and partly because it is difficult or impossible to observe directly.

I have often witnessed over an hour of stroke instruction without hearing any reference to the water or what a swimmer should feel. Many otherwise excellent technical articles make little or no reference to the water. Most descriptions of swimming technique neglect to mention the role played by the water, the very medium in which the activity takes place.

Many highly skilled swimmers are unable to explain why they perform as they do. They may be quite unaware of the particular sensory input that controls their activity, which may be why a skilled swimmer is not always a particularly good teacher. Usually, a skill is taught by demonstrating how the desired movement should *look* rather than by explaining how it should *feel*.

The more purposeful or skilled the movement, the more it depends on sensory impulses, which in swimming are primarily those associated with vision and touch. In learning the more precise movements of swimming, visual information is essential while the degree of muscle tension and amount of muscle contraction are being delicately adjusted to the task, a point we easily appreciate if we try to learn any precise movement with eyes shut.

Voluntary movements are modified by sensory stimuli received from the skin, muscles, and joints. Sensory impulses act at all times to guide muscular contractions. The muscles are under the direct and perfect control of the motor neurons; these neurons never stimulate the muscles to action except when influenced to do so by other neurons.

Water pressure on the sensory nerve endings, the sense of balance, and the relationship of the limbs all help to produce a smoothly coordinated stroke. Attention may be divided between different kinds of sensory messages. Confronted with a mass of available information, a swimmer learns to notice only some of it and ignore much that is irrelevant to the immediate task. Via the process of facilitation at the synapses, repetition causes special pathways to be slowly laid down so that the skilled movements become more accurate.

Muscular movements are driven by a "servomechanism" similar in many respects to the automatic feedback systems used in modern aircraft to control various mechanisms. All these mechanisms have devices (sensors, we may call them) that measure some physical variable and use this feedback information to control the mechanisms that assist the pilot.

Modern aircraft controls are linked by servomechanisms to either electric or hydraulic actuators that automatically maintain the aircraft at the chosen altitude and speed. Servomechanisms sense an error (e.g., departure from the intended course) and apply a correction to the relevant control. Signals from the sensor, called the misalignment detector, activate a small servomotor (from the Latin *servus*, meaning slave), which turns the control surface in the direction necessary to correct the misalignment. Thus, the procedures are performed without the pilot's intervention.

The point is that these devices function automatically to help the pilot. Similarly, in coaching the feel of the water, the aim is to allow a swimmer to rely on only a minimum number of consciously perceived cues and let automatic feedback systems control other functions of the stroke without too much conscious effort.

The Use of Simultaneous Visual and Tactile Impressions

The traditional emphasis when teaching a stroke pattern to a novice has been on the visual. I, too, long believed that the sense of touch was usually too imprecise to be the source of form and shape in the early stages of learning. Furthermore, though some people learn more by means of tactile feedback whereas others receive more beneficial information visually, it is difficult to know whether this difference in perceptual capacity between individuals is significant.

Over a period of about 6 years I experimented with developing a method of coaching stroke technique that would involve using *simultaneous* visual and tactile impressions. I had long before become uncomfortable with merely explaining the shape, form, and pattern of a desired movement without being able to relate its effect on the water. The aim of my method is to teach a swimmer to relate each phase of a swimming stroke with the feel of the flow and thus obtain instant feedback on stroke efficiency.

This method allows a certain amount of individuality. At first, the learner is shown a few sample "flow shaper" skills and left alone to play around with them in the water.

After a week or so, some instruction is begun, usually individual. Not everyone is given the same instruction because each learner is directed to a particular phase of the stroke that appears to need attention. This is generally how the method is applied—not so much on *items* of technique but on particular movement *phases* of the stroke.

Using both visual and tactile impressions *simultaneously* from the start in a definite teaching format causes noted changes in the sensitivity of the learner to particular features of the swimming stroke and its effect on the water.

Tactile perception can be developed to where a swimmer can receive continuous feedback on propulsive effectiveness. This information helps the swimmer to keep adjusting and refining the stroke at the "delivery end" to maintain efficiency. For example, the link between seeing the hand entering the water and bringing the hand into contact with it is somehow obvious. The hand just seems to move in the right way. If the swimmer's hand is "alive" and sensitive to the feel of the water, it acts as a sensing device that transforms the incoming signal into appropriate action. Equally important is that the swimmer has been taught not only to anticipate the oncoming relative flow but also to handle it in the most effective way.

The following sections contain descriptions of the flow-shaping skills and sensitizing techniques used in this conceptualizing process.

Flow Shapers

A flow shaper is an exercise that teaches swimmers to create and detect specific flows in the water. It operates in much the same way as the aircraft servomechanisms already described.

Flow shapers are remarkably effective in helping a swimmer automatically find the most effective path, posture, and attitude of the hand and arm during a swimming stroke; for example, they help the swimmer position the arm correctly at entry, correct a dropped elbow, or, for a butterfly swimmer, know whether to pull wider or narrower. Most important, the flow shaper helps a swimmer find the stroke pattern that accords naturally with the characteristics of individual physique.

Some examples of flow shapers follow.

The Ship Drill

This important exercise teaches swimmers how to insert their hands into the oncoming flow prior to starting the swimming stroke. The swimmer pushes off from the wall with body outstretched and hands back to back and touching, forming a shape akin to the prow of a ship. The swimmer will feel the oncoming flow produced by the push-off as it advances along the palms of the hands and under the forearms and upper arms to the armpits. The pressure sensation of the oncoming flow can be prolonged by continuing momentum with the dolphin kick or by using fins (Figure 5.1a and b).

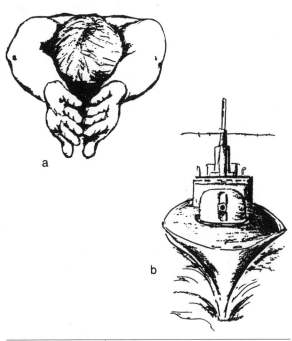

Figure 5.1 The ship drill: (a) ship drill posture and (b) action of the ship's prow.

The ship drill should be performed daily. It is more valuable than any other procedure in teaching a swimmer to feel and recognize the oncoming flow.

Beginning in the ship-drill position, the freestyle stroke should be started with palm turned outward and pressing downward in a curved, diagonal motion. The palm gradually rotates inward as the hand moves inward in the lateral plane toward the center line of the body. During this motion the hand and forearm rotate as a unit. This motion changes the direction of the oncoming flow as it is wrapped around the hand and forearm in a strong swirl.

The swimmer should concentrate on bending the elbow to approximately 90 degrees or as much as feels comfortable. As the elbow bend increases, some individual swimmers may turn the palm of the hand slightly upward toward the chest to obtain maximum forearm rotation, but such extreme rotation may feel comfortable only to tall, lean swimmers.

Destroyer–Ocean Liner–Barge Drill

Practice ship drills with hands in the three different positions shown in Figure 5.2. These drills show swimmers how the changing postures of the hands and arms cause a transition from streamlined flow to turbulent (resistive) flow. In Figure 5.2a there is a free movement of the oncoming flow that is felt on the palms of the outturned hands and along the forearms. In Figure 5.2b and c the flow gradually becomes more resistive as the hand and forearm posture changes.

Half-Ship Drill

Use this drill to enhance feel of the flow at hand entry, especially for swimmers who experience difficulty in feeling the flow. The swimmer kicks while wearing fins and holding one arm out front simulating the entry posture. The hand should be pitched diagonally outward and the elbow up; the other arm is held at the side. The swimmer should feel for the oncoming flow.

Tunnel Flow, or A-OK

Press the thumb against the forefinger to form a "tunnel" through which the flow is channeled as the hand changes direction in the stroke (Figure 5.3). This exercise effectively teaches flow recognition and how to angle the hands efficiently; in fact, it often will "groove" a stroke pattern automatically. If a butterfly swimmer's pull is too wide or narrow, for example, this exercise will direct the swimmer accordingly.

Figure 5.3 Tunnel flow, or A-OK.

This exercise also indicates whether a crawl swimmer is allowing the elbow to drop during the pull, because if so, the flow will not pass through the tunnel. In fact, it should be used in all strokes. Swimmers may try forming the tunnel with one hand while keeping the other hand closed. When both hands are opened and used in the normal fashion, however, the hand

Figure 5.2 Ship drill variations: (a) destroyer, (b) ocean liner, and (c) barge.

that was closed will be found to also have improved its feel.

Piano Playing

In this exercise the swimmer pretends to play the piano by using individual finger movements while swimming. This helps the swimmer feel how separate finger movements influence flow channeling (Figure 5.4).

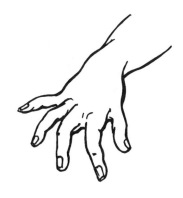

Figure 5.4 Piano playing.

Sensitizing the Sensory Nerve Endings

In developing this method I soon realized that there is no difficulty in increasing the sensibility of the nerve endings. There are many methods to achieve this, including the rehabilitative techniques used after hand surgery and learning to type by touch and to read braille. The heightened tactile sensibility must be related to the various sequences of the swimming stroke, however. The swimmer should be able to recognize and interpret the feel of moving pressure against the hand and forearm during every phase of the swimming stroke.

A vast literature exists on the complex neurological functions of the human hand, which, as we know, is a truly remarkable instrument. Because of the complexity of the subject, I decided to concentrate on a few aspects that I thought most germane to my purpose. I found the experiments of A. Lee Dellon (Dellon, Curtis, & Edgerton, 1974) particularly valuable. As late as 1972, Dellon showed that the sense of touch could be divided into two main areas: moving (*transient*) touch and constant, or *static*, touch.

Using this distinction, I experimented with sensitizing techniques for swimming that alter-

nate the application of transient and static pressures. I found that such techniques as applying different pressures (including static and transient pressures), rubbing the hands and forearms in the desired flow directions, using a loofah as a sensitizing device, and several other procedures very quickly stimulated the sensory nerve endings.

Interestingly, sensitivity to the water appears to decrease as a workout progresses, even for talented swimmers. There also appear to be day-to-day variations. I can only guess at the reason for this—perhaps fatigue or overstimulation of the sensory nerve endings.

Although swimmers have little or no difficulty in learning to recognize the oncoming (distal) flow at hand entry, some do encounter difficulty in recognizing the subsequent flows (radial, ulnar, and proximal) set up by the hand and forearm as they move through the swimming stroke. This can be overcome by teaching swimmers to rub the hand and forearm in the direction of the appropriate flow.

I borrowed from the biomechanists another very effective procedure. Instead of videotaping swimmers underwater *after* they have learned their stroke mechanics, I videotape them *while* they are learning. Instead of the old method of practicing on land in front of a mirror, they practice—still on land—in front of video monitors while they are being videotaped simultaneously from front and side. Three large electric fans (kept well away from the water for safety reasons) are placed around the swimmer to simulate the reacting flows of the water that occur during the various stages of the swimming stroke. Should a swimmer have difficulty in sensing the flow, the palm of the hand and forearm are wiped with a damp cloth to heighten the sense of touch.

A swimmer can thus simultaneously see front and side views of the stroke on the monitors and feel a simulation of the reacting flow. In addition, the swimmer can receive instruction while this is happening. The three stages of "*visualize, verbalize,* and *feel*" (Counsilman, 1968) can occur almost simultaneously.

Sensitizing procedures dramatically enhance a swimmer's feel of the water and should be an everyday feature of the workout. Great emphasis should be placed on sensitizing the hands to the feel of the water and the hands should remain sensitized throughout the workout. When questioned, even talented swimmers admit that their feel of the water tends to diminish as they progress through a workout, however. Whenever sensitivity to the water seems to lessen, a swimmer should resensitize the hands so that the sense of touch becomes more acute as the workout continues.

Fist Clenching

The nerve endings on the palms quickly become highly sensitized when subjected to contrasts between static and transient pressures. Thus, if a swimmer clenches the fists tightly for two or three minutes before starting a swim, the sensory nerve endings overcompensate in reaction to the static pressure. When the hands are opened again, they are particularly sensitive to the pressure of the moving flow.

Swimmers should sensitize the hands at the beginning of every workout by swimming the first 200 meters with their fists tightly clenched. Because they will feel that they are slipping the water they should pull a little more slowly while doing this exercise, concentrating on keeping tightly clenched fists. The swimmer should start the stroke with wrist turned outward, thumb down, and emphasize hand-forearm rotation throughout the stroke while bending the elbow to approximately 90 degrees in midstroke.

Fist swimming was named by the great stroke technician Howard Firby (Firby, 1975). Firby recommended fist swimming to develop ''the *feel* of pulling not only with the hands but with the forearms as well'' and to correct dropped elbows and induce the ''over the barrel'' feeling of the pull (p. 15).

My ''rediscovery'' of fist swimming resulted from reading Dellon's reports and my desire to develop as a sensitizing procedure a method of applying contrasting static and transient pressures on the sensory nerve endings of the hand. Clenching and then opening the hand was a natural choice. I also use fist swimming to show how hand-forearm rotation develops flow circulation. My personal belief, however, is that the greatest value of fist swimming is as a sensitizing procedure for stimulating the sensory nerve endings of the palms of the hands.

An effective exercise for sensitizing both hands and feet is to swim a set distance by alternating fist swimming and overkicking (kicking with more force than necessary) on successive laps of the pool. This can also be a demanding workout. Another variation is to swim with one hand clenched while keeping the other hand open. This contrasts the static pressure on the closed hand and the transient pressure on the open hand, increasing the swimmer's awareness of the water's flow reactions.

The breaststroke and butterfly should frequently be swum with fists clenched. While pulling in the breaststroke the swimmer should use a slight dolphin kick for counterbalance. Emphasis should be on hand-forearm rotation and elbow bending because this action develops the flow circulation necessary for propulsion. This drill highlights the surprising amount of propulsion this mechanism can develop even when the hands are not open to provide as much lift as possible. Although the forearms do not provide a great amount of propulsion, their rotation is necessary and significant in setting up the desired flow circulation.

When the hand is open, the hand and forearm work as a unit. The hand is capable of developing more efficient circulation than the forearm because it has a more favorable shape and can be manipulated on the wrist with more dexterity and through a larger range of movement. When the hand and forearm are used as a unit they form a most effective mechanism for setting up flow circulation.

Fingertip Pressing

These exercises sensitize the fingertips to the oncoming flow as the hands enter the water.

1. Press each fingertip in turn against the thumb (Figure 5.5).
2. Now use both hands. Press the fingertips of one hand against those of the other. Press hard and repeat frequently.
3. Now press each fingertip of one hand separately against its counterpart on the other hand. This develops dexterity.
4. Press the fingertips hard against the pool deck while waiting for the start of next training set.

Simultaneous Sensitization to Static and Transient Pressure

The hand can be held in a variety of postures during swimming to sensitize fingers, individually or in groups, to the sensation of moving pressure. Keeping the palm closed sensitizes it via static pressure. These exercises greatly sensitize the hands to the feeling of moving pressure once normal swimming is resumed (Figure 5.6).

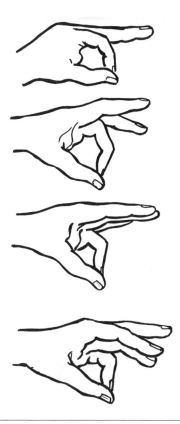

Figure 5.5   Fingertip pressing.

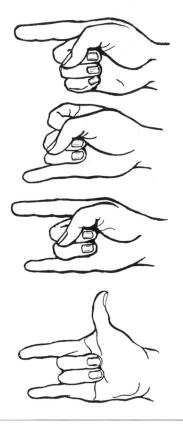

Figure 5.6   Simultaneous sensitization to static and transient pressure.

Hand-Rubbing Exercises

Swimmers find hand-rubbing exercises to be very effective in sensitizing the hands to recognize precise flow reactions. Rubbing one hand against the other can be used to simulate a desired flow direction, which helps make each phase of the stroke consistently efficient.

1. Rub one hand against the other from the fingertips along the palm to the wrist and forearm. This teaches the feel of the oncoming flow as the hand enters the water and is inserted into the oncoming flow at the start of the stroke.
2. Rub one hand *across* the other hand in the desired direction to simulate transverse (lateral) flows as they occur in either an inward or outward pitch of the hands.
3. Rub one hand along the other down the palm to the fingertips to simulate the finish of the stroke.

The Use of a Loofah as a Sensitizing Device

A highly effective method of sensitizing the entire body to the flow of the water is to scrub the skin *lightly* with a *dry* loofah immediately before every practice or competition. (A loofah, or luffa, resembles an elongated sponge and is coarse and fibrous. It is the fruit of a herbaceous plant, *luffa cylindrica*.) The swimmer should scrub the entire body and, in particular, perform a routine in which one arm is held overhead while the loofah is rubbed from the fingertips down the palm of the hand, along the under surface of the arm, and down the side of the trunk to the hips; the same procedure should be repeated on the other side of the body. This exercise will sensitize the hand, arm, and trunk side to the oncoming flow of the water. After several days of using a loofah this way, most swimmers will experience a noted improvement in their sensitivity to the flow of the water.

Daily Application of the Method

Flow Manipulation

Swimmers should be taught always to feel they are inserting the hands into the oncoming flow instead of attacking the water and trying to push it directly backward.

After feeling the oncoming flow, swimmers should be told to wrap, or swirl, the flow around the arm by gradually rotating the hand and forearm. The elbow at maximum bend should reach approximately 90 degrees and be comfortable to the individual swimmer; if it is not comfortable, adjust the amount of elbow bend to suit the swimmer.

After some practice, swimmers will improve in stroke efficiency and be able to recognize weak spots in the stroke through tactile feedback from the flow reaction. They can eliminate weak spots by experimenting with the amount of hand-forearm rotation and the degree of elbow bend they perform.

Timing the Stroke

The timing of the stroke will depend greatly on the desired speed. Swimmers should be told that the entry hand, palm turned outward, acts as a sensor, or "radar," as it accepts the oncoming relative flow and helps them know exactly when to start applying force at the beginning of the stroke. The amount of oncoming flow to accept before starting the stroke will depend on the pace and stroke length each swimmer wishes to establish.

Feeling the differences in pressure on the entry hand at various speeds will help the swimmers learn pacing. Feeling the oncoming flow is an important element in learning split-second timing. The swimmers should be taught to "think momentum." By feeling the amount of stretch in the flow, each swimmer will learn to judge the body's momentum and know when to start the stroke. For example, in a short race, the stroke may be started after allowing the flow to move along only as far as the wrist. Over a longer distance and at a slower speed, a swimmer may let the oncoming flow move along the forearm before starting into the stroke.

Flow Shaper Drills and Sensitizing Procedures

Flow shaper drills and sensitizing procedures should be done every day as part of the regular workout practice.

Fist swimming should be done in *all* strokes at slow and fast speeds. The swimmers should always start the stroke with the hand turned outward. The fists should be kept tightly clenched. Fist swimming in the breaststroke and butterfly is particularly effective for coaching effective hand-forearm rotation and elbow flexion and also has a positive transfer to the other strokes.

Swimmers should be aware that sensitivity to flow will vary from day to day. Every workout should start with skin sensitization—hand rubbing, the use of a loofah, fist swimming, tunnel flow (A-OK), and fingertip pressing exercises. Every now and again during the workout the swimmers should push off from the pool side using the ship-drill posture instead of the conventional locked hands.

These occasional ship push-offs enable swimmers to test hand sensitivity to the pressure of the oncoming flow. The swimmers should always resensitize their hands during the workout, especially during the middle stages of the workout or at the onset of fatigue. If this is done, the swimmers will complete the workout with a greater feel for the water. The coach should not permit the swimmers to regard these procedures as a passing fad because, over the weeks and months, most swimmers will experience a pronounced improvement in technique resulting from their enhanced ability to feel and manipulate the flow of the water.

PART II
TRAINING

Even talented swimmers need years of training under well-integrated controls to produce superior performance. The outstanding feats of the great swimmers attest to the prodigious internal adjustments the human body can make. Their achievements are the result of programs designed to progressively train the body's three energy systems so that eventually a swimmer can cover specific racing distances at maximum capacity.

Although organized competition in track and swimming both started about 150 years ago, training methods advanced more rapidly in track than in swimming, probably because swimmers found they could swim faster merely by improving their stroke mechanics. This approach proved so rewarding to swimmers that they did either very little training or none at all. In addition, the opinion prevailed in many quarters that training too hard would cause "burn out."

Andrew "Boy" Charlton, the great Australian swimmer of the 1920s, is known to have trained for only 4 weeks before a big race, averaging a half mile a day. Another famous Australian, Noel Ryan, Empire Champion and 1932 Olympic finalist, told me that the most he ever swam in a day was 1,000 yards—this was when he was preparing for the 1932 Olympic Games in Los Angeles. When he arrived at the Olympic venue, he reduced his training distance to 440 yards "for fear of burning out."

Ryan said that he used to sit back at the Olympic pool and watch the Japanese team cover up to 5 miles daily. According to Ryan, the Japanese dominance in 1932 and again at the Berlin Olympics in 1936 prompted several theories: that the Japanese had the ideal build for swimming; that they had developed a new stroke; and that they were using drugs. The main reason for the Japanese dominance, however, was that they trained harder than any other team. Few people showed a desire to copy the Japanese methods; in fact, the Japanese effort was dismissed by many as "fanaticism." Either through laziness, jealousy, or genuine belief, people asked, "Who wants to go to such lengths to succeed?" The truth was that the Japanese idea of strenuous training was too far ahead of its time.

Shortly thereafter, World War II produced a brief hiatus in competitive swimming. As interest in competitive swimming revived in the immediate postwar period, swimmers began to realize the importance of improved conditioning. Kiphuth had pioneered supplementary land training for swimmers back in 1917, but a few swimmers now tentatively began to experiment with weight training. Champion swimmer Dick Cleveland, at Ohio State University, practiced weight training 5 days a week under the guidance of Fraysher Ferguson at his gymnasium in Columbus, Ohio. Among other Ohio State swimmers who achieved good results under Ferguson's tutelage was Al Wiggens, who set world butterfly and medley records. In 1952 Walter Schlueter pioneered weight training for women swimmers with his world-record relay team at the Town Club of Chicago (Murray & Karpovich, 1956).

Some swimmers now trained as far as 3 miles daily, but others, attempting to relieve some of the inevitable boredom of swimming long stretches at a comparatively easy pace, introduced periods of intermittent faster activity, which can best be described as a form of intervalization. However, by no stretch of imagination can these procedures be construed as the first structured and formal application of interval training. Nevertheless, during this period there were isolated accounts of coaches and swimmers inadvertently using what can be termed a form of rudimentary interval training.

I mentioned earlier how John Marshall, in his letters home to Australia, described the form of intervalized training used at Yale University. Some accounts credit Marshall's letters with giving Australian coaches the idea from which they developed interval training. In 1956 one of the leading Australian coaches, Frank Guthrie, who spearheaded the Australian revival and coached Lorraine Crappe to become the first woman to beat the then "magic" 5-minute mark for 400 meters, said that the Australians had received the idea from the Americans.

Guthrie's statement may have been partially correct—Sydney University professor Frank Cotton and his understudy, Forbes Carlile, had read of the method in track magazines and research papers. It is also likely that they had discussed the method with world-class Australian track athletes, who were already using interval training.

In 1954, British track athlete Roger Bannister had run the first sub 4-minute mile under the guidance of Franz Stampfl, who advocated a combination of *fartlek* (speed play), interval, and repetition training. Bannister's feat captured the imagination of followers of many sports, causing great interest in Stampfl's training concepts.

Stampfl's book *Franz Stampfl on Running* (1955) and Bannister's *First Four Minutes* (1955) were both instant bestsellers that were intently studied by forward-thinking coaches in swimming as well as track. Bannister described the process whereby he had attacked the 4-minute "barrier" for the mile run. In December 1953, he had started an intensive training program in which he ran a series of 10 consecutive quarter miles, each in 66 seconds, with 2-minute rest intervals between them. Gradually, through January and February, he stepped up the pace until by April he could manage the series in an average time of 60 seconds while keeping to the 2-minute rest intervals.

Information on interval training thus probably reached Australian swimming coaches from several sources. Nevertheless, the Australians were the first to establish a protocol for using interval training as an accepted and regular method of training competitive swimmers.

In the 1950s, Australian swimming coaches, in conjunction with physiologist Frank Cotton, began a methodical study of the interval training method that had been used in running since the late 1930s and applied it to swimming. In a manner similar to Woldemar Gerschler's early research on interval training for track, the Australians attempted to relate heart rate with recorded swimming times at different work:rest ratios. Some coaches used heart-rate checks in establishing interval training as a formal conditioning method for swimmers.

Coincidental or not with the use of interval training, swimming took one of its rare quantum leaps forward. Within a matter of months, in 1956, the Australians almost completely rewrote the world-record books for both men and women. The Australian swimmers, training under six highly innovative coaches—Forbes Carlile, Arthur Cusack, Gus Frohlich, Harry Gallagher, Frank Guthrie, and Sam Herford—made an almost complete sweep of the 1956 Olympic swimming events.

In the first 10 years or so that interval training was used in swimming, there were several phases during which the concept, still incompletely understood, was misapplied. The total training load was often too great, mainly because, in an attempt to strive for even more speed, coaches tended to demand too great a pace for the repeat swims. The result, recognized by only a few at the time, was often an inability by swimmers to recover from what Carlile termed "failing adaptation," a condition that requires either a marked reduction in the intensity of the work load or complete rest. We still have a great deal to learn about the ideal application of the work load, and the important determinant remains quality.

A notable step toward better understanding the effects of varying work:rest ratios in interval training resulted from a simple but highly effective research project conducted at Indiana University by James Counsilman (1968). Three groups of swimmers trained over the same distances for 5 weeks, each group using a different rest interval. The study showed that shorter rest intervals produce greater endurance, whereas longer rest intervals produce greater speed.

In the former East Germany, sport scientists monitored and controlled the intensity and duration of interval training by testing the amount of blood lactate at varying levels of work intensity. As a result, they were able to define more clearly an ideal balance between the duration and intensity of exercise, not only as a broad conceptual exercise but also as a guide to prescribing appropriate training for the individual swimmer. Concurrent with this work was a growing attention on the periodization of the training program with carefully controlled transitions from one phase of preparation to the next.

Although training methods in swimming developed later than in track, the development, when it came, followed a similar evolutionary pattern. In both sports, continued debate marked the search for the ideal balance between the volume and intensity of the workload. The issue is still alive in swimming in the closing decade of the 20th century.

Chapter 6

The Influence of Track Training on Swimming

The training methods of swimming share an origin with those used on the running track. The basic training principles used by modern competitive swimmers were first developed by great track athletes working with renowned coaches and physiologists such as Holmer, van Aaken, and Gerschler.

Obvious differences exist between some of the physiological effects of running and swimming; nevertheless, by looking at the problems that beset the early development of track methods, we may gain greater insight into similar difficulties encountered in swimming. There may be some as yet overlooked aspects of track training that can be beneficially adapted to swimming.

Competitive running started with competitions between England's Oxford and Cambridge Universities. For most of the first 100 years training emphasized developing endurance, but as time passed, it became evident that speed was also important.

Gosta Holmer and the Fartlek Method

Gosta Holmer (1893-1972), the famous Swedish track coach, developed a naturalistic method of training he called fartlek (speed play), which consists of running both quickly and slowly. To some extent, fartlek is an informal type of training in which the athlete jogs, walks, runs, or sprints as he or she wishes. This was particularly true of its use in early season training, for which the method established informal fast and slow cross-country running as a fundamental form of endurance training.

Possibly because the term means "speed play," many people in swimming had the mistaken impression that fartlek was nothing more than an informal and almost inconsequential type of training serving little purpose other than to produce some basic early season fitness. On the track, however, fartlek became a more strenuous and demanding form of training as the season progressed.

The application of fartlek to swimming appears to have been neither properly understood nor taken seriously enough. Perhaps it has been mistakenly interpreted by some as a subterfuge for relieving boredom while accumulating early season mileage. In fact, this kind of training is often termed "bulk mileage" or "garbage," implying a certain mindless approach to the essential task of establishing an extensive aerobic endurance foundation to seasonal activity.

The following are the main features of the fartlek method of training:

1. **Variation of Pace.** The pace varies frequently from short, sharp sprints to long, easy jog-trots, with occasional fast quarter-miles and sustained efforts over distances from a half mile to a mile. This emphasis on pace variation served as an introduction to the more exacting interval training on the track that came later. In swimming, Don Gambril, one of America's all-time great coaches, laid much emphasis in the 1960s on the principle of varying the pace, notably in training such fine swimmers as Patti Carretto, Gunnar Larsen, and Hans Fassnacht.

2. The Importance of Individual Coaching. A defining characteristic of the fartlek method is that it emphasizes the importance of coaching the athlete as an individual. Although the method involves more structure as the season progresses, it provides some opportunity for self-knowledge, producing an athlete who may be more able to judge the effects of exercise through subjective observation. I believe that we have tended to neglect this aspect in recent years when training competitive swimmers. Pope's dictum, ''Man know thyself,'' is as pertinent to competitive swimming as to any other endeavor.

Lactate testing, whatever its value may be in some quarters, may have been overstressed to the exclusion of a more important coaching task: showing swimmers how to recognize, *on their own*, the intensity of effort at different set paces. *Learning to know one's self* is the most important thing a coach can teach an athlete who wishes to compete successfully.

3. Relating Stride to Running Speed. The early season application of fartlek to swimming training has followed formats mostly concerned with developing basic conditioning, but swimming coaches may have neglected the additional pace and tempo teaching possibilities the method presents.

Gosta Holmer began to recognize the important of always relating pace to the training effort between 1921 and 1925, when he lived in Finland, where he had ample opportunity to observe Paavo Nurmi, one of the greatest runners in the history of track.

Holmer correctly believed that a runner learns technique only by running long distances. (This is also true of swimming technique.) Holmer always stressed the importance of relating a runner's stride to the runner's speed. Properly adapted to swimming training, this approach can be used as a challenging and effective training tool. Coaches and swimmers should be aware of the need to relate stroke length and stroke frequency to swimming time

and, as conditioning improves, to assess efficiency by relating these factors to heart rate.

4. The Development of the Will to Overcome Fatigue. Holmer recognized that the will to overcome fatigue is an additional important factor in athletic success. Athletes who use the fartlek method are allowed to determine how far and how fast they wish to run, which teaches them to tolerate fatigue under a variety of physiological stresses.

Similarly, Counsilman recognized the need to motivate swimmers to withstand fatigue. Therefore, he created his ''hurt-pain-agony'' scale to assist sensory perception of fatigue at different levels of work intensity—or, as his swimmers would say, ''at different levels of suffering.'' Counsilman also devised a ''hurt-pain-agony'' chart (Counsilman, 1968, p. 338) that showed the differences in effort expended by ''hard workers'' and ''comfort swimmers'' during practice. Comfort swimmers rarely ventured out of the comfort zone and into the pain zone. But the dedicated, hard workers typically swam straight through the hurt zone, into the pain zone, and finally into the agony zone.

5. Fartlek and the Concept of Tempo Training. Holmer (1972) believed a runner should alternate twice a week between one-quarter and one-half racing tempo and during the last month of training use one-half to three-quarters tempo. Holmer estimated the various tempos as follows: Suppose a runner's full tempo is an average speed of 20 seconds per 100 meters for 1 hour. Increasing this tempo by 2.5%, 5%, and 7.5% produces one-fourth, one-half, and three-fourths tempos, respectively (see the chart at the bottom of the page).

A classic example of how track training methods were successfully transferred to swimming is contained in 1984 Olympic 1,500-meter champion Tiffany Cohen's description of how she used this concept in her training program (Appendix B of this book, the section ''Training for the Distance Events'').

	Distance (in meters)				
Tempo	100	1,000	5,000	10,000	15,000
1/1	20.0	3:20.0	16:40.0	32:20.0	49:00.0
3/4	20.5	3:25.0	17:05.0	34:10.0	51:15.0
1/2	21.0	3:30.0	17:30.0	35:00.0	52:30.0
1/4	21.5	3:35.0	17:55.0	35:50.0	53:45.0

Note. From Holmer (1972). Reprinted by permission.

The Use of Tempo Training in Swimming

In the early years of interval training in the pool, Australian swimming coaches, particularly those most influenced by Frank Cotton around 1955, used a variation of Holmer's long-distance tempo method. To determine the speed and intensity of effort for an interval series, they calculated a percentage of a swimmer's fastest time for a particular distance, for example, 70%, 80%, or 90%. They often compared pulse rate with the recorded time to check a swimmer's fitness. They also predicted performance by plotting recorded time against a total of the heart rates taken at 10-second intervals during the first half minute after exercise (Carlile, 1956b).

The late 1950s and early 1960s were marked by trial and error—mostly error—in the application of interval training to swimming. Because there was a tendency to do interval training at too high a percentage of maximum effort, many teams often had disappointing results. Coaches such as Peter Daland, Sherman Chavoor, Nort Thornton, Forbes Carlile, Don Gambril, George Haines, and "Doc" Counsilman gradually came to appreciate the need for varying the pace and the intervals according to the physiological effects they wished their swimmers to achieve.

Summary of Holmer's Fartlek Method

The gradual seasonal progression used in the Holmer method can be easily adapted to the training of competitive swimmers. Above all, the method is simple. All too often a swimming training program begins to look more like a detailed thesis or an exposé of a coach's knowledge of exercise physiology than a plan whose purpose is plain and can be easily followed. The importance of simplicity in program planning is often overlooked, which is particularly a problem when coaching the younger swimmer, who should be able to recognize at a glance both the purpose of each phase of a program as well as the progress made.

Study of Holmer's plan for a training season shows an initial concentration on building a broad and well-planned endurance base by means of fartlek training. Later, precise paces and tempos are gradually introduced. At first, paced work is done at one-fourth tempo; then, as the athlete's fitness increases, the speed increases to one-half tempo; finally, speed work is done at three-fourths tempo over almost the full racing distance. Thus there is a subtle change in the specificity of the training program as it moves from the development of general aerobic conditioning to establishing the peak season's final race pace. The work is applied in cyclic phases, however, depending on each athlete's individual reactions from session to session, day to day, and week to week.

Holmer's program is all-embracing yet notable for the simplicity of its application; indeed, it would have been surprising had outstanding results not resulted from a program so clearly modeled on everyday common sense. Most coaches who have produced top world athletes and swimmers will confirm that their most successful seasonal programs were those characterized by an essential simplicity that nevertheless took into account a few basic principles of exercise physiology.

Ernst van Aaken's Speed Through Endurance Method

Ernst van Aaken was a general practitioner in the small German town of Waldniel. He developed the "pure endurance" method of training after seeing Paavo Nurmi break the world record in 1928 for the one-hour run, but he did not make his methods public until 1947, when he wrote the article "Running and Record" in *Sport und Gymnastik* (van Aaken, 1947). The adherents of his methods were known as "The Waldniel School" after the town where he lived.

Van Aaken's endurance method was adapted to the training of swimmers by the Australian coach Forbes Carlile with great success during the 1970s. Carlile showed that the concept of speed through endurance very much applied to his protégés Karen Moras, Shane Gould, and Jenny Turrell, world-record holders, at distances from 400 meters to 1,500 meters and for Gould at all distances from 100 meters upward (Carlile, 1976).

The Concept of Training for Pure Endurance

According to van Aaken, Emil Zatopek, who ran long distances with rhythmical changes of speed, exemplified the Waldniel method or "classical" form of interval training. This method enabled Zatopek to win Olympic supremacy in 1948. Van Aaken said that the method introduced the important new concept of training for pure endurance.

Zatopek covered distances at relatively slow speeds. He daily performed 400-meter runs broken by 200-meter jogs at subracing speed over distances between 36 and 50 kilometers. Occasionally, he would run 400 meters at increased speed.

According to van Aaken, critics of the Zatopek method claimed that it not only takes up too much time but also does not sufficiently overload the body, so they increased the quality of the work by introducing breaks and reducing the distances run under stress to 100 and 200 meters. This work was done in a long series of repetitions. They believed this method would develop greater endurance, speed, and strength. They maintained that, for middle- and long-distance racing, it ensures a very quick and effective increase in heart size and also improves the so-called muscle endurance.

Van Aaken's Criticism of Interval Training

Van Aaken (1947) says that the whole concept of interval training is based on becoming used to oxygen debt by doing *mainly anaerobic work*. According to van Aaken, this "improved" interval work, developed, propagated, and made obligatory in Germany, only shows what acute stresses athletes are capable of bearing.

Van Aaken reports that marathon runners training with the interval method performed 200-meter runs 170 times in 33 seconds each. He claims that the interval training method developed the capacity for recovery after heavy stress, but *this capacity is not specific to performance*. He adds that it is incorrect to assume that increasing total intermittent stresses necessarily results in increased capacity to withstand the *continuous and accumulative* stress that occurs when covering full distance at racing speed.

Van Aaken also says that even Herbert Reindell, one of the developers of interval training, showed interval training over short and middle distances caused only moderate increase in heart size. Van Aaken points out that marathon runners, as well as long-distance cyclists and rowers, were found to have the largest hearts. He expresses doubt as to how a long series of short, fast runs could bring about the necessary *long-lasting* endurance effects.

Steady State Training

Van Aaken's pure endurance training involves daily training at a steady state with the most favorable respiratory conditions, without an increase of initial oxygen debt and formation of lactic acid and with an average pulse rate of 130 beats per minute. To achieve this, the athlete performs long runs, initially with short breaks, after the principle of interval training. Later, the athlete runs continuous distances of between 6 to 50 miles. This training method was used for the marathon distance. Note: At the end of the daily run, the method requires a fast run at *not faster* than race pace over *part* of the racing distance.

The Use of Part Distances for Tempo Training. Van Aaken set the ratio of long unbroken runs to shorter distances covered at pace (tempo) at 20:1. The mileage is shortened or extended according to an athlete's preferred racing distance. The pace is determined by the runner's best time.

A 5,000-meter runner capable of 15 minutes would frequently be asked to do five 1,000-meter runs in 3 minutes each, an 800-meter runner capable of 1:44.0 to do six 200-meter runs in 26 seconds, and so on. After some practice, the tempo for the part distances will be set *by instinct* instead of using a stop watch. In addition, all athletes train for the next event above their racing distance ("overdistance"): An 800-meter runner is expected to be able to achieve a reasonable time over 1,500 meters.

The longest distance to be covered in training is many times longer than the racing distance. Van Aaken scheduled runs over these distances at either the beginning or the end of the week. The 800-meter specialist will run at least 12 to 15 miles; the marathoners, 36, 40, even 48 miles, to build the foundation that will last through 26 miles at racing speed. During the first years of such training, the distances are covered in segments of 2 to 3 miles interspersed with walking recovery breaks.

Speed Through Endurance Training Applied to Swimming

Carlile (1971) believed that swimmers should also train over long distances and that if the distance is reduced and the quality element becomes too intense, a swimmer very easily will go into failing adaptation. In fact, almost all of Carlile's work in physiology was oriented to avoiding too much high-pressure training.

Carlile believed there to be a limit to the amount of training that should be done at high speed. Carlile's methods were instead based largely on the simple concept of keeping a constant duration for the twice-daily training sessions (approximately 2 hours per session) and encouraging swimmers to gradually increase the distances they were capable of covering within that fixed time.

Carlile was greatly concerned at the time about the extent to which training in swimming should be specific to sprint and distance racing. He disagreed with coaches who came up with complicated "special programs" for their sprinters, commenting that it must have disturbed these coaches when swimmers who were trained on distance programs won the 100-meter race rather than those prepared specifically for this event. Carlile added that the 50 to 60 seconds taken to swim 100 meters was a pretty long "sprint" compared to the 100-meter dash on the track.

Carlile (1971) criticizes what he terms the "rigid application" of interval training and says that van Aaken had "demolished" the advocates of this method, who had set up a system of training with exact rest periods (irrespective of the individual) and "pseudoscientific" control of training by heart counts, a method he felt was built on incomplete scientific foundations. He points to the effectiveness of empiricist track coaches, citing as examples Percy Cerutty's successes with his pupils John Landy and Herb Elliot and the New Zealander Arthur Lydiard's success with Peter Snell and others.

According to Carlile (1971), the success of endurance training methods indicates that the interval principle should not be carried too far. He notes that endurance-trained runners had succeeded even in relatively short distances when interval-trained athletes had virtually stopped in their tracks. Carlile says that enthusiasm, nonconformity, and empirical observation had succeeded where science had fallen short. (In later years, Carlile came to recognize that there was more of a place for the development of *all* the energy systems—provided the swimmer did not go into a state of reduced physiological adaptation by training at too high an intensity.)

In the 1960s, Sherman Chavoor, one of the most highly successful coaches in the history of American swimming, was an early advocate of training swimmers along the lines van Aaken suggested for track athletes (Chavoor, 1967). Chavoor trained all youngsters for distance swimming. He felt that once they could successfully cover long distances, they could work back to 400s, 200s, and 100s. Chavoor would point out to those youngsters who initially did not like doing 1,500-meter swims in training that swimmers such as Don Schollander, Mark Spitz, Carl Robie, and Roy Saari could swim fast at all distances from 100 to 1,500 meters. He added that there were very few swimmers who were just sprinters.

Summary of van Aaken's Speed Through Endurance Method

1. Athletes learn running mainly by running. Track running is mainly learned by training on level ground.

2. The most important factor in training for middle and long distances is endurance, which is a function of maximum oxygen intake capacity, low body weight, and economical application of the laws of leverage.

3. Endurance is mainly acquired by endurance exercises at medium speed. This speed is determined by personal endurance limit; during training the athlete should always perform below this limit. Only occasionally should the endurance capacity be tested at racing speed.

4. *Continually* practicing at speeds faster than race pace is uneconomical and leads to a decrease of reserves.

5. Speed runs are best practiced at race pace but only over part of the racing distance. The number of repetitions and breaks and the length of the breaks are determined by the recovery period.

6. The interval principle in endurance training is used only to enable the athlete to cover more distance without fatigue.

7. All relatively severe anaerobic stresses (e.g., speed runs) should be preceded and followed by aerobic functions (e.g., light jogging)—that is, the athlete should warm up before speed work and cool down after it.

Woldemar Gerschler's Interval Training Method

Woldemar Gerschler (Gerschler, Rosskamm, & Reindell, 1964) says that he developed interval training through trial and error. He claims that interval training produces greater endurance than running long unbroken distances—and in a shorter time. When interval training was first introduced it was a radical departure from traditional endurance training, yet it often brought dramatic results. Gerschler attributes this to a greater control over the training overload.

Using interval training, Gerschler's protégé Rudolf Harbig set world records before World War II for the 400-meter (46.0), 800-meter (1:46.6), and 1,000-meter events (2:21.5) that were far in advance of the existing standards. When Gerschler died in 1982, he was acknowledged as "Gerschler: The Innovator" (Horwill, 1982), recognized as being 30 years ahead of his time when he pioneered his interval training methods in 1932.

Pulse Rate as a Guide to Training Intensity

Departing from the general trend of his time, Gerschler shortened the distance of the longer training runs. Simultaneously, he increased the speed for these reduced distances. His formula for interval training was to have the athlete run 100 or 200 meters at a pace 3 and 6 seconds slower, respectively, than the athlete's best time for the distance. This gives a pulse rate of 170, plus or minus 10. After the pulse drops to 120 beats per minute within a 1-1/2–minute rest period the athlete runs again.

This routine continues until the heart rate fails to recover to 120 beats within 1-1/2 minutes. Gerschler et al. (1964) claims the daily repetition of this routine for 21 days can increase the heart volume by one fifth. Gerschler says that it is the *recovery* period that strengthens the heart, that is, while the pulse returns from 180 beats to 120.

The Importance of Relating Heart Rate to the Individual. Counsilman (1967) describes how he talked to Gerschler, who told him that swimming coaches did not apply the interval training method properly because they did not make swimmers wait until the heart rate dropped from 180 to 120 beats per minute. Counsilman

explained to Gerschler that swimmers working to develop endurance rested for 10 seconds, those working for both speed and endurance rested for 30 seconds, and those working for top speed rested from 1-1/2 to 2 minutes.

Gerschler adamantly maintained that the heart rate must return to 120. In reply to Gerschler, Counsilman posed hypothetical cases of two different athletes, one with a resting pulse rate of 50 and the other with a pulse rate of 70 and asked whether both should try to attain a 180 pulse rate and wait for it to return to 120. Gerschler replied that this was just a norm. Counsilman went on to point out to Gerschler that heart rate targets must always be specific to the individual and that pulse rates will vary according to the work:rest ratio and the conditioning effect the swimmer wishes to achieve.

The Merits of Different Types of Training

In the 1980s the Russians Viru and Urgenstein confirmed Gerschler's findings, which were based on checking 3,000 athletes (Horwill, 1982). Over a 3-month period, groups of athletes were given hill training, interval training, steady running, and sprinting. The hill runners improved most, followed by the interval trainers. Few runners today do only one type of training, but though they do not regard interval training as the *only* method to use, it remains an important part of their training schedules.

Gerschler's Views on the Benefits of Interval Training. Gerschler et al. (1964) states that interval training is more advantageous than continuous training because

1. it is more intensive and therefore more powerfully stimulates the musculature, and
2. it provides the opportunity to control more precisely the duration of the effort and the intensity of the stimulus.

Gerschler objected to long, slow, uninterrupted running because he felt the training required to obtain the necessary stimulus is excessively long. He believed that the monotony of running for hours on end, day after day, is more tiring than the running itself and that the stimulus provided by long, uninterrupted runs produces neither high enough oxygen debt levels nor a demand sufficient to improve the condition of the muscles. According to Gerschler, interval training provides a balance of both requirements.

Gerschler refers to Reindell's findings, saying that deep breathing during the interval causes venous blood to return to the heart in greater quantity; the tension diminishes and the systolic volume increases, resulting in an active stimulus for increasing heart volume (this is now generally known as "Reindell's heart expansion stimulus").

Basic Elements of Gerschler's Interval Training Method

According to Gerschler, the speed at which a distance should be covered depends on the recovery of the heart beat. The character of interval training changes when training for sprints because longer rests are needed for higher speeds. As for the number of times a training run should be repeated, Gerschler says that there is no fixed answer because the number of repetitions increases with an athlete's adaptation to training.

Gerschler et al. regarded the duration of the rest interval as an important factor. The recovery interval is based on the time the heart takes to recover. Using 5-second pulse rate counts he conducted a 1-year study in which he tested the cardiac frequency of hundreds of specialist runners of all distances, ranging from world-class performers to relatively unknown athletes (1964).

Gerschler concluded that the stimulus resulting from a correct combination of distance, speed, and rest interval produces pulse rates around 180 beats per minute. According to Gerschler, these findings compare favorably with the continuous clinical controls established by Reindell. Gerschler et al. (1964) thus claims that the elements of interval training are effectively proportioned when the heart rate is around 180.

Summary of Gerschler's Interval Training Method

1. Having conducted several studies on the heart rate recovery that occurs between interval training repetitions, Gerschler (Gerschler et al., 1964) claims to have obtained "positive fixed numbers" that put, "for the first time in the history of training, exact values at the disposal of the coach" (p. 31).

2. He timed the recovery interval, which he defined as the time necessary for the heart rate to fall from 180 to 140-120 beats per minute. Trained runners who jogged between efforts required from 90 to 45 seconds recovery, whereas those who rested passively needed from 70 to 30 seconds.

3. Gerschler felt that applying interval training to adolescents requires considerable care because young persons in full development are subject to the inexorable demands of growth and maturation. Comparisons were needed between the postexercise resting heart rates of young people and those of well-trained adults.

4. According to Gerschler, interval training is superior to long-distance running for increasing endurance because 1) interval training takes less time than any other method; 2) interval training can be "dosed" precisely and measured accordingly; and 3) interval training provides more stimulus than long-distance running by itself. Gerschler (1964) says these claims are substantiated by research on endurance and interval training conducted in the former East Germany (Schleusing, Rebentisch, & Schippel, 1964).

A Comparative Appraisal of Track Training Methods

Track authorities have conducted a long-lasting and sometimes even acrimonious debate concerning the most effective training methods, some promoting continuous long-distance running with occasional speed bursts, as advocated by Holmer, van Aaken, and Lydiard and others favoring the classic interval training of the Gerschler method, also known as the "Freiburg school."

In fact, a detailed look at the training methods used by the different schools of thought show that they all used a mix of distance running and intervalized speed work. Although this speed training did not always include actual breaks between runs, the interval was marked by a period of easy jogging or walking also known as "active rest."

Apparently, a tendency by popular writers to play up the more obvious characteristics of a particular method to the exclusion of other components left many with a less-than-complete understanding of the total programs. For example, the mention of Holmer instantly produced the notion of fartlek, or speed play. Van Aaken's name became synonymous with "mileage mania," and Arthur Lydiard's with marathon training for middle distance athletes. In spite of this, their programs were in fact much broader and heterogeneous than cursory study would first indicate.

The Search for an Ideal Training Format

It gradually was recognized that correct sport-specific proportions of *both* endurance (aerobic) training and speed (anaerobic) training are necessary. What this "correct proportion" is remains largely unknown, however, for both track athletes and competitive swimmers. Furthermore, many authorities doubt that a selective method for applying the training program will ever be found.

When interval training was first introduced many advocates emphasized that it enables "more work to be done in much less time" than does prolonged long-distance training. A survey of the writings and presentations at major international conferences by the originators of interval training leaves little doubt that by "more work" these individuals meant a greater stimulation of the heart as well as a more immediate and intensive overload of the working muscles.

At the Duisberg Congress on Running, Gerschler, Rosskamm, and Reindell (1964) presented a paper titled "Das Intervaltraining" ("Interval Training") setting out the principles of the Freiburg method. At this conference, Herbert Reindell, one of the founders of the interval training method, sounded a note of warning to those who would mercilessly and too liberally apply it.

Possible Adverse Effects of Interval Training

Reindell expressed concern that interval training, with its potential for producing severe anaerobic metabolism, very easily could lead to results other than expected if incorrectly applied. He said that although heart volume increases quickly through the interval training method, performances often remain static or actually regress.

Many athletes trained in this method had quickly become expert at interval training but little more. They had developed a *specific* capacity for quick recovery between heavy work loads, but though this may have indicated superior physiological conditioning, there often was not a corresponding improvement when racing. Obviously, either something was wrong in the seasonal application of training methods, or the work load was incorrectly applied in the actual interval training sessions, or both.

Learning From Practical Experience

As mentioned earlier, advocates of the fartlek and speed through endurance training methods were not slow to criticize interval training using the previous arguments.

Similarly, the proponents of interval training returned the volley by saying that long-distance aerobic training makes not only expert joggers but also expert conversationalists because of the ease with which athletes can talk to each other while running at such slow paces. They said that to run distances from 400 to 1,500 meters requires more than a daily training base of "steady state" running with no oxygen debt and an average pulse rate of 120-130 beats per minute.

Most of the popular systems in use on the track were improved by learning from practical experience, especially that of talented athletes. Knowledge probably advances best in this way because scientific explanation can hardly be expected to keep apace with the successful methods discovered in practice—it nearly always follows later. Track coaches nevertheless felt caution necessary in extolling the virtues of any particular approach to the exclusion of new ideas.

Interval Training in Swimming

The Australians were the first to regularly use interval training in swimming as a structured and formalized method. According to Forbes Carlile, the method was learned mainly from the European runners and their coaches. Frank Guthrie, of Sydney, Australia, is generally credited with being the first swimming coach to prescribe miles of interval training with short and long rest periods interspersed between repeated 50 meter swims.

Forbes Carlile describes how he and Frank Cotton used major training items called "efforts" and "repeats":

The "efforts" were made at race distances, often in threes or fours, perhaps 80%, 85%,

90% and then 80% of the maximum heart rate (checked with 10 second carotid pulse counts), usually swum towards the beginning of the training session. There would be one or two minutes rest periods or two laps of slow recovery swimming.

The "repeats" were usually at distances from 100 meters to 400 meters allowing from 10 seconds to 30 seconds rest periods. Generally, there would be a "mile" of such repeat *interval* training. "Long swims" of 1,500 meters or 800 meters at from 80% to 90% effort were introduced regularly.

"Efforts" and "repeats" were also used in separate pulling and kicking drills. The "pulling," using sections of car tubes around the ankles, was performed over 50 meters or 100 meters with short rests. Kicking was usually done between other items and consisted of 50-meter sprints with short rests. Sprints, using the full stroke, often a mile or so of 25-meter swims, were tacked on at the end of the program. (Personal communication, June 15, 1988)

By and large, this program represents in principle the training carried out in Australia by top groups in the 1950s. A wide variety of distances, rest periods, and strokes were used. In retrospect, probably all the energy systems were given reasonable "workouts," although because "aerobic," "anaerobic," and "lactates" were not then the buzzwords they are today we did not look at the training strictly in this way. The sprinters usually swam more slowly most of the time, coming to life in the short sprint section of the program.

As just observed, however, there are most likely important factors other than training that explain the huge improvements today's swimmers have shown on the performances of the 1950s, when Murray Rose, a superb athlete, could win the 400 meter Olympic gold medal in 4 minutes, 27.3 seconds, a time many 12-year-olds can achieve today and one that Murray himself could better some 20 years later!

Chapter 7

Basic Principles of Training

In a trained athlete all the physiological mechanisms involved in exercise appear to function more effectively. Although the details of this process of adaptation are not yet fully understood, many specific effects are now well substantiated.

Broadly stated, these include

1. increased cardiac output and reduced pulse rates for any given workload, as well as increased muscular capillarization and more effective oxygen utilization and energy expenditure mechanisms;
2. increased local (skeletal) muscular strength and endurance; and
3. improved neuromuscular coordination and greater mechanical efficiency for any given work load.

The Overload Principle

The overload principle accounts for the general phenomenon of adaptation to stress. *Overload* refers to a work load greater than that to which the body is accustomed, or more precisely, one for which the oxygen intake is inadequate to supply the needs of the body. The overload principle states that increases in muscle size (hypertrophy), strength, and endurance result from an increase in work intensity within a given time unit.

Hypertrophy occurs only when a muscle performs work at an intensity greater than usual. An increase in the work duration without a corresponding increase in intensity produces no effect. In general, training effects are specific to the work load. For example, an increased training effect cannot be obtained merely by prolonging the activity; the speed of the activity must also be increased to produce a training effect.

Progressive overload is the gradual and progressive increase in work load in accordance with the body's capacity to resist stress. To improve performance, training should aim at progression, but always within the individual athlete's fund of adaptive energy.

Adaptation is the gradual process of the body overcompensating to overload stresses, during which the body undergoes various functional and constitutional changes. In making these adjustments to increased stress the body draws on its fund of "adaptation energy."

Failing adaptation is the body's inability to cope with overload stress. It can result from any number of causes, particularly a too rapid increase in the training work load based on a seriously misjudged ideal balance between volume and intensity, but also from such "hidden stresses" as inadequate rest or nutrition, emotional stress, or the inexorable demands of growth.

Forbes Carlile was the first to apply the work of Hans Selye, author of *The Stress of Life* (1956), to swimming training. Selye's ideas provide a scientific basis for applying the training work load; his "general adaptation syndrome" proposes that stressing agents not only have their own quite specific actions as parts of the organism but also have stereotyped nonspecific effects.

The body makes certain adjustments and changes in adapting itself to prolonged stress. Coaches must be able to recognize differences between individuals in this respect. Applying the proper volume and intensity of exercise stress will produce the optimum amount of specific adaptation for each person.

Failing adaptation may be countered by reducing the work load—by swimming at a slower pace, increasing the amount of rest, or reducing the distance swum in training. Excessive local stress should be diverted but excessive total stress requires complete rest (Selye, 1956). Diversion can consist of varying both the format of the training schedule and the strokes swum in training. In extreme cases where diversion is inadequate to counter failing adaptation to stress, the athlete may require complete rest from both training and unnecessary daily activities. Some swimmers have been shown to benefit from bed rest immediately before a big meet, but an intelligently planned training program will not require such extreme measures.

Specificity of training is a fundamental principle of training, but one that was only vaguely understood in the early days of formal training programs. People realized that to be able to swim fast athletes should practice swimming fast and that to have endurance they should practice swimming long distances, but the principle of specificity is far more complex than merely following these two concepts.

Training effects are specific to the type of work load placed on the body. Brouha (1945) studied this concept of training and reports that athletes in one sport require considerable time to adapt to and reach maximum efficiency in another sport, even when equally skilled in both activities. Indeed, specificity applies not only *between sports* but also *between events within sports*; it applies not only to learning the precise skills and paces of a sport but also to conditioning the body to perform at maximum capacity in the different events within a particular sport.

According to Selye (1956), specificity refers to a few units within a system, implying that training should be planned according to a specific purpose, whether it be to establish desired physiological effects by training the appropriate energy systems of the body, to form skills, to swim a race at a certain speed, or to use certain strategies and paces in competition. Within a single daily workout, appropriate time should be allocated for training specific aspects of the body. As the season progresses the emphasis given to specific physiological requirements should gradually change according to the swimmer's improving fitness and the event(s) to be swum in competition. Each event of the competitive swimming program requires a certain balance between speed and endurance, which naturally varies between individuals.

Specificity does not refer merely to preparing for a particular competitive event, nor is the establishment of general physiological fitness the only "specific" requirement; rather, specificity takes the form of whatever particular quality is being emphasized during any phase of seasonal activity, whether it be endurance training or specialized training for the season's important competitions. A swimmer should thus first build a broad base of endurance. Once this base has been established, the program gradually changes in format to include a carefully planned balance between duration and intensity of effort. These considerations are vital because training at too high a level of intensity easily can result in failing adaptation to the exercise stress; in fact, training at very high levels of intensity should form only a small percentage of the seasonal activity.

Establishing a Training Effect

Different types of work produce different physiological effects. The different systems of the body do not adapt to training at the same speed. An increase in capillarization, for example, may take place within a matter of days, whereas heart muscle takes years to condition properly. The "establishment of effect" is a loose term used to describe specific adaptation resulting from training.

Training has an accumulative effect. The positive effects of training do not appear the very next day after a work load has been applied. Adaptation to the stress of training is a gradual process and requires time to produce the desired biological changes.

Interval Training

Interval training superseded the older type of training in which swimmers did long continuous distances at a comparatively slower pace. The originators of interval training found that by breaking up the training into comparatively shorter periods of activity with intervening rest periods of varying duration, it was possible to place a greater training overload on the swimmer. Swimmers were found capable of withstanding much greater work loads than hitherto believed possible.

Interval training involves swimming *fixed* distances at a *fixed* pace with *fixed* rest intervals, thus providing control of the duration and intensity of effort. Increased *quality* of effort should result when a *longer* rest period is provided between swims. Generally speaking, the higher the quality of a set of interval swims, the *fewer* the repetitions that can be accomplished.

Conversely, it is possible to produce a greater *quantity* of work when *shorter* rest periods are set between *longer* sets of interval swims. The prolonged activity reduces the intensity of effort.

In summary, the two options are as follows:

1. *Quality swimming* involves *long rest periods*, which permit *high-speed* activity but the intensity of which *limits* the *duration* of the activity.
2. *Quantity swimming* involves *short rest periods*, which permit only submaximal speeds to be maintained. The reduced speed enables the activity to be prolonged, thereby enhancing development of the *endurance* factor.

The preceding sketches the ideal criteria for producing specific training effects, but the human factor—the individual swimmer's level of motivation, drive, and dedication—will contribute to the success or otherwise of the activity.

Various training effects can be achieved by applying different work:rest ratios. There are four basic types of interval training:

1. sprint training,
2. repetition training,
3. fast interval training, and
4. slow interval training.

Sprint Training

Sprint training consists of short distances swum at top speed. Although speed starts to fall off after about 50 meters has been covered, distances up to 100 meters are commonly called sprints and are treated as such for the purpose of speed training. Sprint training is usually done in multiples of 25-, 50-, or 100-meter sets. The heart rate should be allowed to recover to 100 beats per minute or below after each swim.

Work:rest ratios from 1:5 to 1:10 should permit adequate rest to enable training to emphasize speed. The ratio chosen will depend on what percentage of top speed the swimmer wishes to attain. In sprint training the swimmer on occasion may attempt to swim at 100% of best time, especially over 25s and 50s. Sprint training attempts to develop speed and muscular strength as well as the ability to tolerate oxygen debt.

Basic examples of sprint training sets are as follows:

1. 8 × 25 (2 minutes rest)
2. 4 × 50 (5 minutes rest)
3. 4 × 100 (10 minutes rest)

Repetition Training

Repetition training consists of simulating the race pace by swimming distances shorter than the racing distance at a pace faster than the pace of the total racing distance. However, any kind of training in which the heart rate is permitted to recover to approximately 110 to 100 before the next swim may be classified as repetition training.

When performed at high enough speeds, repetition training will accustom the swimmer to *anaerobic exercise* in that there is an increase of oxygen debt and an accumulation of higher levels of lactate in the working muscles. Repetition training also increases speed and muscular strength and power.

The work:rest ratio should be at least 1:3 to permit speeds approximately 90% to 95% of a swimmer's racing speed. To develop a high level of blood lactate it is essential that a swimmer exert close to 100% effort. The heart rate also should reach maximum, somewhere in the range of 190 to 200.

So that the swimmer can maintain a high enough level of work intensity, the distances used in high-lactate repeat swimming ideally should not exceed 250 to 300 meters. Because high-intensity repeat swimming can be very stressful and send a swimmer into failing adaptation, the training set should not exceed a total distance of 1,000 meters or be presented more than twice a week in the workout schedule.

Basic examples of repetition training sets are as follows:

1. 15 × 50 (3 minutes rest)
2. 10 × 100 (5 minutes rest)
3. 6 × 150 (5-10 minutes rest) (The last two 150-meter swims should be faster than the swimmer's 150 split recorded on the swimmer's fastest 200-meter swim.)
4. 4 × 250 (10 minutes rest) (The last two 250 repeats should be faster than the swimmer's 250 split recorded on the swimmer's best time for 400 meters. The swimmer's time at the 200 mark will usually accord with the 200-meter pace recommended to the swimmer by physiologists for the purpose of high-lactate training.)

Note: Applying items 3 and 4 twice weekly during the hard training season can be particularly effective in improving a swimmer's times for the 200- and 400-meter events, respectively, possibly because a swimmer becomes accustomed to tolerating the higher levels of lactate that probably start to accumulate around the 150 mark in the 200 and the 250 mark in the 400.

Fast Interval Training

Fast interval training consists of work:rest ratios of about 1:1, permitting the swimmer to develop speeds approximately 80% of best pace. At least theoretically, this ratio enables the equal development of speed and endurance.

Fast interval training introduces a significant element of speed to any prolonged activity. It simulates to a high degree the type of stress experienced in racing events, which makes great demands on both aerobic and anaerobic endurance. In fast interval training the heart rate after each swim will be around 160 to 190. The heart rate should be permitted to recover to approximately 120 to 130 before the next swim.

Although the rest period in fast interval training is shorter than that permitted in sprint and repetition training, it is much longer than in slow interval training. Fast interval training develops heart muscle and the ability of skeletal muscle to tolerate oxygen debt.

Basic examples of fast interval training sets are as follows:

1. 30 × 50 (30-60 seconds rest)
2. 15 × 100 (30-120 seconds rest)
3. 8 × 200 (30-120 seconds rest)
4. 8 × 400 (1-3 minutes rest)
5. 4 × 800 (3-5 minutes rest)

Slow Interval Training

Slow interval training consists of relatively slow activity designed to improve aerobic endurance. It is based on the endurance development principle of prolonging the activity and gradually trying to increase the speed of the prolonged activity as the season progresses. Slow interval training involves swimming at speeds ranging from approximately 60% to 70% of best pace for the distance. The speed of the swims is also limited by the short rest periods. The activity continues for at least 20 minutes to ensure that the intensity of effort is kept primarily at the aerobic level. It may continue for 1 to 2 hours when used to lay the early season endurance foundation. The heart rate after each swim will be approximately 160 to 170, but the recovery will be in the range of 150 to 160.

Basic examples of slow interval training sets are as follows:

1. 30 × 50 (10-15 seconds rest)
2. 15 × 100 (10-15 seconds rest)
3. 8 × 200 (10-20 seconds rest)
4. 8 × 400 (15-30 seconds rest)
5. 4 × 800 (15-30 seconds rest)

Various Applications of Interval Training

Interval training can be applied in many ways. A few of these variations follow.

Straight Sets. A straight set is a series of swims done at near constant speed, for example, 16 × 100 (each 100 in 62 seconds) with 30 seconds rest.

Descending Sets. A descending set is a series of repeat swims in which each subsequent swim is done progressively faster, for example, 20 × 50 (30 seconds rest) descending (first 50 in 35 seconds, twentieth 50 in 28 seconds).

Note: A variation of the method is to post the workout item on the board as 20 × 50 (30 seconds rest), 1-4 descending. This means that the swimmer will decrease the time over the first four 50s and repeat the process four more times until 20 swims have been completed.

Yet another variation of descending sets is to decrease the average time for each set of repeat swims by starting each subsequent set with a faster first 50 than in the preceding set and then continuing to decrease the second, third, and fourth 50 accordingly.

In this type of training, however, the first repeats in a set sometimes are swum too slowly to warrant intervening rest periods. In the previous example, namely, 20 × 50 for a total distance of 1,000 meters (or yards), it might be better to swim the first half of each set continuously without rest intervals and then complete the second half of the distance as a descending set of equal multiples.

For example, the athletes would perform a 250 continuous swim at a fast pace followed immediately by 5 × 50 descending (30 seconds rest), repeating the set for a total of 1,000 meters.

Broken Sets.   A broken set is a series of swims in which the total distance is broken into sectors with short rest intervals between them, for example, 400 meters broken at each 100 with 10 seconds rest. At the end of the swim, deduct 30 seconds (the total amount of rest) from the gross time to obtain the actual swimming time.

Broken swims are highly motivating and can be used to break up all training distances. Several broken swims can be used to form a training set by providing a long rest after each swim, thus combining repetition training and interval training. Another interesting variation is to perform a set of broken swims in a descending series, reducing the gross time for each subsequent swim.

The following are some further examples:

1. 8 × 400 broken at the 50 with 10 seconds rest and 5 minutes rest after each 400
2. 8 × 200 individual medley broken at the 50 with 10 seconds rest and 3 minutes rest after each 200 medley
3. 2 × 150 going straight through into 2 × 50 (a broken 400 with 10 seconds rest between each sector) and 5 minutes rest after each 400

4. 8 × 100 with 10 seconds rest after each 100, and 5 minutes rest after each set, and sets 1 through 4 descending

Pyramid.   This format consists of a set of swims divided into irregular distance sectors and rest periods. The swimmer may either keep the same pace in each swim or vary the pace by going faster on the shorter sectors. Three examples follow.

1. Swim 50, rest 10 seconds
   Swim 100, rest 20 seconds
   Swim 200, rest 40 seconds
   Swim 400, rest 1 minute
   Swim 200, rest 40 seconds
   Swim 100, rest 20 seconds
   Swim 50
2. Swim 400, rest 3 minutes
   Swim 2 × 200, rest 2 minutes
   Swim 2 × 100, rest 1 minute
   Swim 2 × 50, rest 30 seconds
3. (Individual medley in 25-meter pool)
   Swim 400 medley, rest 5 minutes
   Swim 200 medley, rest 3 minutes
   Swim 100 medley, rest 1 minute
   Swim 200 medley, rest 3 minutes
   Swim 400 medley

Permutations.   Permutations are swims broken at irregular sectors of the total distance. The following are examples of permutations of 400 meters in a 50-meter pool (8 lengths of the pool to complete 400 meters). The workout items are posted on the board as 4 × 400 meters (perm) (5 minutes rest after each 400).

1. 2-2-2-2 (10 seconds rest)
2. 4-2-1-1 (10 seconds rest)
3. 1-2-3-2 (10 seconds rest)
4. 4-1-1-1-1 (10 seconds rest)

The pace is kept constant on 3- or 4-length segments but increased on the 1- and 2-length segments.

I developed and use this method. It is effective for developing a swimmer's ability to change pace or accelerate tactically at any stage of a race; alternatively, the pace can be held constant for all sectors. It can also be used for teaching "negative splitting" (see "Negative Split," p. 120). Whatever procedure is used, permutations, or perms, provide an opportunity to practice a variety of paces.

Simulators. The simulator is a method used to simulate the desired pace of a specific racing distance (Counsilman, 1968). Basically, the procedure is to cover half the racing distance at the desired pace before stopping for a short rest that will permit the heart rate only a slight recovery. The swimmer then covers half the amount of distance already covered before stopping for another short rest. The pattern continues until some arbitrarily small segment remains for the total to equal the racing distance.

For example, suppose the racing distance being practiced is 400 meters.

Swim 200 meters, rest 10 seconds

Swim 100 meters, rest 5 seconds

Swim 50 meters, rest 5 seconds

Swim 25 meters, rest 5 seconds

Swim 25 meters

Note: The rest interval is reduced in this example from 10 to 5 seconds before the shorter segments of the racing distance.

Negative Split. Swimming the second half of a racing distance faster than the first half (usually 2-3 seconds faster) is known as a "negative split." Its purposes are to delay the onset of oxygen debt and to teach evenly paced swimming. The negative split also in a sense "pays back" the momentum of the starting dive in the first half of a racing distance.

Other Types of Training

Many of the following options provide unique training benefits as well as add variety to the training schedule.

Overdistance Swims. Broadly stated, overdistance swims are twice as long as the distance for which a swimmer is training. For example, a swimmer whose specialty is the 100-meter event would practice overdistance swimming by doing 200-meter swims. (A 1,500-meter swimmer would also be doing overdistance training when swimming 3,000 meters continuously, although there is no 3,000-meter event in the competitive program.)

Locomotives. Locomotives provide pace variations over different segments of a total nonstop swim. They are an excellent early season conditioning exercise and a useful diversion

during the stress of hard midseason training. The following is one example.

Swim 1 lap fast, 1 lap slow,

Swim 2 laps fast, 2 laps slow,

Swim 3 laps fast, 3 laps slow,

Swim 4 laps fast, 4 laps slow,

Swim 3 laps fast, 3 laps slow,

Swim 2 laps fast, 2 laps slow,

Swim 1 lap fast, 1 lap slow

Time Swimming. Time swimming is an effective method of developing increased endurance; it basically consists of increasing the distance a swimmer can cover within a prescribed time, which, after all, is what speed swimming is about.

Fartlek. Fartlek was adopted by swimmers as an informal early season conditioning exercise. Used this way, most of the distance is covered at an easy pace with intermittent bursts of speed using such devices as changing stroke and pace after a certain number of lengths. However, chapter 6 describes how to use fartlek training to greater purpose and effect by setting more definite requirements.

Tethered Swimming or Sprint-Resisted Training

Tethered swimming was first used 50 years ago at the Chicago Towers Club when Stan Brauninger, coach to 1936 Olympic backstroke champion Adolph Kiefer, attached canvas belts with long elastic bands around the midriffs of his swimmers. In the 1940s, coach Harold Minto of the Firestone Country Club, Akron, Ohio, trained the first postwar Olympic 1,500-meter champion, James McLane, in a canvas harness connected to several yards of elastic aircraft shock absorber cord. In the 1950s, Robert Kiphuth suspended scores of elastic stretch bands from the balcony of the Yale University pool for the use of his swimmers in the water below. In similar vein, Santa Clara's George Haines had his swimmers use latex surgical tubing (type 202) for stretch cord exercises on land.

In the late 1950s and the 1960s the use of tethered swimming became sporadic, but it was revived in the mid-1970s by Randy Reese, the renowned University of Florida coach. Reese experimented with several new in-water drills using 1/8-inch thick surgical tubing that had a 3/32-inch inside diameter and was cut into sections of 18 to 22 feet. He repopularized the use of tethered swimming throughout the world (Colwin, 1984c).

Tethered swimming (also known as sprint-resisted training) was used originally to improve the muscular power necessary for sprint swimming, but research suggested that swimming against an increased resistance actually slowed muscle speed instead of increasing it (Maglischo, 1982). In light of this, Counsilman (1986) used this method for aerobic training of *distance swimmers only*. He prescribed selected periods of activity such as three 5-minute segments with 1-minute rest intervals and cut rubber stretch cord to approximately one third the length of the pool, with allowances for the size and strength of the swimmer and the elasticity of the cord.

Speed-Assisted Training (SAT)

Like so many other swimming training methods, the concept behind speed-assisted training came from track—in this case, the use of such methods as towing, downhill running, and treadmill running at accelerated speed. Ernest Maglischo (1982) refers to a variation of the use of tethered swimming for improving sprint swimming speed. He describes how leading coaches Randy Reese and Nort Thornton each used this method in their programs. The swimmer first swam down the pool, stretching the tubing, and then allowed it to snap back on the return, thus assisting the swimmer to swim at a faster speed than would normally be possible. Counsilman (1986) developed a system of anaerobic lactate training by having the swimmers use repeat swims such as 10 × 50 on 2 to 3 minutes or 5 × 100 on 3 to 5 minutes while attached to stretch cords. He instructed the swimmers to swim diagonally across the pool to avoid becoming entangled in the cords when returning down the pool. The method was not practical in a 50-meter pool because the cords would not stretch tightly enough and the course was too long for sprinting.

Counsilman (1986) devised another variation of the method wherein the sprinters pulled themselves along the lane markers to the other end of the pool and then rested before allowing the taut stretch cord to snap back and give them a speed-assisted sprint back to the starting point.

The Use of a 16-2/3–Meter Course for Sprint and Short-Distance Training

During the 1960s, when I lacked access to a larger training pool, I experimented with the use of a 16-2/3–meter course at the Hillbrow Club, Johannesburg (6,000 feet altitude), when preparing swimmers for international competition in the standard Olympic 50-meter course. One of the swimmers in the group, Ann Fairlie, swimming in Beziers, France, 7 days after completing 3 months of continuous training solely in this 16-2/3–meter course, succeeded in breaking the world 100-meter backstroke record, which had been set by all-time great Cathy Ferguson when she won the 1964 Olympic title. Other swimmers on the team appeared to derive similar benefit from training in this ultra-short course.

I based the method on a procedure used by John Devitt, former world-record holder and 1960 Olympic champion in the 100-meter freestyle. In 1959 Devitt had told me how he had trained for the 100-meter event by marking off on the wall of the pool intermediate distances of 60, 70, 80, and 90 meters and then trying to reduce his time for each of these marks, which enabled him to learn the exact stage of the 100-meter race at which his speed would start to slacken off. In this manner, Devitt trained himself to maintain his initial speed farther and farther into the full 100-meter distance.

Faced with the lack of a suitable training venue and remembering the method explained to me by Devitt several years earlier, I encouraged my swimmers to improve their speed over each of the following intermediate distances on the way to the 100-meter mark: 16-2/3 meters, 33-1/3 meters, 50 meters, 66-2/3 meters, and 83-1/3 meters.

In preparing for the 200-meter event, the distances swum were extended to include 100 meters, 116-2/3 meters, 133-1/3 meters, 150 meters, 166-2/3 meters, and 183-1/3 meters.

This method of training appears to have the following advantages:

1. When swimming 16-2/3–meter sprints a swimmer can achieve the *highest possible rate of speed* while at the same time learning to improve

starting time off the block as well as the importance of accurate timing of the first few strokes of a race.

2. By improving speed over smaller increments of the total racing distance the swimmers learn a greater refinement of pace than would be possible in a larger training pool. One reason is that these conditions allow easier detection of the exact stage of the race at which speed starts to deteriorate.

3. The increased number of turns provides extra turning practice, improving the speed of the turn and the muscular strength and power specific to performing it.

4. The method enables the introduction of different breathing patterns into practice routines, with the swimmer using a different pattern on each length of the pool.

5. The method provides a particularly rugged and arduous form of training and is therefore an excellent conditioner when used judiciously. Short sets of repeat swims, such as 4 × 100 meters with 5 to 10 minutes rest, can be done with great benefit 4 to 3 weeks before tapering for a major event.

Periodization of the Training Program

Varying the intensity and duration of the workouts from day to day and week to week results in a long-term cyclic application of the training program. The days of easy, moderate, and hard work ought not be planned more than one week in advance; even then a coach may decide to change the intensity of a workout based on on-the-spot observation of a swimmer's reaction to a previous work load. Workouts are monitored by means of measuring blood lactates in only a few teams, and for most programs, this phase of coaching remains an art instead of a science. When a program is under the direction of an experienced coach, however, it is often remarkable how a well-balanced pattern of easy, moderate, and strenuous sessions will appear consistently over a period of many weeks.

Several researchers, notably Kindermann (1978), Matveyev (1981), Harre (1982), and Berger (1982), have studied the periodization of the training program. As a result, it is common in Eastern Europe for training preparation to be viewed in the context of three distinct cycles, namely

1. microcycles of 1 week duration,
2. mesocycles of 3 to 7 weeks duration, and
3. macrocycles, one to four per year up to 4 years.

Spirals and Mesocycles

During the 1960s and 1970s several leading programs, mainly in Europe, adopted a new terminology to describe the various phases of seasonal training. For example, Igor Koshkin (1985), coach of the great Soviet 1,500-meter world-record holder Vladimir Salnikov, described a typical training year as being divided into five *spirals*, each having a duration of 8 to 12 weeks, and ending with a 1- to 3-week competition period.

Each spiral comprises 2-week development stages called *mesocycles*. Each mesocycle concentrates on developing specific qualities in the swimmer. During the last mesocycle—the preparation for major competition—the aim is to integrate all the specific qualities developed in the four or five preceding mesocycles.

The Search for a Selective Method of Applying the Training Work Load

The introduction of the interval training method in the 1950s soon showed that the *quality* of the overload stress was the determining factor in producing a desired training effect. What is the proper proportion of quality work? How much is too much and how much is too little? This was the question that continued to puzzle swimming coaches as they sought the ideal balance between quality and quantity in designing training work loads for their athletes.

In the second half of the century, sport doctors in the former East Germany, realizing the importance of determining the stage of the workout at which the athlete arrives at the lactate/ventilatory threshold, introduced their now famous method of regular blood lactate analysis. Previous to the introduction of blood lactate testing, however, many talented coaches as well as swimmers were able to judge intuitively when the lactate/ventilatory threshold had been reached and to adjust the pace of the workout according to the training quality they wished to develop.

The East Germans, under the direction of Lothar Kipke, Alex Mader, and others, developed a very practical method of blood lactate analysis. One method for determining the lactate/ventilatory threshold* involves timing evenly paced swims at 200 or 300 meters, some of which are done at an easy pace. The pace is then slightly increased to a moderate intensity just above the lactate/ventilatory threshold. Finally, much faster swims at almost 100% of maximum effort are performed.

As few as two blood lactate concentrations are plotted against the velocities of the test swims, and the lines joining them are extrapolated to cut the 4 mmol/L blood lactate level. The estimated velocity at 4 mmol/L is read off to predict the exercise intensity for each individual swimmer's lactate/ventilatory threshold.

East German coaches regularly used the 10 × 200 anaerobic test on their swimmers. Studying the nature of the lactate velocity curve helped them assess at regular intervals the changing aerobic and anaerobic capacities of individual swimmers throughout the training season. In addition, they were able to determine a swimmer's ability to reach a high lactate level with a maximum effort performance. The purpose of the procedure was to test a swimmer's ''mobilization capacity,'' or the highest level of blood lactate the swimmer is able to generate. The East Germans maintained that this scientific approach to training enabled them to make very accurate judgments concerning the training condition of each individual swimmer right through the season, up to and including the final precompetition tapering-off period.

Should All Swimming Coaches Use Lactate Testing?

In 1983, Counsilman told me that he believed lactate testing to have limited applications and that too much depends on where and how lactate measurements are taken (Colwin, 1983a). He added that just from normal observation a coach will know the training load better and that it is not a good measure because a swimmer can get the same high lactate level by doing

a few strenuous 50s or a moderate 30 × 50 series.

According to Counsilman (Colwin, 1983a), a study of pH would, however, show something quite different. He said that the pH factor is important and also that physiological researchers had failed to test many other possibilities. To continually test $\dot{V}O_2$max and all the other popularly tested things is a waste. He cited the need for new approaches that would involve a little creative thinking and cooperation with coaches, saying that in the United States the coach and scientist had not worked together.

Counsilman (1984) says that during the spring of 1983 at four swimming clinics he asked over 1,000 coaches whether they had ever used blood lactate measurements to help them evaluate their training programs. Only two people raised their hands. Counsilman says that at Indiana University he took blood lactate measurements off and on since the era of Mike Troy and Chet Jastremski (the mid-1960s). The procedure was expensive because of the necessary equipment, personnel to draw blood, and medical supervision. He indicates his intention to continue to take blood lactates for research purposes but not as a means of evaluating his swimmers' progress, adding that even the East Germans test for blood lactate only with their elite swimmers. According to Counsilman, all these reasons render it unlikely that the method will become common practice.

Tapering for Competition: Origin of the Taper

In the early years of competitive swimming swimmers took little if any extra rest prior to a major competition other than retiring earlier on the previous night. It was not uncommon for training, such as it was, to be continued up to the day before a meet.

Fifty years ago swimmers rarely did more than 1,000 yards in daily practice, often resting 5 minutes after swimming ''300 yards easy.'' Individual swimmers were thought to vary in their ability to swim distances between 1,000

---

*Note. Once again following the lead of track and field athletics, swimming scientists are beginning to replace the term *anaerobic threshold* with *lactate/ventilatory threshold*. The former term refers nonspecifically to the upper limits of aerobic work, whereas the latter refers to measurable levels of blood lactate and ventilatory capacity.

yards to a mile and a half. The emphasis in daily practice was on stroke improvement. Training swims were kept to moderate speeds so as not to interfere with maintaining good stroke mechanics and accurate timing (Armbruster, 1942).

Swimmers were cautious about training too strenuously because coaches constantly warned them about the danger of overexertion. A common dictum in the day's coaching parlance was "training should be *training* and not straining!"

The tendency was for training intensity to be increased rather than decreased during the 10 days prior to a championship meet. In the 1940s it was common practice to do repeated time trials in one's specialty events as late as 10 days before the meet. Coaches and athletes believed this method would provide ample time to do specialized training for an event, particularly if the swimmer was behind in preparation (Armbruster, 1942).

This "specialized training" took the form of having the sprinters swim three fast 100-yard swims with a 20-minute rest between trials. The middle distance swimmers did two 220-yard swims with a 30-minute rest between them. The distance swimmers and backstroke and breaststroke swimmers (there was no butterfly stroke then) were advised also to attempt the middle distance schedule but with a 45-minute rest period instead (Armbruster, 1942).

In the early 1950s swimmers began to increase the distances covered in training. As the quantity of work increased they found they could swim faster. At this time, the tendency was to swim long, unbroken mileage with "wind sprints"—usually a series of 50s interspersed with rest periods—performed at the end of a workout to introduce an element of speed.

Some thought that if a lot of mileage gave good results, then more would give even better; of course, this was not always true. What they found was that swimmers often carried considerable residual fatigue over long periods. They saw that they needed an adjustment to the training regimen that would enable swimmers to produce their best performances in important competition.

The introduction of alternating "easy" and "hard" training days was an attempt to permit a measure of adaptation in the midst of strenuous training, but swimmers still did not obtain sufficient rest to perform at their best. Nevertheless, the idea of alternating days of easier and harder work was to lead to experiments with even longer rests.

Basic Concept of the Taper

Carlile's interest in Selye's concepts of stress (Selye, 1956) combined with his own studies of failing adaptation to stress (Carlile, 1963) prompted him to provide his swimmers with far more rest before competition than was previously thought necessary. This period of reduced activity became known as the *taper*. The beneficial effects of tapering on performance became clear to coaches once they learned to taper swimmers skillfully.

During the 1970s and 1980s the tapering process grew more complex for several reasons, one of them being the increased frequency of top international competition. Often, radical changes had to be made to already busy regional and national schedules. Preparing swimmers to compete successfully in a series of top-flight competitions became a fine art—and only partially a science. Many swimmers chose to "swim through" (either not taper or use a reduced taper) for some meets and then taper completely to swim at a higher level in others. In addition, many lower-ranked swimmers tapered in midseason attempting to meet required qualifying times for entries to championship and major meets.

Principle Considerations in Tapering

Before a major competition swimmers gradually reduce their heavy work load and increase their rest. This period is known as the taper (Carlile, 1963) or tapering off. The transition to easier work causes the adaptive processes of the body to overcompensate as the swimmer prepares for maximum effort. The word "taper"—diminishing toward the end—aptly describes the process. Its use in training was coined by Frank Cotton, professor of physiology at the University of Sydney, Australia, and his understudy at the time, Forbes Carlile, now the dean of Australian swimming coaches.

These two pioneers discovered that for physiological adaptation to occur, arduous training must be tempered with adequate rest. The concept of tapering is based on this realization, and over a period of more than 30 years, it has proved to be one of the most significant contributions to the progress of competitive swimming. Tapering was first described in the literature—and in detail—by Carlile (1963). Not only the concept but also the term was quickly accepted and employed worldwide.

A successful taper results from good judgment and careful planning. The taper should be planned carefully for each individual swimmer. It is rare that a swimmer will taper in exactly the same way every time. Variations in the taper will arise from different factors that have acted on the swimmer during the period preceding an important meet, several of which must be considered on every occasion. Planning an effective taper requires of the coach not only technical skill but also an acute insight into the state of individual swimmers, particularly their reaction to precompetition anxiety.

The taper should be relevant to the work done in the preceding months. Its duration and the amount of rest it provides should allow complete recovery from accumulated fatigue. The body will then overcompensate in its adaptation to stress, enabling a superior performance.

During the taper, attention should be given to every aspect of preparation—mental as well as physical—including mental attitude, physical conditioning, stroke technique, pace, and strategy. Finally, the effects of rest on adaptation should be understood. Rest is a vital determinant of performance and just as important as an ideal balance between different levels of work intensity.

A note of caution: For young swimmers, the excess energy levels that result from tapering often cause a tendency to indulge in horseplay. The coach should forewarn the team against wild or unruly behavior—calling it "excessive exuberance"—that could cause injury and the consequent waste of a whole season of preparation.

The entire season should be mapped out in advance and major and minor meets decided. The program design should include the duration and emphasis of each training cycle with adequate time for the final taper.

Typical Questions on Tapering

The following are typical questions concerning the taper phase of the season that often will confront a coach:

How long should each swimmer taper?

Should all swimmers taper the same length of time?

Should all swimmers perform the same preparation items, irrespective of the events in which they will compete?

Should there be a difference between the taper for a swimmer who is competing only on the fourth day of a meet and, for example, one who is competing on the first day and probably on other days, too?

What is the swimmer's capacity for recovery from hard work?

What allowances should be made for individual temperament?

Has enough time been built into a tapering period to counter any possible errors of judgment?

None of these questions is purely hypothetical; on the contrary, they enter into nearly every planning of a taper period. They constitute only a few examples of possible circumstances that may arise; experience will teach a coach that these circumstances appear to be unlimited.

General Guidelines on Tapering

What worked last season may not work as well—or at all—this season. Any number of changes in conditions can cause this, including alterations in the annual program of competitive events, the available time for workouts, absenteeism, conditioning emphasis, swimmers' levels of development, temperament, and many other factors. Although a coach may recognize recurring situations, it is wise to be alert for new sets of circumstances likely to influence tapering decisions.

Before I identify situations that need special attention in the tapering decisions, it may be helpful to provide a few general guidelines.

1. The shorter the race, the longer the taper; conversely, the longer the race, the shorter the taper. Distance swimmers and sprinters need different tapers.

2. The more races to be contested, the shorter the taper.

3. The younger the swimmer, the shorter the taper. Younger swimmers have a higher level of vital energy; moreover, they tend to lose the feel of the water quickly if they taper too soon. Conversely, an older swimmer may need a longer taper. Swimmers who have com-

peted for many years appear to need a longer taper with each successive season.

4. Nervous athletes need a shorter taper.

5. Large, well-muscled athletes generally need a longer taper.

6. Swimmers with an adequate background of hard work will usually obtain good results if tapered fairly early. Those who have been overstressed in training will show dramatic adaptation and recovery from accumulative fatigue after a long, well-planned taper.

7. Swimmers who have done only a moderate amount of work through the season often will not show great improvement when tapered because they lack the background training.

8. Seasonal goals should be established at the start of the training program when the coach first meets the swimmers. At this time, the coach should identify and outline to the swimmers the type of work and the duration of each training cycle necessary to achieve these goals. Early on, the coach should decide which meets the swimmer will enter and the level of importance to be accorded each competition. More important meets require more complete tapers (major taper). The importance of the meet and the stage of the season will determine whether to use major, minor, or mini tapers.

A meet may be used to check the progress of the team as a whole toward its established goals or to provide opportunities for certain individual members. In particular, the coach may decide to rest a swimmer who lacks confidence so that the swimmer will be able to record a morale-boosting fast time. It is sometimes necessary for an up-and-coming youngster to record a fast swim to encourage continued dedication to a demanding program of hard work.

9. An ideal psychological "climate" should be nurtured and every effort made to foster a positive team spirit. Physiological and psychological preparation should keep apace of each other throughout the season and into the tapering period, resulting in a well-conditioned athlete with a strong, positive mental attitude.

10. An ideal taper, from the physiological standpoint, is when a swimmer has had just the right amount of rest. Sometimes a swimmer will appear unaffected by the taper and show no improvement in speed. There is not much to do in such a situation except be patient and wait for the taper to take effect.

It is just as possible to have too much rest as to have too little. Usually, a swimmer who has had too much rest will lack the conditioning to finish a race strongly; conversely, the swimmer who has had too little rest may not have sharp speed initially but may still be able to finish a race strongly. If competing in a 3- to 4-day meet, for example, the under-rested swimmer may improve over the subsequent days as a result of having more rest. The outlook for the over-rested and underworked swimmer will not be as optimistic, however, as there obviously would be insufficient time to become conditioned.

Maglischo on Lactate Testing During the Tapering Period

One of the best treatments of the use of lactate testing as a guide to anaerobic training occurs in Ernest Maglischo's landmark book *Swimming Faster* (1982). Seven years after its publication, however, when asked whether lactate testing had taught him anything about the taper, Maglischo admitted that "the more I do lactates, the more confused I get" (Muckenfuss, 1989, p. 19).

Maglischo (Muckenfuss, 1989) says that coaches typically started out doing lactates using the information provided by other people. When the process failed to work, they spent all their time trying to figure out their errors in technique. According to Maglischo, they had not necessarily committed any errors. As more and more research came out, it appeared that much of the information just wasn't as good as originally believed.

Maglischo says that lactate testing did identify some of the physiological changes that swimmers went through, but a very intuitive and perhaps very self-assured coach might have been aware of these changes anyway as a result of experience.

He also says that he found the taper allows swimmers to hold their endurance with very little work. Swimmers who did "incredibly easy workouts" during the taper maintained and even increased their endurance. During the taper, the swimmers generally swam 4,000 to 6,000 yards a day until the last week. Most of the time the swimmers swam below their aerobic pace.

Preparing a Basic Plan for the Taper

A basic plan for the tapering period should be mapped out at the beginning of the season when the number of training days and competitions leading to the major meets first become known. The plan should include an outline of each phase of the season together with the duration of each training cycle, as well as adequate time for the tapering period.

Nearly all coaches will agree that tapering is a complex phase of the season—in fact, the word "complex" seems most readily to spring to mind in any frank discussion of the topic. The challenge, then, is for the coach to ensure clear communication on all the important aspects of the planned taper with individual swimmers and the team as a whole. Team meetings and clearly drawn charts will help explain the tapering plan to swimmers at all levels. Not least of all, the coach should warn the swimmers about overeating and becoming overweight as a result of the reduced energy demands placed on the body. The importance of early bedtimes and adequate sleep should also be stressed.

Super-Adaptation

At some stages of the season, many swimmers work so hard that they are unable to approach their best times in training or competition before they taper for the season's most important meets. Counsilman (1968) calls this phase of training "the valley of fatigue" and considers it necessary for what he terms super-adaptation. The reasoning behind its use is that when the work load is finally reduced in the taper period, the body's adaptive mechanisms will continue to overcompensate at the same high level even though the unusual stress of the hard training period has suddenly been removed. If the taper is well planned, the result is a superior performance.

The Warm-Up

The benefits of the warm-up procedure include the following:

1. The resultant increase in body temperature and pulse rate, combined with dilation of blood vessels in the muscles, takes the body from its "resting state" to the physiological level needed for the competitive event.
2. It loosens the muscles and increases flexibility.
3. It familiarizes the swimmer with the pool conditions in which the competition will take place.

4. The swimmer gets into stroke rhythm and feels out the required pace of the race.
5. Muscle fatigue occurs later in the race after adequate warm-up.
6. A muscle that is warmed and stretched prior to maximum exertion is less likely to sustain injury.
7. The warm-up induces a sense of well-being.

During the workouts of the hard training season, a swimmer should cultivate a feeling for how much swimming is sufficient for warm-up. This will significantly aid a swimmer in tapering and warming up before meets.

In some teams, the amount of swimming needed to warm up in daily training sessions is the amount of swimming used in each session during the taper period. The swimmer does just enough work to be able to swim at pace. This is usually followed by some short, sharp work, a loosen-down swim, and practice in starts and turns.

Warm-up procedures vary according to a swimmer's racing events. Short distance swimmers and sprinters will include some short speed work—mostly 25-meter and 50-meter efforts—whereas distance swimmers will establish their race pace by covering a few 100-meter sections.

The warm-up should last 20 to 45 minutes, and the swimmer should be out of the water at least 20 minutes before the meet starts. A swimmer preparing for morning competition may need more warm-up time to "wake up." In the evenings, before swimming in the finals, a shorter warm-up usually will suffice because of the swimming done earlier in the day.

After warming up, a swimmer should don warm, dry clothing, gloves, socks, and shoes. The swimmer should stand up and become active just before the race starts by walking around and doing mild stretching exercises.

As the season progresses, each swimmer should determine his or her best "basic" warm-up. Every competitive session should be preceded by a warm-up and followed by a loosen-down; this helps eliminate stiff or sore shoulders, hips, knees, and ankles.

Effects of Massage

One of the benefits of massage is its effect on the circulation of the area treated. By improving the circulation of blood and lymph, it facilitates the removal of deleterious substances formed in excess by injury or liberated by movement.

Superficial light massage affects only the skin circulation, specifically, the skin capillaries, superficial veins, and lymphatics. The former two, however, hold so much blood that massage in the direction of their flow will materially increase the return of blood to the heart and produce an effect rather like exercise without the more exhausting effects of fatigue. Because the superficial veins draw blood from the muscles as well as the skin, the muscles of the massaged area will drain somewhat. Massage of the lymphatics increases the flow of lymph and the removal of tissue fluid, the accumulation of which causes pain and stiffness. In injury, this fluid contains an abnormally large amount of protein, and if it is allowed to remain stationary it may be converted into fibrous tissue and cause permanent stiffness. Merely rubbing the skin also sends a vast number of beneficial impulses into the nervous system.

Deeper massage hastens circulation through the muscles and the soft tissues because each compression tends to drive the blood toward the veins where the pressure is least. It similarly facilitates the dispersal of accumulated lymph or blood in the deeper parts. It cannot be overemphasized, however, that loosening movements, either on land or in the water, best stimulate the circulation.

Chapter 8

Outline of the Training Program

Planning a successful seasonal training program entails more than designing a series of workouts that will bring a team to peak form at the championship season. A systematic approach should consider all the other factors that may influence performance.

These factors include the type of meets in which the team intends to compete; the particular league or conference and the specific events for which the swimmers will need to prepare; the dates of major competitions; the amount of pool time available for training; and the training background of each swimmer on the team. To provide motivation for purposeful effort throughout the season, team as well as individual goals should be established soon after the team has gathered to begin training.

The Individual Swimmer

Because there is no "average person," you cannot uniformly apply a single method. What is good for one may not be good for another. Albert Einstein, just before he died, said that one of the few things that he felt sure about was that the individual is unique. And the individual changes with time—no person is the same person today as last year. We cannot successfully train swimmers with canned, cut-and-dried, overstandardized methods. Swimmers' development, or any human development for that matter, can never be an assembly-line or stamping-machine process.

The coach should know the training history of every swimmer. This knowledge will let the coach carefully plan work loads in accordance with each swimmer's own capacity. To set a training program that is beyond a swimmer's ability invites failure, but too easy a program does not offer a realistic challenge.

Swimmers react differently to the same training work load, and they have different potentials for improvement. Genetic factors set limitations, both physiological and psychological, on one's level of achievement. It also appears that not too much can be done to change temperament. A coach may encounter a wide range of temperaments among swimmers on a team, from unstable neuroticism to the spontaneous cheerfulness that is so often characteristic of the physiologically robust.

A coach can usually expect different responses from athletes at various levels of maturity, especially in their reactions to stress and their abilities to handle the training work load. The coach should recognize and respect these differences and avoid treating younger athletes as miniature adults.

The importance of good nutrition as a major factor in performance should not be overlooked. And for athletes to maintain improvement within a regimen of hard training, adequate rest is a prime essential (see the comments on nutrition by Forbes Carlile and Richard Telford in chapter 9). Many athletes, trying to keep pace in modern urban society, tend to neglect the importance of rest, both at night and between twice-daily workouts. Quality rest allows for regeneration of the body and adaptation to stress. In fact, rest can be regarded as "unseen" training.

A coach should observe each swimmer's reactions to training, particularly during the most demanding phase of the season, so as to plan workouts compatible with each individual's ability to tolerate stress. The coach should assess the accumulative stress placed on the swimmer and use this knowledge to plan the tapering period as carefully as possible.

Individual Capacity For Training

It is not understood what makes a great athlete different from a mediocre one of similar physique; skill, economy of movement, and tenacity must all play a part. It is difficult enough to find out how any muscle works—subtle differences between individuals are still beyond our means. It is thus a mistake for swimmers to copy the training methods of champions slavishly. Many years of conditioning are necessary before a swimmer can hope to emulate their work loads.

The coach should understand the athlete's present state of training; the fitter the athlete, the less the improvement that can be expected. Effective coaching requires that the training overload be applied carefully until the coach knows how an individual athlete reacts to stress. Another reason why coaches should study and understand individual reactions is that athletes differ in their reactions not only to stress but also to training formats.

The constitutional limitations of the individual constrain the rate of improvement and the amount of training that can be absorbed. A coach who knows the maximal capacity of an athlete can carefully plan the intensity and duration of the training effort. If the athlete does not appear to be adapting to the training work load after a period of around two weeks, the type of stress placed on the athlete should be reassessed. Although physiological monitoring—particularly blood lactate measurement—may indicate a swimmer's reaction to training, most teams lack ready access to facilities for it. Counsilman's (1968) three basic tests for assessing a swimmer's progress are easily applied, however, and provide an effective measure, especially in that the results can be readily compared with a swimmer's previous workouts using the same repeat sets. The tests are

1. the average time for a set of repeat swims;
2. the pulse rate after exercise; and
3. the swimmer's stroke rate counted on the last length of every second, third, or fourth repeat swim.

The Individual Swimmer in the Team Setting

Should practices be scheduled for the team or for its individual members? This simple question may give rise to a battery of further questions that touch not only on the training policies within different teams but also on important aspects of the philosophy of swimming. Non-state-controlled programs have tended to skirt this important issue. The large size of many teams, often an economic necessity, and the consequent wide range of individual ability often present a formidable challenge to the coaching staff.

It is important to remember that competitive swimming is ultimately an *individual* sport. Particularly at the higher levels of competition where really talented athletes are involved, it has become absolutely necessary to know a great deal about the individual athlete to develop that person's potential fully. Not only do we need to know more about each individual swimmer, but we need to schedule training along individual lines, yet this does not happen in most teams. Although there are many coaches who *think* that this is their approach, close scrutiny will often reveal that it is not.

In fact, most schedules take form either around the requirements of a few champion athletes or, at the other extreme, where a team has no outstanding swimmers, around the average needs of the group, which is at best a shotgun method.

During the development of the novice competitor, the shotgun method may produce improvement for a while. But regardless of a swimmer's level of maturity, it will not produce the best possible results; rather, it creates swimmers all cast in the same mold with little regard for their individuality.

In this type of program it is common to hear much about the success of a few outstanding swimmers but little about those who fail. The pity is that youngsters seldom learn to enjoy and appreciate fully the subtle challenges of the sport. Many young swimmers do not flourish as they should because they are in a program with little if any instruction in stroke techniques or the whys and wherefores of training, paces, strategies, and so on.

The first pitfall for a coach is thus the standardized workout in which an entire group is subjected to the same schedule. This standardization of workouts has become traditional in many teams at all levels, from local to international. The coach walks on deck and writes the workout on the board for the *whole* team. Nevertheless, the idea that what is good for the champions is good for everyone is not necessarily true.

Training Formats

Although the formats of most top-level training programs often have a distinct similarity, differences in planning arise from the specific requirements of each team. Other modifications may occur as a coach tries out new ideas.

Many considerations will affect the design of a training program. For example, when coaching older athletes an effort must be made to help them effectively balance their available time between academic obligations and the demands of training. Older athletes have no time to waste on training items of doubtful value. It is especially important that each of their workouts be as specific as possible with no extraneous items.

A well-planned conditioning program should enable a swimmer gradually to improve the physiological qualities necessary to produce peak performances in the season's major meets. Effective training consists of cycles of varied activity, each aimed at a specific purpose.

Weight Training

Weight training is done for a half hour *every day* for the first 8 to 12 weeks of the season. Later in the season the frequency is reduced to 3 days a week. Some type of weight training should continue to within 14 days of the national championships or whatever major meet the team may enter. It is important that strength work continue as late as possible into the season to retain strength gains.

Stretching exercises to keep the joints flexible should always be an integral part of any weight-training program. Nort Thornton (1979), one of the pioneers of weight training for swimming when coaching world-record breaker Steve Clarke in 1961, stresses that strength training and flexibility work should always be done to-gether and that it is a big mistake to do one without the other.

Swimmers on Thornton's team at the University of California at Berkeley lift very heavy weights 3 days per week, on Monday, Wednesday, and Friday. The other days—Tuesday, Thursday, and Saturday—are devoted to work done on the "biokinetic swim bench" and geared toward developing speed and strength.

Ron Johnson (1978), another expert conditioner of swimmers and a renowned master swimmer, also insists that deck training must include exercises for the development of strength, endurance, and flexibility. He says that though not all teams can afford expensive and often elaborately equipped exercise machines, it is possible to do effective strength training with free weights. Johnson maintains that most strength programs for swimming do not provide enough sets or repetitions, and he points out that emphasis should be changed from one muscle group to another after a particular muscle group has been broken down through strenuous exercise.

Not all leading coaches have used weight training to the same extent, however. For example, Jochums (1982) expresses the view that weight training provides psychological benefits and uses it only with his sprint swimmers who will look at their arms in a mirror and believe they have become stronger and therefore will swim faster.

Jochums believes weight training transfers only a very slight gain to swimming, but probably enough to make a difference. He adds that women swimmers may need weight training, but his personal preference is for swimmers to do pulling drills with their feet immobilized in a tube or to use paddles and the pull buoy. He says that these methods are a form of resistance training and as such fit his definition of weight training.

The Biokinetic Swim Bench. Counsilman (1979) refers to biokinetics as the "ultimate exercise" in that it permits a swimmer to accelerate the simulated swimming stroke while recruiting muscle fibers in the same sequence as actual swimming. The biokinetic machine is said to be the only exercise machine capable of measuring work done in terms of *force, time,* and *distance.*

Counsilman reports that swimmers at Indiana University were tested once a week to assess the total amount of work that they could create in 10 seconds, 30 seconds, and 90 seconds. He found that sprinters had the best scores for work done in 10 and 30 seconds and the middle distance swimmers performed best over 90 seconds. When tested over 5-minute periods, the distance swimmers had the best results.

Misconceptions Concerning Strength Training. Counsilman (1979) points out certain misconceptions concerning strength training. He says that it is possible to improve either slow strength or fast strength with specific types of exercise and that contrary to general belief, there is not only one type of strength. Counsilman mentions another misconception—namely, that a muscle or muscle group can be strengthened by prolonged exercise—citing the case of a woman diver at Indiana University who had a low score when tested for the vertical jump. After 5 months of running 5 miles a day her vertical jump and leg strength tests had further decreased. The obvious reason for her failure to strengthen her legs for diving was that prolonged running is not an activity *specific* to the task.

The third misconception Counsilman discusses is the common opinion that *strength is speed*. He claims instead that strength developed at slow speeds is slow strength for performing slow movements, and strength developed at fast speeds is fast strength for performing fast movements. He mentions in this regard a doctoral study by Jan Prins (1978) undertaken at Indiana University under Counsilman's direction in which it was found that fast exercise caused hypertrophy of fast twitch muscle fibers and a corresponding decrease in the size of slow twitch fibers.

The condition was reversed when exercises were done at slow speed. (The size of the fibers was determined by histological examination of biopsy samples taken from the *vastus lateralis* muscle of the leg.) Counsilman points out the lack of research or practical experience indicating ideal proportions of fast and slow work for specific racing events.

The Importance of Efficient Stroke Mechanics

Much emphasis should be given to establishing efficient stroke mechanics in the early season, impressing on the swimmers the importance of feeling for the ideal flow of the water (see chapter 5, ''Coaching the Feel of the Water''). Unfortunately, stroke technique is often neglected in many senior teams, particularly by coaches who regard the correction of faulty technique as ''age-group stuff.'' It makes little sense, however, to spend hundreds of hours conditioning and training a swimmer who does not apply the new-found strength and power to the water in the most efficient way. In other words, neglecting stroke technique partially defeats the purpose of training. For many years I have used as an effective criterion of stroke efficiency the simple truth that *visible effort is unproductive, self-defeating effort*. Conversely, an easy, effortless-looking stroke indicates that power is being efficiently applied through good stroke mechanics.

A foundation of effective technique should be laid during the early season. It is good policy to include practices aimed at improving a swimmer's ability to feel and control the flow of the water. This should be done not only during warm-up but throughout the workout.

Emphasis should be placed on taking fewer strokes per length of the pool at a given speed. In other words, keep the speed constant and reduce the number of strokes per length. As the season progresses speed should be increased while the number of strokes either remains the same or is reduced. The ability to reduce stroke frequency while increasing speed is a reliable indication of a swimmer's improving fitness and efficiency.

The Two Main Aspects of Training

Most descriptions of training routines refer to the differences between the duration and intensity of exercise, but Nort Thornton, one of America's most consistently successful coaches over a 30-year period, brought these two terms into a more practical focus by referring to them as *base training* and *sharpening training*, adding that a correct combination of these two aspects of training give a swimmer the overall capacity to swim a particular race in the most effective way (Thornton, 1987). Thornton describes base training as

that inner basic strength of the athlete that produces a performance *without specific muscle adaptation* for that event as the result of years of training, overall stamina and conditioning. Such a base is usually best built by long slow distance training at a pace well within one's capacity for a long period of time.

By sharpening, I mean those training techniques that produce efficient muscular coordination for a chosen event. Pacework, such as broken swims or ideal pace rehearsal swims, will condition the reflexes for peak efficiency at this speed. Sharpening work is basically muscular and neurological in nature, whereas base training results primarily in the conditioning of the circulatory system. (Thornton, 1987, p. 11)

Thornton also says that a swimmer's future capacity to perform well in a given race depends on "ideal proportions of base work and sharpening. Too many swimmers were constantly sharpening and devoting very little time to developing the essential base conditioning. It was important that enough time should be devoted to building the ideal base of aerobic endurance necessary for world-class performance" (1987, p. 11).

He adds that

any good engineer can tell you the approximate height and size of a new building by looking at the size (depth and width) of the new foundation. You can't expect to put up a skyscraper without a large enough foundation, and nor can you expect to go for world-class performance without an adequate base. (1987, p. 11)

Thornton points out that, although both base training and sharpening training are necessary for best results, they are in many ways opposites. His experience was that the two types of training could not be combined for optimum results over a long period of time because improvement in base conditioning requires a large reserve of adaptation energy. (Adaptation energy permits the body to respond favorably to increased stress overload.) This reserve is quickly depleted by the fast swimming needed for sharpening work. Base training is like money in the bank; sharpening, when done properly, is like taking out the accumulated interest. When done improperly, sharpening is like draining one's financial reserves.

Thornton (1987) outlines the following characteristics of base training and sharpening training.

Base Training

The swimmer's base conditioning can be measured by the performance he or she can produce without specific muscular adaptation for an event. This is best achieved through long, controlled swimming. The base has the following features:

1. It can be improved continuously, even over many years.
2. It can only be developed at a slow rate—in fact, much more slowly than the observed improvement from sharpening training.
3. Its effects are long lasting and not easily destroyed. Swimmers who have taken the time to build a good base often observe that competitive performance remains essentially the same even after a considerable reduction in training.
4. The slow pace used in its development and the requirement of freshness reduce the likelihood of injury or illness.

Sharpening Training

Sharpening adds muscular and neuromuscular efficiency to the circulatory efficiency gained from the swimmer's base training. Sharpening training involves numerous repetitions of a short distance at a racing pace or faster. The essential features of sharpening are as follows:

1. Its effects are short-lived and at times appear volatile. The high performance level resulting from this training rarely persists more than 3 months.
2. When it is done properly, astonishing improvement can be observed in just 6 weeks.
3. Special care is necessary when attempting this type of conditioning, for if it is not done properly it can result in performances inferior to the athlete's base.
4. The faster pace of this training more easily provokes injury and illness, which therefore must be consciously avoided.
5. Sharpening training can drive the athlete into a slump if continued for too long a period. Consequently, it must be terminated after about 3 months or when the symptoms of energy depletion are first noticed.

In his classic presentation, Thornton (1987) outlines three hypothetical case histories in which swimmers A, B, and C use different combinations of base training and sharpening training while training for the same event.

Swimmer A trained only at race pace or faster using successive short-distance repetitions. A's performances, which were erratic and sometimes totally unpredictable, showed little basic improvement from freshman through senior year.

Swimmer B wisely used a combination of various forms of interval training throughout the year but did not swim as hard or as fast while training as A. B did not swim to depletion and maintained a wise balance between stress and recovery. B also did not experience extreme slumps as A did. Swimmer B's base level improved significantly over 4 years and, when combined with sharpening, resulted in greatly improved performance in the senior year.

Swimmer C used the type of training that produces optimum results over many years because it most dramatically improves the base level of the swimmer. Swimmer C did sharpening training only before the most important races. The rest of the year, C trained at a slower pace to improve the base level. Although C spent much of the year training at base level, this swimmer performed better in the senior year than A or B because C's base level was higher than either of the other two. When sharpening was added, optimum performance was attained.

Thornton summarizes his three hypothetical case histories by saying that the swimmer who conditioned first with long slow distance (LSD) is like a builder who lays a strong and deep foundation for a skyscraper. Swimmer A, who began with speed work, is like a builder who lays a weak foundation to get the first few stories of the structure up quickly. Swimmer A showed the fastest initial improvement. However, just as the weak foundation severely limits the height to which the builder can build, so too the inadequate conditioning limits the hasty swimmer's future performances. Swimmer B, who combines base training and sharpening training throughout the year, eventually builds to greatly improved performance in the senior year. However, swimmer C, who did sharpening training only before the most important races, was more successful than swimmers A and B. Swimmer C started slowly and eventually surpassed the others because this swimmer's larger foundation provided the base from which higher and higher performances could be launched.

Three Types of Training: Good and Bad Effects

No one form of training suits every situation: Knowing the pros and cons of each regimen helps coaches maximize the training effect (Thornton, 1987).

Long and Slow Distance Training

Long and slow distance training involves long swims at a steady pace, well within the capacity of the swimmer yet still requiring a real swimming effort (such as 1:00 to 1:15 per 100 yards). Usually, the swimmer stops long before becoming exhausted.

Good Effects

1. Conditions the cardiovascular system
2. Helps develop robust health
3. Helps prevent injuries
4. Produces continuous improvement, although at a very slow rate
5. Develops a swimmer's base level
6. Has a desharpening effect, thus permitting the swimmer to conserve adaptation energy

Bad Effects

1. Has little effect on muscle strength and thus does not prepare a swimmer for fast racing
2. Does not develop efficiency and coordination for swimming at race pace
3. Has a desharpening effect, resulting in slower racing times during midseason

Race Pace Training

Distances covered in race pace training should be about three-fourths of the racing distance. This is perhaps the most taxing of all training techniques.

Good Effects

1. Develops a keen sense of race pace
2. Teaches the swimmer to relax at actual racing pace and to master efficiency of movement

Bad Effects

1. Is very taxing to the swimmer
2. Will quickly break the swimmer down if done frequently
3. Increases the likelihood of illness and injury by producing greater fatigue than usual

Interval Speed Training

This method, also known as repetition training (see chapter 7), refers to frequent repetitions of a short distance at a speed faster than race pace.

Good Effects

1. Teaches the swimmer to relax when swimming at speed
2. Helps the swimmer to learn efficient co-ordination when swimming at speed
3. Develops muscle strength
4. Has a fast sharpening effect
5. Often results in astonishingly rapid improvement

Bad Effects

1. Robs the swimmer of adaptation energy and thus, if continued, could cause illness, injury, or poor performances
2. Places a great strain on tendons because of its fast pace and can easily result in injury; can draw a swimmer into a slump quickly if done improperly
3. Therefore, great care must be exercised to see that this type of work is effectively performed, as it can improve a swimmer who uses it well

The Energy Continuum in Relation to the Duration and Intensity of Swimming Exercise

ATP (adenosine triphosphate) is a nucleotide compound found in all cells but chiefly in striated muscle. It is the energy source of the muscles and is supplied to them in three ways. In two of these ways oxygen is *not* a prerequisite in producing ATP; these two methods are called *anaerobic*, meaning "without oxygen." In the third method oxygen *is* a prime ingredient in manufacturing ATP; this method is called *aerobic*, meaning "with oxygen."

The body's three chemical systems for producing ATP are

1. the ATP-CP system (anaerobic);
2. the lactic acid, or LA, system (anaerobic); and
3. the oxygen system (aerobic).

The duration of a swimming event determines which of these three methods comes into effect during the activity.

Most swimming events engage at least two of the energy systems; swimming events of ap-proximately 1 minute involve all three systems. One system will usually predominate over the other systems during any one event, however. Therefore, if the energy system predominant in an event is improved through specific training, the swimmer's performance in that event will also improve.

The ATP-CP System (Anaerobic)

Creatine phosphate (CP) and ATP are stored in the muscles in relatively small quantities. Energy can be supplied by this system for a short time only, for example, a 25-yard sprint. If all-out effort is continued for longer than approximately 10 seconds, energy will be drawn increasingly from the LA system.

The Lactic Acid or LA System (Anaerobic)

After ATP-CP has been depleted the production of ATP depends on energy in the form of sugar (glucose) stored in the muscles. When the supply of oxygen is inadequate, glucose is broken down to lactic acid, allowing ATP to be produced. The accumulation of lactic acid and oxygen debt become limiting factors to performance and are associated with painful fatigue. All-out swimming for periods of 1 to 3 minutes draws energy primarily from the LA system.

The Oxygen System (Aerobic)

ATP is manufactured most efficiently and abundantly in the presence of oxygen. Lactic acid and glycogen are resynthesized by the supply of oxygen. The aerobic system predominates in work over 2 minutes in duration.

Chemical Changes in Muscle

The primary chemical change in a contracting muscle is the oxidation ("burning") of the carbon and hydrogen in the carbohydrate glycogen and the production of carbon dioxide and water as in any other engine. In the case of a muscle, however, energy is stored in advance of combustion in a readily available form, just as an automobile battery is charged so that electricity is immediately available for starting.

The substance stored in the muscle is adenosine triphosphate. Through its two molecules of high-energy phosphate, ATP liberates much more energy when split up than any other phosphate. Applying ATP to threads of acto-myosin (the sliding filaments in muscle fiber) causes them to contract. ATP is made fairly rapidly from ADP (adenosine diphosphate) and from creatine phosphate, both of which have high-energy phosphorus.

Storing energy as organic compounds of phosphorus enables a muscle to continue contracting in the absence of oxygen for quite a long time—indeed, until all its creatine phosphate has been converted into creatine. It cannot, however, recover without oxygen, for this is necessary to recharge the creatine and adenosine with the high-energy phosphate. The muscle may therefore accumulate considerable oxygen debt. Although a swimmer may take in a large amount of oxygen during a race, this may not be nearly enough to recharge the chemical system. The swimmer will have to pay off the oxygen debt by taking in a large amount of oxygen after the race is over, which is often indicated by continued breathlessness, for example, after a 100-meter swim.

Anaerobic Metabolism

When the oxygen supply is insufficient to provide all the needed energy from aerobic metabolism, the balance of the energy requirement is derived from anaerobic metabolism. Contracting muscles produce lactic acid when their supply of oxygen is inadequate to meet energy requirements. Pyruvic acid is formed by glycolysis and converted to lactic acid, and this action regenerates one of the factors (NAD^+) required to maintain glycolysis. The rise in the concentration of lactic acid in the blood indicates the amount of anaerobic metabolism involved.

The disadvantages of anaerobic metabolism are the low yield of ATP (two molecules per molecule of glucose utilized) and the formation of a strong acid, namely, lactic acid. A further disadvantage under some conditions is that only carbohydrate can be used in anaerobic metabolism. In spite of these drawbacks, anaerobic metabolism is indispensable in two circumstances: first, as an immediate source of energy at the beginning of exercise, before oxygen supply has been increased by circulatory and respiratory adjustments; and second, during exercise intensity in which all the energy cannot be supplied by aerobic metabolism.

During oxygen deficiency the body does in fact make a little high-energy phosphate as a result of the anaerobic breakdown of carbohydrate to lactic acid, which accumulates in the blood as lactate. This waste of combustible lac-

tate is uneconomical, but it makes the body more capable of withstanding a physical emergency. Figure 8.1 diagrams the chemical changes that take place.

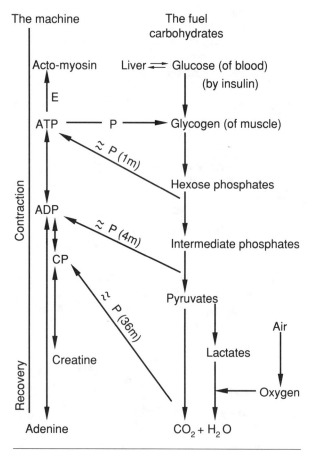

Figure 8.1 The chemistry of muscle contraction.

The Lactate/Ventilatory Threshold

The more arduous the exercise, the more the lactic acid accumulates in the muscle cells and diffuses into the bloodstream. Performance declines once the amount of blood lactate reaches a certain level.

By measuring heart rate and blood lactate it is possible to assess a swimmer's response to different work loads. Pyne and Telford (1989), who did continuing research work on the pool deck for 8 years with Australia's leading international swimmers, confirmed that although lactate measurements have contributed to a better understanding of the physiology of swimming training, coaches without access to lactate testing will find that simply measuring heart rate provides very useful information in training classifications.

The exercise rate at which an athlete's blood lactate level, although elevated, will not continue to rise is known as the *lactate/ventilatory*, or *anaerobic, threshold*. The average value is 3.5 to 4.0 millimoles per liter and upward for all swimming distances, although Pyne and Telford mention that this threshold can vary between 3 to 6 millimoles in well-conditioned middle-distance swimmers.

Some physiologists maintain that 80% to 90% of training should be done at this level. Improved speed over longer distance results from being able to swim faster while retaining a lactate level equal to or lower than that previously produced at lower speeds. Years ago, I coined a saying in this connection: "The anaerobic work of today is the aerobic work of tomorrow." A good example of this is that there was a time when beating 60 seconds for the 100-meter crawl was considered a notable feat for a male swimmer and also was one that put him into severe anaerobic distress. Top swimmers now regularly average well under 60 seconds for each 100 meters over 400 meters, and Vladimir Salnikov, Glen Houseman, Kieren Perkins, Joerg Hoffman, and Stefan Pfieffer have accomplished this feat over 1,500 meters.

The lactate/ventilatory threshold is not really a new concept but merely a new term for what physiologists used to call "maximum steady state work" (Morehouse & Miller, 1971) and what some coaches still term "fastest comfortable pace." Morehouse and Miller (1971) say that a constant level of oxygen intake during exercise is not sufficient evidence of a steady state: The oxygen consumption may be constant simply because the athlete has reached the maximal level of oxygen intake, yet lactic acid may be accumulating.

According to Morehouse and Miller, the maximum rate of sustained work describes a person's ability to maintain steady state activity at high levels of exertion. The aim of such training is to improve the athlete's physical condition so that the organs can sustain a physiological equilibrium at increasingly higher levels of activity. In the process, a swimmer learns to recognize the maximum rate that can be maintained in a physiological steady state.

Pyne and Telford (1989) make the important observation that swimmers who swam so-called threshold sets often did not achieve their lactate and heart rate targets. They emphasize that swimmers need to swim very fast when doing threshold workouts, adding that *well-conditioned* swimmers should attain heart rates of 180 to 190 beats per minute because when swimmers improve their aerobic fitness, higher speeds and heart rates can be achieved before the lactate/ventilatory threshold is reached.

Work Time at Maximal Effort (Approximate Distance).   According to Counsilman (1975):

In events of under two minutes duration [approximately 200 meters], the work is predominantly anaerobic. After this period the aerobic ability of the swimmer becomes more important. In the 1500 meter swim approximately 90% of the energy used is developed via the oxygen system. Obviously a person training for this event should stress training that improves the ability to transport oxygen and to use the oxygen at the cellular level, such as overdistance training and short rest interval training [Figure 8.2]. (p. 20)

Most of the literature on the topic states that up to a pulse rate of 150 beats per min-

Process	10 sec/25 m	60 sec/100 m	2 min/200 m	4 min/400 m	20 min/1500 m	120 min/6000 m
Anaerobic work	85%	60-70%	50%	30%	10%	1%
Aerobic work	15%	30-35%	50%	70%	90%	99%

Figure 8.2 Work time at maximal effort (approximate distance). *Note.* From Counsilman (1975). Reprinted by permission.

ute, the source of energy is aerobic. Above this rate the shift is toward an anaerobic source of ATP. Many factors, however, enter into determining the pulse rate. Such factors as state of emotion, age and individual differences, elapsed time since eating, elapsed time since intake of coffee, and so on, must be considered. If the swimmer and the coach want to use the pulse rate as an indicator in determining roughly whether the swimmer is performing aerobically or anaerobically in practice, they should use [Figure 8.3]. (p. 25)

In short sprints this table has little validity. For example: in a sprint [25 yards] the work is almost completely anaerobic, but there is little increase in pulse rate.

The Three Main Types of Training

There are three main types of training, the effects of which combine in proportion to the specific energy demands of the different swimming events. These three types of training are aerobic, anaerobic, and sprint training. Aerobic training enables a swimmer to maintain a faster rate of speed through the middle stages of a race whereas anaerobic training helps a swimmer better withstand the accumulative effects of fatigue. Sprint training assists a swimmer in developing faster initial speed.

Aerobic Training

Aerobic training is performed at submaximal levels of intensity. The primary aim of aerobic training is to build endurance, that is, to enable the athlete to swim farther and faster before lactate build-up in the muscles, with its consequent lowering of the pH level. The gradual improvement in aerobic fitness eventually enables a swimmer to achieve a higher percentage of race speed before reaching the lactate/ventilatory threshold, at which point the body begins to experience difficulty in supplying energy to the muscles by means of aerobic metabolism. The modern theory of endurance training is based on the belief that much of the work should be performed at or slightly below the lactate/ventilatory threshold. This is commonly believed to occur when the blood lactate has reached approximately 4 millimoles per liter. This type of training is known as "threshold training," and its aim is eventually to produce *less* lactate at higher rates of speed. Training at the lactate/ventilatory threshold is intended to improve *aerobic function* and will *not* improve a swimmer's anaerobic capacity. An improvement in aerobic fitness is indicated by faster swimming times accompanied by lower blood lactates and heart rates. The development of improved aerobic capacity is a long, slow process requiring a carefully devised long-term plan based on gradual progression, year in and year out; by the same token, the resulting adaptation will be retained for a long time.

Anaerobic Training

Whereas the aim of aerobic training is to produce *less* lactate, anaerobic training aims to produce *more* lactate by having the athlete perform work at greatly increased levels of intensity with the deliberate purpose of building a high

Pulse rate per minute	% Aerobic/anaerobic
Under 120	Probably 100% aerobic. Little or no benefit will be derived insofar as developing the anaerobic systems is concerned.
120-150	90-95% aerobic/ 5-10% anaerobic
150-165	65-85% aerobic/ 15-35% anaerobic
165-180	50-65% aerobic/ 35-50% anaerobic
Over 180	Over 50% anaerobic

Figure 8.3   Pulse rate related to aerobic/anaerobic work. *Note.* From Counsilman (1975). Reprinted by permission.

accumulation of lactic acid in the muscles. The goal is to enable the muscle to tolerate a high level of lactic acid and to improve its capacity to buffer the accumulating lactic acid effectively while also stemming to some extent a decrease in pH. Work performed at this higher level of intensity is often referred to as "lactate training."

The chemical changes resulting from severe anaerobic training occur more quickly than the changes associated with aerobic training, but the effects are lost just as quickly with a subsequent reduction in training. The intensity of the anaerobic work load should be carefully monitored. This type of training should be introduced in the training schedule at the appropriate stage of the season, and even then it should not be used in more than two workouts a week because of its highly stressful nature.

Sprint Training

Sprint training is anaerobic and uses ATP and creatine phosphate, which are stored in the muscles in relatively small quantities. Only very short distances, for instance 12-1/2 to 25 meters, should be used in sprint training because energy is drawn increasingly from the lactic acid system if all-out effort continues for more than approximately 10 seconds, and the resultant fatigue prevents the maintenance of a

swimmer's top speed. For the same reason, the intervals between swims should be long enough to ensure that the swimmer is able to continue working at maximum speed.

Effects of Varying Training Intensities

Although the preceding sections outline the differences among the three main forms of training, research has enabled further delineations between relative levels of training intensity (Figure 8.4).

Aerobic Low Intensity

Easy swimming—a comparatively relaxing activity—can be used as a warm-up, as "active rest" immediately after completing a race, or as partial recuperation between high-intensity lactate swims. The heart rate may vary between 120-150 during the activity.

Aerobic Endurance

Swimming at a high, steady pace provides a level of intensity just below or at the lactate/ventilatory threshold. The heart rate may vary between 160-170. The following sets are some examples.

1. 30 × 50 (10-15 seconds rest)

Stage	Type of training	Energy source	Heart rate (bpm)	Maximal blood lactate (mmol/L)	Percentage effort	Perceived exertion
1.	Low intensity	Aerobic	120-150	1-3	80%	Comfortable
2.	Aerobic endurance (maximal equilibrium)	Aerobic	160-170	2-4	85%-90%	Somewhat uncomfortable
3.	Anaerobic endurance	Aerobic/anaerobic	160-190	6-10	90%-95%	Hard work
4.	Race pace simulation	Anaerobic	190-200	8-12	100%	Hurtful
5.	Short sprints (10-25m)	Anaerobic lactic	160-180	3-5	100%	Fast but comfortable

Figure 8.4 Effects of varying training intensities. *Note.* From Absaliamov (1984) and Pyne and Telford (1988). Adapted by permission.

2. 20 × 100 (10-15 seconds rest)
3. 8 × 200 (10-20 seconds rest)
4. 8 × 400 (15-30 seconds rest) (any stroke)
5. 4 × 800 (15-30 seconds rest)
6. 8 × 200 individual medley (20 seconds rest)
7. 1,500 meters freestyle (After the first 250, overkick and fist swim on alternate laps.)
8. 4 × 1,500 freestyle (30 seconds rest)
9. 2 × 3,000 freestyle (2 minutes rest)
10. 3,000 swim (first 1,400 freestyle, last 1,600 individual medley in reverse order with continuous 400 on each stroke)
11. 10 × 100 kick (20 seconds rest) (choice of specialty)
12. 10 × 100 pull (20 seconds rest) (choice of specialty)

It is important that aerobic training not be done entirely in freestyle to ensure that the muscle fibers used in the other strokes are also mobilized.

Anaerobic Endurance (Aerobic/Anaerobic)

This type of training consists of fast swimming in which the energy demands are met both aerobically and anaerobically. The heart rate will be in the range of 160 to 190, depending on the individual and the level of fitness. This type of training may produce blood lactate concentrations of 6 to 10 millimoles per liter. The following sets are some examples.

1. 30 × 50 (30-60 seconds rest)
2. 15 × 100 (30-120 seconds rest)
3. 8 × 200 (30-120 seconds rest)
4. 8 × 400 (1-3 minutes rest)
5. 4 × 800 (3-5 minutes rest)
6. 5 × 300 (8 minutes rest) (faster than 400 pace)
7. 8 × 150 (7 minutes rest) (4 × 150 on specialty, 4 × 150 in freestyle)
8. 8 × 200 specialty (last 50 of each 200 on butterfly) (2 minutes rest) (1-4 descend)
9. 8 × 200 individual medley (1 minute rest) (1-4 descend)
10. 4 × freestyle 500 (3 minutes rest) (1-2 descend)
11. 8 × 200 (2 minutes rest) (alternate 200 freestyle, 200 specialty)

Race Pace Simulation

Race pace simulation involves swimming sections nearly as long as the racing distances at race speed or faster. This type of work will produce severe anaerobic metabolism. The heart rate, and probably the lactate concentration as well, will reach maximum. The heart rate will be in the range of 190-200, again depending on the individual and the level of fitness. The lactate concentration will reach levels of 8 to 12 millimoles per liter.

All swims should start from a dive and be accurately timed for future comparison against other race pace simulations. A swimmer's average time per set will indicate progress or lack thereof, so great importance should be placed on this type of training, which should be undertaken only when a coach feels reasonably sure that the swimmer is motivated to the task. The following sets are some examples.

Sprinters:

1. 15 × 50 (3 minutes rest)
2. 10 × 75 (3-1/2 minutes rest)
3. 10 × 75 specialty with 25 freestyle easy ''swim-back'' after each swim as active rest (Sets 1-5 descend. On each fifth repeat try to improve on the 75 split recorded on swimmer's best-ever 100 swim.)
4. 6 × 100 (5 minutes rest)
5. 5 × 150 (5-10 minutes rest) (Last two 150 swims should be faster than the 150 split recorded on the swimmer's best 200 swim.)
6. 4 × 200 (5-10 minutes rest)

Middle-distance swimmers:

1. 20 × 50 (2-1/2 to 3 minutes rest)
2. 14 × 75 (3-1/2 minutes rest)
3. 10 × 100 (5 minutes rest)
4. 7 × 150 (4-5 minutes rest)
5. 5 × 200 (5-6 minutes rest)

Long-distance swimmers:

1. 10 × 200 (3 minutes rest)
2. 8 × 250 (3-1/2 minutes rest)
3. 7 × 300 (3-1/2 minutes rest)
4. 5 × 400 (5 minutes rest)
5. 4 × 500 (6 minutes rest)

Short Sprints

Short sprints are short bursts at maximum speed over distances ranging from 10 to 25 meters but no farther. Depending on the swimmer and the stroke swum, a swim will seldom last longer than 10 to 15 seconds. This type of work serves to develop speed and is not exceptionally fatiguing unless carried out for a long time.

All swims start from a dive. The following sets are some examples.

1. 32 × 12-1/2 (2 minutes rest)
2. 16 × 25 (2-3 minutes rest)
3. 16 × 25 (3 minutes rest) (Alternate 25 freestyle with 25 specialty. Start from a dive and finish each 25 with a turn and complete push-off.)

Shorter sprints, such as 12-1/2 meters and 25 meters, are more effective than 50s and 100s for developing pure speed and the ability to swim without a build-up of blood lactate. Because creatine phosphate in the muscles tends to last for only 1/4 minute at most, the intervening rest intervals, even for these very short swims, should be about 2 to 3 minutes to permit its replacement.

Proportions for the Training Season

The percentage of varying training intensities when averaged out in terms of a total *seasonal* training program will be approximately as follows:

- Stages 1 and 2 (aerobic training): 50% to 60%
- Stage 3 (aerobic/anaerobic training): 20% to 25%
- Stage 4 (anaerobic training): 3% to 5% only
- Stage 5 (short sprints): 5% to 10%

Heart rate will provide useful information when access to lactate testing is unavailable.

Outline of the Annual Training Program

The annual training program (macrocycle) is built on a series of microcycles (1-week periods), which in turn form mesocycles (blocks of several weeks) devoted to distinct phases of preparation. Each phase should exhibit an ideal balance between the volume and intensity of training specific to the development of desired physiological qualities. An excellent model of ideal daily, weekly, and seasonal planning designed by Ernest Maglischo (1985) is shown in Figure 8.5.

It should be emphasized that Figure 8.5 represents an *ideal*, and that much always depends on a coach's skill, ''feel,'' and plain common

sense in correctly proportioning the work load and controlling the subtle transitions from one phase of the season to the next. In addition, as the program enters its competitive phase, the requirements of preparing for specific events will need to be considered. The transitions from one phase of preparation to the next are reflected in the size of the general work load as well as the volume and intensity of work and are shown in the chart by Tudor Bompa (1985) (Figure 8.6).

The Need for Interspersed Regenerative Periods

One of the problems with designing charts and ideal training configurations is that swimmers cannot be relied on to perform like clockwork machines. Consequently, we can neither synthesize training methods mechanically nor put them into neat pigeonholes to be used willy nilly, irrespective of situational needs. Most experienced coaches develop a natural feel for the changing mood tonus among the members of a team and may alter a planned workout simply as a result of this type of empathy. This approach is not witchcraft but merely the application of everyday common sense.

Paul Bergen (1985) says that some coaches fail to address the need for recovery and regeneration time within the training program. Bergen suggests that microcycles be grouped in periods of 3 building weeks followed by 1 regeneration week. This method can be varied as a season progresses, for example, 4 weeks of building followed by 1 week of regeneration, then 3-1, 4-2, 2-2, and 1-1 as the major competition of the season approaches.

The Number of Training Sessions in a Week

Bergen (1985) draws attention to the work of Tudor Bompa (1985) in classifying frequencies of training sessions within a 1-week microcycle (Figure 8.7a-c).

The first chart in the figure shows eight workouts in a microcycle with only 1 day containing two sessions. Although there is no complete day off, the absence of morning sessions during the week enables the swimmers to sleep a little later before leaving for school.

The second chart depicts 3 workouts and 1 off. This means that there is one day of two workouts followed by a day with only one workout. Then the swimmers have a complete day off at the end of the week.

Planning the Season

1. Adjustment phase—2 to 4 weeks
3. Competitive phase—4 to 6 weeks
　　Transition to competitive phase—1 to 2 weeks

2. Endurance phase—8 to 10 weeks
4. Taper phase—1 to 3 weeks
　　Transition to taper phase—1 to 2 weeks

Weekly Planning

Endurance phase

Mornings—Emphasis on aerobic endurance
1. Stroke drills
2. Aerobic training
3. Occasional short sprints
4. Occasional long sprints

Afternoons—Monday, Wednesday, Friday:
1. Long aerobic sets at optimal pace mix kicking, pulling, and swimming
2. Short sprint sets
3. Occasional long sprint sets

Afternoons—Tuesday, Thursday, Saturday:
1. Stroke drills and aerobic endurance sets at a slower pace
2. Major sprint sets
3. Occasional long sprint sets

Competitive phase:

Mornings—Same as endurance phase

Afternoons—Monday and Wednesday:
1. Major anaerobic sets
2. Aerobic sets at optimal pace
3. Some short sprints

Afternoons—Tuesday and Thursday:
1. Stroke drills
2. Aerobic sets at slower pace
3. Pace work
4. Some short sprints

Afternoons—Friday or Saturday:
1. Major sprint sets
2. Stroke drills
3. Aerobic sets at slower speed

Daily Planning

1. Warm up
2. Short sprints
3. Major aerobic set or minor aerobic set
4. Recovery set—pulling, kicking, or stroke drill

5. Major aerobic, anaerobic, race pace, or sprint set
6. Recovery set
7. Sprints, relays, fun sets
8. Cool down

Figure 8.5 Outline of an annual training program. *Note.* From Maglischo (1985, p. 62). Reprinted by permission.

The third chart shows five training sessions followed by a 1/2 day off. This pattern is repeated and then followed by one day off.

There are several other permutations for applying the number of workouts in a microcycle.

Altitude Training

Altitude training has been conducted with a number of purposes in mind but chiefly

1. to improve performance at sea level;
2. to enable competition at moderate to high altitudes; and
3. to build a higher than normal aerobic base for early season endurance training.

Variation in the reactions of individual athletes has made it difficult to form an assessment of the effects of altitude training. Other variables have included differences in the altitudes at which studies have been conducted, the time spent at the venue, the type of training performed, whether testing was done immediately after arrival at altitude and whether at rest or during exercise, the effects of mountain sickness, and other unforeseen circumstances.

Research studies frequently have neglected to set up sea-level control groups, rendering it difficult to differentiate between improvement caused by the normal effects of training and the improvement caused by training plus the possible extra adaptations resulting from altitude training.

Effects of Altitude

At any altitude there is a lower pressure and volume of oxygen than at sea level, yet there are over 100 million people in the world living at or above 7,000 feet. Life at this altitude presents no great medical difficulty, however, although the respiratory rate must be increased. For example, in Mexico City (7,300 feet/2,300 meters), one fifth more air is needed.

At 7,000 feet/2,100 meters there is no evidence of distressed breathing (dyspnea) until one walks or runs faster. At 14,000 feet/4,200

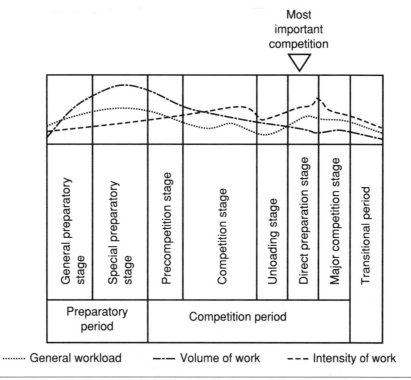

Figure 8.6   Major training cycle: basic year-round training plan. *Note.* From Bompa (1985).

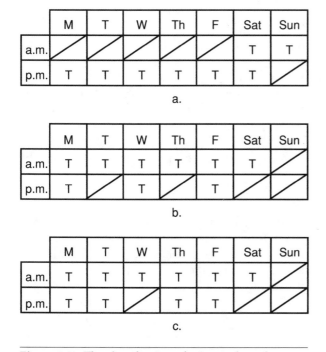

Figure 8.7   The classification of microcycles—the number of training lessons. (a) Microcycle with eight training lessons. (b) Microcycle with a 3 + 1 structure. (c) Microcycle with a 5 + 1 structure. *Note.* From Bompa (1985).

meters dyspnea occurs in a resting situation. At 23,000 feet/6,900 meters there is severe distress with such symptoms as vomiting. It is impossible to exist at this altitude for long.

Adapting to Altitude Training

The minimum altitude at which hemoglobin (red blood cells) appears to increase is about 5,800 feet/1,740 meters. Swimmers should try to train at an altitude higher than this for the best adaptation to take place. However, the higher the altitude, the less the work that can be done. The appropriate altitude will allow enough work stress for adaptation to take place: Mexico City is ideal (Jackson & Balke, 1971). Karikosk (1983) recommends that athletes prepare for sea-level competition at altitudes from 5,760 feet/1,800 meters to 8,000 feet/2,500 meters.

The following symptoms occur when athletes first start training at altitude:

1. Heart rate increases for a given amount and intensity of work.
2. The effects of endurance training are completely different; the heart rate recovery is

slower and the early morning heart rate is probably also elevated.

3. Respiration becomes difficult, which is perhaps the most serious symptom and can have an adverse psychological effect on the athletes unless handled sensibly.

4. Maximum heart rate is reached at a lower rate of work.

5. Blood pressure does not usually change in a uniform manner.

6. Blood lactate is higher and longer recovery periods are necessary. The maximum work possible at altitude is markedly less than at sea level.

Adaptive Effects of Training at Altitude

After an adequate period of acclimatization, most swimmers will improve their aerobic performance at altitude.

1. With adaptation, the blood cell count increases after 14 to 21 days. At 9,500 feet/ 2,850 meters there are significant blood cell increases after about a week.

2. After 10 to 20 days at altitude, the heart rate at rest begins to decrease.

3. Swimmers who adapt best at altitude are also those who tend to compete best at altitude by pacing themselves efficiently.

4. Evidence strongly suggests that if swimmers are not in good condition before going to altitude, a 4-week adaptive period is necessary; 3 weeks is probably the minimum effective period.

5. When first going to an altitude of 7,000 feet/2,100 meters, for example, an athlete is working at approximately 65% of maximum. With acclimatization the maximum can be brought up to approximately 80%.

6. At 7,000 feet/2,100 meters, athletes tend to encounter difficulties after 2 minutes of activity; for less than 2 minutes of activity, performance times are not much affected but a longer rest period is needed. Performances are adversely affected proportionate to duration for any activity of more than 2 minutes.

Effects of Altitude Training on Sea-Level Performance

There appears to be scientific evidence that athletic performance at level can be improved by training at altitude. Maximum oxygen consumption ($\dot{V}O_2$max) can be increased by about 4% in 1 week of training at ideal altitude (Balke,

Nagle, & Daniels, 1965; Bannister, Jackson, & Cartmel, 1968; Daniels & Oldridge, 1970; Dill & Adams, 1971; Klausen, Robinson, Michael, & Myhre, 1966).

When first competing at altitude athletes often suffer a big decrease in performance times: for example, a 3:59 mile runner was capable of only 4:29. At Mexico City (alt. 2,200 meters) Jim Ryun could not finish the mile—he ran 600 meters and stopped because he tried to run at his sea-level pace. A week after returning to sea level, Ryun set a world record for the mile run and two other athletes, who also trained at Mexico City, set personal best times after years of training. In his next race Ryun set a world record for 1,500 meters (Daniels & Oldridge, 1970).

My experience over many years of training swimmers at altitude is that most altitude-trained swimmers will improve their performances at sea level at all distances from 100 meters upward. Although altitude training appears to favor the development of endurance, short-distance swimmers have broken long-course world records at sea level within 7 days of completing several weeks of high-altitude training. For unknown reasons, however, a few swimmers fail to benefit from altitude training. In such instances a psychological aversion to the effects of altitude training should not be ruled out. On one occasion, swimmers from coastal cities who had spent at least 28 days training at altitude did not do as well as anticipated on returning to sea level. However, most of these swimmers competed in their first sea-level meets more than 14 days after returning from high-altitude work. It is possible that the effects of their adaptation to altitude training had either diminished or begun to diminish by this time.

Haymes, Puhl, and Temples (1983) suggest that suboptimal hemoglobin values (14 to 15 grams per 100 milliliters for men, 12 to 13 grams per 100 milliliters for women) on arrival at altitude may be responsible for the inability of some individuals to benefit from altitude training. Smith and Sharkey (1984) recommend that future studies include actual performance measures because laboratory tests might not adequately portray the effects of training or altitude.

Considerations

Preparing at altitude for subsequent sea-level competition should be distinguished from acclimatization at altitude for an upcoming competition at altitude.

Karikosk (1983) says that Soviet distance runners normally spend 14 to 28 days at altitude when preparing for *sea-level* competition. When preparing swimmers for a major meet *at altitude* (6,500 feet/1,950 meters) my experience has been that swimmers, who are well trained at sea level, especially those preparing for events from 200 meters upward, ideally should acclimatize to altitude over a period ranging from 14 to 28 days before the meet. Conversely, swimmers who have trained extensively at altitude for sea-level competition should not arrive at sea level more than 3 to 4 entire days before a major meet. I believe that for swimmers training to compete at sea level the ideal duration of altitude training at 6,500 feet/1,950 meters is at least 21 days.

Track athletes appear to require more time for readaptation to sea-level competition after prolonged training at high altitude, probably because of the greater thickness of the air at sea level (Travers & Watson, 1972). However, there seem to be conflicting opinions on this topic among track athletes; Dick (1979) reports that the Romanians recommend 2 to 3 days for reacclimatization to sea level, whereas the Soviets are said to prefer a period of 14 to 21 days.

For best physiological adaptation to occur the altitude should be above 6,000 feet/1,800 meters and below 9,000 feet/2,700 meters. At too low an altitude, it takes too long to effect adaptation; at too high an altitude, the amount of work stress that can be placed on the athlete is restricted and detraining may occur.

One of the biggest problems of training and competing at altitude is dehydration because there is less moisture in the rarer atmosphere. It is important to take enough fluid to increase the blood volume, so coaches should emphasize this. West German scientists suggested drinking tea or milk instead of carbonated drinks (Colwin, 1975a, p. 24).

Bronchial troubles and irritations occur because of the dry air and hyperventilation. On first going to altitude, common problems include headaches, dizziness, insomnia, poor recovery, muscle soreness, and dehydration. The West Germans suggested a diet rich in carbohydrates and protein. Athletes should avoid vegetables such as cauliflower, cabbages, and turnips, which may cause gas. All athletes—especially females—should take iron supplements.

Coaching at the Olympic Games

One of the big challenges facing an Olympic head coach and the staff of assistant coaches is handling swimmers from a variety of different programs and becoming acquainted with their needs and idiosyncracies over the comparatively brief period of 1 month or so. According to George Haines (Staff, 1980) the first thing the Olympic coaching staff must do is obtain all the information possible from the swimmers' regular coaches.

Fortunately, many of the Olympic assistant coaches are chosen because they have helped their swimmers to place on the Olympic team and are therefore readily available to advise the head coach on the needs of the swimmers concerned. Even so, it is helpful to obtain a written outline on each swimmer, whether or not the regular coach is a member of the coaching staff.

According to Haines, the coaching staff should also ask swimmers what training they think they need; sometimes what the home coach wants and what the swimmer wants differ completely. The coaching staff should then try to blend the workouts so that there is occasionally something in the daily training schedule that reminds the swimmers of home.

Another major challenge that may confront the Olympic coaching staff is simultaneously conducting mens' and womens' team meetings when the men and women are in separate parts of the village. According to Haines (Staff, 1980), "The coaches can't get in with the women; what women we have along as managers are *not* the coaches and the girls don't want to meet with the managers, they want to meet with the coaches, so it becomes a little more difficult" (p. 11).

Haines maintains that the coaches' biggest job at the Olympics is to ensure that every swimmer is provided with a good program of preparation. If an individual swimmer is not getting along in a particular group, the coaching staff may decide at their daily meetings to move a swimmer to another group within the team. The coaches consult among themselves to solve the difficulty, usually with good results.

One of the necessary decisions is how to divide the team for training purposes. The division may be based on the strokes swum by individual members. For example, it is possible that the male and female distance swimmers may be grouped together while the breaststroke and individual medley swimmers may form a group under an assigned coach, and, similarly, the backstroke and butterfly swimmers may form another group under the charge of a couple of other coaches.

Haines mentions that another option is to put any swimmers whose regular coach happens to be on staff under that coach's care and then to add to that group a few more swimmers who fit the same category. However, Haines says that many coaches think that no matter how swimmers are grouped it will always be possible to consult other coaches on each swim-mer's needs and exchange ideas back and forth on each swimmer's progress.

Olympic Coaches' Questionnaire

James "Doc" Counsilman, head coach of the 1964 and 1976 U.S. Olympic men's swimming teams, sent out a precompetition questionnaire to both the college and summer club coaches of each swimmer who was selected to the team. This questionnaire, a model of its kind, is reproduced here.

Coaches' Questionnaire
U.S. Olympic Men's Swimming Team

(Reprinted by permission of Dr. James E. Counsilman.)

1976 United States Olympic Swimming Team

1. Name: _____

   Address: _____

   Phone: Home _____ Office _____

2. Name of swimmer: _____

3. Events in which this swimmer will compete in Montreal: _____
   _____
   _____
   _____
   _____

4. Does this swimmer have any physical problems we should be aware of? _____ Please specify:
   _____
   _____
   _____

5. Do you anticipate the need for any medical care for this swimmer during the next six weeks?
   _____

   If so, please specify:_____
   _____
   _____
   _____

6. To your knowledge, is this swimmer taking any medication for any reason?_____
   If so, please specify:_____
   _____
   _____
   _____

7. Does this swimmer have any emotional or psychological traits we should be aware of?_____
   If so, please specify:_____
   _____
   _____
   _____

8. In your opinion, what is the most favorable training program for this swimmer three weeks
   prior to competing in his event in the Olympic Games? _____
   _____
   _____
   _____
   _____

9. In your opinion, what is the most favorable training program for this swimmer two weeks prior to competing in his event in the Olympic Games? _____

_____

_____

_____

_____

10. In your opinion, what is the most favorable training program for this swimmer one week prior to competing in his event in the Olympic Games? _____

_____

_____

_____

_____

11. In your opinion, what is the most favorable training program for this swimmer 48 hours prior to competing in his event in the Olympic Games? _____

_____

_____

_____

_____

12. Will you be in Montreal? _____ If so, where can you be reached? _____

_____

_____

Additional Information:

Distance:

On an average, how far does your swimmer work out during mid-season?
a.m. _____ p.m. _____
How far does he swim during the taper period?
a.m. _____ p.m. _____

Please list three to four workouts each for a.m. and p.m. that you would like to see your swimmer do during training camp (June 22 to July 7).

1)   a.m.   p.m.
2)   a.m.   p.m.
3)   a.m.   p.m.
4)   a.m.   p.m.

Tapering for the Olympics.

Your swimmer will be competing on the following days:
July   18   19   20   21   22   24   25
When do you want him to begin his taper?   July _____
List two to four workouts each for a.m. and p.m. that you would like him to do during the taper.

1)   a.m.   p.m.
2)   a.m.   p.m.
3)   a.m.   p.m.
4)   a.m.   p.m.

Do you have any particular suggestions about the manner in which we should handle the taper insofar as nervousness, fatigue, tendency to overwork or to loaf, etc., are concerned? _____

_____

_____

_____

_____

Warm-up.

Outline the warm-up you want your swimmer to follow before his competition. List such items as whether he should get up early and get in the water twice before he swims in his event. How many sprints (if any) he should do. _____

_____

_____

_____

_____

Stroke Mechanics.

We don't plan to change your swimmer's stroke mechanics, but if there are any tendencies you would like us to watch for and correct, please list them. We should also appreciate any suggestions you might have on this subject that relate to your swimmer. _____

_____

_____

_____

_____

Race Strategy or Pace.

We would like to know as much about your swimmer's race as we can: his strategy, the pace he wants to hit, his splits, and so on. Any suggestions would be appreciated. _____

_____

_____

_____

_____

Psychology.

Are there any particular hints that you can give us on how to handle your swimmer? That is, what do you want to do when he gets nervous? Does he need constant reassurance or does he like to be left alone? _____

_____

_____

_____

_____

PART III

SWIMMING RESEARCH IN THE 20TH CENTURY

In this part of the book Forbes Carlile describes the history of swimming research, starting with the early attempts to learn more about the physical characteristics of successful swimmers. What type of build and combination of height, weight, shape, and body composition enable a swimmer to float well and offer minimum resistance to the water? What are the physiological and anatomical characteristics required for success in particular events? Because the people asking these questions were coaches mainly working with young, still-growing swimmers, they also needed to learn more about how growth affects the work capacity of boys and girls at different ages and levels of development (Faulkner, 1967).

With the development of more sophisticated and successful training methods came a need to analyze both the physiological and psychological effects of the increased work loads. Although the new training methods generally resulted in a steady improvement in swimming performance, there were many occasions when the results were other than anticipated.

The phenomenon of failing adaptation to stress served notice that training methods cannot be used haphazardly. Coaches and scientists recognized a need for a greater understanding of training methods and good nutrition. Carlile traces the history of swimming research in the 20th century in all its disciplines with the expertise of both a prominent sport scientist responsible for landmark swimming research and a successful Olympic coach of many great swimmers.

The story is taken up by Carlile's compatriot and fellow scientist Richard Telford, head of the department of physiology and applied nutrition at the Australian Institute of Sport. Telford provides a thought-provoking summary of the meaningful research conducted with Australia's top swimmers in collaboration with leading coaches over an 8-year period and also offers some insights into the possible future course of research in competitive swimming.

Mindful of the effects of the so-called information explosion, both Carlile and Telford restrict their discussions to research having positive, practical results. Much has been made of the significance of the information explosion. But what we have really been facing is an exploding mass of data, and not information. Ideas are necessary for data to be converted into information. We can use information, but data on its own is useless. Once we have enough information we are well set to convert relevant information into *concepts* that may have beneficial practical applications.

The intrinsic nature of concept formation should be recognized not only by scientists but by swimming coaches, who are also very much at the receiving end of this data bombardment. In fact, Carlile states that if coaches had to read all the material that comes their way, it is likely that they would have little time left to coach. Counsilman once said that the most valuable research he had ever conducted was contained in his daily training log of every workout he had set during his coaching career. This trial-and-error process has been followed throughout the history of swimming, with coaches experimenting with new ideas and accepting or rejecting them until gradually a pattern of workable concepts evolved. Of course, at their pool-side "laboratories," the final arbiter was—and is—the stopwatch, often referred to as the "George Washington of Swimming" because it never lies about performance.

Chapter 9

Selected Topics on Swimming Research

Forbes Carlile, MBE, MSc
Head Coach of the Carlile Swim Club and
Consultant in Sport Science, Australian Institute of Sport

Selecting various studies and concepts as benchmarks in swimming research will always be a subjective exercise of personal interest and judgment. Still, I apologize if I have been less than strictly objective as to the value of the ideas that follow.

An overwhelming volume of swimming research took place during the second half of the 20th century, so much that no coach on the pool deck could keep up with it, much less apply it, without help from full-time resource staff.

The Slow Adoption of New Ideas

For a long time swimming coaches tended to adhere to what seemed to work well with their most successful swimmers, but rarely could they claim with certainty that a particular training method was scientifically justified. They instead preferred to retain apparently successful procedures.

The general application of a new concept was often a delayed process. The slow adoption of weight training for preparing competitive swimmers is a good example. Coaches believed that the use of heavy weights would reduce flexibility and cause "bulking-up." In the early 1950s, world-record holder Dick Cleveland lifted weights, bench pressing over 100 kilograms as part of his sprinter's preparation, but it took a long time for other coaches to follow through with something that should have been obvious. Although we still have much to learn about it, we know now that sprint ability and power are closely related.

Technique, Training, and Science Are Important Success Factors

The most important factor in the continued improvement in speed and endurance has been the increase in the quantity and intensity of training, which in the 56 years between 1932 and 1988 has improved the world 1,500-meter record by 31% from 21:35.3 to 14:58.27.

A better understanding of stroke techniques has also been an important factor, but for the greater part of a century, observation and trial and error (empiricism) contributed more than scientific theory to the development of more efficient stroke mechanics. Only in recent years did studies of hydrodynamics and biomechanics contribute information of practical use to coaches.

Of course, facilities and adaptations such as deeper pools, wave-reducing lane dividers, and sloping starting blocks also improved racing conditions.

Pioneers in Swimming Research

Though no one could give credit to all those to whom credit is due, some 20th century pioneers in swimming should not be overlooked.

Karpovich and the Resistance of the Water

Karpovich (1933) derived the constant K (for crawl K = 3.17) in the formula $R = K \times V^2$, which indicates a disproportional resistance for higher speeds because the forces of resistance increase geometrically, in proportion to the square of the velocity, rather than linearly. At speeds greater than 2 meters per second—the velocity of the present world record for 100 meters—an even greater disproportion in resistance appeared likely, necessitating energy release related to the cube of the speed. This suggested that lowering the world record much below 48 seconds would be difficult.

Recent studies in swimming biomechanics question the validity of passive towing to determine resistive forces because of body instability and complications introduced by moving parts in the swimming action. Magel (1970) has used tethered swimming experiments to investigate swimming performance, but Scheuzenzuber (1975) claims that the application of forces when the body is held stationary are not well related to the free swimming situation.

The solution to this difficulty appears to be the swimming flume (or ''mill''), which was developed in Sweden in 1968. According to Holmer and Haglund (1977), the Åstrand flume, which enables the swimmer to work against a well-controlled moving current, in most respects is identical to swimming in a pool, and the stroke dynamics are not significantly changed.

Professor T.K. Cureton

Thomas Kirk Cureton might well be called the ''Father of Swimming Research.'' He started his work at Springfield College in the 1930s and moved to the University of Illinois in the 1940s, where he became the director of the Physical Fitness Institute and professor of physical education.

Cureton retired in 1980 after making prolific contributions to the science of swimming and to the understanding and measuring of physical fitness. Only one aspect of Cureton's work is discussed here, namely, his contributions to swimming, which only now are slowly coming to be appreciated.

Cureton published more than 1,000 scientific studies and articles; he followed his first important textbook, *Physical Fitness, Appraisal and Guidance* (1947), with the most comprehensive work on the testing of athletes yet published, *Physical Fitness of Champion Athletes* (1951). In these two books Cureton broke new ground; much of his work continues today as it is rediscovered. For instance, in 1932 and 1936 he carried out tests on the American swimmers and the emerging Japanese swimmers, whose men swept away all before them at the Los Angeles and Berlin Olympic Games.

In 1932 Cureton concluded that the Japanese would beat the Americans (Cureton, 1974), apparently much to the surprise of the American Olympic coach, Bob Kiphuth. Cureton showed that the Japanese, particularly their sprinters, were significantly stronger than the Americans in their arm pulls and were also superior in other physiological measurements. It is interesting that Cureton remarked then on the fact that the *bent* arm pull was the most effective.

The Japanese males in 1936 averaged only 5 feet, 6 inches (1.68 meters) and weighed on average 141-1/2 pounds (64 kilograms); the Americans, 6 feet (1.83 meters) and 172 pounds (78 kilograms). The resting pulse rates of the Japanese averaged 56 beats per minute instead of the 65 of the Americans, suggesting greater circulatory fitness of the Japanese.

Cureton paid attention to ankle flexibility, where the Japanese scored much higher than the Americans (74.8 degrees of movement on average versus 65.4), and it seems that the Japanese developed much more propulsion from their leg actions because of this superior ankle flexibility.

All Cureton's tests pointed to the same conclusion—Japanese swimming superiority—which the Olympic finals confirmed.

Cureton's Tests.   Cureton and his co-workers followed, with slight modifications, the somatotyping procedures proposed by Sheldon, Stevens, and Tucker (1940) and still used today to describe general body types, whether endomorphic (analogous to the hippopotamus), mesomorphic (the ape), or ectomorphic (the greyhound).

With few exceptions, the swimmers were predominantly mesomorphic, muscular types, but they were not as strong as gymnasts or track and field champions per pound of body weight. Cureton found a more endomorphic nature for the distance swimmers. They had greater buoyancy and horizontal floating capacity. It is unlikely that today's champions can be so neatly categorized because the muscularity and power of practically all top swimmers have increased.

John Marshall. The swimmers in Cureton's study were mainly American champions, but one subject was the Australian John Marshall, who died as a result of a car accident in 1957. Marshall leapt to prominence in the Australian national championships in 1947. The results of tests on Marshall revealed several reasons why he was the world's best swimmer by 1950, holding every world freestyle record from 200 to 1,500 meters. There are also good clues as to why he did not swim even faster. Here, in summary, are some of Cureton's findings (Cureton, 1951, pp. 80-83).

John Marshall was found to have one of the largest hearts per pound of body weight of any person tested in Cureton's laboratory, although the heart size of Cureton's sample did not correlate highly with athletic performance. John Marshall's heart stroke volume was very high.

Marshall ranked on top for aspects of heart function on *all* tests. In the basal state his electrocardiogram deflections were the highest ever measured in T-wave and R-wave amplitudes.

His oxygen uptake per minute was the highest ever measured on Cureton's apparatus at Illinois.

Marshall had extreme chest, back, shoulder, and ankle flexibility, again at the top of the Cureton scale. His hyperextension of the back was remarkable (Figure 9.1).

Then we come to what most likely were John Marshall's weak points. Although he had a low specific gravity and floated high and at an angle of 45 degrees to the surface (10% from the top of the table), this was because he was relatively fat. His buoyancy and high floating ability no doubt meant less water resistance, but Marshall was *not* strong, even though resistance exercises with Kiphuth from 1949 to 1951 had improved his strength. Marshall was 21 pounds overweight compared to the average man with the same size skeleton. His fat accumulation on the hips and buttocks was considerably more than a man of his build usually carried. (Cureton measured the fat component of athletes with calipers. The possibly more accurate weighing-in-water technique, with the nitrogen or helium gas method used to estimate the residual air left in the lungs, had yet to be developed.)

In a series of motor fitness and strength tests, Marshall demonstrated strength about the same as only the normal, nonathletic young

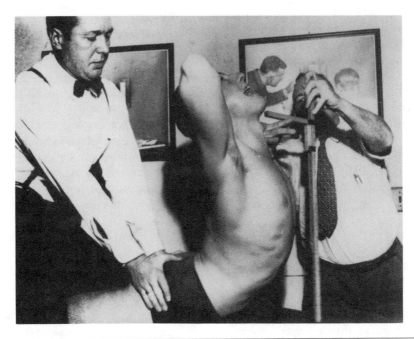

Figure 9.1 Extreme hyperextension of the spine in the late John Marshall. *Note.* From Cureton (1951). Reprinted by permission.

man; he was superior only in rhythmical *endurance* exercises. I remember that when I coached the 1948 Olympic team, John, urged on by teammates in the YMCA gymnasium in Melbourne, could not chin the bar even once. When tested in Illinois he had improved to four chin-ups, but this was still well below average. He was only average in the vertical jump at a height of 20 inches (50.8 centimeters).

There was a good physiological basis for Marshall's endurance tests. Cureton measured the swimmer's blood pH following a hard swim at 6.74, the lowest ever measured in the laboratory. Moreover, before the swim the blood alkaline reserves tested out on the top of the scale, indicating a great buffering capacity for lactic acid during exertion.

Frank Cotton

Frank Cotton died in 1955, a year before the Olympic Games were held in his own country in Melbourne, Australia. If Tom Cureton can be called the father of swimming research, then Frank Cotton well deserves to be considered the father of sport science in Australia; he was also important in the world scene. At the University of Sydney, where he became head of the department of physiology in 1950, I had the privilege of working under his guidance for 13 years, first as a student and then as a lecturer.

Frank Cotton was an outstanding swimmer in his youth; in fact, into his early 30s he was next in line for the Australian 800-meter relay team, which won the silver medal at the 1924 Olympic Games. He always trained with a stopwatch propped up at the end of the pool. Cotton was basically an academic specializing in circulation, although in the last 10 years of his life he contributed a great deal to a number of Australian sports, including swimming. His thinking at the time was revolutionary. I remember as long ago as 1945 being called to his office to go through Bob Kiphuth's book *Swimming* with him, selecting those exercise *specific* to strengthening the swimming action. It was an idea before its time.

We used what was probably the first timing clock made especially for swimmers in training. It was installed in 1947 at the North Sydney Olympic pool near the Harbor Bridge and it is still there. In retrospect, it can be seen that Australian swimmers in those days were at the forefront in applying new methods of training.

They swam repeat "efforts" (as we called them) at various intensities monitored by taking heart rates. Cotton used to amuse bystanders by tossing the end of a long-tubed stethoscope toward swimmers as they finished and counting heart beats to measure the "effort" expended.

Warming Up.   I recall in the 1940s experimenting with warming up. Because there were not hot showers at the North Sydney pool (at that time an unheard of luxury at most Australian pools), I procured a bathtub with a large immersion heater to hold the water at a temperature of 112 degrees Fahrenheit. Just 8 minutes of submersion was enough to raise the core body temperature of the "guinea pig" swimmers considerably. I am sure that this improved the swimming performance of the red, perspiring, and often protesting swimmers.

Although there have been a number of articles denying any beneficial effects of warming up, a study (Carlile, 1956a) initially on passive warming up and later extended to include the effect of active muscular exercise on the 3-centimeter deep internal temperature of the muscles (using thermocouple needles) showed *both* procedures to improve performance. The general useful effect of passive and active warm-up was confirmed much later by physiologist Herbert de Vries (de Vries, 1974). (See Figure 9.2.)

James E. Counsilman: Physiology and Swimming Biomechanics

James E. Counsilman of Indiana University made an enormous contribution to swimming in the 20th century. "Doc's" testament lies in his two great books, *The Science of Swimming* (1968) and *Competitive Swimming Manual* (1977), which contain much of his accumulated research not only in swimming biomechanics and physiology but in almost every phase of competitive swimming. Counsilman developed a format for the application of interval training that was of great practical value to the coach on the pool deck, but he also revolutionized the then infant science of swimming biomechanics. His important contributions in these fields are discussed in depth in other parts of this book.

To cap it all, at his first attempt at the age of 59, Counsilman became the oldest man to swim the English Channel.

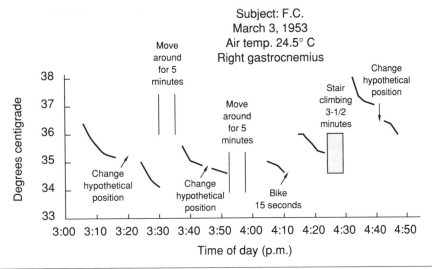

Figure 9.2 Muscle temperature changes at rest and after exercise. *Note.* From unpublished work done by F. Carlile at the University of Sydney.

Published in December 1969, Counsilman's article "The Role of Sculling Movements in the Arm Pull" drew the analogy of propeller blade action. In 1970 and 1971 he used the Bernouilli principle to explain lift forces compared with "straight back" drag-force propulsion. These revolutionary papers opened the way to a better understanding of stroke mechanics.

Talking in terms of the changing pitch, or angles, of the hands, Counsilman began to illuminate the meaning of "feel of the water." Encouraged and inspired by Counsilman, Robert Schleihauf (1974, 1977, 1979) also made valuable contributions to swimming biomechanics. Counsilman (1977) reprinted Schleihauf's important papers in his *Competitive Swimming Manual*. Schleihauf (1979) recognized that Counsilman had revolutionized current thinking on propulsion techniques. (Schleihauf's research is discussed in depth in chapter 2, "Principles of Stroke Mechanics.")

Counsilman and Wasilak (1982) published "The Importance of Hand Speed and Acceleration in Swimming the Crawl Stroke." Photographic analysis of the underwater stroke at two angles indicated a marked difference between the hand acceleration of world-class swimmers such as Mark Spitz and Jim Montgomery and that of less successful swimmers. In their article, Counsilman and Wasilak claim it possible to improve the stroke effectiveness of university swimmers by simply drawing their attention to the acceleration aspect of stroke mechanics.

Classifying Different Types of Interval Training. In his many articles and in his two major books (Counsilman, 1968, 1977), Counsilman first systematized various training items for improving both the sprint and endurance capacity of swimmers through his consideration of *interval*, *repetition*, and *continuous* training.

Developing Muscular Strength and Power. Counsilman was the first to systematize ideas on the strength and power of swimmers. The Counsilman-sponsored "Isokinetic" minigym and electronic "Biokinetic" apparatus, which develops and accurately measures power of the swimming arm action, both made significant contributions to swimming.

Jack Wilmore and Gender Differences

Jack Wilmore and David Costill led a scientific testing program on swimmers in the United States after the 1976 Olympic Games. Wilmore (1979) asked whether, in spite of the substantial differences between male and female records, the sexes are more or less equally endowed with the physical and physiological characteristics that affect performance. In America, East Germany, and the Soviet Union, there was a growing tendency to train and strengthen women and men similarly.

Lean Body Mass. According to Wilmore, the average 20-year old woman has about 24% relative body fat and the average male of similar age has 14%. Is this difference primarily genetic in origin or environmental and cultural? The amount of body fat can make a significant difference to performance, even helping in long-distance swimming. Allowing for the higher amount of essential fat in females, however, with its contributions to the contours, especially of the breasts, at what point does the addition of fat become unessential and limiting to athletic performance?

The relative body fat of the average female long-distance runner studied closely resembled the average male runner's of around 7.5%, which suggests that many women carry more fat than biologically necessary and certainly more than is required for optimum athletic performance. Swimming coaches regularly monitor the fat percentage of their swimmers, often by using laboratory weighing-in-water techniques. As a rule, they require their female swimmers to be below 12% or 13%. Paul Bergen (1979) reports that none of the female winners at the 1978 World Championships exceeded 14.5% fat. As well as restricting calorie intake, many coaches use land programs, including running, to help maintain a high lean body mass. This leanness presumably means better streamlining and less water resistance.

Fast and Slow Twitch Muscle Fibers. Wilmore refers to the relative distribution of slow twitch and the two or three subtypes of fast twitch muscle fibers and points out that, because this procedure is a comparatively new technique, there is an inherent complexity in the analysis of results. Russo et al. are reported by Wilmore (1979) as giving a correlation coefficient of only 0.56 between percentage of slow twitch fibers and endurance performance in athletes competing in various sports and events.

So low a predictive value suggests, along with other reports, that at this stage, knowledge of the muscle composition in an isolated muscle group will give little practical information as to whether a 100-meter or 200-meter swimmer needs a good supply of slow twitch fibers for endurance capacity to supplement sprint capacity. Training increases blood capillarization and even changes muscle fiber type ratios. In fact, the effect of training is believed to be very much at the muscle cell level.

The extremely explosive contractions seen in the 100-meter runner or weight lifter are not required in swimming events. Many outstand-ing 200-meter performers have had close to equal distributions of slow and fast twitch fiber. Basic muscle fiber types seem to be only one of a number of factors contributing to superior swimming performance. Wilmore (1979) reports no difference between the sexes in fiber types, but he did review several studies that showed men to be on average 30% to 40% stronger than women. However, Wilmore demonstrated that the mean strength of non-athletic women can be improved by as much as 30% with a 10-week training program.

Addressing the concerns of many girls in swimming programs who do not want to finish up looking like heavyweight wrestlers, Wilmore (1979) says that although strength training did produce large increases in the female subjects' total strength, it did not appear to result in concomitant gains in muscle bulk.

The females' relatively low amounts of the hormone testosterone accounted for their inability to add much muscle bulk. Allowing for body size, however, females probably can become very nearly as strong as males, but males will have greater total strength through greater muscle mass.

Cardiovascular Efficiency. Wilmore summarizes the cardiovascular differences between males and females and points out that the female's smaller cardiac stroke volume is probably related to her smaller size. For equivalent submaximal levels of work, the female can compensate by increasing her heart rate, but at maximum effort, once maximum heart rate is reached, the female has "nowhere else to go."

The females studied had blood hemoglobin levels on the average 10% lower than the male. Combined with the smaller stroke volume it was not surprising that the females had a lower maximum rate of delivery of oxygen to the muscles. These differences appear to be generic and argue *against* most female records ever matching those of the males, with the exception of long-distance cold water swimming, where fairly large fat distribution is essential for heat conservation.

Although highly trained men were shown to be distinctly superior to well-trained females in total body oxygen utilization, with an average utilization of close to 70 milliliters per kilogram per minute (about 16% higher than a comparable group of highly trained female runners), Costill and Wilmore (1970) showed the top three women averaged 67.5 milliliters per kilogram per minute, only 4% below the men's average. Thus, it appears that when women are highly trained they can come close to top male athletes in cardiovascular function on a per-body-weight basis.

Wilmore concludes his general review by pointing out that what once appeared to be dramatic biological differences in physiological function between the sexes in fact may be related to cultural and social restrictions placed on females as they reach puberty and assume a sedentary lifestyle. As women train and compete more their performance goals clearly can be set very high.

Applying Physiology to Swimming Training

As we approach the physical limits of the athletes and their medium (water), we clearly need not more training but better training. In spite of the search for physiological signs of overtraining, as well as of target intensities, they remain elusive.

The Brachial Pulse Wave

Cureton (1951) examined the brachial pulse wave recorded from the upper arm with the Cameron heartometer (Figure 9.3).

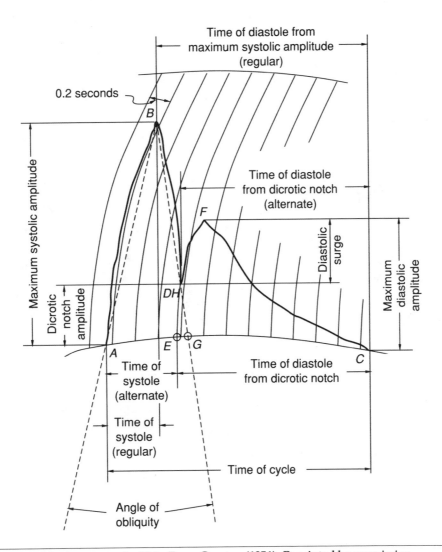

Figure 9.3 Notation of the heartograph. *Note.* From Cureton (1951). Reprinted by permission.

He found a high correlation (r = 0.88) between the Grollman acetylene determination of the stroke volume (a fairly complicated laboratory procedure) and the area of the brachial pulse wave. According to Cureton, this mechanical record of pressure changes from the partially inflated pressure arm cuff yields important information about the state of training of the circulatory system. Changes in this pulse wave and its area, as well as increases in the size of the systolic wave and the diastolic surge wave, reflect closely the strength of the heart beat and blood flow through and resilience of the peripheral vessels (Figure 9.4).

Cureton (1951) summarizes that out-of-training athletes suffered loss of diastolic surge to a remarkable degree, if not entirely, and that the gradual restoration of this characteristic through training demonstrates this measure to be one of the best indicators of the trained cardiovascular system.

Testing Australian Swimmers. Carlile and Carlile (1961) investigated the physiological progress of the 28 members of the Australian Olympic team over an 8-week pre-Olympic training period using the Cameron heartometer. A gradual positive change in all six as-

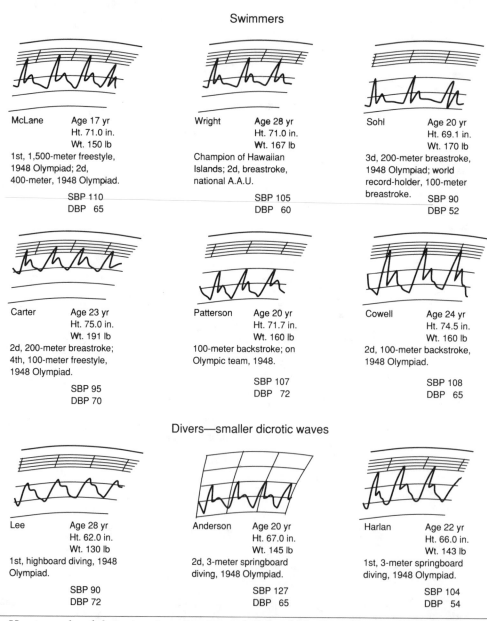

Swimmers

McLane   Age 17 yr
Ht. 71.0 in.
Wt. 150 lb
1st, 1,500-meter freestyle,
1948 Olympiad; 2d,
400-meter, 1948 Olympiad.
SBP 110
DBP 65

Wright   Age 28 yr
Ht. 71.0 in.
Wt. 167 lb
Champion of Hawaiian
Islands; 2d, breastroke,
national A.A.U.
SBP 105
DBP 60

Sohl   Age 20 yr
Ht. 69.1 in.
Wt. 170 lb
3d, 200-meter breastroke,
1948 Olympiad; world
record-holder, 100-meter
breastroke.
SBP 90
DBP 52

Carter   Age 23 yr
Ht. 75.0 in.
Wt. 191 lb
2d, 200-meter breastroke;
4th, 100-meter freestyle,
1948 Olympiad.
SBP 95
DBP 70

Patterson   Age 20 yr
Ht. 71.7 in.
Wt. 160 lb
100-meter backstroke; on
Olympic team, 1948.
SBP 107
DBP 72

Cowell   Age 24 yr
Ht. 74.5 in.
Wt. 160 lb
2d, 100-meter backstroke,
1948 Olympiad.
SBP 108
DBP 65

Divers—smaller dicrotic waves

Lee   Age 28 yr
Ht. 62.0 in.
Wt. 130 lb
1st, highboard diving, 1948
Olympiad.
SBP 90
DBP 72

Anderson   Age 20 yr
Ht. 67.0 in.
Wt. 145 lb
2d, 3-meter springboard
diving, 1948 Olympiad.
SBP 127
DBP 65

Harlan   Age 22 yr
Ht. 66.0 in.
Wt. 143 lb
1st, 3-meter springboard
diving, 1948 Olympiad.
SBP 104
DBP 54

Figure 9.4   Heartographs of champions in swimming and diving. *Note.* From Cureton (1951). Reprinted by permission.

pects of the brachial pulse wave completely confirmed Cureton's claims. This simple apparatus has given way to more complex (and expensive) electronic equipment, which I suspect means only that a very valuable tool to quite easily measure cardiovascular condition has been neglected.

Champion swimmers in Cureton's studies showed no difference in heart size from normal young men, but he did find electrocardiogram differences in the form of larger resting R and T waves for the athletes, indicating strong and well-trained hearts. Probably because his subjects were not in strenuous training when they came to be tested at Illinois in 1951, Cureton did not observe the flattened and inverted T waves later reported by Carlile and Carlile (1961). (See Figures 9.5a-c and 9.6a-c.)

Overtraining

Brachial pulse wave anomalies point to another area of concern—overtraining. A swimmer who is carrying a heavy training load may at any

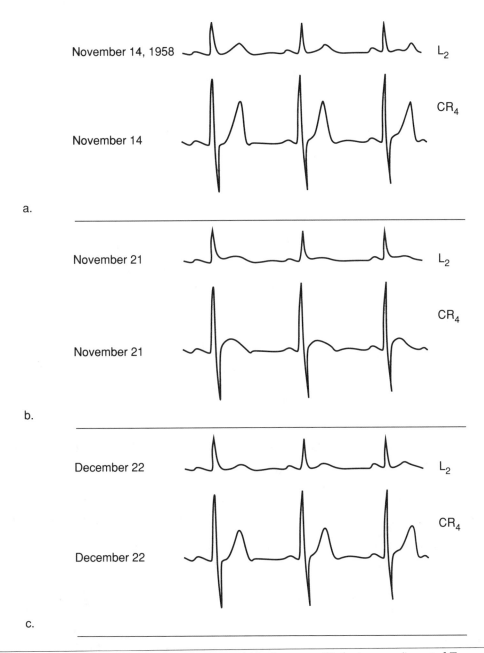

Figure 9.5 Electrocardiograms of cyclist Ian Chapman: (a) before race, (b) during race (inverted T wave, lead 2; flattened T wave, lead CR$_4$), and (c) one month after race (recovery).

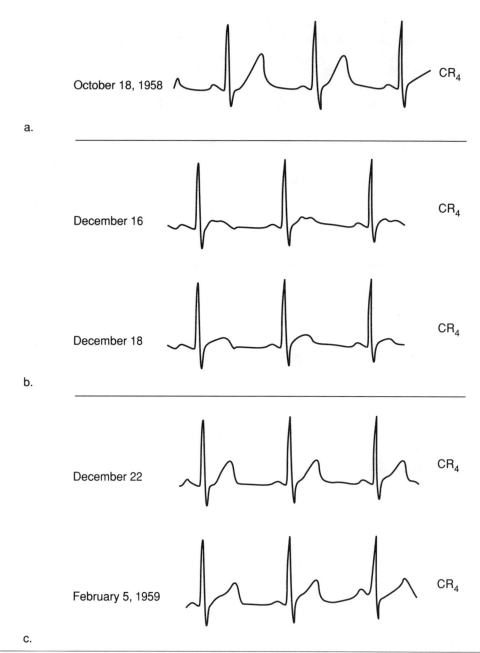

October 18, 1958 CR_4

a.

December 16 CR_4

December 18 CR_4

b.

December 22 CR_4

February 5, 1959 CR_4

c.

Figure 9.6 Electrocardiograms of swimmer Brian Hallinan: T wave changes in lead CR_4 caused by hard training. (a) Light training, (b) strenuous training, and (c) light training.

time begin to suffer from overtraining and failure of adaptation, accompanied invariably by worsened performance. Most coaches have sought tests for early assessment of the ideal training load to enable a swimmer to benefit continually from exercise stress. When does the training load become too great and lead to chronic fatigue and eventual breakdown? Can objective tests tell coaches when to back off from very strenuous training?

For years my main interest in physiological research has been to find objective tests that

signal failing adaptation and oncoming staleness. After 30 years of looking at this problem, my search has been disappointing, which, as we shall see, has been the experience of others, too.

Testing for Overtraining. Two highly significant papers (Hansen, 1980; Morgan, 1980) may shed light on the problem of the overstress syndrome in sport and exercise.

Working from a clinical perspective, Hansen concludes that, even when there were marked manifestations of overtraining and staleness, the results of physiological testing, comprehensive physical examinations, and laboratory studies invariably showed up as *normal*, even though performances may have been greatly affected.

Levels of muscle-related enzymes such as creatine phosphokinase (CPK) and the enzyme SGOT were occasionally elevated, but this varied, and in the case of CPK is to be expected with an athlete's increased muscle activity. Hansen says that there was little evidence showing any consistent alteration in oxygen transport, cardiac output, or blood picture (including blood hemoglobin level), even when performances were at their worst.

Clinically, the swimmers in the studies usually appeared normal, even though it was clear to the athletes and coaches that everything was by no means normal. As mentioned, such changes as marked deformation of the electrocardiogram's T wave, gross falls in the blood hemoglobin level, and alterations in blood pressure *may* occur in similar cases, physiological and clinical observation and testing produced no "golden cord" of consistent response that could guide coaches objectively. Of course, the physician should test for the results of infectious diseases in such cases because there is always a possibility that postviral fatigue may show up with long-term effects on training and performance.

A wide variety of responses to overtraining can occur, but few consistently. These responses are as varied as the many target organs likely to be affected.

Until now coaches have been able to obtain practical guidance only from performance and from the subjective reports of *how the athlete feels*. Laboratory tests seldom have been able to guide the coach with any certainty. Indeed, it appears that how an athlete feels may be the best guide for controlling overtraining and its subsequent state of staleness.

Depression.   Hansen (1980) suggests that the "profile" of moods—tension, anger, fatigue, confusion, and particularly depression—are the common denominator of symptoms in overtrained athletes.

Morgan (1980) rightly points out that the modern coach must push modern athletes "right to the brink" and then back off. This sums up what is happening today. However, the coach may not back off soon enough. Preferring not to rely entirely on intuition, the coach may choose scientific guidance. Of course, it is also possible that the athlete may resist being overdriven by exhibiting negative responses to the demands of the training schedule.

According to Morgan the problem is to monitor the athlete so as to *prevent* staleness, which he regards as the next step in an overtraining-staleness continuum. Physical testing often reveals nothing about the overstressed athlete, which leaves psychological factors as the possible common denominator of overtraining. Emotional changes should be monitored as well as physiological parameters.

Morgan (1980) says that he never encountered an athlete with deteriorating performance clearly associated with overtraining who had *not* shown marked and significant changes in "mood profile," something he claims to be an excellent measure of overtraining staleness. The athlete in a state of staleness shows all the psychological symptoms of a state of depression. Morgan says that a psychiatrist examining a stale athlete would report the athlete to be a clinically depressed person requiring psychiatric treatment. Fortunately, a long layoff is often enough to cure the condition. Very stale individuals who do not respond to taper usually will not return to normal condition until the next season.

Rushall (1979) offers a more or less similar means of assessing psychological stress. His "General Health and Stress Level Check-List" inventory (Carlile, 1980) is very much on the same lines as Morgan's work. Psychological inventories are important at least in opening lines of communication between coach and swimmer.

The General Adaptation Syndrome.   Selye (1956) pioneered the concepts of the "general adaptation syndrome" and "failing adaptation." His work deals with generalized, nonspecific biological reaction to a variety of stresses. A coach should watch athletes in training for a number of possible indications of failing adaptation to the sum of stresses on the body.

In midcentury I drew attention to some possible symptoms of failing adaptation, including chronic loss of weight; joint and muscle pain not attributable to any local injury; intestinal upsets; swollen lymph glands; blocked nose and 1-day colds, skin rashes; hives and general muscular tenseness; and what I called "psychic unrest, irritability, insomnia, and general fatigue often referred to as staleness'' (Carlile & Carlile, 1955, 1956a & b)—perhaps even then I was not too far off the mark. At that time, there was no systematic attempt to quantify the mood states.

Successful coaches know they must press swimmers hard to satisfy modern training demands. The art and the science are to detect those who will not easily recover from strenuous training once the tapering period commences. This is where we need scientific enlightenment—to make coaching more science and less art.

Prevention of Staleness. For all the expensive electronic testing equipment now available, observation and testing with psychological inventories still appear to be the best ways to monitor the staleness syndrome so as to take appropriate preventative action. This in no way repudiates the hard-won physiological and medical knowledge that has provided us a better understanding of the training process, but at our present state of knowledge there seems to be a good case for monitoring training closely by observing psychological as well as physiological parameters.

Joint Overuse Injuries

For a swimmer in heavy training each shoulder joint rotates about 100,000 times a week, over 2-1/2 million times in a 6-month season. It should not be surprising, therefore, that muscles, tendons, and ligaments around the shoulder joint become subject to wear and tear problems. Basically, overuse and persistent rubbing lead first to inflamation of bursas and so on and then to pain, which eventually can be severe and cause great limitation in range of movement. This can greatly interfere with proper stroke mechanics.

Richardson (1979a,b, & c) points out the problem as being the large number of tendons and muscles packed between the bony acromium and corocoid process of the scapula and the capsule covering the head of the humerus. The crowding causes impingement, which causes bursitis or tendonitis. Dominguez (1980) says that up to 60% of high-quality competitors and age groupers become affected at some time.

Complete rest from the pain-producing action will usually effect a cure, but this is not easily carried out with ambitious swimmers. Apart from rest, preliminary stretching, physiotherapy, drugs, and finally surgery, the most

highly acclaimed and accepted method of treatment is *ice*. Richardson and other very experienced authorities in this field, Kennedy, Hawkins, and Krissoff (1978) and Dominguez (1980, pp. 35-42), agree. Dominguez says that

ice is the therapeutic agent of choice. Experienced athletic trainers who have treated swimmers recommend application of crushed ice, preferably in a bag or in styrofoam or paper cups, 10 to 15 minutes a session, 4 or 5 times a day, if possible. Ice massage can be applied to the tender area . . . ice should be the prime treatment besides rest.

''Cryotherapy in Sports Medicine'' (Knight, 1978) also contains an excellent consideration of the physiology and medical aspects of ice therapy.

All these experts agree that such resistance work as weight training and Nautilus pullovers help prevent the shoulder pain syndrome. The exact mechanism for this is unknown, although the multiple strengthening of various muscles around the shoulder joint is recommended.

More recently, Foley (1987) suggests that the impingement syndrome can be remedied by strengthening the *serratus anterior* muscle, which permits it to better pull the scapular away from the impingement area around the joint.

Knee injuries are remarkably present among breaststroke swimmers. The condition of ''breaststroke swimmer's knee''—usually inflamation and pain from the tibial collateral ligament (Kennedy et al., 1978)—is often treated successfully by ice therapy and rest.

Heart Rate Response

Heart rate response to exercise has long been accepted as the best and most easily obtained physiological guide to cardiovascular condition. Cotton (1932) first reported on the low resting heart rates of athletes. He found that eight champion swimmers, mainly highly trained Japanese, had average heart rates of 47.5 beats per minute on waking in the early morning before competition.

Cotton showed that normal men with little training had basal heart rates of 66 beats per minute whereas Olympic swimmers with about 10 years of swimming experience had 47. The slow resting heart rate is taken to indicate a powerfully beating heart with a high stroke volume for each beat. At submaximum work loads in well-conditioned subjects a relatively low energy cost is reflected in a low working heart rate and a quick return to the resting level. By taking immediate postexercise counts, a coach can monitor fairly accurately the energy cost of the training effort.

In 1956 I studied the use of postexercise heart rate counts in the prediction of maximum performance (Carlile, 1956b). The physiological basis of this approach is that heart rate, oxygen utilization, and swimming velocity are linearly well related to one another and the "line of best fit" can be extrapolated to cut the maximum heart rate. However, although this provides a good approximation, it is an oversimplification because the swimmer can still swim more quickly even after reaching maximum heart rate by using the lactate anaerobic energy-production system.

The Treffene Formulas. Treffene (1978) and Treffene, Alloway, and Shaw (1977) investigated crawl stroke efficiency using the linear relationship between heart rate and swimming velocity. The subjects reached personal maximum heart rate at a velocity coincident with maximum oxygen intake. Treffene called this the "target velocity" (Figure 9.7).

Treffene claims that before reaching maximum heart rate most of the energy requirements were met with a combination of aerobic breakdown of carbohydrate and fat (using available oxygen delivered to the muscles) and some anaerobic breakdown of glycogen, producing lactic acid. Treffene, Craven, Hobbs, and Wade (1979) modified the earlier theory after conducting a study using Australian swimmers that showed sprinters to have considerably higher blood lactate levels at the velocity of reaching maximum heart rate than endurance swimmers. As will be seen later, this was not an unexpected finding in terms of our understanding of the lactate/ventilatory threshold, which occurs at relatively low velocities for sprinters.

Treffene devised a series of formulas for predicting swimming times at various distances from sprint to 1,500 meters. Carlile (1979) discussed Treffene's work and pointed out that the formulas were those fitting the mathematical form of the rectangular hyperbola and that their predictions of swimming times will be accurate only for subjects with well-balanced release capacities for both sprint and endurance.

Plotting average velocities of individual world-record holders from 100 meters to 1,500 meters, the *performance curve* (distance versus average velocity) followed very closely the form of the rectangular hyperbola. But it appeared that only certain types of swimmers had the inborn capacity for their individual performance curves to fit. However, Australian specialist distance swimmer Max Metzker's performance curve up to 400 meters failed to fit the rectangular hyperbolic curve as did the curves of the world-record breaking sprinters of the time,

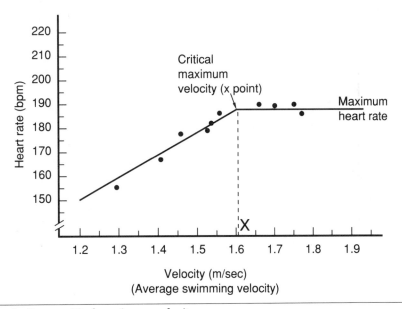

Figure 9.7 Target velocity, or critical maximum velocity.

Jonty Skinner and Barbara Krause, for events from 100 meters to 1,500 meters (Figure 9.8).

Depending on the distribution of their sprint and endurance aptitudes, most swimmers varied from the rectangular hyperbola at one end or the other of their performance curves, and hence the formulas did not have reliable predictive value. However, Brian Goodell, Olympic 400-meter and 1,500-meter winner in Montreal in 1976, had best performances from 100 meters to 1,500 meters, which *did* closely fit the rectangular hyperbola; therefore, the Treffene formulas could quite accurately predict his performances at various distances (Figure 9.9).

"Target Velocity."   Treffene (1978) and Treffene et al. (1979) say that with proper training of the energy systems the swimming velocity at which the maximum heart rate is reached should gradually increase with well-trained swimmers throughout a season, indicating improved potential performance. They call this critical velocity the "target velocity," implying the desirability of training mostly at a velocity close to the "target."

In an unpublished study of the effect of training on thirteen state- or national-level swimmers, all of whom improved in their various events, I could *not* confirm the significant increase in "target velocity" reported by Treffene. However, the subjects were male swimmers who were not particularly unfit at the beginning of the study. In 20 weeks no swimmer showed a significant change from the first determination of his "target velocity." I concluded that swimmers who are relatively fit in the first place would be unlikely to have further improvement consistently linked with heart rate, as Treffene had claimed, but this does not mean that other physiological parameters had not improved in capacity.

There have been a number of studies showing that training causes the *power* of the heart beat to increase, indicated by increased stroke volume. Cureton (1974) cites Shepherd and Faulkner as having independently shown that stroke volume typically *increases* even after the maximal pulse rate and the oxygen intake have leveled off. By the mechanism of increased stroke volume alone, the oxygen transport will be enhanced without necessarily affecting the heart rate response in highly trained swimmers.

Cureton (1947) says that the heart increases its output by increasing the pulse rate and also by increasing the amount of contractile force per stroke (shown by changes in the brachial pulse wave). The pulse rate is not always di-

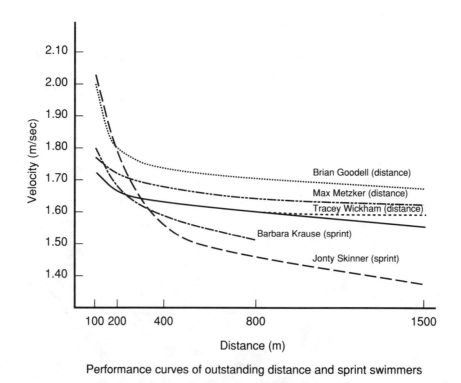

Performance curves of outstanding distance and sprint swimmers

Figure 9.8   Performance curves of outstanding distance and sprint swimmers.

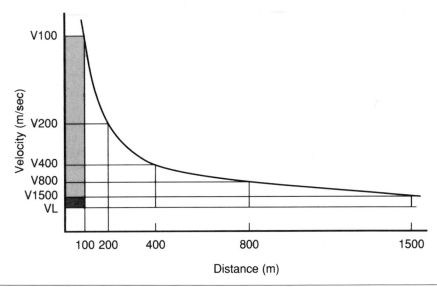

Figure 9.9   The form of a rectangular hyperbola.

rectly proportional to the severity of the exercise, however, because skill and other physiological adjustments are contributing variables. He adds that it is never quite certain whether increased blood flow in response to exercise is caused by increased heart rate or increased contractile force, which makes exact interpretation of pulse rate changes difficult.

The Lactate/Ventilatory Threshold. Given a known "target time" for an individual, Treffene et al. (1977) recommend that a substantial portion of the training for aerobic capacity be carried out at an intensity between 85% and 100% of this "target." The defect in this approach, which Treffene later partially recognized (Treffene et al., 1979), lies in the nature of the lactate/ventilatory threshold, an important consideration in the physiology of the athlete that is dependent on whether sprint or endurance capacity predominates.

The lactate/ventilatory threshold can be defined as that point (in velocity or rate of oxygen uptake) where levels of anaerobic by-products (e.g., lactic acid) in the blood, lung ventilation, and so on, rise steeply. The lactate threshold (the point of rapidly rising lactic acid) is *not* closely related to either the maximum heart rate or maximum oxygen uptake. It usually lies between about 60% and 90% of the $\dot{V}O_2$max. With training this threshold will move closer to the $\dot{V}O_2$max.

Heart rates clearly have meaning mainly in *the context of the individual*, and even then they should be interpreted with care. At a heart rate fairly close to maximum, one athlete may have

relatively little accumulation of lactic acid whereas another might have so high a level as to make training at that rate difficult—or even harmful if perseverance at this intensity leads to failing adaptation.

According to Alois Mader (Carlile & Carlile, 1978), the East German swimmers and coaches, who paid particular attention to lactic acid levels, were advised to regulate training so as not to create "pressure" to train too much at intensities that might overdo anaerobic stress. They perceived a distinct danger in setting "target" times that might be easily attained by some but only at considerable physiological cost by others.

Maximum Oxygen Utilization ($\dot{V}O_2$max)

Exercise physiologists have long been interested in $\dot{V}O_2$max, which mainly depends on the efficiency of the cardiovascular and respiratory systems. Astrand (Åstrand & Rodahl, 1970) and others have shown $\dot{V}O_2$max to be an important performance predictor, though it is by no means infallible. It is believed to be of less importance in swimming, but as already mentioned, a high aerobic capacity is desirable even in a sprinter, for generous delivery of oxygen to the active muscles will postpone the need to switch to the less efficient lactic acid system to meet energy demands.

An important factor for predicting performance is how close the lactate/ventilatory threshold is to the $\dot{V}O_2$max. Training this anaerobic aspect of an individual's physiology is part of the modern concept of specificity of training and something about which we have much to learn if we are to construct the best possible training schedules. At present we can deal only with principles—we lack an exact and complete knowledge concerning the interaction of the many factors involved.

Measuring Strength in Swimming

Some coaches and sport scientists have asked themselves why swimmers who are running up stairs, climbing ropes, working with very heavy weights, performing chin-ups and push-ups, running cross-country, and carrying out all manner of apparently *nonspecific* exercise *are succeeding*—many doing very well indeed, despite all the good arguments for developing *specificity*. Much has been written on specificity, but we still know very little about how to optimally strengthen swimmers who compete at varying distances and who have varying degrees of initial "strength."

The effect of strengthening exercises no doubt lies *beyond* their effect on the structure of the muscle. Among the reasons that have been suggested for the apparent beneficial results of heavy nonspecific activity are that it facilitates neural "inhibition" and teaches the athlete to recruit fast twitch fibers in muscle groups. More than 40 years ago Frank Cotton suggested that perhaps heavy weight lifting trains the "effort centers" in the brain. We still do not know.

Evidence, however, seems to point to the importance of specificity, so the question becomes *what* unspecific work is beneficial and how much. So far there are few scientific answers, and as usual, what is good for one individual may not help another.

There have been excellent review articles in *Swimming Technique* summarizing scientific knowledge on resistance training: "Getting a Grip on Strength" (Hopper & Bartels, 1980) and "Biokinetic Strength Training: A Compilation of Scientific Papers" (Counsilman & Favell, 1980). In an important paper by Costill, Sharp, and Troup (1980) based on a well-controlled experiment, the authors conclude that the subjects' upper-body strength as measured electronically on the Biokinetic Swim Bench is a major determinant of freestyle performance in events from 50 yards to 500 yards.

The researchers report that sprinting potential was quite predictable, improving on the average 1.3% for every 10% increase in biokinetic swim bench strength (strictly speaking we should call it *power*, because strength for *single* lifts was not measured). The implications for both increasing power and measuring accurately are clear: Increasing biokinetic bench power is closely related to sprint speed; this study showed a very high correlation ($r = 0.87$) with 200-yard swimming time.

Another, independent, study (Hopper, Hadley, & Piva, 1980) on 26 top-level college swimmers comparing power generated in tethered swimming with power on the Biokinetic Swim Bench found that strong, skilled swimmers swam faster than weak skilled swimmers. This was indicated by the fact that their power to sprint speed correlation coefficients were 0.71 for the bench and 0.85 for "in water" testing.

This suggests interesting possible uses of tethered swimming for highly specific strengthening. For example, a digital display of work output visible on the floor of the pool could help a swimmer learn optimum stroking techniques. The work output could be displayed on a 5- or 10-second basis. The individual could test subtle stroke changes while at the same time increasing power potential by doing "weight training in water."

There seems to be one clear principle for increasing swimming power: *The resistance exercise should duplicate both the form and speed characteristics of the swimming movement.* The Biokinetic bench is believed to do this and seems to be the best such device now available; although it is not exactly the same as free swimming, I believe, however, that tethered swimming provides a nearly ideal strengthening exercise for swimmers. Accurate measurement *with feedback*—allowing modifications to be made and tested—is an important way for swimmers to learn about the relationship of the water's "feel" to work done in the stroke.

Flexibility and Strengthening Exercises. Cureton (1947, 1951) was the first to draw attention to the superior joint flexibility of top swimmers. In the 1970s interest revived in this aspect of fitness. Hogg (1977) delivered an excellent and comprehensive paper on this subject, and Snelling (1980) contributed a valuable discussion of the practical aspects of administering a stretching and weight-training program.

Training the Human Energy Systems

The combinations and arrangements of the training items in a swimming program must be based ultimately on the understanding of how muscle fibers function. The more we understand of the physiology, the more we can learn about how best to specifically stress the various systems, thus bringing about optimal enzyme and other adaptations for maximum performance. A special issue of *Swimming Technique* (Georges, 1981b) contained excellent review articles on this topic under the general heading "Energy Sources for Swimming Events," including articles by Hopper, Georges, Richardson, Bonner, Prins, Bartels, and Atterboom, with practical suggestions for distance and sprint workouts by Hill, Shoulberg, and Griner.

The following issue of *Swimming Technique* (Georges, 1981a) contained equally important articles, one by Bob Hopper and others on the rational use of training aids and another on "The Age Group Swimmer: Considerations for Training and Performance" by Troup, Plyley, Sharp, and Costill. Again, it should be pointed out that *no* program design will improve the individual if it imposes too great a stress load for the individual at that time. This concept has led to *cyclic training*; that is, rhythmic increase and decrease of the training work load on a "mini" (in each training session) to a "maxi" (weekly and yearly) basis.

The aim of coaching today lies in using scientific knowledge of the mechanisms of the energy systems to appropriately train individual swimmers. This entails also providing adequate recovery periods. *Many otherwise excellent training routines are rendered less so by a combination of too much work and too little recovery time.*

Nutrition

One of the best basic sources of general nutrition information is the comprehensive textbook *Exercise Physiology, Energy, Nutrition and Human Performance* (McArdle, Katch, & Victor, 1981). The book begins with an excellent section, "Nutrition: The *Base* for Human Performance," that points out the importance of proper nutrition and describes it as basic to all physical performance. The authors maintain that the key to adequate nutrition is *variety*, which reminds me of how Henry Priestly, professor of biochemistry at Sydney University, summed up nutritional needs in a conversation many years ago: "a wide variety of foods as close as possible

to their natural states." All modern evidence concerning optimum nutrition confirms this. In recent years, nutritionists have placed great emphasis on unrefined, fiber-rich carbohydrates and restricted fat intake with food fats contributing not more than about 30% of food energy.

Swimmers are no different from others as regards these nutritional needs. Ideally, swimmers should eat a regular balanced diet and avoid the "empty calories" in the relatively fat- and sugar-laden "junk foods."

Unfortunately, swimmers do not always follow such a well-balanced diet and hence resort to the "insurance policy" of supplementary vitamins, even though this is condemned by many nutritionists and physicians. Nevertheless, a good deal of literature continues to describe research indicating that some disease states are brought on by deficiencies of various trace vitamins and minerals, so many coaches understandably recommend their pupils be "safe rather than sorry," especially in the belief that the stress of heavy exercise may bring about extra demands. Coaches generally recommend supplementation of C, B complex, and carefully administered iron.

A study by Åstrand (1971) of top Swedish girl swimmers found that in spite of advice to the contrary they still consumed the contemporary young person's good measure of "junk" foods, so he recommended extra B complex and C. However Fitch (1978), Australian Olympic team head medical officer, scathingly criticizes the practice and claims that not only is there no evidence of benefit from supplementation but also that there is a potential danger from megadoses. He further claims that Australian athletes probably vie with the Americans in excreting the most expensive urine in the world.

However, it is possible that deficiency in individuals can easily be missed in mass trials. For instance, it has been shown that potassium deficiency, which can result in muscle weakness, occurs in some individuals during heavy exercise in hot climates (Lane & Cerda, 1979) and in those who sweat profusely. These individuals may at times need up to 5 or 6 grams per day. Between 5 to 8 servings of high-potassium fruits such as oranges and bananas are recommended rather than chemical supplementation with potassium. The overwhelming majority of reports on vitamin E supplementation do not show it to be an ergogenic aid, but Cureton (1974) maintains that taking a related substance, octocasanol, results in measurable benefits to circulatory function. However, only a few studies support the claim that vitamin E supplementation can improve athletic performance. Our knowledge is far from complete in this area of human nutrition.

Because lean red meat is high in assimilable iron, which is an often needed element for adequate blood hemoglobin production, it should be consumed about three times per week.

Enhancing Performance Through the Mind

The most highly acclaimed book on general mental training and "programing" for success is *Psycho-Cybernetics* (Maltz, 1960). Tutko (1976) and Rushall (1979) have made outstanding contributions in sports psychology; Rushall more specifically on swimming.

It has been known for many years that the physical process of muscle relaxation in itself has a normalizing, beneficial effect on the physiological reactions of the body (Jacobson, 1938). Suggestion, whether given in the waking state (Benson, 1975) or in the hypnoidal state (Cunningham, 1980), can have far-reaching effects on thought processes and performance.

The concept of positive thinking is also important in this context. Stanton (1979) contributes a helpful, easily read work on the subject, and *Psyching in Sport* (Rushall, 1979) is an excellent book on the psychological aspects of race preparation for competitive swimmers.

The Swimmers' Memorandum on Mental Training (Ronan, 1977) provides good coverage of self-image, visualization, and other aspects of mental training. However, this book, which was produced as part of the American scientific drive to do well at the 1980 Moscow Olympic games (although the United States ultimately did not compete there), was placed on a restricted circulation list and sold only to American coaches. It is a comprehensive and recommended treatment of a subject of increasing importance in maximizing performance as physical limits are approached.

Madsen and Wilke's Age Group Multiyear Training Plan

In their paper "A Comprehensive Multi-Year Training Plan," Madsen and Wilke (1983) set out a model for training age groupers for high-level performance. The plan starts with systematic training at the age of 7 or 8 years and culminates after 8 years of progressive skill learning in varied activities and increasing swimming work loads (Figure 9.10).

The principles outlined essentially review the research findings reported since 1973 by some 20 East and West German scientists who systematically studied the development and physical performances of boys and girls of various ages. From what we know of East German age group preparation, their training procedures are well in accord with these principles. The remarkable success of the older German swimmers in itself argues convincingly for the soundness of the "comprehensive" plan that Madsen and Wilke put forward as a model for age group preparation.

It should be said, however, that the model considers an almost idealized situation. Unlike East German and Soviet teams, training squads in the more affluent West rarely have well-coordinated and school-sanctioned schedules balancing time for study and athletic preparation, high coach:swimmer ratios, or ample water space for training elite swimmers. These appear to be first considerations and taken for granted in the fully state-supported systems of Eastern Europe. Further, in the West parents rather than the government usually must pay for full-time, well-trained coaches to take on relatively small groups. This makes high-level competition swimming a sport for the upper-middle-class, relatively affluent families, which means that a great many athletically talented boys and girls never become exposed to the important initial preparation.

And in many countries, beyond basic learn-to-swim instruction there is no further systematic teaching of swimming techniques easily available inside or outside the school system.

There are advantages in the "private enterprise" system, however. For instance, very late developers are able to stay in swimming schools and not be cut from the squad because of poor performance. In the West, providing fees are paid, swimmers can continue in a program simply because they like training and swimming on a team. Provision is usually made for these swimmers at all levels of achievement.

In contrast, Madsen and Wilke, in line with the principles they enunciate, set out an 8-year plan "to foster a successful swimming career for athletically talented boys and girls" at the international level; of course, the key words are "athletically talented." Those who recognize

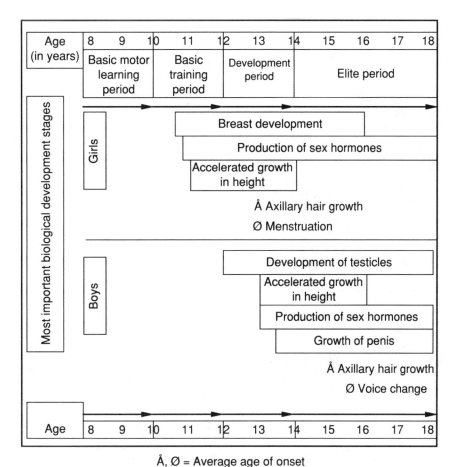

Figure 9.10 Chronological relationship between processes of maturation in boys and girls.

the individual social and developmental benefits of swimming and support programs that persevere with swimmers of varying ability and dedication, simply because it is good for the general development of children, will find it difficult to reconcile their view with this seemingly intrinsic demand for excellence in Madsen and Wilke's "idealized" 8-year development approach.

A compromise between the typical private enterprise system and the model government-supported situation may yet be found that will yield the best from both worlds. Of course, this will require of the private enterprise club system a sound basic philosophy and enough pool space and financial subsidy.

"Elite" programs for those with the aptitude and desire to be champions could be set up parallel to the more orthodox swim club coaching, which caters for those of all ability levels. These elite programs could be fairly demanding. Madsen and Wilke's plan recommends that even 7- and 8-year olds attend as many as three to four 40- to 50-minute swimming sessions per week and three to four 15- to 25-minute sessions of land exercises.

The recommended optimum commitment increases progressively with each developmental age group, quickly requiring time and facilities beyond the capacity of most families and privately operated swim schools. There seems to be a clear need, then, for two complementary strands—for the "average" child, on the one hand, and for the "committed" and talented child, on the other.

There is the further difficulty of differential development. It is a recognized and accepted fact of fundamental importance in the application of training programs to individuals that children mature at different chronological ages (Figure 9.11). This complicates the application of any training plan designed for the "average" boy or girl.

Despite these difficulties in the application of any multiyear training plan, there are good reasons to believe that the principles that Madsen and Wilke extract from the conclusions of the many research scientists and enunciate in their plan are sound and provide an essential working basis for the training philosophies of swimming school coaches, both government and private, and for swimming associations and

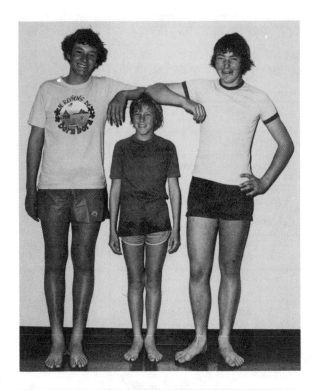

Figure 9.11   These boys are all 14 years old. *Note*. Reprinted by permission of P. Russo.

other administrative bodies. The implications are far-reaching.

The Effect of Science on Swimming Progress

Considerable advances have been made in the scientific analysis of swimming and training mechanisms, particularly during the period that seemed to mark the birth of the so-called information explosion, namely, 1976 to 1981. Yet it is a sobering thought to ask ourselves this cynical question: Why did these advances in swimming times not continue in the 1980s? In fact, the *rate* of progress decreased.

There is very good evidence for the decreased rate of progress. Over the past 70 years, despite the setbacks of two World Wars (when progress in all sports was understandably slowed) there has been a remarkably constant *linear* improvement. This was the case only up to 1976, however, as measured either by Olympic record performances *or* by averaging the top six world times in a number of events.

Obviously, a constant rate of improvement cannot continue indefinitely: For one thing, resistance to movement through water increases

with roughly the *square* of the velocity, making advances difficult beyond proportion to the gain, and for another, if the rate did continue, distances would be swum in *no* time at all. So sooner or later, progress must "flatten out." It really boils down to *when*.

A study of the winning times for the men's and women's 400-meter freestyle at the Olympic Games from 1904 to 1976 shows remarkably consistent improvement in performance of about 3% every 4 years. Only once has the "expected" improvement not taken place, at the 1980 Moscow Olympic Games. It is possible—even likely—that the boycott by some leading swimming nations, particularly the United States, affected the winning times there. The question is by how much? Was this but a "hiccup" in the march of progress? At the 1984 Olympic Games, this time without the Soviet Union or East Germany, the 400-meter freestyle times were again little improved.

Graphing the progression of winning Olympic times leads to some startling conclusions. Extrapolating the trend established between 1948 and 1976, it appears that by about the year 2000 the winning Olympic times for *both* men and women for the 400-meter freestyle will be approximately 3 minutes 10 seconds! In addition, the intersection of the male and female graph lines indicates that the women will have caught up to the men (Figure 9.12).

Probably neither the most positive-thinking and optimistic swimming coach nor the most militant feminist would predict *either* of these—the best women will *not* overtake the best male swimmers even though they have steadily closed the gap since the 1920s, and the time for the men's record will *not* drop to 3 minutes 10 seconds, an average of 47.5 seconds for each 100 meters! If these two judgments are correct, we must come to the inescapable conclusion that either we are already in a pronounced flattening period, as the 1984 winning times indicate, or that this flattening will happen very soon.

The data for the Olympic 400-meter freestyle are perhaps not conclusive evidence of an imminent fall-off in improvement rate, but there is additional statistical evidence of this.

Six male events and five female events that were common to the Olympic years since 1924 were chosen for comparative purposes and the averages taken of improvement or otherwise for these events (Table 9.1). The swims were made at all times of the year. The source of in-

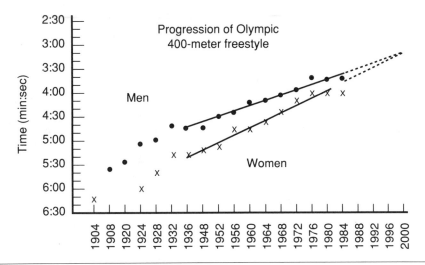

Figure 9.12 Progression of Olympic 400-meter freestyle record.

formation was *Swimming World* magazine, 1964. The Moscow Olympic boycott in 1980 is unlikely to have accounted for any substantial fall-off covering the period 1976 to 1980 because the times considered were made throughout the world at *any* time in the twelve months.

Table 9.1
**Average Improvement
of the Top Six World Times**

	Comparing			
	1964 to 1968	1968 to 1972	1972 to 1976	1976 to 1980
Men	+2.63%	+2.87%	+3.14%	+0.31%
Women	+3.88%	+1.36%	+4.30%	+1.26%

Note. Six men's events and five women's events are considered and the averages shown. The events considered for comparison are men's 100, 400, 1500FS, 100BK, 200BS, 800 teams; women's 100, 400FS, 100BK, 200BS, 400 teams.

The Moscow boycott by some strong Western nations, principally the United States, was not raised until the USSR-Afghanistan situation arose in January 1980. However, to find whether this caused a significant difference to the progress in 1980, progress between 1975 and 1979 was looked at using the same principle of comparison, the best world-class times each

year for the selected events. The improvement averaged 1.24% for males and 2.34% for females, which confirms the conclusion that improvement was less in this 4 years than in any 4 years since 1964; in fact, it was less than half the improvement shown in the 4 years previous to 1975.

Comparing Predicted and Actual 1988 Olympic Winning Times

These predictions were made on the basis of five male and four female times in events contested since the 1924 Olympic Games.

Table 9.2 shows a comparable improvement in line with the linear performance graph already discussed from 1952 to 1964 and from 1964 to 1976. The average improvement from 1964 to 1976 was 8% for men and 8.5% for women. Assuming the same general improvement over the next 12 years, Table 9.3 lists the times that would have been anticipated at Seoul in 1988.

None of these predicted times were even approached at Seoul; in fact, it is likely that they will *never* be attained, with the possible exception of the men's 100-meter freestyle time.

The disparity between the predictions and the actual times appears to reduce to absurdity the proposition that improvement will continue at the pre-1976 rate. There must be a flattening in progress. Because women started only relatively recently to prepare like men, their improvement rate might be expected to fall off rather more slowly than the men's, but the slowing down process seems to be well under way for the women, too.

**Table 9.2
Comparison Over 12 Year Span[a]
of Improvement in Olympic Races**

	Comparing			
	1924 to 1936	1936 to 1952[b]	1952 to 1964	1964 to 1976
Men	+6.4%	+3.0%	+7.2%	+8.0%
Women	+9.1%	+3.3%	+8.6%	+8.5%

[a]Five men's events and four women's events are averaged.
[b]World War II years were excluded.

**Table 9.3
1988 Olympic Performance Projections
From Past Gains in Speed Compared
With Actual Times Recorded
at the 1988 Seoul Olympic Games**

Men's events	Predicted	Actual
100m freestyle	45.99	48.63
400m freestyle	3:33.38	3:46.95
200m breaststroke	2:04.30	2:13.52
100m backstroke	51.05	55.05
1500m freestyle	13:50.21	15:00.4

Women's events	Predicted	Actual
100m freestyle	50.92	54.93
400m freestyle	3:48.85	4:03.85
200m breaststroke	2:20.32	2:26.71
100m backstroke	56.27	1:00.89

Some Conclusions

Forecasting improvement in swimming times is an interesting pastime. Reason alone tells us that it must become ever more difficult to break world records, if only because the increased velocities needed through the relatively dense medium cause a disproportionately increased resistance and consequently require a greatly increased energy production.

There clearly has been a great decrease in rate of improvement since 1976. I have, as it were, played devil's advocate by drawing attention to this flattening out in swimming performance at the top level, and it might be said that the explosion of sport science applications during this same period does not argue strongly for its influence on progress. It is, however, nearly impossible to quantify the effect of various factors affecting swimming progress.

Strenuous and consistent training has been a major factor contributing to the consistent linear improvement for decades, but judging by the rate of "breakdown" in swimmers with very heavy training, we seem to have reached a stage where the answer cannot be to stress swimmers with more work.

A nation can exert a major influence in the level of its top swimmers' performance by the systematic identification of talent from the broadest possible base—the regular swimming of all its young. We know that selecting young swimmers for more intensive and specialized training must be a major concern of any country seeking competitive success internationally. This "search" must surely be most fruitful, however, if it is a spin-off from regular and extensive physical education programs in schools whose primary goal is health and general fitness. *This* is the lesson that East Germany taught us by dominating international competition with its relatively small population.

The involvement of science in swimming should thus be accompanied by a sound governmental philosophy: the provision of swimming as a prominent core in physical education at school having the same status as academic subjects—at least through the first 6 years of primary school. *Then* science in swimming can come into its own.

We are only at the dawn of significant and greatly expanded knowledge, waiting for present and fresh insights to be assimilated and applied universally by coaches. After selecting the best talent, coaches, with the help of science, can continue to add something to the gifted heredity with which some enter the world, extending the limits and making new records possible. (*Note.* Used by permission of Forbes Carlile.)

Physiology and Swimming at the Australian Institute of Sport

Richard D. Telford, PhD, FASMF
Head, Department of Physiology
and Applied Nutrition and
Physiologist, Olympic Swim Team 1984, 1988

Rather than attempt to summarize the vast amount of excellent research applied to swimming, in this section I will describe how one physiology unit operates with a swim team, confining my comments to the work by staff at the Institute of Sport in Canberra, Australia.

The institute's department of physiology and applied nutrition has been working with swim coaches and swimmers for 8 years. The work can be classified into two sections: first, the monitoring of swimmers' responses to training, and second, the projects that attempt to systematically answer questions raised. Before any work is undertaken the question is asked "Does this directly help the swimmer?" If the scientist and coach do not agree that it does the work does not proceed. This ensures that the research is very much "applied" rather than purely academic.

Although I have classified the work into "monitoring" and "projects" it is all research. Even "routine" monitoring of heart rates, lactates, and so on should constitute part of an overall project that attempts to elucidate an aspect of training. For example, heart rates and lactates may be measured to discover what a particular training set is achieving or how a swimmer is responding to a particular training microcycle.

Too often swimmers have been subjected to testing for testing's sake, with time and energy spent determining, say, the strength or power of a swimmer without there being a question to be answered or a hypothesis to prove or disprove. No coach wants to have a swimmer spend time in a laboratory or pool simply to receive a report that the swimmer has, for example, above average strength. If the swimmer is big and an excellent sprinter the coach may already expect above average strength. Instead, the coach wants to know how to get the swimmer to go faster over a given distance. Any measure of, say, strength, must be performed as part of a project which, for example, provides the coach with information about the efficacy of the training program. Does the training improve strength? Is this improvement correlated with improved racing ability? Which individuals responded best and why? Which type of weight training elicited greatest strength gains? Was there a concomitant weight gain? How much was fat? To answer such questions in relation to performance requires careful planning and control.

On the other hand, coaches must be prepared to allow for time and planning by scientists if solid conclusions are to be drawn. Many coaches want answers but are not prepared to modify their training plans to facilitate execution of a controlled project. Projects have been thwarted and much time wasted by coaches reneging on promises to rest up swimmers in preparation for testing at a particular time. I am continually amazed at how difficult it seems to be for some coaches to prepare easy recovery sessions for their swimmers. It's as though it irks their conscience when they record light training. This "training diary syndrome" can be the coach's worst enemy. But aid is available. The following is a review of some of the methods that our department has employed in an attempt to help the coaches.

Laboratory Testing

During the first 2 years of the department's existence, a battery of laboratory tests was used to develop a data base to facilitate future work, particularly in the talent identification area. Regular tests included blood hemotology and biochemistry, 10-second maximal swim bench work and peak power, 60-second swim bench maximal work and blood lactate accumulation, isokinetic strength, heart rate response to submaximal cycle ergometry, vertical jump, and skinfold measures for body fat estimation (Telford, Tumilty, & Damm, 1984; Telford, Tumilty, Kupkee, Woolston, Burton, & Damm, 1984) (Figure 9.13).

There were some important findings. Firstly, it became evident that full blood counts did not seem to explain nor predict the many cases encountered of overtrained or tired swimmers. In many cases, hemoglobin concentrations were lowered although swimmers were training exceptionally well. (I will return to this point when discussing more comprehensive blood testing for nutritional deficiencies.)

The largest gains detected in the 8 months of training studied were in peak power and isokinetic strength. This was particularly true of those who previously had not worked with specific weight training and swim benches. The sprinters always achieved the highest values of power and strength, indicating the relative importance of these characteristics in the short events.

However, the 60-second tests and blood lactates provided perhaps the most enlightening information. During periods of high-volume endurance training, 60-second work capacity and blood lactate accumulation decreased dramatically in most swimmers. This was interpreted as a loss of anaerobic capacity. During the taper period, where volume was reduced and faster training employed, both 60-second work capacity and postexercise lactate accumulation recovered, but several swimmers did not regain their pre-endurance-training anaerobic capacity and consequently did not swim competitively to expectations. We learned that anaerobic energy production must be nurtured to a degree throughout endurance buildup phases and that sufficient time must be allowed to develop anaerobic capacity fully during the precompetitive phases. Of particular interest in this regard is the more recent finding (Telford, Hahn, Catchpole, Parker, et al., 1988; Chatard,

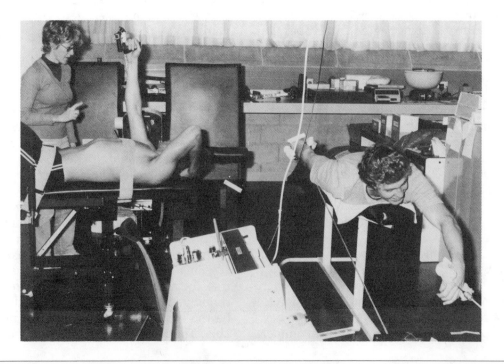

Figure 9.13   Laboratory testing at the Australian Institute of Sport, Canberra.

Paulin, & Lacour, 1988) that the fastest swimmers in most events accumulate the highest blood lactate concentrations. This indicates the extreme importance of anaerobic energy systems in winning races at all distances.

Poolside Testing

Following these laboratory assessments the physiology unit's work moved more toward poolside assessments (Figure 9.14). In recent years we have regularly monitored blood lactate and pH responses to training and competition. Other applications of these measures have been directed at monitoring fitness by way of heart rate and lactate responses to swims of varying intensity.

There is no doubt that the use of lactate and heart rate measures to determine the precise nature of training benefits coaches considerably, but there are questions concerning the validity of the lactate-speed curves in measuring changes in swimming fitness. The reliability of such measures is also questionable, particularly when prior training, diet, and sleep are not (and usually cannot be) well controlled. Furthermore, it is uncertain whether a curve should "shift" toward lesser or greater accumulation of lactate for better performance. Al-though a lesser blood lactate accumulation seems to indicate better aerobic capabilities, aerobic endurance, as previously pointed out, is only part of swimming fitness and probably a minor part in events of 200 meters or less. Perhaps one should aim to decrease lactates at submaximal speeds and increase lactates at maximal effort—but is this possible?

Irrespective of difficulties in interpretations of lactate-velocity curves, monitoring lactates and heart rates during training has contributed much to the program. For example, on many occasions where a coach believed that he or she was directing a "lactate tolerance" set, blood values of considerably less than 5 millimoles indicated that the set was in fact predominantly aerobic. The coach then had the option of resting the swimmer more to achieve a true tolerance session or being satisfied with the mainly aerobic training. Poolside lactate and heart rate measures are also regularly used at the Australian Institute of Sport to ensure that "threshold" sets are just that. During longer all-out steady pace trials over 800 meters to 1,500 meters individual threshold speeds, heart rates, and lactates are measured. This information is then usefully applied to evaluate the validity of sets aimed at threshold intensity. In this way, coaches can use speeds, poolside lactate, and heart rate measures to adjust training either

Figure 9.14   Testing $\dot{V}O_2$max at the Australian Institute of Sport, Canberra.

during the session itself or at least in subsequent sessions.

Helping to Predict Overtraining

Other useful measures are resting electrocardiograph (EKG) values and blood pressure responses to standard exercise. It can be argued that more overall stress is placed on the cardiovascular system of a swimmer than, say, a distance runner, whose training duration and intensity are more limited by weight-bearing stresses. We have extended the work of Carlile and Carlile (1961) in investigating the magnitude of the T waves of the EKG in relation to training fatigue (Telford, Zhang, et al., 1987). This information, together with a record of swimmer's subjective feelings and the coaches' assessments, has been used to modify intensity and volume of training.

Nutrition and the Swimmer

Applied nutrition continues to be an important area of research. As mentioned previously, apart from exceptional circumstances, hemoglobin, packed-cell volume, and red cell concentrations do not appear to provide much indication about a swimmer's current state of adaptation to training. It soon became apparent that iron deficiency without anemia was present in many athletes at the Institute of Sport (Telford, Hahn, & Parker, 1987), and serum ferritin measures by radioimmunoassay soon became part of the regular battery of blood tests. Modification of diet (particularly inclusion of lean red meat) and supplementation of iron (along with other minerals) gradually overcame the problem. In certain nonanemic but iron-deficient individuals the response to iron therapy was very encouraging as training improved considerably within periods as short as a week. Some individuals were prescribed intramuscular iron injections if ferritin did not respond to oral therapy; these injections, however, were only in the order of 0.2 milliliter or 25 milligrams elemental iron and were administered only after appropriate testing for adverse reactions to such a procedure.

It occurred to us that if iron was a potential problem even in those who consumed the recommended dietary allowance (RDA), then a similar problem might be occurring with other minerals or vitamins. Perhaps the many hours of training and study and failure to consume nutritious food consistently was compromising nutritional status, so we set up a 12-month study of the blood vitamin and mineral status in swimmers and other athletes (Telford, Hahn, Catchpole, Plank, et al., 1988; Telford, McLeay, et al., 1988). Blood measures, although not without problems of interpretation, are currently the best method of objectively assessing nutritional status (Sauberlich, Dowdy, & Skala, 1974). In particular, we investigated the effect of a wide spectrum of vitamin and mineral supplementation on nutritional status and performance. Our findings indicate that although the athletes regularly consumed the RDA, many individuals showed unacceptably low vitamin or mineral levels. We also discovered sport-specific as well as sex-specific differences in the mean blood levels of many of the vitamins and minerals. This data base has been used for national team nutritional assessment before important competitions and objective prescription of vitamin and mineral supplementation if necessary.

Special Projects

A final example of a project carried out in response to coaches' questions is our investigation of the effect of alkaline salt ingestion on 200-meter freestyle swimming. In an unpublished report we note a small but significant improvement in 200-meter time using a double-blind crossover study design incorporating a placebo. Although overall race time improved for those who ingested the alkaline drinks, the first 100 meters was slightly slower. The faster final 100 meters for the experimental group was accompanied by a greater blood lactate accumulation following the race.

A current study by the Australian National University biochemistry department investigating the effect of strenuous training on the immune system could lead to further insight into the problems associated with the prediction of overtraining. To date we have shown that chronic endurance training tends to have a depressive effect on the white cells' ability to fight infection. We have also shown that a bout of moderate exercise (60% $\dot{V}O_2$max for 1 hour) tends to prime up the white cells' immune response (Smith, Telford, Hahn, Mason, & Weidemann, 1988; Smith, Telford, Mason, & Weidemann, 1988; Smith, Telford, Mason, &

Weidemann, 1990). It appears, therefore, that the strenuously training swimmer may have a fluctuating immune response to invading pathogens. Our current work suggests that stressful anaerobic swimming may also depress the immune response and adds further support for ensuring that intense anaerobic sessions be carefully positioned in a training program. It seems, then, that monitoring white cell response to stimulation in vitro may also have some application in the early detection of overtraining.

Interestingly, the studies of immunology are closely related to the studies of exercise-induced free radical production in the human body, for the neutrophils themselves, on stimulation, produce their own burst of reactive oxygen species to destroy invading particles. Among others, Demopoulos, Santomier, Seligman, Pietrogro, & Hogan (1986) allude to the potential damaging effect of similar exercise-induced, highly reactive species on our own tissues. The role of antioxidants such as the vitamins E, C, and A seem critical in protecting the strenuously training swimmer. Was it coincidence that we found blood vitamin levels of vitamin E in swimmers often to be significantly lower than other, less active sportspeople? Perhaps this area of study will increase our knowledge of methods of regeneration after strenuous training.

The application of science to swimming is never-ending. There are always questions to pursue, and it becomes increasingly evident that there is much room for improvement in training programs. We still cannot determine the optimal ratios of a swimmer's aerobic, anaerobic, and strength components for a particular event. Even if it is idiosyncratic, we still do not fully understand how to determine the ratios of aerobic, anaerobic, and strength training to achieve that individual's best results. In the future we must also learn more about tailoring training to individual physiology using aerobic and anaerobic stress indicators together with anatomical stress indicators. There is still too much of the "survival of the fittest" approach by coaches who work programs on a group basis even at the elite level, but swimmers who train the hardest are not necessarily the fastest in a "once-off" competition event, especially in the shorter events. Reliable and valid tools for monitoring training adaptation must be further developed, particularly in the elite swimming category. However, the measurement procedures must be such that they do not interfere with optimal training programing, and it is critical that these measures provide information in which the coach can have full confidence.

Increased efficiency in techniques such as nuclear magnetic resonance (NMR), echocardiographs, bone scans and bone density estimations, and blood and tissue micronutrient analysis will enable some of these to become rapid routine monitors of swimming fitness adaptation. The optimization of blood cellular components, blood volume, and viscosity by training and environmental and dietary manipulation may offer a chance for further progress in the record book.

Some advances in medical science will inevitably be applied to improving human performance. Nevertheless, it will be a sad day when genetic engineering is used to produce a "super swimmer"; it is similarly sad that many athletes are currently willing to risk their health with illegal performance-enhancing pharmacological agents. In any case, it stands to reason that there will be a natural tendency toward improvement in the potential for humans to swim faster as the human population continues to increase and pairs of talented athletes themselves produce offspring—a common occurrence these days. Nevertheless, the vast amount of science and coaching energy being applied to the modern swimmer clearly shows that although exceptional inherited talent is required for international success, it is simply the beginning prerequisite. (Note. Used by permission of Richard D. Telford.)

PART IV

THE HUMAN DYNAMIC

The phenomenal progress of competitive swimming in the 20th century owes much to modern technology. Swimming pools designed for speed with wave-reducing lane markers significantly improved standards. In many parts of the world, designing a beautiful and practical modern swimming stadium became an advanced art. The Speedo company of Australia pioneered form-fitting racing swimwear that reduced the drag resistance around a swimmer's body. And streamlined swimming goggles eliminated the often painful eye irritation caused by chlorine, enabling swimmers to increase greatly the amount of training time they could spend in the water.

In the early part of the century a long sea voyage was necessary for swimmers to compete in major overseas meets, but the advent of air transportation, especially jet travel, increased the frequency of international competitions. Rapid communications, television, and other mass media spread technical knowledge around the world and popularized swimming

to the extent that by midcentury countries with no previous record of success were producing world-class swimmers.

In 1952 the start of a formal age group program in the United States led to similar programs in many other countries, causing a dramatic world-wide surge in participation. Competitive swimming now annually attracted thousands of children generally too young to be recruited by other sports. Important incentives included fun, challenge, travel, athletic scholarships, and public recognition. Because of the youth of the participants, swimming became a family activity. Many parents gave valuable support by assisting with club administration.

Why the steady and unwavering improvement in performance? First, the catchment area for attracting athletic talent had become far greater. The 285 participants in the 1896 Olympics were drawn from 50,000 athletes in training; the 10,000 participants at the 1964 Tokyo Olympics represented 100 million possible competitors (Smith, 1968). The XXIV Olympic Games at Seoul, 1988, proved to be the largest ever with 13,626 participants from 160 countries. Chinese swimmers, competing in their first Olympics at Seoul, reached several finals and served notice that China could well achieve a rapid rise to world prominence even before the end of the 20th century.

The Development of Multilevel National Programs

The growth of the sport and the desire to excel led to the development of multilevel national programs and the employment of professional administrators, often university-trained in sport leadership. Assisting these professionals were prominent people in commerce, industry, and the professions, who were termed "lay volunteers." In the more advanced countries, the better-organized lay volunteers, contributing their expertise and guidance, supplanted the old part-time "amateur" hobbyist. In a sense, the administration of swimming was taken off the kitchen table and into the board room.

In some countries, competitive swimming, like all sports, was organized and centrally controlled by the state. Elsewhere, governments directly involved in funding national programs tried to give an impression of "remaining at arm's length," but often it was apparent that who paid the piper called the tune. When opening the IOC's 94th session at the Seoul Olympics, its president, Juan Antonio Samaranch, saw fit to plead with governments to "respect the independence of the national Olympic committees."

The Role of Science

Scientific research assisted some programs despite a tendency to cause confusion through "information overload" and lack of simple communication. Most research, however, had little or no use in actual practice because its primary aim generally was not to help swimmers go faster. Where coach and scientist cooperated at training venue and competition site, however, more positive results were achieved; this approach gradually becoming common in several countries.

Most technical improvement, however, continued to result from practical coaches and talented athletes learning through trial and error.

It became clear from past achievements that when the need was imperative progress could not wait for the development of theory. More often than not, the search for theory was inspired by practical success.

Continuing improvements were implemented by coaches who were inspirational and innovative leaders and often natural practical psychologists. They encouraged their swimmers to believe that there were no limits to improvement and that limits were yet to be found. This intrinsic quality—the striving by the human spirit to excel, to surpass previous achievements, and to seek new horizons—has been the most important factor in the remarkable progress of the sport.

The Information Explosion

After James Counsilman's innovative work revolutionized the technical approach to swimming and showed how science, *useful science*, could be beneficially applied, a spate of scientific papers followed from a variety of sources. Novice coaches apparently were dazzled by the volume of scientific "results" and "evidence" placed before them. They didn't realize that most research is a progress report rather than a conclusion. Perhaps the classic quote of the 20th century on the subject of the "information explosion" came from a Canadian coach, Alain Lefebvre: "Years ago there was a desert of information. Now it is a jungle. The question is how to get through it" (Young, 1990).

The Need for Motivators and Innovators

Many beginning coaches really didn't know how to start coaching, what information to accept as appropriate and what to discard as inappropriate. They came to expect more from science than science was capable of providing. In the late 20th century young coaches have grown up in the sport expecting that science should supply them with all the answers instead of trying to become more competent and self-sufficient by testing new ideas as part of their daily practical coaching.

As competitive swimming reaches the doorstep of the 21st century some penetrating questions are being asked. Have modern coaches been caught between two approaches, the pool-deck empirical and the scientific? Have modern coaches lost the ability to innovate? Do young coaches in particular rely too much on the scientific research papers and not enough on developing their own ability to innovate?

A trust in science does not imply the abandonment of hunch and intuition. On the contrary, the history of science itself is studded with cases of important discoveries made through chance, hunch, serendipity—even dreams. Most coaches who use their hunches well also seem to possess a high level of knowledge and understanding about their activities. So the question is not when to apply science and when to rely on intuition, but rather how to *combine* them effectively.

The history of swimming has shown time and again that the leadership of capable and inspired coaches can help a country consistently produce elite swimming teams despite a mediocre or even self-serving administration at the helm. In any country the future starts with the coaches—not administrators, not scientists, but inspirational coaches working with talented swimmers. This is the first essential: The future starts on the pool deck. Only after this come the administrators who plan the programs and the possible assistance that science can provide. The future of swimming depends on the coaches.

Chapter 10

The Growth of the National Program Concept

It is a surprising fact that swimming has been an organized sport in Japanese schools since *A.D.* 1603 as a result of an Imperial edict issued in that year and the Japanese interschool competitive swimming program has continued to the present time (Oppenheim, 1970). But Japan's early start did not influence other countries to follow suit, probably because of the isolated nature of Japanese culture for many centuries.

Although a giant 3-day swim meet was staged in Japan in 1810, competitive swimming was not placed on a regular organized basis until more than 20 years later. In 1837, under the leadership of one John Strachan, a body called the National Swimming Association conducted swimming races in London, England (Oppenheim, 1970).

Continuing this trend, the first modern championship race was held in Sydney, Australia, at the Robinson Baths. The race was over 440 yards and was won by W. Redmond in 8 minutes 43.0 seconds. The first attempt to stage a "world championship" race was at St. Kilda, a southern suburb of Melbourne, Australia, on February 9, 1858. Joe Bennett of Sydney scored the victory over the Englishman Charles Stedman (Oppenheim, 1970).

Designing the First Rules

On January 7, 1869, competitive swimming was first placed on a properly organized basis as a result of a meeting at the German Gymnasium in London, where a group of representatives from various London swimming clubs met to design rules for the conduct of the sport.

The Metropolitan Swimming Club Association was formed at this meeting, and adopted a motion by one of its members, W. Ramsden, to establish rules of competition. A month later, on February 11, 1869, the club drew up a definition of amateurism and agreed on rules for conducting swimming races. Prior to this, amateurs and professionals competed together, and many swimmers accepted cash prizes. Within 5 years, in 1874, this London group became a national association known as the Swimming Association of Great Britain, the first such national governing body of swimming in the world (Oppenheim, 1970).

On the European continent swimming gradually grew in popularity, with the Erste Wiener Swimming Club of Vienna organizing so-called European Championships. These "European Championships" were held annually until 1903, when they were discontinued. It was not until 1926 that the European Championships were organized in their present form.

Around 1900 so-called World Championships were held. The first Olympic swimming events were those staged at the first modern Olympics in Athens, 1896, in open water at Zea near the Piraeus (Oppenheim, 1970).

As we have seen, competitive swimming was placed on an organized basis only in 1869; as such, it is a comparatively young sport. It is difficult to imagine competition without regulation-size pools, standardized racing distances, and precise time measurements, yet these were the challenges facing the organizers of the first swimming competitions.

Races were held in courses ranging from canal locks, rivers, and local ponds to swimming ''baths'' of assorted sizes. Swimmers competed wherever there was a suitable stretch of water, and the length of the race was governed by the size of the course. The variations in the racing distance affected even the swimming events at the Olympics in Athens, Paris, and St. Louis and made a uniform list of records impossible.

Early references suggest that the typical contest was a match or challenge race between two or more contestants, more often than not for a money purse collected by the spectators. Races were not timed for the simple reason that the stopwatch had not yet been invented.

The stopwatch was a cheaper version of the chronograph developed by E.D. Johnson in 1855; it was not until a few years later that an affordable stopwatch became generally available for timing sporting events. According to records, the first timed swimming race was the English 1-mile championship of 1869 swum in the River Thames from Putney Aquaduct to Hammersmith Bridge. As far as can be ascertained, the winner of that event, T. Morris, was the first champion ever to be timed (27 minutes 18 seconds).

Official lists of records were soon published. The first official swimming record belonged to Winston Cole, who in 1871 swam 100 yards in 1 minute 15 seconds, this time being ratified by the recently formed Metropolitan Swimming Club Association.

The stopwatch was to swimming what the wheel was to civilization. Greater emphasis was placed on speed and not only who placed first, second, or third. The efficiency of the evolving speed strokes—overarm sidestroke and crawl—could be tested more accurately and scientifically. An additional benefit was the possibility of comparing performances produced in different towns and even countries, provided that they were recorded over the same distances and in the same size pools.

The need for standardized racing distances grew, but it was a long time before authorities constructed pools of standard dimensions to ensure uniform racing conditions. Even when these facilities were built, architects frequently failed to consult with the potential users, resulting in the omission of features necessary for competitive swimming.

The New Laws of Amateurism

The industrial revolution in the mid-18th century and Thomas Arnold's introduction of sports as regular extracurricular activity in English public schools spurred a great development of sports during the Victorian age. This athletic revival of the 19th century led to the restoration of the Olympic Games at Athens in 1896. It also brought with it the revival of what was said to be ''the classical ideal of amateurism.''

For the first 17 years of its existence, the Amateur Swimming Association of Great Britain was preoccupied with establishing a definition of an amateur which could be open to no variant interpretations. For a time the future of the Amateur Swimming Association (A.S.A.) was in jeopardy because, for often profitable reasons, not everyone wanted to be an amateur. It was only when its membership had spread sufficiently that the A.S.A. finally had the power to enforce its amateur laws. This caused much friction between the predominantly amateur southern counties and the north of England, where there had been laxity in the matter of mixed races for money and other prizes.

It was not surprising that the northerners rose to combat the inroads—in the form of suspensions—made by the interfering southerners. On their side, the southerners had felt for some time that their movement to purify the sport merited the support of the northern and midland swimmers. Enforcing the amateur definition throughout the country was an extensive and often wearisome undertaking, especially as many local corporations held out the temptations of money and value prizes at their ''regattas.''

The A.S.A. eventually won the day, but not before such fine swimmers as T. Cairns, J. Nuttall, W. Evans, S.W. Greasely, J.H. Tyers, and D. Billington had been declared professionals. Among them they had shared most of the championships from 100 yards to 1 mile. Although their departure from the amateur ranks was hailed as indicating the existing spirit in favor of amateurism, the wisdom of hindsight leaves one wondering whether the zeal of those who strove to establish *their* ideal of amateur sport was not misplaced. To what extent did the exclusion of such talented and prominent swimmers retard the development of competitive swimming in England?

The Myth of Amateurism

In recent years the supposed ancient Greek origin of amateur sport has come to be seriously questioned. At the University of California at Santa Barbara, classics professor David C. Young published a study (1984) that threw much light on this hitherto sacrosanct subject. ("The Olympic Myth of Greek Amateur Athletics"; D.C. Young, Aries Press, Chicago, 1984.)

Another professor of classics, Trevor Hodge of Carleton University in Ottawa, Canada, published an article in *The Ottawa Citizen* (1988) entitled "The Ancient Olympics: A Run for the Money," in which he summarizes and comments on Young's revealing book.

> The whole concept of amateur sport is entirely a late Victorian invention, and began around 1870. No ancient Greek could have even understood the idea, so foreign was it to antiquity and the ancient Olympics. It did not exist in Britain or America either, where cash prizes and betting were, before 1870, a regular feature of sporting events.
>
> But the money aspect is in fact a red herring. The distinction between amateur and professional was in reality a reflection of something else. The real distinction was between gentlemen and the working classes. An "amateur" was really a Victorian upper class English gentleman, who sometimes dabbled a little in sport on the side, and the professional was the socially inferior son-of-toil, who was in it for the money.
>
> But the gentleman amateur was caught in a cruel dilemma. The axiom was that he could always beat a working man, because his breeding made him innately superior. This meant not only [that] the gentleman would win, but could do it without really trying.
>
> The only escape for a gentleman facing a working class opponent he couldn't beat was to rule him out altogether. Thus was born the amateur/professional distinction (which had not existed before), and it was into this atmosphere that the modern Olympics were born.
>
> And what of the money? Let it be clearly understood, there was no monetary prize in the ancient Olympics, any more than today. But this did not mean that there was no money in winning. Athletes were honored by the cities they represented, and at rates of pay we now associate only with rock stars and pop groups. (p. B3)

(The preceding is quoted directly from Hodge's article, reprinted here with permission, but anyone interested in the origins of amateur sport is encouraged to read Young's book for a more complete account.)

Swimming Baths

In 1846, a bill "Promoting the Establishment of Baths and Wash-houses for the labouring classes" passed the British parliament. The term "bath" referred not only to a bathroom fixture for performing ablutions (known in North America as a "tub") but also to a swimming pool. To further confuse the issue, the term "baths" or "bath house" also applied to establishments containing both public baths in which to wash and "swimming baths" where people enjoyed themselves by swimming after they had taken a bath.

Even after most homes contained their own bathrooms the term "swimming bath" remained in vogue to describe a place for swimming and spread with emigration to several countries of the then British Empire, where it is often used to this day.

The first public bath in England was erected by the Corporation of Liverpool in 1828; subsequently, there was a steady increase in the number of baths built in London, Manchester, Liverpool, and other important towns. One of the main objectives of the A.S.A. was to stimulate public opinion in favor of building swimming pools. The A.S.A. published a list of 800 "bathing places" that existed in 460 towns. Of these, almost 600 contained swimming baths. According to Sachs (1912), although a large number of baths were built, most of them were "totally inadequate" for the purpose of competitive swimming.

Criticisms included irregular pool dimensions, impractical and inconvenient location of spectator and dressing room space, inadequate facilities for the growing number of female swimmers, uncomfortable water temperature, and lack of lane lines on the floor of the pool. An uninterrupted view could rarely be obtained "without fear of splashings and drenchings'' (Sachs, 1912, p. 242). Dirt and grit were carried into the baths by people wearing muddy boots. The entrance was often a large door opening directly onto the pool deck through which icy blasts caused swimmers extreme discomfort.

Competitive swimming in its present form largely resulted from the evolution of the artificial environment of the measured pool. The modern swimming complex is a far cry from the first public bath halls and washing houses or even the first public swimming baths, divided as they were according to social class and sex and built in a diversity of sizes. At the international level, it was to be a long time before competitions were held over standard distances. Some 28 years passed after the revival of the Olympic Games at Athens in 1896 before the Olympic swimming events were conducted in the 50-meter course we know today.

Early Promotion of Swimming

In the Victorian period swimming was encouraged in most English public schools. Although a growing appreciation existed of the health benefits of the sport, the main consideration was that of safety. Death from drowning was common because most of the population could not swim.

The Royal Life Saving Society encouraged the teaching of swimming because it viewed swimming as a way to save life, which it held should be the main objective of the activity. It promoted competitive swimming because the speed and endurance developed by racing would enable a rescuer to reach a drowning person quickly. The ability to swim quickly was encouraged by holding school ''swimming sports'' at set periods of the year.

The first promoters of swimming realized that the future of the sport depended on introducing swimming to school children. Reports of the time suggest a certain social tinge to the developing structure of the sport; ''the records of the Public Schools gives assurance that the future at any rate of one class of Englishmen as swimmers is secure'' (Sachs, 1912, p. 39). Not all parents encouraged their children to swim; many withheld permission because of superstition concerning imagined ill effects of prolonged immersion and physical strain, and the risk of contracting disease from water. Ac-

cording to Brasch (1970), as late as 1880 a rhyme of unknown authorship was popularly quoted:

> Mother, may I go out to swim?
> Yes, my darling daughter;
> Hang your clothes on a hickory limb,
> But don't go near the water.

This common fear of swimming prompted the Southern Counties Branch of the A.S.A. to publish a small pamphlet entitled ''Can You Swim?'' containing articles by eminent doctors on the benefits of swimming.

The Growth of International Swimming

After January 7, 1869, when competitive swimming was first placed on an organized basis at a meeting in the German Gymnasium in London, England, the sport spread gradually to other countries. Initially, the two big centers were England and Australia, and it is interesting to note the influence of the one on the other, even though separated by thousands of miles.

Each new country to adopt competitive swimming inevitably followed the constitutional formula designed by the officials of English swimming. They also applied the definition of amateurism which was apparently based in large measure not on altruism but on the prevailing class-consciousness in Great Britain.

The Birth of F.I.N.A., the International Governing Body of Swimming

With the rebirth of the Olympic movement, it became clear that universally accepted rules would be necessary if Olympic competition was to be conducted on a consistent and equable basis. In 1908, at the Olympic Games in London, George Hearn, president of the English Swimming Association, was asked to establish an Olympic Swimming Code. Assisted in his deliberations by the Englishman William Henry, Max Ritter (U.S.A.), and Hjalmar Johnson (Sweden), Hearn realized that a more farsighted policy would be to establish rules that could be applied on a permanent basis and not only for the Olympic Games.

To achieve this, Hearn decided to use the opportunity to form an international swimming association. Because representatives from ten nations (England, Germany, Denmark, Sweden, France, Ireland, Finland, Hungary, Belgium, and Wales) were participating in the Olympic meeting in London, George Hearn called a meeting to set up an international governing body of swimming with a set body of laws. On July 19, 1908, at the Manchester Hotel in London, F.I.N.A. (Federation Internationale de Natation Amateur) was formed; the swimming code of F.I.N.A. was based on the model of the English Amateur Swimming Association.

Discrimination Against Career Coaches

Although F.I.N.A. stipulated only who could and who could not *compete* as an amateur, particularly in Great Britain and other countries of the former British Empire, the amateur laws were applied in such a way as to exclude paid coaches and instructors from official positions within the governing bodies of swimming. In fact, until quite recently, paid coaches were often treated in many countries as pariahs and "lesser breeds without the law." "Professional coaches," as they were quaintly termed, were excluded from the governing bodies of the sport and from official coaching assignments with international teams, despite the fact that much of the progress in the sport and the development of leading swimmers was directly attributable to their efforts. It is to the credit of many of these coaches that, throughout their careers, they nearly always traveled to national and international meets at their own expense to assist their swimmers.

In some countries, discrimination against career coaches to some extent must have had a retarding effect on the development of swimming, especially when compared with the giant strides made in the United States, where career coaches were officially recognized as a welcome and integral part of the swimming organization. A particularly significant example of this was the appointment of the dynamic Ray Essick, a leading coach, to the position of Executive Director of United States Swimming, Inc.

Competitive Swimming in the 20th Century

The dominant nations in world swimming in the 20th century have been the United States, East Germany, Australia, Japan, Hungary, and Holland. Other occasionally successful nations were Germany (up to 1939), the Soviet Union, Great Britain, Denmark, France, Sweden, West Germany, and South Africa.

In the 1960s the United States accumulated 80 individual medals at the three Olympic Games (Rome, 1960; Tokyo, 1964; and Mexico City, 1968); other nations claimed the remaining 61 medals (Thierry, 1972). At the Montreal Olympics in 1976 the U.S. men's team under head coach James Counsilman won 12 of 13 gold medals, the first time in Olympic swimming history that this had been accomplished.

Throughout the years, by personal contacts and lecture clinic visits, swimming coaches in the United States and Australia readily made their experience and expertise available to all countries, irrespective of their forms of government or political affiliations, solely for the general benefit of the sport. In particular, the American Swimming Coaches Association (A.S.C.A.) for more than a quarter century provided leadership and coaching education not only in the United States but also worldwide by conducting its well-attended annual World Swim Clinics and making membership open to coaches from all countries. In any given year, about 10% of the coaches attending the A.S.C.A. Annual World Clinic were not U.S. citizens. Similarly, in any given year, foreign membership of A.S.C.A. numbered about 350 coaches, mainly from Europe and the undeveloped countries.

Swimming Publications

Swimming World magazine (published by Richard Deal and edited by Robert Ingram) has been an important influence in spreading swimming information internationally. It was founded by Bob Kiphuth and Peter Daland at Yale University in 1952 as a mimeographed newsletter and was later developed into a fullfledged magazine by Albert Schoenfield with the assistance of his indefatigable wife, Faye. Schoenfield, a swimming parent and advertising executive, made the magazine his life's mission and was inducted into the International Swimming Hall of Fame in 1983 in recognition of his great contribution to international swimming.

Swimming World has appeared as a monthly magazine for the past 28 years. Together with *Swimming Technique* (edited by Brady Bingham and Brent T. Rutemiller), which is published by the same house, it has been a vital agent in the continuing international dissemination of technical knowledge on swimming. In the mid-1980s, two periodicals published by the American Swimming Coaches' Association became valuable technical resources: *The American Swimming Coaches' Association Magazine*, founded by the late Keith Sutton and now edited by A.S.C.A.'s dynamic Executive Director, John Leonard, and the *Journal of Swimming Research*, founded by the late Keith Sutton and first editor Mary F. Sutton and currently edited by Rick L. Sharp.

Other swimming magazines of note in the English-speaking world are the British *Swimming Times*, the world's oldest swimming magazine, founded in 1923 by its first editor, Capt. B.W. Cummins, now edited by Karren T. Glendenning; the Australian *International Swimmer*, published by Speedo Racing Swimwear, founded in 1963 by its first editor, John Devitt, 1960 Olympic 100-meter freestyle champion, present editor Paul Moorfoot; and the Canadian *Swim Canada*, founded in 1974 by its publisher and editor, Nick Thierry, probably the world's foremost swimming statistician.

Swimming Knowledge Circles the Globe

After the 1960 Olympic Games in Rome it was apparent that technical knowledge on swimming had spread worldwide, with the result that international champions could now be expected to come from almost any country. The dramatic rise of the East German swimmers strongly proved the point, and such countries as Romania, Yugoslavia, France, Brazil, Spain, Mexico, West Germany, Switzerland, and the Soviet Union showed that no one nation owned swimming expertise.

Different Types of National Program Structures

The history of competitive swimming in the 20th century shows that great swimmers can be produced in a variety of programs ranging from those with little if any sponsorship by government or the private sector to highly organized national systems, underwritten, designed and controlled in their entirety by the full authority of the state.

It was not unusual for most planners of national programs to speak about building a *pyramid* with a broad base that gradually tapers to the pinnacle from which the nation's talented

and future elite athletes would emerge. In this respect the "superpower" nations with their colossal populations theoretically should possess an insurmountable advantage over smaller nations.

However, the consistent successes of the East German swimmers showed there to be other approaches to national development that could even the odds. Vanek (1971) presents several variations of national organizational structures that can be used to develop top athletes. His ideas are predicated on the necessity of first evaluating the conditions, talent, and resources in a particular country before deciding on the most suitable format for that country.

Vanek outlines four different types of pyramids (Figure 10.1) that can form the basic developmental structures for developing champion athletes.

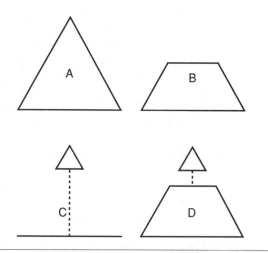

Figure 10.1 Vanek's four pyramids of development. *Note.* From Vanek (1971, p. 255). Reprinted by permission.

1. *Pyramid A* represents the typical pyramid previously mentioned, in which there is some relationship between the many average performances at the base and the superior ones at the top. Selection is through a tough competitive system and a long, hard climb to the top. This used to be the situation in American swimming, especially in California; this was also the pyramid of Swedish cross-country skiing. Vanek whimsically suggests this to be a system of natural selection that perhaps does not need amenities such as coaches and psychologists.

2. *Pyramid B* represents natural selection without the elite emerging at the top as seen in Pyramid A. This situation has occurred in many

countries where there has been little desire to achieve excellence and no great motivation or national plan that offered well-organized competition as well as fine coaching and training. According to Vanek, there should be a "whipping up" of the milk at the base to create the cream at the top.

3. *Pyramid C* has no base of many competitions and facilities as in A or B but concentrates on developing a few talented athletes. Vanek says that the cream is selected first and made into very good cream. This was how they produced high-tower divers in his native Czechoslovakia. There were few divers, no special diving pools, and no base of average divers—yet they produced gold medals in international competition, including the Olympics.

4. *Pyramid D* has a broad base of competition but is not merely a natural selection system coming through a refining system, because when the cream rises to the top it is given extra special treatment. The best emerge from the base of the pyramid and are given special attention, which includes analysis of individual needs and an intense scientific approach with the aim of developing the athlete to top international caliber. This was the East German system. In a sense, this is a "dictatorial" approach, with five or six people at the top given the responsibility for achieving results with adequate funding, all facilities provided, and a power structure to develop coaches and scientific support staff.

Four countries—Australia, the United States, Japan, and the former East Germany—established a particularly fine tradition of success in international swimming, each in turn rising to pre-eminence at various times during the 20th century. Although their individual programs have had distinct and characteristic differences from one another, each country has contributed to the growing concept of building a nation's swimming strength by means of a definite preconceived plan. It is appropriate to examine the contributions made by each of these four countries.

Swimming in Australia

Forbes Carlile, MBE, MSc
Head Coach of the Carlile Swim Club
and Consultant in Sport Science, Australian Institute of Sport

Although there was swimming in Sydney harbor from the time the First Fleet arrived in 1788, the first pool was built in 1879 by "Professor" Fred Cavill when he immigrated from England. Cavill, the father of six famous swimming sons and three daughters (including the first great crawl exponent, Richmond "Dick" Cavill) built a "swimming bath" in Sydney harbor at Rushcutters Bay. He later built another pool at Lavender Bay, which was near the site of the present North Sydney pool, scene of many world-record swims. Cavill's pool at Lavender Bay was a famous landmark in swimming history until its demolition in the early 1940s.

There are, however, counterclaims that Melbourne, the site of the 1956 Olympic Games, had the earliest swimming pool and swimming club in Australia, namely the Emerald Hill Baths, where the club was said to have conducted its first carnival on March 3, 1877.

The First Golden Age of Australian Swimming

The first regular championships were held in Australia in 1889. Championships held during this era produced world-record holders and leaders in swimming such as Dick Cavill, Barney

Kieran, and Freddy Lane. Later, the early 20th century saw such swimmers emerge as Cecil Healy, Frank Beaurepaire, and Fanny Durack.

The first golden age of Australian swimming covered the period from the start of the century to World War I. Swimmers such as F.C.V. Lane, Dick Cavill, Barney Kieran, Frank Beaurepaire, and Cecil Healy were prominent in the world-record books. Cecil Healy was renowned as a great stroke innovator, writer, and student of swimming; Fanny Durack and Mona Wylie were the top women swimmers of their era and first and second at the 1912 Stockholm Olympics.

The great Australian distance swimmer, Andrew "Boy" Charlton, won the 1,500-meter race in Paris in 1924. Although 16-year-old Clare Dennis won the 1932 Olympic breaststroke championship at Los Angeles, Australian swimming went into partial eclipse during the 1930s.

At the 1948 London Olympic Games Judy Joy Davies, Nancy Lyons, and John Marshall won medals. Training in the United States at Yale University in the early 1950s, Marshall set scores of world records at all distances from 200 to 1,500 meters. At the Helsinki Olympics in 1952, John Davies, who had trained at Michigan University, won a solitary medal for Australia, the gold in the 200-meter breaststroke, swimming the old "butterfly-breaststroke," which consisted of the butterfly arm action combined with the breaststroke kick.

The Rise of Australia in 1956

Australia's winning bid to conduct the 1956 Olympic Games in Melbourne proved to be the impetus for the second golden age of Australian swimming.

The Australian revival surprised the swimming world: Australia won eight gold medals for swimming at the Melbourne Olympics and provoked a great worldwide interest in how it had been able to do so well again after so many years in the doldrums.

There were probably a number of reasons.

Swimming Out of Season. First of all, the Australian swimmers were competing before home crowds and they were prepared systematically and well. Further, the Americans, who had won the lion's share of swimming medals in 1948 and 1952, were caught out of season with the games set for November in the Southern Hemisphere.

The young Australians who swam so well were almost all the result of an extensive club system with large numbers of competing young swimmers. This type of club system was then in its very early stage of development in the United States.

Shaving Down. Another important factor was that probably for the first time an international team of male swimmers shaved down. The Australians had experimented with ways of decreasing skin resistance, and shaving off body hair seemed an obvious procedure.

Swimming Techniques. We know with retrospect that the Australians swam with better crawl stroke and backstroke techniques than their rivals—underwater films clearly indicate this. Their arm recoveries were the high-elbow "boomerang-shaped" type in the crawl and, more importantly, their arms pulled through the water with a bent-elbow pull in an S-shaped path. In this they contrasted with most of their rivals, particularly the Americans, who obviously had been taught to make long levers by keeping their arms straight.

The techniques of such swimmers as Murray Rose, Dawn Fraser, Jon Henricks, and backstroker David Theile, winner of the 100-meter backstroke in 1956 and 1960, would still look efficient today. John Devitt, however, who was second in the 100-meter freestyle in Melbourne and won the Olympic title in this event at Rome in 1960, swam with an unorthodox high-revving stroke that nevertheless was recognized as being highly efficient for his individual physique. Devitt, with typical whimsy, claimed to have "perfected an imperfect stroke."

Interval Training. The Australians in the early 1950s were probably the first swimmers to adopt the principle of *interval training* originally used by European runners. They used it in nearly every training session. It was really quite simple; they often did a mile of 50s, starting each 50-meter swim every 60, 45, or even every 40 seconds.

Frank Guthrie was the Australian coach who introduced this sort of interval training, that is, miles of repeat 50s with short and longer rest periods. His outstanding pupil of that era was Lorraine Crappe, the first female to break 5 minutes for 400 meters and the winner of this event at the Melbourne Olympics as well as a very close second to Dawn Fraser in the 100 meters.

The 1956 Olympic champions trained only about half as much each day as top swimmers of the 1980s and they also swam at a much lower intensity. They trained no more than 6 months in an "off year" when there was no scheduled international competition; when preparing for the Olympic or Commonwealth Games they trained for about 8 months of the year.

Administration. The administration of Australian swimming remained much the same from 1909 to 1983, resisting all efforts for change in its monolithic national organization. It permitted several state delegates to control and resist progressive ideas as well as choke the emergence of "new blood" in the Amateur Swimming Union of Australia (A.S.U. of A.). It is a matter of speculation as to the extent to which maladministration and lack of vision over the years contributed toward the steady drop in Australian standards since the brilliant successes in 1956. In August 1985 the newly constituted Australian Swimming Incorporated, masterminded by Peter Bowen-Pain, replaced the old Amateur Swimming Union of Australia. Professional coaches were at last granted the opportunities to make significant input into the administration and planning of Australian swimming.

Coaches. The first breakthrough for profes-sional coaches came in 1956, when four professionals—Harry Gallagher, Frank Guthrie, Sam Herford, and I—were appointed to coach the Australian team at Townsville in tropical Queensland during its 12-week preparation for the Melbourne Olympics, but it was not until the 1964 Olympics that Australian professional coaches were officially appointed to an Olympic team, namely, Don Talbot and Terry Gathercole as men's and women's coaches, respectively. The most successful coach produced by Australia was Don Talbot, who has been head coach in both Australia and Canada.

Brisbane coaches Joe King and Laurie Lawrence were highly successful coaches in the 1970s and 1980s. Lawrence, a master motivator, produced such swimmers as world champion Steve Holland (1973) and Olympic champions Jon Sieben (1984) and Duncan Armstrong (1988). Bill Sweetenham, head coach of the Australian Institute of Sport and the 1988 Olympic team, was responsible for bringing Australian swimming back into the modern international scene. He coached such outstanding Australian swimmers and world-record breakers as Tracy Wickham and Steve Holland. In the late 1980s Sweetenham said that Australia still had a long way to go to recapture her past glories. *Note.* Used by permission of Forbes Carlile.

The Australian Institute of Sport (A.I.S.): An Example of State Support in the Western World

The greater part of the 1970s saw a rapid decline in Australian swimming. In fact, Australia's poor performance in the 1976 Montreal Olympics finally brought home to the Australian authorities the need for drastic action to remedy the situation. They realized that it would take more than talented swimmers to bring their country back into the Olympic spotlight. On Australia Day, January 26, 1980, the federal government established the Australian Institute of Sport in Canberra to provide first-class coaching and training facilities for athletes (Schoenfield, 1987).

The athletes at the institute receive scholarships that may include board, educational allowance, training and competition clothing and equipment, coaching, and domestic and international travel and competition, plus the support services provided by sport science and medicine. The Australians knew they had a lot of catching up to do, and the $100 million institute has now become the world's best training facility.

Apart from its mind-boggling facilities for other sports, the institute's features include an ultramodern complex with a 50-meter Olympic-size pool that can be divided into two 25-meter pools for water polo, a 25-meter training pool, and a complete diving well. There is ample spectator seating, lighting, an electronic scoreboard, and an excellent PA system. One of the most outstanding features of the institute is the two-story Sports Science and Medicine Center, which accommodates the sciences of physiology, biochemistry, biomechanics, and psychology and possesses unique, state-of-the-art equipment.

Money seems to be no obstacle; funding for the institute is $11 million per year administration costs and $2.2 million per year to run the facilities. A sum of $100 million has been spent on capital works and equipment. The federal government provides 95% of this funding and 5% comes from commercial sponsorship.

How the A.I.S. Operates

In May, 1987, I was a guest of the Australian Institute of Sport, where I spent several days observing the program in action. I discussed the program with the institute's head swimming coach, Bill Sweetenham. Sweetenham, who was also head coach of Australia for the Seoul Olympics in 1988, said:

The program is not designed to be the savior of Australian swimming but to supplement, complement and support existing programs and encourage Australian senior athletes to continue swimming while pursuing their long-term career goals.

The advantage we have over the American collegiate system is that we can take young *or* older swimmers into our program at the Institute. We have a policy that we don't recruit or accept people into our program who are younger than seventeen. However, in the case of a swimmer from a very backward or remote area where the coach is very supportive of the swimmer coming in, we provide them with the opportunity of visiting the Institute for short periods at a time, be it for one week or three weeks and even on a full-time basis.

Basically, we have 37 full-time scholarships. Each scholarship-holder receives a full study grant, all educational costs, free coaching, free food, housing, about $1,000 to $1,500 worth of training equipment, free medical services. Injuries are treated immediately. Five or six full-time masseurs or trainers are in attendance and about the same number of physiotherapists, biomechanists filming at our request whenever we need their services for in-depth stroke analysis . . . and individual as well as team work with the psychologists.

Swimmers on full-scholarships come into the program for the academic year. In Australia that ranges from after the national championships, the last week in February, through to the end of November. Sometimes, for those who are working, we send them home after the winter nationals which are usually held in early September.

We continue to support the swimmer in the home program even while they are not attending the Institute. If the swimmer and coach feel that additional competition is needed then this is provided. In 1986 we had, apart from 37 full-time scholarships, 270 visiting scholarship holders, people who had been in for more than one week, and we had 66 visiting coaches who were here for more than one week.

Sport Science Testing Performed at the A.I.S.

On arrival at the institute all swimmers receive a full medical examination; immediately after the national championships swimmers receive a full blood profile. Richard Telford, the institute's exercise physiologist, accompanies the swimming team to the national championships, where he and his team conduct blood lactate and heart rate speed/curve testing on each of the participating swimmers. In this way, the institute coaches are provided with each swimmer's physiological history.

Because the swimmers train very strenuously the institute's staff carefully monitors their ability to adapt to the work load in order to achieve the maximum adaptation for each swimmer.

A method of testing first used by Forbes Carlile on Australian Olympic swimmers back in the 1960s has been reinstituted. This method uses the Cameron heartometer to look for inverted T waves, which are a sign of overstress. It provides a very effective 2-minute guide to whether the swimmer is in failing adaptation as a result of too heavy a work load.

The institute's coaching staff uses a wide range of evaluation processes: biomechanical analyses, psychological profiles, complete medical examinations, and both in-water and laboratory physiological testing. Lactate testing is done twice a week, on Tuesday and Thursday afternoons, or whenever specially requested by the coaching staff.

Other measures include blood pressure testing, electrocardiogram, and heart rate testing.

The records of all swimmers are stored in online computers, making the information immediately available to the coaching staff in individual offices at any time. In fact, 2 minutes after an athlete completes a physical examination in the laboratory the coach can read the result on the computer in a poolside office.

The liaison with sport medicine and sport science people heightens the coaches' awareness to their swimmers' needs by giving them as much information as possible to make the best decisions as soon as possible.

The swimming program at the institute works very closely with the national coaching director, Paul Quinlan, who acts as a liaison officer between the clubs and the institute. Basically, the national coaching director supervises two important programs that attempt to identify the Australian coaches who are producing the most significant results. These programs are the national events program and the satellite coaches program.

Dedication to a Common Goal

The Australians realize that because there are only 16 million people in Australia, to challenge the world in swimming they need to build a system that will work better than any other. To achieve this goal they believe it vital that, despite being fiercely competitive among themselves, they should try to inspire all their coaches to work toward a common goal with a unified approach to international-level swimming. The institute's program has the flexibility to supplement or work with outside clubs in whatever way best serves their individual interests. There is also a very strong relationship between the head coach of the institute, the national coaching director, and the official state coaches.

Although some countries such as Canada have long had a state-sponsored support system for athletes and clubs based on achievement, the Australians appear to have developed a more practical approach that typifies the inborn Australian aversion to the paralyzing effects of bureaucracy. Like Canada, Australia has a limited talent pool, but because it has a much smaller population than Canada, Australia has of necessity devised a system that, as far as possible, tries to ensure the best swimmers are coached by the best coaches.

Swimming in America

William "Buck" Dawson
First Executive Director,
International Swimming Hall of Fame

Organized competitive swimming meets started in North America in 1876 (the Montreal Swimming Association) and in the United States 1 year later (the New York Athletic Club). The first municipal swimming pool in the United States was built in Brookline, Massachusetts, in 1896, but an even older pool, the Detroit "Natatorium," had existed since 1816; its dimensions were 16 by 33 feet.

The Start of Mass Swimming

The first YMCA swimming "bath" in the United States was built in Brooklyn, New York, in 1885. It measured 14 by 45 feet. By 1909, when the "Y" officially launched its National Swimming Campaign, there were 293 pools in YMCAs. Sometime around 1905 a "swimming missionary" named George Corson introduced mass swimming classes throughout eastern North America. Corson was a horticulture professor at the University of Toronto. A showman, publicist, and traveling teacher, Corson is generally credited with increasing the number of swimmers throughout the YMCA movement in eastern North America.

The More Advanced Styles of the North American Indians

Unfortunately, early organized swimming in North America copied the European swimming style, particularly the methods brought to America by the colonial English. This was a pity, because more advanced styles already existed in North America, as noted in 1739 in the diary of the English colonial William Byrd, founder of Richmond, Virginia and a planter, satirist and writer of diaries (Byrd, 1928). Writing on September 30, 1739, Byrd noted:

> This being Sunday, we were glad to rest from our labors; and, to help restore our vigor, several of us plunged into the river, not withstanding it was a frosty morning. One of our Indians went in along with us, and taught us their way of swimming. They strike not out both hands together but alternately one after another, whereby they are able to swim both farther and faster than we do. (Byrd, 1928)

Even when the better American style was exported to England 100 years later in a 1844 London exhibition by two traveling Native Americans, Tobacco and Flying Gull, the English paid little attention and refused to change, despite the obvious superiority of the Native American swimming style. This forerunner of the modern crawl stroke was described in the London *Times* (April 22, 1844) as being totally ''un-European,'' declaring that ''the Indians thrashed the water violently with their arms like sails of a windmill and beat downward with their feet blowing with force and performing grotesque antics'' (Carlile, 1963, p. 126).

First World Records Set by Americans

In spite of the writings and teachings on the subject of swimming by Benjamin Franklin in 1821, Americans trailed behind the English in swimming for a long time. The Americans set their first world records using the English trudgen stroke in 1899 (Midget Schaefer) and 1903 (Harry LeMoyne).

Although Charles Daniels, influenced primarily by the Australian Cavill, set world records with the ''American crawl'' from 1905, it was not until the great Duke Kahanamoku came to the mainland from Hawaii in 1911 that the true American crawl took over. When ''The Duke'' was asked in 1912 who had taught him to swim the crawl he replied that the stroke was ''natural to the Hawaiians'' (Kiphuth, 1942, pp. 3, 4).

Factors Leading to Rapid Progress

The competitive motivation prevalent in American society also had its effect on U.S. swimming, causing improved swimming pools to be built. Ultimately, vast numbers of people were attracted to the sport, if only as a recreation. After a late start, American swimming enjoyed rapid progress from the beginning of the 20th century, mainly because of

1. the elevation of the swimming coach's status from that of bath house attendant to that of professional teacher;
2. the vast number of competitions;
3. the continual improvement in swimming techniques and training methods;
4. the institutional backing of both secondary school and university competitions; and
5. the use of administrative methods of the English Amateur Swimming Association.

By the late 20th century American swimming had become a colossal structure, as shown in the organizational chart in Figure 10.2.

With its headquarters at the high-altitude Olympic Training Center in Colorado Springs, United States Swimming, Inc., under Executive Director Ray Essick, provides multifaceted leadership not only in the financial and administrative side of the sport but also in program planning at many different levels under such experts as chief coach Dennis Pursley and domestic technical director Bob Steele. Scientific research and physiological testing is conducted by physiologist John Troup and his team working in liaison with the University of Colorado at Colorado Springs. A state-of-the-art swimming flume is used for physiological testing and also provides assistance to biomechanists for analyzing stroke mechanics. In 1990 a 50-meter pool was being planned for construction on the grounds of the center.

American Domination of World Swimming

America's eventual dominance of world swimming, indicated by world records and Olympic

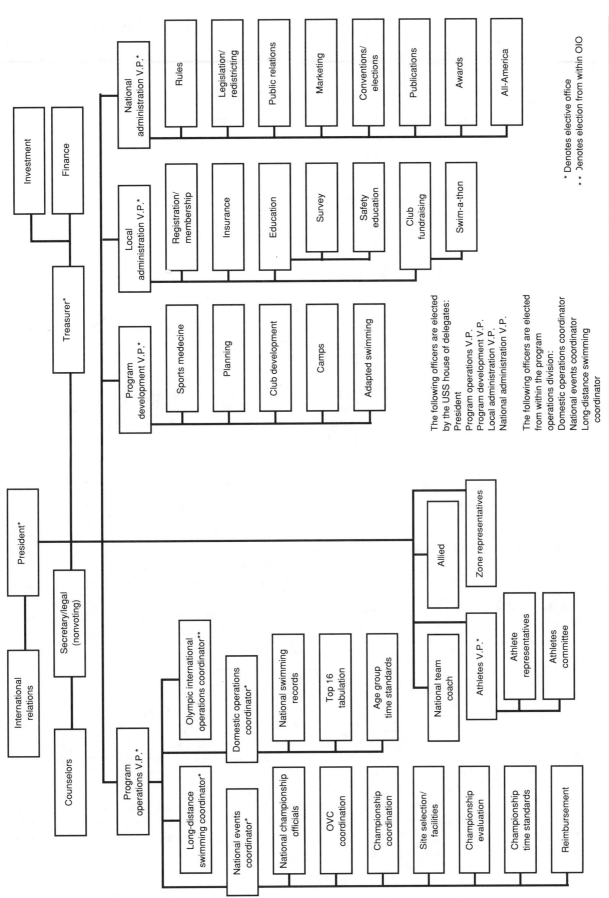

Figure 10.2 Table of organization for United States swimming. *Note.* Reprinted by permission of United States Swimming, Inc.

performances, by such all-time greats as John Weissmuller, Mark Spitz (7 gold medals at the 1972 Olympics), and many other illustrious American swimmers, both male and female, began hesitantly with world records by Schaefer (1899) and LeMoyne (1903) but really took off with Charles Daniels (1906) and subsequent performances by Duke Kahanamoku in the 1912 Olympics. The United States took charge in the 1920 Olympics and dominated between 1924 and 1928, but it dipped to second as the very young Japanese swimmers took over in 1932 and 1936. It resurfaced as number one in 1948 and 1952 but lost to the interval-training and shoulder-rolling Australians in 1956, started to come back in 1960, and dominated again in 1964, 1968, 1972, and 1976. The United States currently remains a force to be reckoned with, but the rest of the world has caught up, particularly in womens' swimming, where the East Germans were still dominant at the time of the German reunification on October 2, 1990.

There is every indication that for centuries the Native Americans of both North and South America swam in great numbers with a superior crawl stroke. While the so-called civilized world persisted with breaststroke and sidestroke, Native Americans were using a crawl that included even the roll and shoulder dipping, which U.S. swimmers and others did not adopt fully until the 1950s.

The Diversity of United States Swimming Programs

American competitive swimming was dominated first by the East Coast, then by Chicago and the Midwest, and finally by California. The Hawaiian influence was strong from 1911 to 1956. There is no longer one area that dominates United States swimming, however. Good coaching has spread nationwide and good programs spring up wherever good coaching exists.

Similarly, United States college swimming, which started with a Yale, Pennsylvania, and Columbia meet in 1896, went through a long period—1924 to 1958—during which six universities dominated the scene: Navy, Northwestern, Rutgers, Michigan, Ohio State, and Yale. It is now becoming more balanced after recent dominance by Sunbelt schools. The total United States swimming picture was dominated by the urban, private-membership athletic clubs from 1875 to 1940 and by the colleges from 1936 to 1960.

High school swimming in the United States became a major development program, as did the YMCA and Boys' Clubs. More recently, community recreation swim clubs have played a big part in America's learn-to-swim program, which continues through to the structured high school and college programs and ultimately to *U.S. Swimming* (formerly A.A.U.), the F.I.N.A.-recognized governing body of American senior swimming.

Americans also originated age group swimming, an exposure and developmental program begun in the 1950s through Carl Bauer at the Missouri Athletic Club in St. Louis and developed by Beth Kaufman in California. The impact of United States age group swimming was so great in the 1960s that swimming became a kindergarten sport with world-record holders as young as 12-years old and Olympic champions in their teens. (*Note.* Used by permission of Buck Dawson, First Executive Director, International Swimming Hall of Fame.)

Age Group Program: Revolution in American Swimming

The biggest single factor in the tremendous growth of American swimming in the post WWII years was the development of age group swimming. Peter Daland, coach of the University of Southern California and one of the prime movers in American swimming during the second half of this century, told me that the first result of the new program showed up at the Melbourne Olympic Games in 1956, when Sylvia Ruuska, an age group product, won the bronze medal in the 400-meter freestyle.

According to Daland, the first results of real depth from the new age group program were at the Rome Olympics in 1960. The United States had seen a great upsurge of swimming, particularly in California, with Daland coaching at both the University of Southern California and with co-coach Don Gambril at the Los Angeles Athletic Club and George Haines at

Santa Clara developing the most successful homespun team of all time.

Two of Haines's Santa Clara swimmers, Chris von Saltza and Don Schollander, made an important impact on world swimming in the 1960s when they helped the United States to break the Australian stranglehold on the sport. In 1959 von Saltza had become the first American woman to break 5 minutes for the 400 meter freestyle when she set a world mark of 4 minutes, 45.5 seconds. At the Rome Olympics the following year, she went on to win three gold medals and one silver medal, thus ending the domination of the great Australian female swimmers. In 1963, Don Schollander, a consummate stylist, became the first swimmer to beat 2 minutes for the 200 meter freestyle and, for almost 4 years, remained the only swimmer in the world to have achieved this feat. Schollander emulated his Santa Clara teammate, Chris von Saltza, by leading United States men's swimming back to the forefront of the world scene by winning four gold medals at the 1964 Tokyo Olympics. Between 1957 and 1974, the Santa Clara swim club, coached by George Haines, achieved the remarkable tally of winning 43 national titles, developing 55 Olympians, and winning 33 Olympic gold medals, 11 silver medals, and 7 bronze medals—an achievement rivaled only by coach Mark Schubert during his 13 year tenure at Mission Viejo, California, where Schubert's swimmers won 44 national titles.

Starting in the years 1957 to 1959, a number of age groupers began to break world records. The age group program spread across the United States, causing a great influx of young swimmers. The large increase in numbers was not without attendant difficulties, particularly those of administration and coaching development. The swimming population of America multiplied about tenfold between 1956 and 1964. What had been small meets soon became *huge* meets; for example, in southern California, a senior meet that at one time had usually had 1 heat or sometimes 2 but rarely 3, soon came to have 10 or 12 heats, even with set qualifying times.

Although Carl Bauer, Beth Kaufman, and Peter Daland are generally acknowledged as the pioneers of the age group movement, its expansion largely resulted from development by the local swimming committees in Sunbelt states such as Texas, Florida, and California. It was promoted mainly by age group parents, upper-middle-class people who had taken over the leadership role in swimming administration.

American University Swimming

As the age group youngsters became older there was an influx of swimmers into American university swimming programs. It was not long before university swimming, which deals with the oldest swimmers in the sport, benefited from the dynamic age group program that had taken shape beneath it. Soon there were many hard-working former age group swimmers participating in the college ranks, which caused a revolution in the size of college teams, the size of competitions, and the number of good swimmers.

Athletic Scholarships. Athletic scholarships were offered as inducements to swimmers to continue competing while pursuing their academic careers. According to Daland (personal communication, June 1984), athletic scholarships had existed for 50 to 60 years but became more numerous in the 1950s and 1960s. In the mid-1970s, however, with the financial crisis that developed in American colleges, there was a very severe cutback: the National Collegiate Athletic Association (N.C.A.A.) removed 40% of the aid in non-revenue sports. However, there always has been a high percentage of non-scholarship swimmers in American universities—the majority, in fact.

N.C.A.A. Proposes Unpopular Legislation. At the N.C.A.A. Convention in January 1991, legislation potentially injurious to Olympic (non-revenue) sports like swimming, was adopted, effective in the 1991-1992 school year. The N.C.A.A. adopted a series of sweeping legislative reforms for intercollegiate athletics. The full effects of this legislation will not be known for several years, but it may limit coaching staff size and reduce scholarships and time devoted to athletics by student athletes. (Dale Neuburger, personal communications, October 8, 1990, and April 22, 1991.)

The N.C.A.A. Presidents' Commission originally proposed that

- all athletic-related activities be limited to 20 hours per week, including workouts, weight training, competition, meetings, and physical therapy;

- the required training and competition season be limited to 24 weeks;
- during off-season, 3 days per week be free of required athletic and related activities, and practices be limited to 8 hours per week;
- student athletes may use facilities and equipment on a voluntary basis if a member of the coaching staff is present, and the coach is permitted to impart skill instruction; and
- participation on outside teams be prohibited, and coaches not be involved with outside teams that have enrolled student athletes during the academic year. (Dale Neuburger, personal communication, April 22, 1991)

Dale Neuburger, Executive Director of the College Swimming Coaches' Association of America, said

Leaders within the swimming community see this movement as destructive to the sport of swimming, while continuing to miss opportunities for real reform in football and basketball. Young coaches will find their chances for graduate assistantships and even volunteer coaching assignments limited. Prospective student-athletes will see less scholarship opportunities. But, perhaps most destructively, swimmers will receive the very clear message that reaching for goals and attempting to fulfill potential will become secondary to arbitrary time limitations. Americans have been successful because they were willing to outwork their competition; now, mirroring political changes, athletes are being told that there should be tangible limits on how hard and how long they should train and prepare for competition. (Personal communication, October 8, 1990)

Women's Athletic Scholarships. In the United States school system, swimming did not take hold for girls until the federal government passed Title IX, which mandated all programs to have equal opportunity for women in publicly-funded schools or colleges/universities that receive funds from the federal government. Female swimmers have tended to drop out of the sport earlier than their male counterparts, and many in America saw athletic scholarships for women as providing a strong incentive for women to remain longer in the sport. According to Karen Moe Thornton, Olympic 200-meter butterfly champion at Munich in 1972 and later women's swimming coach at the University of California at Berkeley, women dropped out earlier because they started earlier than men (personal communication, April, 1984). The difference in the longevity of men and women swimmers was that most women started at 12 or 13-years old, whereas most men don't really start pushing at their swimming until about 15 or 16 years. (Thornton said that this may be related to rates of physical development.) By the time a woman starts college, she has invested much more time than most men. Thornton said that at that point a different type of motivation is required to keep women interested in swimming a little longer.

The Professional Development of American Swimming Coaches

John Leonard
Executive Director, American Swimming
Coaches Association

Begun in 1985, the American Swimming Coaches Association Certification Program is a voluntary system designed to identify professionally prepared swimming coaches. By 1989 over 1,800 coaches had applied for certification and over 1,725 had been granted it at one of five different levels.

The program began in a spirit of compromise between an old guard of professional coaches who felt strongly that true coaching was best identified by results and coaches who felt that professionalism is best developed through education. The primary compromise was the inclusion of elements of education, experience, and coaching achievement in the certification requirements. A.S.C.A. staff operating certification noted some evidence of division along the lines of competencies: academicians favored education and "seat-of-the-pants" coaches favored experience and achievement.

The program grew steadily, with the upper-level coaches (3, 4, and 5) generally coming into the program first, as might be expected, followed by the newer coaches in subsequent years. The statistics are revealing: In 1985, over 74% of the coaches certified were levels 3 or higher; in 1987, this percentage had dropped to 39%; and in 1988 and 1989, over 80% of the coaches certified were at levels 1 and 2. This indicates that the program has received considerable acceptance by the coaching community. The A.S.C.A. certification program was accepted by every organized coaching group in the United States, beginning with National Interscholastic Coaches Association (N.I.S.C.A.) and followed by Masters coaches, YMCA coaches, and the College Coaches' Associations.

Following initial compromises to get the program started, the certification committee moved steadily toward an education-based program while retaining requirements for coaching achievement at levels 3, 4, and 5, as well as experience requirements at all levels. Thus, a coach needs some credentials in all three areas and cannot receive certification with only an experience background, say, or only an academic education; certification requires both education and practical experience. To reach the upper levels of the profession it is necessary to have worked successfully with some excellent athletes.

Certification was extended to non-U.S. coaches who were A.S.C.A. members, with requirements based on world ranking athletes rather than on U.S. achievements and education and experience requirements similar to their U.S. counterparts. Initial response to this program has been very positive, especially from coaches of non-elite swimming nations without certification programs.

It became clear that the independent and internal professional organization of the certification process is quite important to the A.S.C.A. membership. Regulation from within is seen as preferable to regulation from outside.

Clinical education testing is required. For a coach to receive credit for attending a clinic it must offer a test on the material taught, and the individual coach must successfully complete that test. All tests and scores are recorded at the A.S.C.A. national office. In 1990 the certification committee began categorizing educational units as either lifetime units or units since 1988 (the previous 2 years) to encourage coaches to stay current with information available in the profession.

Three areas were expected to play major roles in certification. The first is the application of an ethical standard for coaches. To be certificated and remain so, a coach must meet a determined standard of ethical conduct. The method and the standard have to be developed as well as the strictures to be imposed and procedures to be followed in the case of a breach of ethical conduct. It is anticipated that this will be a difficult task.

The second important concern is the creation of an awareness among employers of swimming coaches in all segments of the aquatic community of what coaching certification means to them. Financial and employment issues will play a major role; A.S.C.A. salary and compensation surveys were keyed to certification levels.

Finally, the use of certification by the coaches themselves will be a major issue. To provide coaches with a truly professional image and lifestyle the issue of professional preparation and conduct with their peers, employers, and clients must be forced. Whether coaches will be willing to do so will determine the future of swimming coaching as a profession. (*Note.* Used by permission of John Leonard.)

The Golden Era of Japanese Swimming

From 1932 to 1936 Japan reigned supreme in world swimming, but after World War II, with the exception of producing such great swimmers as Furuhashi, Hashizume, Yamanaka, Taguchi, Tanaka, Suzuki, and a few other outstanding competitors, Japan never regained its former depth in world swimming.

The dramatic rise of the Japanese to world

supremacy at the Los Angeles Olympics in 1932 marked the first occasion that a single country had put into effect a definite national plan with the aim of achieving complete mastery. It also was the first time that the motion picture camera was used as a scientific device for improving swimming technique on a national scale. The Japanese made extensive motion film studies of leading American and European champions from both above and below water. In particular, they concentrated on filming the technique of 1924 and 1928 Olympic champion Johnny Weissmuller, who, under the guidance of his coach, William Bachrach, was considered to have developed the classic crawl style (Armbruster, 1942). The films were then shown to schoolchildren throughout Japan to give them a visual idea of good technique.

These children were carefully nurtured in sound stroke technique from an early age. The American crawl was cleverly adapted to the shorter Japanese physique, but the Japanese crawl, as it came to be called, was not fundamentally different from the American style. Not only were the Japanese youngsters taught well from an early age, but they trained harder than swimmers had ever done before. Good technique and strenuous training were consistently applied. The results of this first conscientious application of a national development plan were outstanding.

In the Amsterdam Olympics in 1928 the breaststroke swimmer Tsuruta was the only Japanese to win a title. His success inspired all Japan. Only 4 years later Japan brought a team of young teenagers to the 1932 Los Angeles Olympic Games and shook the whole world of swimming by the heels. They won every swimming event with the exception of the 400-meter event, which was won by Clarence "Buster" Crabbe, an American from Hawaii.

The American team coach, Bob Kiphuth, was said to have been pleased by the fact that the 1932 American Olympic team had beaten the 800-meter relay record in practice by over 15 seconds, but this improvement was not enough to beat the Japanese team, which eclipsed the old relay record by over 37 seconds to establish an undreamed-of mark (Cureton, 1934). In all, the Japanese accumulated 86 points versus the American total of 33. Japanese swimmers won first and second in every race but one; in that they placed third, fourth, and fifth. These results showed a Japanese team of unusual mass strength (Cureton, 1934).

- 100-meter freestyle—first, second, and fifth (new Olympic record)
- 800-meter relay—first (new world and Olympic record)
- 400-meter freestyle—third, fourth, and fifth (all under the old Olympic mark)
- 200-meter breaststroke—first, second, and sixth (new Olympic record by both Tsuruta and Koike)
- 100-meter backstroke—first, second, and third
- 1,500-meter freestyle—first and second (new Olympic record by both Kitamura and Makino)

One of the most amazing features of the great Japanese rise to victory was that it all happened within only four years, between the Olympic Games of 1928 and 1932, and there were no warning signs whatsoever of their pending breakthrough to world dominance.

Suggested Reasons for the Japanese Success

Thomas Cureton (1934) comments that a great number of guesses were made by various authorities as to the reasons for the Japanese success. Speaking as a scientist, he says that it was "really unfortunate" that no comparative measurements were available for 1928 to show exactly wherein the Japanese had made their advancement. However, from various publications of the time, Cureton grouped all the suggested reasons under the following four major heads:

1. Attitude
   a. Superior financial backing and national interest resulting in better organization for the task
   b. Superior unity of purpose in conquering for Japan resulting in a higher quality of loyalty to purpose and seriousness for the requirements of training
   c. Eager open-mindedness to the results of research in training and stroke mechanics

2. Stroke Mechanics
   A new stroke, the Japanese crawl, claimed to be an improvement over the American style (This was reputed to have been developed from careful study of American swimmers and tests on the Japanese swimmers.)

3. Organic Condition
    a. Social customs facilitating utter simplicity and lack of sophistication in matters of diet, sex, and entertainment
    b. Strenuous practice, up to four times as hard as the American swimmers
4. Structural Aptitude
    Better buoyancy and flexibility of the Japanese

Cureton's final comment is significant:

Older books on swimming explained the performances of champions largely upon the basis of differences in stroke mechanics. Recent tests show that much must also be attributed to training methods which build endurance. (Cureton, 1934, p. 107)

The Japanese success in the 1930s was the first example in competitive swimming of what can be achieved by careful planning and specialized training that works purposefully rather than hopefully toward a set goal.

They were not to know it at the time, but the Japanese had developed what would prove to be a basic recipe for national success in international sport. They set the scene for the Australian resurgence in the 1950s and the rise to eminence of the East German program, the most thorough of all time for developing elite athletes in all Olympic sports.

The Success of the East German Swimming Program

The former East Germany dominated women's swimming during the 1970s and 1980s. At the Seoul Olympics in 1988 their men and women swimmers finished first in the medal tally with 11 golds, 8 silvers, and 9 bronzes. They won 10 of the 15 women's events.

Although the basic structure of East German sports was similar to that of their Warsaw Pact allies (Childs, 1969), the question frequently asked was how a country with a population of only 17 million and an adverse climate could consistently dominate world swimming (Cichoke, 1977).

Students of German sporting history believe that the East German success can be attributed to a strong German sporting tradition with experience in sport administration over nearly 150 years. In sports, as well as in arts and science, the Germanic peoples as a whole had a reputation for efficient and methodical planning (*grundlichkeit*). Moreover, this history shows that sports in Germany have been efficiently *controlled* by the state at many junctures for militaristic and propaganda purposes; first by the Prussian military machine, then by Hitler and the Nazi party, and then in East Germany by the Communist party.

The question that immediately springs to mind is why the same heritage did not make West German sports as consistently successful as their East German counterpart. The answer is that West German sports did well in the postwar years, although not on a par with East Germany's, but in a free society it was impossible for the state to exercise central control over every aspect of a nation's sporting activities, methodically sifting through the entire population to seek potential champions and meticulously controlling their training and education for 4 to 6 years or more.

Historical Background

Before World War I Germany had become a leader in science and the arts and was also becoming prominent in sports. The Germans realized that scientific research in sport could improve performance. An important development in this period was the establishment of a special commission for scientific research into exercise and sporting techniques (Childs, 1969).

Germany staged the 1936 Olympic Games in Berlin because Hitler wanted the propaganda value for his new regime. A nationwide talent search was conducted and the Olympic competitors were prepared in special camps. Hitler ordered Olympic athletes in government employ to be given all the free time they needed to train. The final medal count showed that Germany had improved from sixth place at the 1932 Los Angeles Games to first place in Berlin.

One noteworthy trend that emerged as part of the state's methodical and efficient interest in sport was the introduction of scientific investigation to improve performance, a development thoroughly in keeping with the great importance German society attached to medicine and science generally.

Many experienced and capable sports administrators who survived the war understood the potential value of sport science, disciplined effort, and efficient planning and implementation.

German athletes had developed a pride in their tradition of high achievement in international sports. These factors should be considered in any appraisal of the postwar East German success.

The Soviet Influence on East German Sport

Immediately following World War II sports participation in the Soviet zone of Germany was limited to members of the trade unions and a new organization, the Free German Youth (F.D.J.), which had been set up by the Communists in 1946.

The F.D.J. followed a deliberate policy of indoctrinating German youth through the medium of sport. It generously provided equipment and lavish facilities that the sports-loving Germans could not have afforded otherwise. To conduct their new sports programs the Communists had no alternative to using the expertise of closely supervised former Nazi sports officials.

In August 1948 the German Sports Committee, *Die Deutscher Sportausschuss* (D.S.A.), was formed. The state gave a far-reaching mandate to the D.S.A., granting it virtual control not only over all sports but also over *all educational institutions involved with sports*. This included universities as well as schools. Furthermore, the D.S.A. was to be responsible *for every aspect of the national life affected by sports*: scientific research in sports, the sports media, the manufacture of sports equipment, and the construction of sports facilities (Childs, 1969).

Among the new facilities built were the University for Physical Culture (*Hochschule für Körperkultur*) in Leipzig; sports schools at Hamberge, Bad Blankenburg, and Werdau; the Hallen swimming pool at Rostock; and several sports stadia in various parts of the country. In addition to the Leipzig *Hochschule*, which started with an initial enrollment of 400 students, other university-level institutes were planned. Along with the use of these facilities sports participants were given greatly reduced rail fares.

Of great significance was the inauguration of a policy enabling control over the schooling and training preparation of highly talented children. New provisions detailed the establishment of special boarding schools for children 14 years old and up. These schools were designed to meet the demands of both general education and specialist preparation for high-performance sports. They not only enabled the authorities to monitor and control every aspect of a young athlete's life but also provided ideal conditions for training. It was no longer necessary to travel vast distances to twice daily training sessions or to train early in the morning before school. The first training session of the day would take place in midmorning during a break in school lessons rather than at an early hour, when a swimmer's metabolism is still functioning at a low rate. Unlike many Western countries, coaches and swimmers did not come under a daily barrage of parental pressures or interference in the program. The general health as well as the diet and rest habits of the swimmers were closely and continuously supervised by experts.

The Central Organization of East German Sport

On March 17, 1951, the Socialist Unity Party (S.E.D.) adopted a resolution that made the German Sports Committee (Deutscher Sportausschus, or D.S.A.) the supreme governing body of sport and physical education in East Germany.

Apart from establishing the previously mentioned sports boarding schools, the S.E.D. Resolution of 1951 made sports compulsory in all schools. A national sports program was established based on three stages of awards according to age. Childs (1969) lists these stages as follows:

1. 10 to 14 years: ''Be ready for Peace and Friendship.''
2. 14 to 16 years: ''Be ready to Work and Defend Peace.''
3. 16 to 18 years: ''Ready to Work and Defend Peace.''

Clearly, this is a philosophy of sport based largely on ideology and politics and the value of the talented athlete to the state. Sports in East Germany already bore a strong resemblance to sports in Nazi Germany in that they were centrally organized and controlled in a one-party state.

The Structure of East German Swimming

The East German sports system worked closely with the schools. Children received swimming classes in the second and third grades; at this time, the more talented youngsters were identified and put into a group that trained once or twice a week. The better swimmers eventually were selected to proceed to one of the nine sports centers situated in the bigger cities and affiliated with local clubs. There were 10 swimming clubs: Vorwaern Potsdam, Chemie Hallen, Dynamo Berlin, Einheit Dresden, Empor Rostock, Magdeburg, Turbine Erfurt, Karl-Marx-Stadt, Leipzig, and Berlin (the last two were based at the *Deutsche Hochschule für Körperkultur* in these sites). Each club had an average membership of approximately 100 swimmers and the entry age was 11 years for girls and 12 for boys. Each of these clubs produced a number of prominent international swimmers (Colwin, 1975b).

I asked Gert Barthelmes, Secretary General of the East German Swim Federation, whether it was true that families moved with youngsters who were farmed into sports centers. Barthelmes replied that this was not true ''as a rule.'' Most of the swimmers chosen to go to the sports centers were already boarding school students so they went to the boarding school nearby. Around 80% of the swimmers came from the big cities and only 20% from the smaller towns (Colwin, 1975b).

Barthelmes said that they had thousands of children to work with and did not have the capacity to do research with all of them. He added that there were ''more general ways of estimating who may have more chance of success than others'' (Colwin, 1975b, p. 13).

When youngsters entered the program they were given a thorough physical examination and extensive testing of their sports skills. Once accepted they trained twice a week for 2 hours each session for a total training distance of 300 kilometers or 190 miles per year (Cichoke, 1977).

After 2 years those children who could not swim the 100-meter freestyle in 1:30 or faster were weeded out and the more talented swimmers were accepted into a sports school. Between the ages of 9 and 10 years the annual training program was more than doubled to 800 kilometers (approximately 500 miles). At the age of 12 years the annual distance covered was increased to about 1,000 kilometers (600 miles). By this time the youngsters swam for 3 to 5 hours on weekdays and 2 hours on Saturdays. Around 90% of the twelve-year olds were weeded out of the program.

Another weeding out process occurred between the ages of 12 and 15 years of age, this time with a training distance increase to over 1,000 miles a year. At 14 to 15 years of age the girls would show a marked increase in performance; the boys reached a similar stage of improvement about 2 years later.

About the ages of 14 to 16 years boys and girls covered about 1,500 miles per year. The East Germans were said to have experimented from time to time with even greater annual distances, about 3,500 kilometers in 1973, but the outcome of this experiment is unknown in the West. The aim of the developmental phase of the East German program was to train their swimmers to cover long distances at high speed (Cichoke, 1977).

Program Control

The training of East German swimmers resulted from teamwork in a group of highly trained specialists working in liaison: coaches, trainers, biochemists, biomechanists, psychologists, and physicians.

The entire program was carefully monitored, with special attention given to biochemical and medical control of the swimmers. This program control was accomplished by the following means:

1. Tests to detect possible disturbances and deviations in physiochemical areas such as electrolytes, serum urea, and CPK
2. Control of the duration and intensity of daily workouts, lactate level, acid-base state, and so on
3. Other medical control examinations

The results of these regular tests were given to the club physician, who then passed the information on to the coach. Depending on the nature of the report, there would be either an adjustment in the swimmer's work load or appropriate rehabilitative therapy. The results of the blood tests (lactic acid, urea, creatinine, phosphokinase, oxygen, carbon dioxide, and pH) were fed into a computer. It has been claimed (Cichoke, 1977) that this information was analyzed and a recommended program was thereupon produced by the computer.

During strenuous training, a swimmer's lactic acid level was observed over 2-week periods. The data for each swimmer were fed into a central computer in Leipzig, and based on the results the swimmers' training programs were revised. Diet was also calculated by computer.

Muscle biopsies of East German swimmers were examined using photomicrographical techniques that split muscle fibers longitudinally and horizontally before enlarging the samples for examination. The East German swimmers monitored their early morning basal heart rate as a check against overtraining, a technique introduced to swimming by the Australians in the 1950s.

Finally, the East Germans had six swimming flumes (a specially designed tank in which a swimmer is tethered while swimming against a regulated flow of water) in which stroke techniques were analyzed and physiological tests conducted.

Effects of Political Changes

The dramatic political changes in East Germany and other Eastern European countries in 1989 gave rise to much conjecture concerning the extent to which sport in those countries would remain under state control. There was doubt as to whether sports facilities would continue to be reserved for the exclusive use of top athletes, and soon there were reports of leading East German swimmers and coaches moving to the West.

In the past, the ability to travel outside their country to international meets—a privilege associated with being a top state athlete—had been a big incentive to work hard at sports. With the removal of travel restrictions, an important motivational factor had suddenly been eliminated. The biggest question asked by the international swimming community, though, was whether the reunification of Germany would produce a swimming superpower rarely seen before in the history of the sport.

Starkman (1990) reports that the famous training center in Leipzig is in a state of decline. Although West German sports officials have been anxious to preserve the East German's scientific approach and their system of training coaches within a reunified Germany, they believe that this aim could already be too late. Furthermore, many West Germans think that the East German system will have difficulty in surviving for long within the framework of a free enterprise democratic society, saying that there will not be the same need or motivation to show off the system to the rest of the world.

As far as producing a swimming superpower is concerned, the general opinion appears to be that, although some "stored fat" may yet remain from the previous East German standard, there probably will be a gradual diminution of the previous levels of performance.*

Finally, Starkman produces confirmation of what the world of swimming had long suspected, namely, that East German swimmers had definitely been given steroids on a consistent basis since the early 1970s. Professor Hermann Buhl, in charge of medical research at the Leipzig institute, in a "frank hour-long discussion" with Starkman, freely admitted that "specific research on anabolics came directly from East Germany's pharmaceutical industry" and that part of his medical research at the Leipzig institute had included "devising steroid programs for East German athletes." However, Buhl chose to credit an "excellent coaching system" as the main reason for the East German success, saying that steroid research had not played the key role in the East German success.

---

*Note. With the reunification of Germany on October 2, 1990, literally thousands of sport administrators, coaches, and sport scientists automatically became unemployed. Only a few hundred of them will probably find employment within the new Germany. Therefore, many countries may benefit from an influx of highly trained personnel.

Chapter 11

The Future Belongs to the Innovators

As competitive swimming prepares to enter the new millenium it is clear that progress is slowing down. Although international competition has intensified, most world records, especially in the women's division, have become more difficult to beat. Any country seeking complete dominance will need to produce innovative techniques on a scale unequalled before.

This text has examined the nature of change so that we may better predict how new trends will develop. It is unlikely that future change will be in the form of a quantum leap forward. Neither will it be the result of the astute use of technology alone. Change will not be dramatic but rather a gradual transition resulting from the accumulative effects of small improvements in almost every phase of technical preparation.

Purposeful Planning for the Future

It is possible that most short-term progress could come mainly from the seemingly unlikely area of program planning. Particularly in the West, many facets of national preparation have yet to be adequately addressed. The planning of competitive programs that ideally match each stage of seasonal training preparation has presented a perennial challenge. But this challenge is a relatively mundane one compared with other possible developments.

Recent modifications to the previous rigid laws of amateurism now permit funds to be held in trust for a swimmer against retirement. This development has resulted in a new trend: regular international match races between the great swimmers of the world.

In March 1990, Marcel Gery of Canada collected the special prize of £10,000 for breaking the world 100-meter butterfly mark at the Leicester short course meet in England—the final event in the World Cup and the fourth in the "Milk in Action" British Grand Prix series. Similar prizes were offered for world records by swimmers in other events.

Across the Atlantic well-known Olympic swimmers such as Matt Biondi, Tom Jager, Tracy Caulkins, Mary T. Meagher, Rowdy Gaines, and Mark Stockwell also competed in match races for prize money. For example, in the U.S. Swimming Sprint Championships Jager out-touched Biondi while breaking the world 50-meter record to pick up $12,000 in prize money—$10,000 for first place and $2,000 for holding the world record at the end of the competition. For coming in second Biondi received $5,000. Although there were only 800 spectators at the Nashville Sports Complex, the championships were televised live and seen by an audience of millions.

Nearly 100 years after the first amateur laws hounded many great swimmers out of the sport for accepting prize money, the wheel turned full circle. In the late 20th century a whole new elite category of competition emerged that could well result in lower grades of competition for those less talented or committed.

Training the Elite Swimmer

Under these altered circumstances training the elite swimmer could become even more specialized. The coaching and support staff attending the needs of the superathlete would need to be of the highest possible caliber. With the peaking of world swim records in the 1960s and 1970s, great coaches are needed all the more (see Figure 11.1). Also, with the changing face of world politics, expert coaching can play a significant role in the share each country has in world records (Figure 11.2). Only time will tell whether these expert coaches and their assistants continue to be available to swimmers of lesser talent.

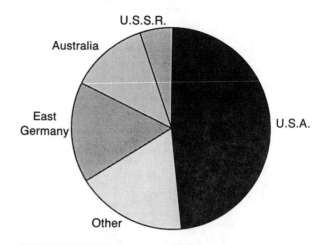

Figure 11.2 World swimming records, by country, from 1950 to 1990. In the past, the U.S.A. has seized nearly half of the world swimming records. But with the dissemination of the U.S.A.'s swimming science knowledge to the world and the greater access to methods of the former East German sport system, expert coaching could change this distribution dramatically. *Note.* Reprinted by permission of N.J. Thierry.

Planning Various Tiers of Competition

Many coaches automatically assume that all swimmers in their charge desire to become champions, but this is simply not true. The level of aspiration varies from swimmer to swimmer, and coaches and administrators should come to a greater recognition of this. It is sound educational practice always to allow a child to find his or her own level. Perhaps various tiers of competition and training intensity could be designed according to individual talent and commitment; such a move would result in a dramatic change in the entire framework of national programs.

Following this trend, the structure of age group swimming may change with the advent of graded competition according to timed performance only, *without reference to age*. Instead of the present systems that usually classify different grades of ability *within* each age group, young, developing swimmers could be grouped by means of *across-the-board* graded competition only.

When to Reach a Peak Performance

Another aspect of program planning that needs more in-depth study is the question of how many times a year a swimmer should peak. In the past, a swimmer usually had the choice of peaking either once or twice a year, but now

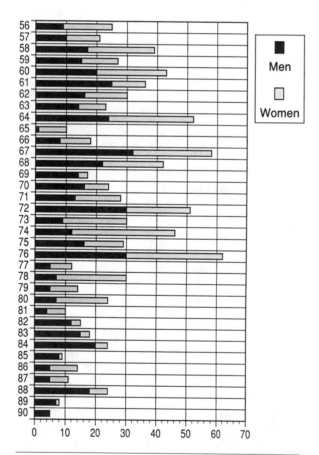

Figure 11.1 World swimming records from 1956 to 1990. This graph shows the combined totals for men's and women's records for each year. Men's records have remained more or less steady with Olympic and world championship years showing a natural increase. Women's records peaked in the 1970s. *Note.* Reprinted by permission of N.J. Thierry.

there are many swimmers, particularly in North America, who peak three or four times a year. A better understanding of this phase of preparation will result in progress.

A swimmer may need to vary the number of peaks in a year; for example, after competing in the Olympics a swimmer may need to rebuild gradually by undertaking only one peak during the following year. Young, developing swimmers may benefit more from the long, gradual buildup of a one-peak year, whereas a swimmer preparing for the Olympics may derive greater benefit from a two- or three-peak year.

The Role of the Human Dynamic

Purposeful planning for the future will require a greater appreciation of the role of the human dynamic. Too many administrators have placed blind faith in shibboleths: management by objectives, feasibility studies, goal selection, evaluation procedures, and so forth. Consequently, administration of the sport often has become so overstructured as to lose its capacity to impart momentum. Many otherwise conscientious and capable planners have tended to forget the important axiom that it is people who make plans work. The sport of swimming will need to find as many people as possible who are capable of innovative thinking in their disciplines and, more importantly, able to convert their new ideas into positive action. Appreciation of this fact could open up new vistas for swimming in the 21st century.

Sport Science and the "Information Explosion"

We have seen how the nature and character of competitive swimming changed enormously over a period of 150 years. But progress was slow and gradual, with the greatest improvements in swimming knowledge coming from imaginative coaches working with talented swimmers. Progressive coaches accepted or rejected new ideas and methods and intuitively modified and developed them with the conscious goal of making swimmers faster. Thus, the world of swimming was offered an ever-expanding range and variety of inspiration for its future development.

Coaches and swimmers have been the greatest innovators and contributors to swimming knowledge, despite claims that may be made on behalf of formal scientific research. And it is important to note that when science did have an impact on swimming methods, the most significant contributions were made by scientists such as Carlile, Costill, Cotton, Counsilman, Cureton, Kipke, Mader, Madsen, Maglischo, and Schleihauf—all of whom were coaches, swimmers, or both. These intuitive coach-swimmer-scientists understood the needs of the sport, and thus their research aimed at providing specific information essential to progress.

The Processes of Change

Increased quantities of scientific research and the "information explosion" were expected to intensify and accelerate the processes of change. Contrary to expectation, technical progress has become trapped amid a great logjam of diverse junk information. The purpose and potential usefulness of this information is not always clear, but it is certainly not aimed directly at solving practical problems.

Although science has acquired a rich heritage of ideas from coaches and swimmers from which to work, the specific problems that face the coaching practitioner have not always been fully recognized nor adequately addressed. Although science has developed many ways of acquiring new knowledge and invented increasingly flexible and efficient instruments for using it, it is still far from being used in the most effective and practical manner.

The last decade of the 20th century will be an age of transition for competitive swimming. Progress has slowed down, probably because humans are reaching their physiological limits but also because coaches no longer use their natural intuition to the fullest extent. They rely excessively on scientific research that often is not relevant to the most pressing practical needs of the sport; its irrelevance largely stems from the failure of coaches and scientists to work together continuously in the practical pool-deck setting.

Bridging the Gap Between the Swimming Coach and the Sport Scientist

For years many swimming coaches have had an aversion to working with scientists, mainly because they perceived the scientists to be patronizing or condescending toward them and they noticed that many scientists doing so-called swimming research were rarely seen at a swimming pool from one year to the next.

Scientists were often accused of being cold and unemotional people who lived in a remote world of their own.

Scientists may have built a barrier to understanding between themselves and laypersons simply because they use a special written language for which there is no spoken equivalent, no popular slang, no easy colloquialism. Scientific literature must leave no doubt about what the scientist means when describing a particular study. Scientific language and the scientists who use it thus may appear to the layperson to be stilted, pompous, and remote from the practicalities of pool-deck coaching.

The Need to Produce Meaningful Research

McPherson (1980) says that sport scientists need to produce meaningful quality work. The fact is that there are few productive scholars within the physical activity sciences; recruitment has been haphazard and few departments provide rigorous research training.

Hay (1986) says that although there has been obvious progress in swimming research over the last decade or so, the rate of progress is unlikely to increase until the number of trained researchers in the field increases. Those who wish to see improvement in swimming research would do well to consider what might be done to attract established scientists and identify and train young scientists interested in swimming. A well-reasoned, carefully planned approach to this problem seems to offer the greatest single opportunity for progress; without it we are unlikely to see a marked change in the present rate of progress.

Coach and Scientist Should Become More Familiar With Each Other's Disciplines

It is significant that much of the comment on the role of science in the three main scientific disciplines concerned with swimming—biomechanics, physiology, and psychology—emanated from James Counsilman, the person most influential in the 20th century in making the swimming world recognize the practical value of a properly implemented scientific approach.

Counsilman (Kimiecik & Gould, 1987) says that most researchers are in a difficult situation. Most of them work in academia and must comply with what other academicians consider to be standards of good research. In contrast, So-

viet sport scientists do very few experimental studies but are out in the field with the coaches and athletes compiling notes and getting a first-hand look at training; from this they develop concepts that coaches can incorporate in practice sessions. This kind of research is simply not being done in the United States.

Biomechanics. Referring to the practical application of biomechanical research, Counsilman (Colwin, 1983a) says that instead of mathematical models of stroke mechanics or other information expressed in scientific terms researchers need to present practical applications that a coach can use in the pool. Counsilman says that research pays off in only a small percentage—about 5% at the most.

Physiology. According to Counsilman (1988), there is a halo effect around research that makes it difficult for coaches to discriminate between sound and unsound advice. Many coaches hold researchers in awe—particularly if the researcher has a doctorate in exercise physiology—because they use terminology alien to the coach's vocabulary. Indeed, some researchers become adept at enhancing the halo effect in the minds of coaches; one method is to ignore equivocal data that would diminish the impact of the researcher's statements if included.

Counsilman (1988) claims that it has been primarily the coaches who through trial and error have developed the currently used concepts of training. By helping a coach understand the need for an integrated program, however, the exercise physiologist can provide necessary help—for example, finding the appropriate mix of anaerobic training, anaerobic lactate training, and aerobic training for swimmers specializing in specific events.

Psychology. Counsilman denies that sports psychology is far behind the other two key disciplines, physiology and biomechanics, because he believes that some of the best psychologists are coaches (Kimiecik & Gould, 1987). He adds that some coaches are such good motivators it is "almost frightening" what they can get their swimmers to do. Still, the field of sports psychology might lag behind the other two disciplines from the standpoint of being accepted by coaches and athletes. Commenting on psychological testing, he says that tests provide some standard information on all the athletes and the athletes enjoy taking them—it makes them think and they learn a little about themselves.

According to Counsilman, the best way to build confidence is to ensure that the swimmers know they have been well-prepared physiologically (Kimiecik & Gould, 1987). If swimmers believe in their training program they inevitably will feel confident before they compete.

The Human Factor

Stroke techniques and training methods will continue to improve as competitive swimming moves into the 21st century. Scientific research will become more rewarding and national development programs will be designed to better effect and purpose. However, I believe that not all improvement will be the result of these emphases. We need to learn more about developing the abstract qualities of our athletes; then we will be able to help them develop more fully toward the ideal of the whole, unobstructed personality. Doing so will enable us to release the immense inherent qualities that reside within each individual competitor and that up to now have not been used to their full extent.

The Soviets have experimented with "mind power" in sports since the beginning of the postwar period, and the East Germans and Chinese also include these techniques in their national training programs. In fact, keen observers believe this approach to be widespread throughout the Eastern Bloc. This is often confirmed by the consistency, perseverance, and control under pressure—mental toughness—that result from the unusual powers of concentration shown by such athletes as the East German swimmers, Chinese divers, and Romanian gymnasts.

The significant enhancement of performance to be derived from improving a swimmer's concentration has received scant attention in the West. Without doubt, however, the inability to concentrate throughout a swimming race has been the downfall of many an otherwise talented and promising swimmer. This is a vital defect in a swimmer's competitive makeup. More often than not, a below par performance is attributed to factors such as misjudging the taper, poor warm-up, and so forth—anything but the real reason, which being abstract escapes the notice of the untrained observer.

Although talent identification programs will continue to find bigger, better, and more talented athletes, the odds are that these athletes will be only slightly bigger, better, and more

talented then their predecessors. The focus of the future may be on improving "the human factor" by embracing techniques that will teach even talented athletes how to mobilize *all* the forces that enable the power of the body to fully express itself.

A holistic approach to sports education may permit tomorrow's athletes to tap reserves of power in the human mind and body. It has often been said that we use only 10% of our brains—but the rest must be there for a reason. According to Ostrander and Schroeder, authors of *Super-Learning* (1983) and the best-selling *Psychic Discoveries Behind the Iron Curtain* (1971), the Soviets have long researched and developed sports training programs that show brawn-*plus*-brain to be a winning combination (Ostrander & Schroeder, 1983).

According to Ostrander and Schroeder, Soviet scientists believe that average athletes only realize about half their potential if brain power is not used. At the Advanced Medical Training Institute psychotherapists V. Rozhnov and A. Alexyev have developed methods that teach the brain to take charge of the body and mobilize all the body's organs to work together in the most efficient fashion. These two scientists, both authorities on holistic sports education, insist that training the emotions should be part of the process.

Mind-Calming Programs

Many Soviet athletes perform a 10-minute mind-calming program before they compete in their events to enable them to eliminate tensions and prepare their nervous systems for very rapid reactions. An athlete who becomes nervous or even panicky before competing will perform mind-calming confidence exercises in addition to the usual visualization techniques.

According to Rozhnov and Alexyev, three-way training involving athlete, coach, and mind trainer is used on a large scale in the Soviet Union; the same approach is also widely used in the performing arts, ballet, and music. Even Soviet cosmonauts are trained in mind/body techniques (Ostrander & Schroeder, 1983).

The Soviet methods of mind/body training have become more streamlined over the years and are now applied as a simple step-by-step routine that takes only a few minutes each day. Neither special equipment nor strenuous physical exercises are needed; in fact, no particular effort or any special belief is required. Practice and imagination are the two keys. Through practice, a link with the unconscious gradually is set up, enabling the athlete to tap the reserves of the mind. Gradually, conscious control of so-called involuntary functions develops and relaxation becomes automatic.

Integration of Left- and Right-Brain Abilities

The system of the Bulgarian Georgi Lozanov is based on suggestology, which was first used in psychotherapy to heal disease and control pain as well as to help people improve their intuitive and so-called extrasensory abilities. Suggestology attempts to get the body working together with left-brain and right-brain abilities as an orchestrated whole to make people more capable of doing whatever they are trying to do (Ostrander & Schroeder, 1983).

Left-brain specialties are involved with logical and factual learning and remembering; right-brain activities deal with intuition, creativity, and (it is claimed) extrasensory abilities. Proponents of the method maintain that the ability to learn and remember can be increased 5 to 50 times. Lozanov claims that both history and experimental data show humans to possess vastly larger capabilities than those they now use (Ostrander & Schroeder, 1983).

From the Lotus Position to the Starting Blocks

In 1975 an American coach, Joan Lyons, experimented with teaching yoga to preteen swimmers, combining yoga techniques and swimming disciplines. The approach concentrated on developing ''calm strength, resembling that of a ballet dancer taking command and moving with purpose and determination'' (Lyons, 1977, p. 126). Lyons maintains that a program of yoga for swimmers alleviates the pain of stress and strengthens the body, mind, and spirit.

Far from interfering with each other, yoga practices are compatible with competitive swimming disciplines and training. Both activities stress the same course of development.

Swimming Training	Yoga Practices
Perfection of strokes	Perfection of postures (asanas)
Breathing techniques	Controlled respiration (pranayama)
Concentration	Meditation (dhyana)

Whereas swimming and other sports involve external actions that develop the muscles, yoga postures work in depth on the interior being. They work partly in the physical plane (viscera, endocrine glands, brain, and voluntary and involuntary nervous systems) and also on the mental level, where they produce the sort of calm and serenity that may be the key to energy and intense concentration.

Lyons (1977) says that yoga postures purify and give maximum flexibility and strength to the skeletal, muscular, and nervous systems. Yoga lays great stress on the effects of having a very supple, strong back and spinal column. The thousands of nerves that control all the organs and areas of the body can be traced back to the gigantic network of nerves in the spine and the brain.

Lyons taught her swimmers to begin at the top of the spine and work throughout the body by stretching, twisting, balancing, and breathing in a specific manner. This process massages the vital organs and increases blood circulation. The gentle, systematic pressure on the glands and vital organs causes hormones to be secreted, which changes the chemistry of the blood. This in turn causes a balanced chemical change in the brain that alleviates tension and stress.

According to Lyons, swimming coaches can adopt the parts of yoga that best suit the needs of competitive swimmers. One of the most important of these is the final complete relaxation exercise done at the end of the half-hour session. Swimmers arousing themselves from a state of complete relaxation are excited and amazed at the body sensations they feel, not least of all a sense of rest and regeneration. The lightness of their bodies and one-pointed, or centered, concentration are also pleasant. Lyons claims that her swimmers learned to use the state of complete relaxation between swimming events at meets and to apply the same kind of focused concentration to the race itself.

Intuition and the Creative Mind: The Intuitive Coach

Many swimming coaches throughout the history of the sport have achieved consistently successful results and built great careers without the use of a scientific approach. Frequently, they were unable to explain their use of a particular method, no matter how successful it might have been. They were often disparagingly said to be using seat-of-the-pants methods. Leading coaches have always been highly intuitive, however, and have used intuition as a built-in guidance system. Because their methods were successful, they felt no obligation to provide additional justification.

Intuition has been defined as a clarifying idea that springs suddenly to mind, an immediate insight or perception in the absence of a conscious process of preliminary reasoning. Intuition is part of the innovative process and plays an important role in the creation of new ideas, concepts, and methods.

Carl Jung, one of the founders of psychoanalysis, was a pioneer in describing the intuitive personality (Campbell, 1971). His description of the "extroverted intuitive" personality aptly describes many successful and highly intuitive swimming coaches:

> The intuitive is never to be found in the world of accepted reality-values, but has a keen nose for anything new and in the making. Because he is always seeking out new possibilities, stable conditions suffocate him. He seizes on new objects or situations with great intensity, sometimes with extraordinary enthusiasm, only to abandon them cold-bloodedly, without any compunction and apparently without remembering them, as soon as their range is known and no further developments can be divined. (Campbell, 1971, p. 223)

Can Intuitive Ability Be Measured?

Top business executives given personality tests that included measurements of intuitive ability were found often to bypass rational processes altogether, particularly when faced with highly complex problems or issues for which there were no precedents (Isenberg, 1984). Likewise, intuitive ability appears to be an important personality factor contributing to the success of great coaches and swimmers, who so often appear to do the right thing at the right time naturally.

Westcott (1968, p. 24) investigated the relative amount of information people need before being able to solve a specific problem. His results prompted four distinct classifications of problem solvers:

1. *Cautious problem solvers* required considerable preliminary information but eventually are successful in solving the problem.

2. *Cautious failures* require considerable preliminary information but do not use it successfully.
3. *Wild guessers* are prepared to act on the basis of limited preliminary information but often are unsuccessful.
4. *Intuitive problem solvers* are able to solve problems with relatively little preliminary information.

Coaching: Art or Science?

Is coaching art, science, or both? It would be a mistake to think of a scientist as a person who merely follows rules of logic and experiment, because a scientist needs to use both rationality and imagination in drawing conclusions from research data. Consider that the ancient Peruvian language had a single word (*hamavec*) for both poet and inventor (Nicolle, 1932): Both artist and scientist obtain assistance from the sudden and unexpected insight of intuition.

There is fairly general agreement that innovative ideas arise from the subconscious activities of a mind that has continued to turn over a problem even though no longer giving it conscious attention.

Research has been conducted on the relationship of intuition to creative thinking and problem solving (Platt & Baker, 1931). Intuitions characteristically occur following a period of intense work on a problem accompanied by a desire for its solution and subsequent abandonment of the work, perhaps with attention given to something else. The intuitive idea then appears with dramatic suddenness and often a sense of certainty. There frequently is a feeling of exhilaration and perhaps surprise that the new idea was not thought of previously. All ideas, including the simple ones that form the gradual steps in ordinary reasoning, probably arise from intuition.

Sometimes ideas spring straight into the conscious mind without deliberate effort to form them. They evidently originate from the subconscious activities of the mind, which when directed at a problem bring together various ideas that previously have been associated with the particular topic. When a possible significant combination is found it is presented to the conscious mind for appraisal.

Conditions Conducive to Creative Thinking

Certain conditions are particularly conducive to innovative thinking.

1. The mind must first be prepared by prolonged, conscious puzzling over the problem.
2. Competing interests or worries are inimical to intuitions and should be avoided.
3. Most people require sufficient privacy and freedom from interruptions.
4. Innovative ideas often appear when the problem is not being worked on so occasional diversion may be beneficial.
5. Positive stimuli should be provided by contacts with other minds via discussion, critical reading, writing, and so on.
6. New ideas sometimes irretrievably disappear from the mind as they come so they should be written down.
7. The absence of mental and physical fatigue.

Shaping the Future of Competitive Swimming

The ideal situation for the success of any national program would be to have the best swimmers training under the best coaches in the best pools and in the best programs. A study of previously successful national programs showed that the real challenge was not in creating the necessary initial momentum but in maintaining it by constantly introducing improved methods and keeping the program alive and interesting. The wave of success tended to crest and gradually fall off.

In some countries, when a national program met with unexpected setbacks there was a panic reaction, with unimaginative administrators resorting to crisis management. The tendency was to scrub all existing plans immediately and start a long process of obtaining input from as many people as possible before embarking on the old standby of management by objectives. Such people have not learned the most important skill of all: the ability to keep abreast of change.

We live in a world of constant and often dramatic change. Despite the great developments in modern technology, the techniques of the various swimming disciplines have not advanced proportionately. Progress demands that we do more than keep up with change; through the use of innovation in developing breakthrough ideas we can actually create change and shape the future. It will be necessary to make innovation the central theme of our work. By generating new ideas and constantly searching for concepts from other disciplines we will learn to use the information explosion to our best advantage.

Knowledge becomes the implement of progress through an ongoing process: observe, discuss, read, study, experiment, accept or reject. Ultimately, though, both thought and action must be guided by personal judgment based on *intuition*. As the French philosopher Descartes said: "Give unqualified assent to no propositions but those the truth of which is so clear and distinct that they cannot be doubted."

Swimmers, coaches, and sport administrators should all constantly try to improve on present methods. Use the same methods year in and year out and you probably will have the same results year in and year out. The "tried and true" is no permanent guarantee for success: Using yesterday's methods is an invitation to be left on the blocks. Every person involved in swimming is capable of devising innovative strategies that can improve the sport in one way or another; in fact, by using intuitive reasoning to solve problems that arise in administration, coaching, and the actual competitive situation, we can improve our ability to innovate. This is how the sport will continue to develop.

Analyzing the reasons for success is part of competitive swimming, part of the constant drive to improve. Synthesizing is easy; innovating is harder. Using the same methods as others may prove successful for a while, but the real leaders are the innovators. It is they who produce continuing results. It is they who will move competitive swimming forward into the 21st century.

Appendix A

A 400-Year Bibliography of the Historical Development of the Swimming Strokes

Grateful thanks are extended to Thomas K. Cureton, a pioneer of scientific research in swimming, for giving me permission to use as a framework for this bibliography the footnotes originally contained in Cureton's two classic volumes, *How to Teach Swimming and Diving*, volumes 1 and 2 (1934).

These materials were then arranged in chronological order and other titles were added. The materials shown in brackets following a number of the entries are the results of further research (including additions, verifications, revisions, and annotations) conducted by me in the records of the Library of Congress; the British Library Catalogue; the National Union Catalog; the Rare Books Division of the National Library of Canada; the Library of Parliament, Canada; and the North Carolina Collection of the University of North Carolina at Chapel Hill.

The bracketed notes point out items of information that might prove interesting to sport historians and scientists (and anyone else interested in swimming). Also, note that the bibliography covers the 400 years from 1531 to 1930. To be sure, the modern definitive texts on swimming appear after these years, but the bibliography is meant to provide historical rather than state-of-the-art resources.

Elyot, Sir Thomas. (1531). *The boke named the governour*. London: Thomas Berthelet.
[This book on the training of gentlemen included a section on swimming. The popularity of the volume is evidenced in a string of new editions—1537, 1544, 1546, 1553, 1557, 1565, and 1580. Near the end of the

19th century, scholars began a set of reprints—1880, 1906, 1962, and 1970, with translations into German and Italian in the 1930s.]

Wynman, Nicolaus. (1538). *Colymbetes, sive de arte natandi dialogus et festivus et iucundus lectu*. (Dutch Copy). Ingolstadt, Bavaria: H. Steiner
[Wynman's very early text experienced many reincarnations—including three Latin reprints a century after its first publication and even an 1889 extract in a German publication titled *Heidelberg*.]

Magnus, Olaus. (1555). *Historia de gentibus septentrionalibus*. Rome: Magno Gotho.
[Magnus' *History of the Nordic Folk* told (among many other things) of swimming practices in Scandinavia. Magnus, Archbishop of Upsala, went into voluntary exile in Rome after the Swedish Reformation. In 1546 he represented Pope Paul III to the Council of Trent. The first complete Italian translation of his history appeared in 1565, some seven years after his death.]

Dygbeio (Digby), Everardo (Sir Everard). (1587). *De arte natandi libri duo, quorum prior regulas ipsius artis, posterior vero praxin demonstrationemque continet*. London: (s.n.).
[Digby's *The Art of Swimming . . .* was a seminal work that inspired Melchisedech Thevenot's *L'Art de nager* a century later. Unfortunately, the value of the work was long overshadowed by Digby's infamous role in Guy Faulks' Gunpowder Plot. In fact, Digby himself wrote papers about the plot during his imprisonment in the Tower

of London, after which he and seven other conspirators were executed by being hanged, drawn, and quartered—the stipulated punishment for treason.]

Middleton, Christopher. (1595). *A short introduction for to learne to swimme gathered out of Master Digbie's booke of the art of swimming* (trans.). London: (s.n.).

Percey, William. (1658). *The complete swimmer, or The art of swimming.* London: J.C. for H. Fletcher.

Thevenot, Melchisedech. (1696). *L'art de nager.* Paris: T. Moette.

[Thevenot's *The Art of Swimming* took inspiration (and material) from Digby's 1587 work. Thevenot's book was described variously as "advice for bathing," a "discourse concerning artificial swimming," and a guide to "different postures necessary to be used in that art." This popular work went into three English editions (the first in 1699) and was published in a number of abridgments from 1696 to 1972. Thevenot was a distinguished Oriental scholar and a founder of the French Academy of Sciences. In addition to *The Art of Swimming*, he wrote *Recueil de Voyages de M. Thevenot* (discussing the art of navigation) in 1681 and *Bibliotheca Thevenotiana* (a catalog of the valuable books under his care as curator of the Royal Library).]

M'Iver, J. (1764). *The art of swimming, with advice for bathing* (Thevenot, trans.). London: John Lever.

Bernardi, de Oronzio. (1797). *Vollstandiger Lehrbegriff der Schwimmkunst, auf neue Versuche uber die spezifische Schwere des menschlichen Korpers gegrundet.* Weimar: (s.n.).

Muths, Guts. (1798). *Kleines lehrbuch der Schwimmkunst zum selbstunterrichte* (Manual for self-instruction in the art of swimming). Weimar: (s.n.).

Muths, Guts. (1798). *Th. Chr. Fr. Lehrbuch d. Schwimmkunst gr.* Weimar: (s.n.).

Strutt, Joseph. (1801). *Glig-gamena angel-deod*, or *The sports and pastimes of the people of England.* London: White.

[This work outlasted three authors, five publishers, and the whole 19th century with 10 editions spanning 1801 to 1903. Of course it dealt with more than swimming, but the swimming discussion (p. 66 of the original edition) provides some insight into this ancient island nation's perception of swimming.]

Bernardi, de Oronzio. (1807). *Arte de Nadar Compendiada del que Escribio en Italiano.* Madrid: (s.n.).

Frost, J. (1816). *Scientific swimming.* London: (s.n.).

[Frost, Teacher of the Art of Swimming at Nottingham, sought to approach swimming scientifically. His *Scientific Swimming* was described as a series of scientific instructions that facilitated the attainment of the art of swimming.]

Frost, J. (1818). *The art of swimming.* New York: P.W. Gallaudet.

Clias, Peter H. (1825). *An elementary course of gymnastic exercises and a new and complete treatise on the art of swimming with the report made to the medical faculty of Paris on the subject* (4th ed.). London: Sherwood, Gilbert & Piper.

Mason, James, & Payne, A.M. (1839 & 1840). *Prize essays of the national, now the British society on the art of swimming.* London: (s.n.).

Howard, Sydney (pseudonym). (1849). *The science of swimming as taught and practiced in civilized and savage countries.* New York: Fowler and Wells.

Richardson, B.C. (1857). *Instructions in the art of swimming.* London: (s.n.).

Forrest, George (pseudonym for John George Wood). (1858). *A handbook of swimming and skating.* London: Routledge & Sons.

Forrest, George (pseudonym for John George Wood). (1863). *A handbook of swimming.* London: Routledge & Sons.

Steedman, Charles. (1867). *Manual of swimming, including bathing, plunging, diving, floating, scientific swimming, training, drowning, and rescuing.* Melbourne: (s.n.).

Beadle. (1869). *Dime guide to swimming.* New York: (s.n.).

Wilson, William. (1876). *The swimming instructor.* Glasgow: (s.n.).

Wilson, William (1883). *The swimming instructor.* London: (s.n.).

Sinclair, A., & Henry, W. (1893). *Swimming.* London: Longmans, Green.

[By 1912, this volume was in its seventh "impression" with four new editions and three reprinted editions. Sinclair and Henry were both honorary secretaries of the Royal Life-Saving Society, and Henry was one of the founders of F.I.N.A., the international governing body of swimming.]

Riley, Tom. (1903). *Swimming*. New York: (s.n.).

Douglas, W.G. (1903). *How to swim*. New York: American Sports.

Sterrett, James H. (1903). *How to swim*. New York: American Sports.

[As well as covering the by-now standard topics of swimming with various strokes, diving, and floating, Sterrett's book contains "a chapter on modern life-saving, and one for women and girl swimmers." Sterrett was known as "The Father of American Swimming."]

Thomas, Ralph. (1904). *Swimming*. London: Sampson Low, Marston.

[The nonspecific title hides the uniqueness of Thomas' book—a bibliography of swimming books in English, German, French, and other European languages. The book also discusses swimming and resuscitation and includes a history of swimming and biographies of persons important in the field. Under the pseudonym of Hamst Olphar, Thomas also wrote *The Handbook of Fictitious Names* (1868).]

Fountain, P. (1904). *The swimming powers of animals*. London: (s.n.).

Daniels, C.M., Johnson, H., & Sinclair, A. (1907). *How to swim and save life* (Spalding's Athletic Library, no. 21). London: British Sports.

Sinclair, Archibald. (1909). *Swimming*. London: Routledge & Son.

Sachs, Frank. (1912). *The complete swimmer*. London: Methuen.

Daniels, C.M. (1919). *Speed swimming*. New York: American Sports.

Handley, Louis de B. (1920). *Swimming and watermanship*. New York: MacMillan.

Bachrach, William. (1924). *The outline of swimming*. Chicago: Author.

Handley, Louis de B. (1927). *Swimming for women*. New York: American Sports.

Sullivan, Frank. (1927). *The science of swimming*. New York: American Sports.

Cureton, T.K. (1929). Outline of Pageant. *Evolution of swimming*. Philadelphia: P. Blakison's Son.

Handley, Louis de B., & Howcroft, W.J. (1929). *Crawl-stroke swimming*. London: E.J. Larby.

Weissmuller, John, & Bush, Clarence. (1930). *Swimming the American crawl*. Boston: Houghton.

Appendix B

Training Schedules of Top Coaches and Top Athletes

Training for the Distance Events (800- and 1,500-Meter Freestyle)

There are two important factors in developing endurance: increasing the distance swum (prolonging the activity) and increasing the speed over the established distance. Combining these two will enable a swimmer to cover more distance in a given time (Colwin, 1977).

Shoulberg (1983) says that the key to distance training is to increase the number of yards per minute, *not* the number of minutes per day. When Tony Corbisiero set an American record at the N.C.A.A. championships in 1983, his coach, Don Galluzi, attributed Corbisiero's success to the fact that he had increased the yards per minute he covered in training. Shoulberg's point is that there has been an unnecessary tendency to increase the amount of training time instead of concentrating on improving the speed of the long-distance training swims.

Jochums (1982) says almost the same thing as Shoulberg, that too many coaches are still too wrapped up in the yardage syndrome and that the true definition of work is the yardage times the intensity of the effort at which the work is done.

Shoulberg (1985) says that his distance swimmers train for 1 hour before school and again for 2 hours and 40 minutes after school. The additional 40 minutes in the afternoon is used either for training on the biokinetic bench or for doing light weights. Shoulberg uses a variety of pool sizes (e.g., 25 yards, 15.3 meters, 25 meters, 33 meters, 50 meters, and even 80 meters).

Shoulberg's swimmers never do distance training on consecutive days with the exception of Saturdays and Sundays.

Shoulberg's swimmers practice at various speeds and paces to avoid boredom. Sometimes his swimmers will do 5,000-yard straight swims in which they fluctuate their speeds. They vary the time for each 100 by setting different paces; for example, swimming several 100s at 68 seconds, another batch at 1:02 and then easing back to 1:04 for several more 100s before stepping up the pace to full racing speed. Shoulberg says that this type of work is good for heart conditioning.

Shoulberg uses another variation of the straight 5,000-yard swim by setting a prescribed pace for each 500. The first 500 should be covered in 5:08 and then the swimmer changes the time for each 500 by swimming either a little slower or a little faster. Shoulberg insists that his swimmers literally race when doing this particular training item.

Shoulberg also uses "catch-up" swims in which swimmers of *almost equal* ability would start from opposite ends of the pool and swim 5,000 yards trying to overtake each other.

Tiffany Cohen (Schubert, 1985) describes her training under Mark Schubert prior to winning the 1984 Olympic 1,500-meter title. Cohen's favorite training set was a 15 × 300 in which she would try to attain her fastest workout time during the last five 300s. She claims that the key to her success was that she always attempted to record a best workout time for any set she did in training. A favorite item, and one she found to be a very tough workout item, was a 1-hour nonstop swim in which she tried to increase the distance covered. The average 100-meter pace recorded in this 1-hour swim was later incorporated in subsequent workout sets both as a guide to pace and as a challenge. (This last item bears a strong resemblance to the fartlek method of tempo training used on the running track and described in chapter 6, "The Influence of Track Training on Swimming.")

The Speed Factor in Distance Training

Speed is an important factor in 800-meter and 1,500-meter swimming because it gives a swimmer who already has considerable endurance the ability to use a variety of tactics.

Many coaches include fast (rested) swims as part of preparing their distance swimmers. Fast 50s will be part of nearly every workout and there will be a set of quality (rested) 100s, 200s, or 300s two or three times a week. Schubert (1985) stresses the importance of weight train-

ing for 1,500-meter swimmers because, in his view, this work develops the speed necessary in top-level competition.

However, in the late 1980s coaches were not unanimous on whether distance swimmers should train with weights. Jochums (1982) is adamant that distance swimmers should keep out of the weight room. He believes that it is better for distance swimmers to stay on the thin side and adds that the transfer of strength from the weight room to the swimming pool is under 10%. Jochums says that weight-training distance swimmers develop large shoulders and muscles to the detriment of their performance.

Counsilman (1984) expresses the similar belief that some weight-training swimmers had become too strong and that their endurance had suffered severely. He says that although one type of training may have a beneficial effect on a particular trait it will produce an opposite effect on contrasting traits. Therefore, coaches should try to balance their training methods to achieve *optimal* and not maximal adaptations of the desired physiological traits.

Mark Schubert on Training 1,500-Meter Swimmers

Mark Schubert coached Brian Goodell, 1976 Montreal Olympic 1,500-meter champion and world-record holder, as well as Tiffany Cohen, 1,500-meter Olympic champion at Los Angeles in 1984.

All coaches agree that it is important for swimmers training for distance events to develop a good endurance base while still young. Mark Schubert, in conversation with me (Colwin, 1983b, used by permission), said that most of his very young swimmers do far more endurance training than speed work. The speed element is introduced to their training when the swimmers became older.

Schubert believes it important that swimmers train primarily by using descending sets, which teaches them to increase speed at the close of a race. Schubert also emphasizes negative splitting in individual practice swims in 90% of a swimmer's workouts.

Discussing the importance of speed and sprint training for distance events, Schubert said that all his swimmers are taught a six-beat kick for use in the closing stages of a distance race when extra speed was necessary. For the first 1,300 to 1,400-meters of a 1,500-meter race his swimmers typically use an energy-conserving two-beat kick but switch to a six-beat kick for speed over the final 100 to 200 meters. For this reason, Schubert's swimmers work on 25-meter sprints in practice while using a six-beat kick technique.

Schubert's swimmers do many pace-simulated 1,500s during a season in descending sets of two to five repetitions. These sets are always descended and done with negative splitting (for an explanation of these terms see chapter 7, "Basic Principles of Training").

Most of Schubert's pace sessions are done with 1,500-meter swims broken at 50, 100, or

150 meters. These are swum at race pace—sometimes with a short rest, sometimes with a longer rest, and sometimes with an easy swim ("active rest") between the pace work.

Schubert usually tries to keep the swimmers to a fairly challenging rest interval between the 1,500s. When assigning a set of as many as five 1,500s Schubert will descend the rest intervals. For example, the better swimmers might descend the intervals from "on 18 minutes" to "on 17 minutes" or even to "on 16 minutes, 30 seconds."

Sometimes Schubert will encourage the swimmers to take an active rest by swimming lightly between 1,500s. However, he said that it is necessary to be able to simulate the race situation by doing quality work without the benefit of a preliminary active rest.

Schubert's swimmers do not do negative

splitting all the time; he teaches other paces to enable them to counter unexpected situations that arise in actual competition. He believes it very important that a good distance swimmer have a "full bag of tricks," so his swimmers often practice different sets in which a swimmer will go out very fast at the beginning, or work the middle part of a race, or just practice swimming fast at the end. It is also important to practice "sprinting" for 200 meters or so to learn how to pull away from a rival swimmer or wear a competitor down.

To study tactics Schubert said that he tries to attend as many major championships as he can to observe other swimmers and learn how they swim their races and how they can be beaten. Schubert said that he spends much time educating his swimmers on the tactics to be used in competition.

Sherman Chavoor on Training 1,500-Meter Swimmers

Sherman Chavoor, in discussion with me, said that he based his concepts on training for the 1,500 on his observations of two great Japanese swimmers, Furuhashi and Hashizume, when they both broke the 1,500-meter world record at the Los Angeles Coliseum in 1950. Chavoor was particularly impressed that they both broke the world record for 800 meters on the way.

Chavoor, a pioneer of overdistance swimming, coached such great swimmers as Mike Burton, Debbie Meyer, Mark Spitz, John Ferris, Vickie King, and Sue Pederson to swim "farther and faster." Mike Burton was the first of Chavoor's protégés to prove what can be done by overdistance training at speed, after which younger swimmers on Chavoor's team also started working hard and became able to swim a timed 1,500 meters in training three times a week.

Chavoor believes that a swimmer who has learned to swim quickly over long distances eventually will also become a good sprinter. Mark Spitz, an early Chavoor protégé, was to win a record seven gold medals at the 1972 Munich Olympic Games. Not only did Spitz grow up in Chavoor's "overdistance at speed" pro-

gram but he was also a great distance swimmer who at one time missed the 1,500-meter world record by a scant four tenths of a second. Later, when Spitz when to Indiana University and trained under James Counsilman, he cut down to swimming 100s and 200s with the results that the world now knows so well.

Citing the benefits of fast distance training, Chavoor said that Debbie Meyer was a very thin girl when she first started in his distance program but as a result later became very strong. Chavoor added that though Mike Burton was not a very strong boy when he first started, his first impression was that Burton might be able to qualify to compete in the national championships by following a distance program rather than sprinting.

Chavoor's philosophy on the importance of the early long-distance base spread worldwide, and many great swimmers were reared on this type of program. Initially, Chavoor's methods encountered much resistance, but Mike Burton, Chavoor's original guinea pig, inspired other youngsters to attempt the same distance training program. Not only did Chavoor's swimmers start making tremendous improvement through long-distance training, but other coaches eventually were able to encourage their swimmers to follow suit.

All Chavoor's great swimmers were able to swim fast at distances from 25 yards to 3,000. Mike Burton's ability to do such training items as three 1,500s in training, considered unique at the time, soon became commonplace. In midseason Burton would swim daily an average of 10,000 to 14,000 yards.

Chavoor held the view that a great long-distance swimmer can swim a good time at any distance. For example, Mike Burton was a great distance swimmer, the 1,500-meter Olympic champion and world-record holder, yet he was an N.C.A.A. record holder in the 500-yard freestyle in 1970 with a time of 4:37.29 and a fast 200-yard freestyler. He always made the team at 200-yard freestyle and was N.C.A.A. champion at the 200-yard butterfly (1:51.60) in 1970. Burton was a good sprinter, too, with a ranking of seventh in the world at one time. Chavoor also cited Mark Spitz's winning the N.C.A.A. 500-yard freestyle in 1969 as another example of how easy it is for a distance-reared swimmer to move up or down the scale. (*Note*. Used by permission.)

Dick Jochums on Training
1,500-Meter Swimmers

Dick Jochums says that intensity is the key to training for the 1,500-meter event just as it is in preparing for sprinting. (*Note*. From Jochums, 1982. Used by permission of the American Swimming Coaches Association.)

Jochum's swimmers train a maximum of 16,000 meters a day, usually somewhat less. During the college year, his swimmers train 12,000 meters a day. In morning workouts they swim for 1 hour, often completing the difficult task of covering 6,000 yards within that time. The afternoon sessions are a little longer, and the distance swimmers complete about 8,000 yards.

Jochums believes in having his swimmers do many descending series, each succeeding series becoming faster until the swimmer eventually is moving at race pace. Race speed should be achieved at least three times in a workout.

Jochums usually sets his swimmers a triple series with the final series done at race pace to enable them to recognize it in competition. He maintains that by pacing the workout swimmers can achieve quality swims three different times in an afternoon session.

Jochums stresses the important difference between short- and long-course swimming. In long-course training he provides a slightly longer rest period between 100s in interval swimming, increasing it by about 10 seconds, for example. He also stresses the importance of using the pool walls efficiently in long-course swimming, building tempo as the swimmer approaches the wall and emphasizing good swimming technique. Jochums believes that technique and not just sheer power is even more important in long-course swimming than it is in the short course (Jochums, 1982).

Igor Koshkin on Training
for the 1,500 Meters Event

Igor Koshkin describes the training methods of 1980 and 1988 Olympic 1,500-meter champion Vladimir Salnikov, the first swimmer to beat 15 minutes for that event. (*Note*. From Koshkin, 1985. Used by permission of the American Swimming Coaches Association.)

Salnikov's complex program progressed through various stages of preparation that changed in emphasis during the training year. Salnikov's annual training between 1980 and 1984 varied from 3,000 to 3,500 kilometers in the water, 250 to 300 hours of land preparation, and 90 to 100 starts, including time trials. The season was divided into five spirals each lasting 8 to 12 weeks. Each spiral ended with competitions of from 1 to 3 weeks.

Salnikov's land training consisted of four major components:

1. Strength building (60%)
2. Specific flexibility (30%)
3. Game preparation (5%)
4. Cross-country racing (5%)

To carry out systematic development, a system of specific exercises was developed that included 12 exercise programs and 150 different land exercises.

Salnikov's psychological preparation included autosuggestion and relaxation techniques. According to Koshkin, hypnosis was used for mobilizing the athlete to a state of readiness, development of personal qualities, and the improvement of swimming techniques.

Salnikov trained twice daily on four days of the week and once daily on Friday, Saturday, and Sunday. Above and below water filming was used to analyze stroke technique. A system of pulse rate and blood lactate testing was used within each of the five mesocycles. The tests were sometimes conducted on four different days of the week; different training items were tested on each of these days. The tests were always specific to the physiological quality the swimmer was trying to achieve during a particular mesocycle.

Tapering for the 1,500-Meter Event

Most 1,500-meter swimmers who have a solid seasonal background of strenuous training taper very late. Rather than reduce the pace intensity of training during the taper period, the duration of the workout is reduced gradually while the intensity usually remains the same.

For example, Shoulberg (1985) says that a 1-hour swim should be reduced to 45 minutes but the intensity should remain similar to that of a 60-minute swim. By the same token, an afternoon workout of 120 minutes should be reduced to 70 minutes while retaining the same intensity.

Lightly built male swimmers and female swimmers should be tapered later, and the heavier distance swimmers should undergo a greater reduction of workout time: Instead of reducing from 120 minutes to 70 minutes, the heavier athlete should cut down gradually to a 50-minute workout.

Peter Daland (Schubert, 1985) states a simple formula for tapering: The longer the race, the shorter the taper. The heavier the body type, the longer the taper. The more nervous the swimmer, the shorter the taper.

Jochums (1982) uses a basic 14-day taper and reduces the distance swum by about a third as the taper progresses. His swimmers warm up at least 2,500 to 3,000 meters twice a day, totaling about 5,000 to 6,000 meters daily during the taper period. Much of this is easy swimming.

Bud McAllister on Training Olympic Champion Janet Evans for the Individual Medley and Middle- to Long-Distance Freestyle

Bud McAllister coached American star Janet Evans, then 17 years old, to three gold medals at the 1988 Olympic Games in Seoul. Her winning times were as follows:

400-meter 4:37.76

400-meter freestyle 4:03.85 (world record)

800-meter freestyle 8:20.20 (Olympic record)

Janet Evans: Midseason Training Sets and Performance Indications

These schedules are excerpted from an interview with coach McAllister by John Leonard in *ASCA Magazine*. (Note. From Leonard, 1988. Reprinted by permission of the American Swimming Coaches Association.)

Individual Medley

200 at 2:45, 400 at 5:30, 600 at 8:15, 800 at 11:00,

600 at 7:45 (swam 7:38), 400 at 5:10 (swam 4:59), and

200 at 2:35 (swam 2:27)

This set was first swum at 3:00 per 200 on all distances going up, then at 2:45 from the second 600 down.

Also 20 × 400 individual medley, with 4 at 6:00, 4 at 5:50, 4 at 5:40, 4 at 5:30, 4 at 5:20 (last set of 4 were done in 5:12, 5:09, 5:07, 5:04)

Also, 4,000 individual medley—1,000 of each stroke. Time 52:29 (5:13 average each 400 individual medley) (Janet has dropped over 1 minute from her first time through this swim.)

On the following set I gradually lowered the 400 individual medley intervals and watched her go faster.

600 individual medley at 9:00, then 3 × 400 individual medley at 5:25 (5:13, 5:13, 5:11)

600 individual medley at 9:00, then 2 × 400 individual medley at 5:15 (5:06, 5:01)

600 individual medley at 9:00, then 1 × 400 individual medley at 5:05 (4:53)

Butterfly Set: 24 × 100

1 each at 1:30, 1:25, 1:20, 1:15
2 each at 1:30, 1:25, 1:20, 1:15
3 each at 1:30, 1:25, 1:20, 1:15

Janet's last three were 1:12, 1:12, 1:12.

Freestyle Set: 12 × 150

3 at 2:05, 1 at 1:50 then,
2 at 2:00, 2 at 1:45 then,
1 at 1:55, 3 at 1:40

Janet's last three were 1:36, 1:37, 1:38. Janet has done 3 × 150 at 1:40. Also

4 × 100 at 1:25, 3 × 200 at 2:40, 2 × 300 at 3:45 and 1 × 400 at 4:40 (Janet did 4:13)

8 × 300 with 2 at 3:45, then 2 at 3:25, 3:45, 3:20 (on the 3:20, Janet went 3:17, 3:19)

These were some of the toughest and best sets Janet Evans made. She has also done intense middle-distance freestyle sets, such as eight 300s with two at 3:45, two at 3:25, two at 3:45, and two at 3:20. During school vacations, she does slightly more yardage: 14,000 to 15,000 a day rather than 13,000 to 14,000.

Sample Workouts
From World-Record Distance Swimmer
Kim Linehan's Training Program

Note. From Blood (1978). Reprinted by permission of *Swimming World* magazine.

Indoor Season:
Short Course (Yards)

Morning

Warm-up:

500 free, breathe five strokes; eight 25s free, board drill.

Main Series:

(Two sets of each with 15 seconds rest):

500, 400, 300, 200, 100 (first set free swim, descend pace, second set hard swim)

4 × 500, 1-minute rest, hold all times at 5:03

1. 15 seconds rest at 100s
2. 10 seconds rest at 100s
3. 5 seconds rest at 100s
4. straight

8 × 50 breaststroke (odd pull, even kick)

Total: 6,100 yards

Afternoon

Warm-up:

2,000 individual medley reverse with 500 each stroke as follows:

3 × 100 stroke series

200 swim, descend by 50s

Main Series:

12 × 100 free, 10 seconds rest, descend in pairs

6 × 200 free at 2:10

12 × 100 specialty, no free, 10 seconds rest, descend in pairs (butterfly)

6 × 200 same on 2:45 (butterfly)

20 × 50 kick: 1-5 free at 50 seconds, 6-10 choice at 1:00, 11-15 free at 50 seconds, 16-20 choice at 1:00

Total: 8,800 yards

Outdoor Season: Long Course (Meters)

Morning

Warm-up:

4 × 500 with 15 seconds rest

Swim freestyle

Descend by 100s free

Swim backstroke

Descend by 100s backstroke

Main Series:

6 × 800 free at 10:00

1. straight
2. straight
3. 10 seconds at 400s
4. 10 seconds at 200s
5. 10 seconds at 100s under 1:06
6. 10 seconds at 100s at 1:04 or better

1,200: odd 100s kick, 75 hard, 25 medium; even 100s pull, 75 medium, 25 hard.

6 × 150, 6 × 100, 6 × 50: choice of cycle and stroke, no freestyle (each set begins at 6:00)

Total: 8,900 meters

Outdoor Season: Short Course (Yards)

Morning

Warm-up:

12 × 100 with 5 seconds rest

4 sets of 3: 100 kick, 100 pull, 100 swim (one set each stroke)

8 × 100: descend by 2s at 1:30

Main Series:

10 × 225 at 3:00
☐ Odd: 75 each stroke
☐ Even:
   2. 75 fly, 50 back, 50 breast, 50 free
   4. 50 fly, 75 back, 50 breast, 50 free
   6. 50 fly, 50 back, 75 breast, 50 free
   8. 50 fly, 50 back, 50 breast, 75 free
   10. 50 each, 75 weakest stroke

10 × 100 at 1:20
☐ Odd:
   1. 50 fly, 50 back
   3. 50 back, 50 breast
   5. 50 breast, 50 free
   7. 50 fly, 50 back
   9. 50 back, 50 breast
☐ Even 100 individual medley

500 kick, 50 hard free and 50 medium choice

20 × 50 choice at 0:45 second—four sets of five with each set as follows:
1. 25 sprint; 25 easy
2. 25 sprint; 25 moderate
3. 25 sprint; 25 moderate/hard
4. 50 sprint; 27 or under free, 30 or under fly, 31 or under back, 37 or under breast

Total: 6,750 yards

Training for the Shorter Distances

Lars-Erik Paulson's Sample Workout for Short-Distance Swimmers

Bill Sweetenham, head coach of the Australian Institute of Sport, makes the following comparison between sprint and distance swimming: "I always tell my swimmers that sprinting is concentration, energy systems and training fast. This has nothing to do with distance swimming. It's like two different sports, so you shouldn't use one philosophy to train for the other" (Young, 1986b, p. 11).

Patricia Young (1986a) highlights the importance of basic speed to the short-distance swimmer. She cites comments by Lars-Erik Paulson, noted Swedish coach of world-class sprinter Per Johansson, European champion in 1981 and 1983 and Olympic bronze medalist in 1980 and 1984.

At an international coaches' conference in Helsinki, Paulson said that he did not believe in having his swimmers do a great many repetitions but instead aimed for the highest possible quality during each set. He said that "quantity is the enemy of quality." (Paulson's talk was translated by Marek Barlowski, coach of the Y Laser Swim Club in Saskatoon, Canada.) (*Note.* Workout is from *Swim Canada* magazine. Used by permission.)

Midseason Short Course

Morning

500 meter warm-up

20 × 25 1 to 4, descending on 30 seconds

1,000 kick (rarely done)

1,000 pull with pull buoy and sprint into turns

3 × 100 in sets of 4 × 25 "super sprint set" at about 2:40 pace, performed without breathing or all-out

400 swim 10 strokes of each of fly, back, breast, free

10 × 50 fly on 50 second pace

10 × 50 back on 60 second pace

10 × 50 breast on 1:10 pace

10 × 50 free on 45 second pace

200 kick fly with no board

3 × 100 kick on main stroke

3 × 100 pull on main stroke

3 × 100 swim main stroke with long rest; start when swimmer feels ready

Late Season Short Course: 8 Days Before Nationals

Morning

200 swim main stroke, work on technique

4 × 25 sprint, long rest

400 swim easy swim, concentrate on technique, maximum sprint 5 meters in and out of turn

10 minutes rest

3 × 50 "mini-max" swimming (maximum speed with minimum number of strokes)

10 minutes swim easy, any stroke

Testing series (every 2 weeks)

Test to last 1 hour, swimmer to do 4 × 100 with high quality and descending progression of times. Test is done after a regular warm-up.

<table>
<tr><th colspan="4">Example Set Done by Per Johansson
Two Weeks Before Swedish Championships:
Long Course</th></tr>
<tr><td></td><td>First
50</td><td>Second
50</td><td>Final
time</td></tr>
<tr><td>First</td><td>26.55</td><td>29.13</td><td>55.78</td></tr>
<tr><td>Second</td><td>25.52</td><td>28.12</td><td>53.64</td></tr>
<tr><td>Third</td><td>25.10</td><td>28.12</td><td>52.50</td></tr>
<tr><td>Fourth</td><td>24.68</td><td>27.07</td><td>51.75</td></tr>
</table>

Per Johansson's Times From 1980 to 1985						
	80	81	82	83	84	85
50 free				23.35	23.83	23.21
100 free	51.29	50.55	50.19	50.20	50.31	51.02

Training for the 50-Meter Freestyle: Sample Workout Set Used by Tamara Costache

Note. Workout is from *Swimming World* magazine. Used by permission of *Swimming World*. In 1988 Tamara Costache was one of the fastest 50-meter freestyle swimmers in the world with a best-ever time of 25.28 (Ewald, 1988a, b). (This time was beaten by China's Wenyi Yang, who set a world record of 24.98 seconds early in 1988. Kristin Otto won the gold in the 50-meter freestyle at the Seoul Olympic Games in 1988, with a time of 25.49, an Olympic record. Wenyi Yang was second in this Olympic event with the time of 25.64, and Costache [sixth] recorded 25.80.)

Long Course (Meters)

Morning

Warm-up:

400 free

300 back

200 breast

100 fly

4 × 50: 25 fly, 25 free, breathe every 5 to 7 strokes

4 × 25: freestyle without breathing the whole 25

Base training:

4 × (5 × 100 free) in two stages

- stages 1 and 3 with paddles at 1:20
- stages 2 and 4 without paddles at 1:30

2 × (10 × 50 fly)

- stage 1 with fins at 0:50
- stage 2 without fins at 1:00

Kicking for 200 easy

8 × 50 at 1:00 without fins

Arm workout with paddles and float

- 8 × 50 free at 0:50

Intense swim at 85% with start dive

- 4 × 50 at 1:30 (3 free in 26.0 to 27.5; 1 fly in 27.5 to 30.0)
- 6 × 25 (4 free at 11.8 to 11.9; 2 fly at 12.7 to 12.8) *Note*: 25 meters swum fast at times shown and last 25 meters of the lap swum relaxed.

300 free relaxed

The morning session lasts from 6:30 to 8:30 a.m. prior to school. It usually emphasizes physical training and starts with a half hour of exercises to warm up. The total swimming workout covers from 6,000 to 7,000 meters.

The afternoon workout runs from 4 to 7 or 7:40 p.m. and includes weight training for an hour to an hour and a half on 14 different pieces of apparatus designed specially for swimmers. The pool workout consists of longer distances to work on endurance but none more than a 400 free and mostly 200s.

Training for the 100- and 200-Meter Backstroke Events: Theresa Andrews

The following excerpts from the pre-Olympic training program of 1984 Olympic 100-meter backstroke champion Theresa Andrews were provided by her coach, Murray Stephens, owner and head coach of the North Baltimore Aquatic Club, and are reprinted here with his permission. In correspondence with me, Stephens explained that he had tried to show some of the day-to-day-work performed by Andrews in preparation for the U.S. Olympic team at the end of June 1984. The timed workouts show the gains made over a 6-week period as a result of an "interesting balance of endurance training and speed work."

Examples of Pre-Olympic Training

Body Weight

1978 age 16: 128 lbs. 100-meter backstroke 1:06.33

1984 age 21: 131 lbs. 100-meter backstroke 1:02.55

(*Note*: Andrews' weight in college went as high as 145 pounds.)

Schedule

Monday, May 8, 1984:
(Short Course [Yards])

8 × 100 freestyle/individual medley (1:25)

20 × 100 backstroke (1:30) average 1:06

5 × 100 freestyle (1:30) smooth

10 × 50 butterfly (1:00) control

15 minutes practicing backstroke turns and push-offs

Tuesday, May 9, 1984:
(Short Course [Yards])

40 × 50 (10 kick, 10 swim, 10 pull, 10 swim choice)

3 × 200 backstroke pull (1st at 2:18)

8 × 50 backstroke pull fast, average 30 seconds

24 × 25 (swim 3 × [5 × 25 plus 3 × 25 fast]) 30 seconds

Saturday, May 20, 1984:
(Long Course, Wakefield, Virginia) Swim for 2 minutes in between the following sets:

4 × [200 free, 200 individual medley] 1,600

10 × 50 backstroke (0:45) at 37-38

10 × 50 backstroke (0:50) at 36

10 × 50 backstroke (0:55) at 34-35

5 × 50 backstroke (1:05) 34/34/33/32/33

Monday, May 22, 1984:
(Short Course [Yards])

3 × (100 free [10], 100 backstroke [10], 100 breaststroke [10] 100 kick-swim fly [10])

5 × 300 backstroke pull (30) long full pull

16 × 50 backstroke (3 with left arm only, 1 with right arm; all fast and progressive in sets of 4)

10 × 25 backstroke sprints alternate arm swimming—did 15.5 seconds average each arm

3 × (5 × 100 kick) 2:10 backstroke
☐ 1st set: 1:35-1:31
☐ 2nd set: 1:30-1:28
☐ 3rd set: 1:30-1:25

20 × 50 freestyle (40) as a swim down

Sunday, May 28, 1984:
(Short Course [Yards])

400 freestyle 400 ST 4 × 100 (10) backstroke-breaststroke

3 × 100 (10 × 75) backstroke
☐ interval (1:20) did 0:51; (1:15) did 0:48; (1:10) did 0:46; last one in 0:45

24 × 25 (30)

10 × 50 freestyle (40) swim down

Wednesday, June 7, 1984:
(Short Course [Yards])

5 × 100 freestyle (1:30)

5 × 100 paddles (1:40)

5 × 100 kick (2:00)

4 × 100 backstroke (1:13, 1:10, 1:09, 1:07.5)

Four sets of 3 × 50 (50) active rests between sets

Thursday, June 8, 1984:
(Short Course [Yards])

12 × 100 (2 × [3 swim - 3 kick])

3 sets of 5 × 100 (1:40, 1:35, 1:30)

Last set did 1:03.6, 1:03.6, 1:03.6, 1:03.3, 1:03.0

3 × 300 pull easy moderate

10 × 75 swim easy moderate

20 × 50 freestyle—three breaths per 25 (45)

Do 5 starts, 10 turns, 3 × 10 squat jumps on deck.

Saturday, June 10, 1984:
(Long Course, Navy Pool, Annapolis)

300 Swim: 2 × 100 kick

backstroke 3 × (400 [6:40], 300 [5:00], 200 [3:20], 100 [1:40])

4 × 50 backstroke (1:40) 37.6, 35.1, 32.6, 30.9

2 × (3 × 100 fly, 2 × 100 backstroke kick, 2 × 50 butterfly, 100 backstroke drill)

Tuesday, June 20, 1984:
(Short Course [Yards]) (one week before the start of the Olympic trials)

300 swim plus 4 × 50 kick, 4 × 50 pull, 4 × 50 swim

2 × 100 negative (3:00) 33-30.7; 33-29.3

This time seems close to 32 seconds for second 50 of Los Angeles Olympics 100-meter backstroke 6 weeks later.

2 × 50 negative (2:00) 16.3-13.6; 16.4-14.0 (good 25s done from a turn)

6 × 25 descending done by 2s (pairs) from a push

8 × 100 freestyle-butterfly (1:40) changing stroke each 25

Pull 8 × 100 (1:30) BH (breath hold)

300 easy

Steve Bultman on Training for the 100-Meter and 200-Meter Backstroke Events

The following are excerpts from the training program of Andrea Hayes and Cynthia Barr conducted by Steve Bultman at the Greater Pensacola Aquatics Club. (*Note.* From Muckenfuss, 1986b. Reprinted by permission).

Early and Midseason Workouts

Early Season

Warm-up:

300 choice

7 × 300 individual medley (20 seconds rest)
☐ odd: swim and descend
☐ even: 50 stroke drill/25 swim
☐ hold times the same

Kick:

5 × 200—one 200 each stroke
☐ one choice (3:20)

Swim:

7 × 200 backstroke
☐ 1-3 stroke drill/100 swim (2:55)
☐ 4-7 swim (2:45)
25 easy

Kick:

100 freestyle, no board, to loosen

Swim:

12 × 150 freestyle
☐ 1-4 pull buoy, paddles, tube (2:05)

☐ 5-6 pull buoy (1:55)

☐ 7-8 75 stroke drill/75 swim (1:55)

☐9-12 swim (1:45) hold the same time on the last one

50 easy

100 easy

Midseason

Warm-up:

400 freestyle

600 reverse individual medley—50 kick/50 stroke drill/50 swim

200 choice

Swim:

18 × 25 (0:30): six sets of 25 kick, 25 stroke drill, 25 sprint 2/3 lap; one set of each stroke, individual medley order, two sets backstroke

Kick:

400 individual medley

200 backstroke

6 × 50/100 (1:30): 50 is easy choice, 100 is fast backstroke (descend 100s 1-3, 4-6)

50 easy

Swim:

12 × 50 (0:40): odd freestyle; even backstroke

8 × 100/200 (2:30): 100s are 25 easy choice, 50 stroke drill, 25 moderate swim: 200s are timed backstroke, negative split and descend 1-4, 5-8

50 easy

6 × 100 freestyle pause drill (1:20): at the end of each stroke the swimmer pauses before the next stroke is initiated; 25 with 3-count pause/25 with 2-count pause; 25 with 1-count pause/25 swim

3 × 50 (1:30) timed faster than 200 pace; 1 free, 2-3 backstroke; easy 25 between

100 easy

Charlie Hodgson on Important Butterfly Training Concepts

Charlie Hodgson (1984), one of America's foremost coaches of butterfly swimmers, outlines what he believes to be important training concepts. (*Note.* Reprinted by permission of the American Swimming Coaches Association.)

Butterfly Training Concepts

Perfect Stroke at All Times:

Primarily use free/fly by 25s or 50s

Straight fly sets (swimming fly only) only for people like Mary T. Meagher

Too much fly can cause stroke deterioration

Kicking and Fins:
(half of total fly kicking per week should be on the back)

At least a 1,000 per day of fly kick

Twice per week—set of 1,500-3,000 fly kick

Twice per week—set of 500-1,000 high-intensity fly kick with fins

Breaststroke Pull:

3 times per week (700-1,000)

No using legs at all

Pull should be to emphasize outward press from front extension

Examples:
John Sieben, Mary T. Meagher, Matt Gribble, Pablo Morales, Michael Gross

Taper:

Concentrate on technique and drills

Concentrate on speed and acceleration (25s and 50s)

Not much fly

Training for the 100-Meter and 200-Meter Butterfly

Dennis Pursley, coach of the great Mary T. Meagher, believes that coaches "panic unnecessarily" at a loss of technique when butterfly is trained for long periods of time. "I've always found that in a rested situation the style you're looking for automatically comes back. Of course I discourage stroke breakdown. I tell them to concentrate as hard as they can to keep high elbows throughout the stroke, but if they can't keep them up because of the distance of the drill, I'm not going to panic (Pursley, 1986 p. 28).

Early and Midseason Workouts

Here are two examples of what Dennis Pursley's butterfly swimmers would do during a workout. (*Note*. From *Swimming Technique*, Feb./April 1986. Reprinted by permission of *Swimming Technique*)

Early Season (Aerobic Emphasis)

Warm-up:

600 one-arm fly with fins
12 × 50:
☐ 50 dolphin kick (1:00)
☐ 50 freestyle (0:45)
☐ 50 butterfly (0:50)
(repeat three times)
3 × 200 lungbusters (3:30)
☐ 50 free, breath choice
☐ 50 free, breathe every five
☐ 50 free, breathe every seven
☐ 25 free, breathe every nine
☐ 25 fly, no breath

Swim:

8 × 300 butterfly holding fastest pace possible, individual intervals allowing 10 seconds rest

Kick:

400 dolphin kick with fins: 200 moderate/200 maximum;
300,200,100,50
☐ all 1/2 moderate, 1/2 maximum
☐ 30 seconds rest between

Pull:

1,500 freestyle: descend 500s breathe every 7,5,choice, by 500 16 × 50 (1:10): 25 no-breath sprint fly/25 easy free

Midseason

Warm-up:

600 free (9:00)
4 × 150 (2:30): fly/free/fly, by 50
400 free (5:40)
4 × 100 fly (1:50): odd numbers kick/swim, by 50; even numbers swim/kick
200 free (2:40)
4 × 50 (1:00):25 sprint fly/25 easy free (1:00)

Swim:

6 × 200 fly (4:40)—broken swim:
☐ 1 and 4: 50/50/100
☐ 2 and 5: 50/100/50
☐ 3 and 6: 100/50/50
10 seconds rest at each break; each 200 should be within 10 seconds of best time

Kick:

3 × 400 fly, no fins (7:20): descend 1-3

Swim:

300 free (4:30)
4 × 50 fly (1:20): at pace
three sets

Training for Butterfly in the Midseason: An Example From the Curl Swim Club Training Program

John Flanagan, coach of the Curl Swim Club, captured much attention in the late 1980s with swimmers such as Michelle Griglione, the top female individual medley swimmer in America and one of its leading butterfly swimmers. He also coached leading butterfly swimmers T.A. DiBiase, Susan Leupold, and Vanessa Richey. Flanagan himself set a national record for masters swimming in the 30-34 butterfly. When interviewed by *Swimming Technique*'s Mark Muckenfuss, coach Flanagan said:

> We do not swim a tremendous amount of full-stroke butterfly. Of the six kids who were qualified nationally in the butterfly, all of those kids also qualified for either junior or senior nationals, in the 500 freestyle. So what I depend on for our conditioning for fly is a lot of middle-distance freestyle training. (Muckenfuss, 1987b, p. 14).

The following workout is what John Flanagan's butterflyers did on the day he spoke with Mark Muckenfuss. *Note*. Workout from Muckenfuss (1987b). Reprinted by permission.

Sample Midseason Workout

Morning

Warm-up:

10 × 100 (1:30) right arm/left arm/twice
400 free pull (5:15) moderate

200 individual medley kick down/swim back

Swim:

10 × 100 pace:
☐ odd—freestyle (1:15)
☐ even—individual medley (1:30)

Kick:

10 × 50 (0:55) easy/hard by 25

Swim:

10 × 50 free (1:25) 5 seconds rest at 50; out easy, back hard

Afternoon

Warm-up:

6 × 200 free, start at 3:10 and decrease base 10 seconds on each swim

Swim:

40 × 50 fly (0:50)
☐ odd—right arm/left arm
☐ even—kick/swim
6 × 200 fly (4:15) 10 seconds at each 25
10 × 100 (1:30) 25 fly/50 free/25 fly

Kick:

3 × 200 (3:45)

Pull:

5 × 150 free (2:15) with paddles
5 × 150 free (1:45) with paddles

Sample Butterfly Workouts Designed by Coaches Bill Thompson and Mitch Ivey

The following examples of butterfly workouts were set by Bill Thompson and Mitch Ivey, two prominent American coaches, and first appeared in an article in *Swimming Technique*, "Making Best Use of the Elements" *Note*. From Muckenfuss (1985b.) Reprinted by permission.

Sample Butterfly Sets

Bill Thompson, Santa Clara Swim Club

Thompson emphasizes that this is not a sample workout: "We never do a whole workout fly." These are only some of the sets that he incorporates into his workouts.

300 (broken down as follows):

50 one stroke right arm, one stroke left arm, two full strokes

50 full stroke

50 down with the right, back with left

50 full stroke

50 underwater recovery

50 full stroke

10 × 75:

25 kick with hands behind the back (try to flip water off the fingers)

25 two strokes right arm, two strokes left arm, four strokes regular

25 underwater recovery, two strokes head up, two head down

8 × 25:

Down fly, drill on the way back

400 kick:

50 on back, hands at side

50 on back, arms extended

50 on front, arms extended

50 on front, arms at side

(repeat)

8 × 100 kick:

body on its side, lower arm extended, head underwater, resting on arm—down on right side, back on left

400 pull (buoy and hand paddles):

two strokes right, two left, two regular (optional: designate a breathing pattern)

8 × 50 pull (buoy only):
breathing pattern two up, one down

Sample Butterfly Workout

Mitch Ivey

Warm-up:

300 swim

300 kick

300 pull

Workout:

Swim: 15 × 50 (0:45 second base) every third 50 is hard, full butterfly stroke, freestyle or choice on the other 50s

Kick: 6 × 200 (3:30) dolphin on back, descend 1-3, 4-6

100 warm-down

Pull: 8 × 300 free (4:00 minimum base)
☐ descend 1-3, 4-6, 7-8
☐ breathe every third, every fifth, and every seventh stroke on each consecutive 100

100 warm-down

Kick: 8 × 50 dolphin on back (1:30): quality set

Training for the 100-Meter and 200-Meter Breaststroke

Eddie Reese, coach of the University of Texas, trained star breaststroke swimmers Rick May, Stuart Smith, and Spencer Martin. In 1986 coach Reese placed four swimmers in the finals of each race in the N.C.A.A. championships: two in the championship finals and two in the consolation finals. No other university had more than one swimmer in the breaststroke finals.

Early and Midseason Workouts

Asked by Mark Muckenfuss to come up with his "ideal" breaststroke workouts, Reese designed the following schedules. (*Note.* Workout from Muckenfuss, 1986a. Reprinted by permission.) Said Reese: "I'd like you to know that we've never done these workouts and we may never do them because each day's workout is different and many are individualized for each swimmer" (Muckenfuss, 1986a, pp. 16-22).

Early Season

Warm-up:

3 × 100 freestyle (1:30)
200 stroke drill (4:00)
3 × 200 freestyle (2:45)
200 individual medley stroke drill (3:30)
3 × 300 freestyle (4:00)
200 stroke drill (3:00)

Swim:

4 × 400 breaststroke (6:00) start at aerobic pace plus 5 seconds (per 100) pace and descend

Kick:

900 with board (16:30) three sets of 100 flutter kick, 200 breaststroke kick
6 × 100 breaststroke kick drill (1:30) four kicks no breath, arms extended, two full strokes

Drill:

200 individual medley reverse order, stroke drill (3:00)

Pull:

10 × 50 breaststroke with buoy (1:00)

Swim:

100 easy

Drill:

Turns and streamlining

Midseason

Warm-up:

800 freestyle (11:00)
400 individual medley reverse order stroke drill (6:00)
10 × 50 individual medley (0:45)

Pull:

3 × 200 breaststroke with buoy (3:00)
1 minute rest

Kick:

3 × 200 breaststroke with board (3:15)
1 minute rest

Swim:

3 × 200 breaststroke (2:45)
200 easy (3:00)
400 individual medley (7:00) broken: 5 seconds at each 50
3 × 200 breaststroke (3:30) broken:
☐ 1-5 seconds at each 50
☐ 2-5 seconds at first 50, 10 seconds after middle 100
☐ 3-10 seconds at 100
200 easy (4:00) not breaststroke

Pull:

5 × 200 freestyle with buoy (2:30)
breathe every five pulls

Swim:

100 easy (2:00)

Kick:

1200:
- ☐ 100 flutter kick under 1:40
- ☐ 100 breaststroke under 1:40
- ☐ 100 breaststroke under 1:30

- ☐ 100 breaststroke, eight kicks per lap, under 1:45
- ☐ repeat three times

Swim:

16 × 25 (0:30), four of each stroke

200 easy

Paul Bergen on Breaststroke Training

Interviewed by Mark Muckenfuss (1985a), Paul Bergen, coach of such breaststrokers as Nick Nevid, Kathy Treible, and Tracy Caulkins, provided two samples of breaststroke workouts that he set at different times during the season. (*Note.* From Muckenfuss, 1985a. Reprinted by permission.)

Midseason and Taper Workouts

Midseason

Warm-up:

600

Pull:

400 freestyle with buoy and six-inch innertube

Breathing 3,5,7,9 by 100s

8 × 100 breaststroke with buoy and paddles (1:40)

Swim:

3 × 1,000
- ☐ first 1,000: alternate 25 fly/25 free
- ☐ second 1,000: alternate 100 back/100 free
- ☐ third 1,000: alternate 50 breast/50 free
- ☐ descend 200s within each 1,000

Kick:

10 × 100
- ☐ 5 at 1:50
- ☐ 5 at 1:40

Drill:

1 × 200

Sprint:

6 × 50 fast (0:50) alternating with easy 100 freestyle (2:00)

Taper

Warm-up:

400

Kick:

6 × 100 (2:00)
- ☐ progressing 1-3 twice

Pull:

1 × 600 (with buoy)
- ☐ alternate 100 free/50 breast four times

Drill:

1 × 200

Swim:

10 × 100 breaststroke (2:00)

odd numbers easy, even numbered fast

95% of maximum

Drill:

1 × 200 individual medley

Sprint:

24 × 25—six of each stroke (0:30)
- ☐ sprint 15 meters no breath, last 10 meters easy

Mark Schubert on Individual Medley Training

Individual medley training is a very broad subject, but I will give you some of my ideas and some of the things that have worked for us successfully over the years. Our individual medley swimmers follow a dryland training program of free weights and machines three days a week, and swim benches three days a week. On the days that they do the swim benches they also use surgical tubing. The individual medley swimmers work the benches and the tubing with exercises for all four strokes. This program is specialized more for 200 or 400 individual medley swimmers, with the distance swimmers doing longer sets with more repetitions. For example, on the benches, sets range from 2 to 10 minutes and repetitions of 100 to 200 times for each of the four strokes for the distance swimmers. In the sprint training program, which many of the 200 IM swimmers follow, the repetitions are normally from 30 seconds to 2-1/2 minutes in length. The free weight program and machine program for the distance swimmers again varies from the sprinters, in that distance swimmers will lift lighter weight with more repetition, and the sprinters will lift heavier weights with fewer repetitions.

After the first 4 to 6 weeks of the season, where the entire team swims mostly aerobically, the IM swimmers become much more specific in the types of workout they are doing for their event. Of the 11 training sessions per week, for the IM swimmer the workouts are divided as follows: Three will be working strictly on individual medley, where we concentrate on the switching of the strokes and swimming direct IM sets; three of the workouts are primarily freestyle and are aerobic in nature; five of the workouts are spent primarily concentrating on one of the four strokes. Some weeks the extra workout will be spent concentrating on one of the four strokes. Some weeks the extra workout will be spent concentrating on the weak stroke, so they'll have two workouts that week working on the weak stroke. Some weeks the bonus workout will be spent concentrating mainly on the prime stroke. So,

four workouts of the five will be concentrating on one individual stroke and one workout on either the weak or the strong stroke.

Two of the eleven workouts per week are quality or anaerobic in nature, particularly those we do on Tuesday and Saturday nights. Some of those workouts we may concentrate solely on stroke, and some we may concentrate on a type of switching set or an individual medley set. In these high-quality workouts we may concentrate on a set of 1,000 meters, and the distances will emphasize 150 meters or less. So with the IM swimmers, if we're emphasizing switching, we may, for example, go a set of 6 × 150 at 5:00 or 6:00, swimming three fly, back, breast, and three back, breast, free.

For each swimmer I try to identify the weak switching area of the race. It might be the backstroke-breaststroke area, or the breaststroke-freestyle area. By identifying that weak switching area, we try to do a predominant amount of training concentrating on that, particularly when we are doing high quality. For example, if we identified the breaststroke-freestyle area as the weak area, we might do a quality set of a 50 followed by a 100, followed by a 150, three times through. The 50s they would swim breaststroke, the 100s they would swim breaststroke-freestyle, and the 150s they would swim backstroke-breaststroke-freestyle. We're concentrating on that weak area in the quality set.

Once a week I try to give my swimmers what I call a "challenge set," where I try to write a specific set that will push them to the absolute limit of their ability. An example of a challenge set that I gave Jesse Vassallo at the height of his career was 9 × 400 IMs. They were descended 1-3, the first on 4:50, the second on 4:45, and the third on 4:40. He would repeat that three times for nine 400 IMs. So what I try to do with each swimmer is to give a set once a week that will present a challenge to do something in practice that one has never been able to do before. This builds confidence in themselves and their ability to train.

Tapering for the Individual Medley

Normally the taper for the individual medley swimmers is 3 weeks in length. For the female swimmers we taper them on the weights, the benches and the bands. We gradually cut down on the work they are doing. For the male swimmers who are more muscular, we taper the weights beginning about 5 weeks out from the championship meet, and then eliminate the weights the last 3 weeks. We keep them on the swim benches and the bands, but gradually cut down on the work they are doing on them. The work load we reduce about 20% every week from between 14,000 and 16,000 down to about 5,000 a day for the last week of training.

The quality training that is done twice a week is tapered from about a 1,000 set, gradually taking 200 off every week, down to about a week before where they are going a set about 400 yards in distance. One set every day is aerobic in nature, which is fairly difficult, but not 100% swimming. An example of this may be 12 × 100 IMs descended 1-4, or perhaps 6 × 200 IMs descended 1-6. Most of the swimming the last three weeks is easy swimming, drill swimming, stroke work, some aerobic work, quality a couple of times a week, and an occasional 50 or 25 to develop the sharpness of the swimmer.

My basic philosophy in entering competition with individual medley swimmers is that they should enter races in all four strokes through-out the year, as well as the individual medley. So, each competition we choose two strokes, as well as the IM to concentrate on. In the middle of the season I try to put a little more emphasis on the weak stroke, rather than the strong strokes in competition.

Our IM swimmers spend quite a bit of time using surgical tubing bands for tethered swimming, particularly for breaststroke kicking and swimming. All of the afternoon kicking is normally done with fins, and all of the pulling is normally done with a pull buoy and paddles. What I like to do on the days when the swimmers are concentrating on stroke is put them with the best stroke swimmers on the team. For example, if they are concentrating on breaststroke, then they train with the breaststrokers that day. That gives us good competition, not only with the better stroke swimmers on the team, but it gives the better stroke swimmers a chance to race against IM swimmers and see some new faces in the lane.

As far as I'm concerned, the best recommendation I can give to you regarding training IM swimmers is to make sure you train all four strokes on a weekly basis, and to make sure you don't neglect the switching drills. Just training the individual stroke will not mean success. Individual medley is completely different because you need to develop the ability to change from one stroke to the next; this should be the main thing you should concentrate on. (*Note.* From Schubert, 1987. Reprinted by permission.)

Training for the 200-Meter and 400-Meter Individual Medley

Early and Midseason Workouts as Prescribed by Coach Richard Shoulberg

Richard "Dick" Shoulberg has produced such swimmers as Karin LaBerge, Sue Heon, Polly Winde, Erica Hansen, Jeff Prior, Ron Karnaugh, David Berkoff, and individual medley world-record breaker David Wharton. When interviewed by Mark Muckenfuss as part of *Swimming Technique*'s notable series on the training methods of America's leading coaches, Shoulberg said emphatically:

A great IMer is someone who is willing to train on strengths and weaknesses, and when training on the weaknesses doesn't get frustrated and throw in the towel. The great IMers no longer have weak strokes. Years ago an IMer was someone who swam breaststroke and had endurance.

The modern IMer is one who trains in all facets of the event, and when he has to move over (in circle training formations) accepts the challenge of whatever circle he's in. Dave Wharton's weakest part of his IM is his backstroke. But he doesn't mind training with the backstrokers. (Muckenfuss, 1987a, pp. 15-18)

Sample Workouts

Note. From Muckenfuss, 1987a. Reprinted by permission.

Early Season: Afternoon

12 × 75 (0:52) minus 3 SPL (normal strokes per length)

9 × 200, 100 back/100 breast three sets

1. Technique (2:50)
2. Negative split each 100 (2:40)
3. Race (2:30)

1 × super 500, speed kicking: 25 (0:30), 75 (0:95), 50 (0:60), 25 (0:30), 25 (0:30), 50 (0:60), 75 (0:90), 25 (0:30), 50 (0:60), 25 (0:30), 25 (0:30), 25 (0:30), 25 (0:30)

1 × 2,000 (22): 500 (6/6 turns [six kicks on back, six on side, then swim]; 500 race; 500 12/12 turns; 500 race

16 × 75 butterfly (1:02) double circle, straight arm recovery

9 × 250 (3:25), descend by sets of three

1. 75 fly, 50 back, 75 breast, 50 free
2. 50 fly, 75 back, 50 breast, 75 free
3. 100 weak stroke, 75 second weakest, 50 next strongest, 25 strongest (individual medley order)

5 × 50 (1:00)

1. fly/back
2. back/breast
3. breast/free
4. choice
5. choice

Midseason: Afternoon

16 × 25 (0:25): drop 1 second per 25 until failure, rest 10 seconds, begin again

12 × 50/150 (3 sets of 4): 50s at 0:45, one of each stroke, individual medley order, within 3 seconds of life best; 150s:

1. negative split (2:00)
2. technique (1:50)
3. build (1:40)
4. race (1:30)

1 × 4,000 individual medley: 250 each stroke per 1,000, total race

1 × Super 500:

☐ 25s: fly, straight arm recovery
☐ 50s: back/breast, think turn
☐ 75s: any three strokes, IM order

20 × 100: odd ones individual medley (1:18), even freestyle (1:02) fast

6 × 30 (1:00): start five yards from wall, perfect stroke with perfect transition turn, sprint last 25

References and Recommended Readings

Absaliamov, T. (1984). Controlling the training of top level swimmers. In J.L. Cramer, (Ed.), *How to develop Olympic level swimmers*. Finland: International Sports Media.

Alexander, R.M. (1983). *Animal mechanics*. Oxford: Blackwell Scientific.

Armbruster, D.A. (1942). *Competitive swimming and diving*. St. Louis: Mosby.

Astrand, P.-O. (1971). Panel discussion: "General athletic nutrition." In L. Percival & J.W. Taylor (Eds.), *Proceedings of the first international symposium on the art and science of coaching* (pp. 189-208). Toronto: Fitness Institute Productions and the Coaching Association of Canada.

Astrand, P.-O., & Rodahl, K. (1970). *Textbook of work physiology*. New York: McGraw-Hill, pp. 341-369.

*Australian Sports Institute Study Group. (1975). *Report on the feasibility of establishing a national sports institute in Australia*. Canberra, Australia: Department of Tourism and Recreation, pp. 127-129.

Balke, B., Nagle, J., & Daniels, J. (1965). Altitude and maximum performance in work and sports activity. *Journal of the American Medical Association, 194*(6), 646-649.

Bannister, E.W., Jackson, R.C., & Cartmel, J. (1968). The potentiating effect of low oxygen tension exposure during training on subsequent cardiovascular performance. *International Zeitschrift fur Angewandte Physiologie Einschliesslich Arbeitsphysiologie, 26*, 164-179.

Bannister, R. (1955). *First four minutes*. London: Putnam.

Barthels, K.M. (1977). Analyzing swimming performance: General considerations. *Swimming Technique, 14*(2), 51-52.

Barthels, K.M. (1979). The mechanism for body propulsion in swimming. In J. Terauds & E.W. Bedingfield (Eds.), *International symposium of biomechanics: Swimming III* (pp. 45-54). Baltimore: University Park Press.

Barthels, K.M. (1981). Swimming biomechanics: Resistance and propulsion. *Swimming Technique, 16*(3), 66-70, 76.

Barthels, K.M., & Adrian, M.J. (1975). Three-dimensional spatial hand patterns of skilled butterfly swimmers. In L. Lewillie & J.P. Clarys (Eds.), *International series on sport sciences: Vol 2. Swimming II* (pp. 154-160). Baltimore: University Park Press.

Benson, H. (1975). *The relaxation response*. New York: Avon.

Bergen, P. (1979). Workshop: Coaching tips. In R. Ousley (Ed.), *American Swimming Coaches Association world clinic yearbook 1979* (pp. 229-236). Fort Lauderdale, FL: American Swimming Coaches Association.

Bergen, P. (1985). Executing a year training program. In T. Welsh (Ed.), *American Swim-*

Note. An asterisk (*) beside an entry indicates an additional, recommended reading that is not referenced in the text.

ming Coaches Association world clinic yearbook 1985 (pp. 195-204). Fort Lauderdale, FL: American Swimming Coaches Association.

Berger, J. (1982). Die zyklische Gestaltung des Trainings prozesses unter besonderer Beruecksichtigung der Periodiserung des Trainingsjahres (The cyclic establishment of the training process in special consideration of a cyclic subdivision of the training year). *Medizin und Sport*, **22**, 282-286.

Blake, R.W. (1980). The mechanics of labriform locomotion: 2. An analysis of the recovery stroke and the overall fin-beat cycle propulsive efficiency in the angel fish. *Journal of Experimental Biology*, **85**, 337-342.

Blood, T. (1978). How they train: Kim Linehan. *Swimming World*, **19**(8), 17.

Bompa, T.O. (1985). *Theory and methodology of training*. Dubuque, IA: Kendall/Hunt.

Brasch, T. (1970). *How did sports begin? A look at the origins of man at play*. New York: David McKay.

Brouha, L. (1945). Speficite de l'entrainement au travail musculaire. *Revue Canadienne Biologie*, **4**, 144.

*Burke, E. (Ed.) (1978). *Toward an understanding of human performance*. Torquay, Australia: Movement.

Byrd, W. (1928). *A journey to the Land of Eden and other papers*. (Mark van Doren, ed.). (s.l.): Macey-Masius.

Campbell, J. (Ed.) (1971). *The portable Jung*. New York: Viking, p. 223.

Carlile, F. (1956a). Effect of preliminary warming up on swimming performance. *Research Quarterly*, **27**(2), 143-151.

Carlile, F. (1956b). The use of post-exercise heart rate counts in the prediction of maximum performance and assessing the progress of the swimmer in training. *Report of the World Congress on Physical Education* (pp. 102-104). Melbourne, Australia: W & J Barr.

Carlile, F. (1963). *Forbes Carlile on swimming*. London: Pelham.

Carlile, F. (1971). Where do we go from here? American Swimming Coaches Association's first world clinic, Montreal, 1971. *Swimming Technique*, **8**(4), 98-100, 119.

Carlile, F. (1976). The philosophy of speed through endurance. *International Swimmer*, **12**(7), 7-12.

Carlile, F. (1979). The prediction of swimming times with special reference to the Treffene

anaerobic theory and prediction equations, and the significance of the anaerobic threshold in training. *Swimming Technique*, **16**(1), 2-12.

Carlile, F. (1980). *Adaptation by F. Carlile of B.S. Rushall's psychological inventory sheets*. Pymble, Australia: Author.

Carlile, F., & Carlile, U.M. (1955, October-November). The athlete and adaptation to stress: Part 1. The general adaptation syndrome. *Physical Education Journal*, pp. 9-13.

Carlile, F., & Carlile, U.M. (1956a, February-March). The athlete and adaptation to stress: Part 2. Application of the stress concept to training. *Physical Education Journal*, pp. 7-10.

Carlile, F., & Carlile, U.M. (1956b, February-March). The athlete and adaptation to stress: Part 3. Signs and symptoms of stress. *Physical Education Journal*, pp. 11-14.

Carlile, F., & Carlile, U.M. (1959). T wave changes in the electrocardiogram associated with prolonged periods of strenuous exercise. *Australian Journal of Physical Education*, **17**, 10-20.

Carlile, F., & Carlile, U.M. (1961). Physiological studies of Australian Olympic swimmers in hard training. *Australian Journal of Physical Education*, **23**, 5-34.

Carlile, F., & Carlile, U.M. (1978). *New directions in scientific training*. Pymble, Australia: Author.

Chatard, J.C., Paulin, M., & Lacour, J.R. (1988). Postcompetition blood lactate measurements and swimming performance: Illustrated by data from a 400-m Olympic record holder. In Ungerechts, B.E., Wilke, K., & Reischle, K. (Eds.), *International series on sport sciences: Vol. 18. International symposium of biomechanics and medicine in swimming: Swimming science V* (pp. 311-316). Champaign, IL: Human Kinetics.

Chavoor, S. (1967). Sherm Chavoor speaks out on training. *Swimming World*, **8**(10), 5.

Childs, D. (1969). *East Germany*. London: Unwin Hyman.

Cichoke, A. (1977). The German Democratic Republic's planned dominance of the 1980 Moscow Olympics. *Swimming Technique*, **14**(3), 81-85.

Colwin, C. (1969). *Cecil Colwin on swimming*. London: Pelham Books.

Colwin, C. (1975a). Cec Colwin talks on altitude training. *International Swimmer*, **12**(3), 24.

Colwin, C. (1975b). DDR swimming. *Swimming World*, **16**(8), 12-14.

Colwin, C. (1977). *An introduction to swimming coaching*. Ottawa, ON: Canadian Amateur Swimming Association.

Colwin, C. (1983a). Colwin talks to Counsilman. *Swim Canada*, **10**(2), 18-20.

Colwin, C. (1983b). Mark Schubert on training 1,500-meter swimmers. Unpublished recorded conversation.

Colwin, C. (1984a). Fluid dynamics: Vortex circulation in swimming propulsion. In T.F. Welsh (Ed.), *American Swimming Coaches Association world clinic yearbook 1984* (pp. 38-46). Fort Lauderdale, FL: American Swimming Coaches Association.

Colwin, C. (1984b). Kinetic streamlining and the phenomenon of prolonged momentum in the crawl swimming stroke. *Swim Canada*, **11**(1), 12-15.

Colwin, C. (1984c). Tethered swimming. *Swim Canada*, **11**(3), 20-21.

Colwin, C. (1985a, July-August). Essential fluid dynamics of swimming propulsion. *American Swimming Coaches Association Magazine*, pp. 22-27.

Colwin, C. (1985b, September-October). Practical application of flow analysis as a coaching tool. *American Swimming Coaches Association Magazine*, pp. 5-8.

Colwin, C. (1987). Coaching the ''feel of the water.'' In T.F. Welsh (Ed.), *American Swimming Coaches Association world clinic yearbook 1987* (pp. 87-98). Fort Lauderdale, FL: American Swimming Coaches Association.

Costill, D.I. (1987). Building a better mousetrap. *Swimming Technique*, **24**(3), 34-36.

Costill, D.I., Sharp, R., & Troup, J. (1980, February). Muscle strength: Contributions to sprint swimming. *Swimming World*, **21**(2), 29-34.

Costill, D.I., & Wilmore, J.H. (1970). Maximal oxygen consumption amongst marathon runners. *Archives of Physical Medicine and Rehabilitation*, **51**, 317-320.

Cotton, F.S. (1932). The relation of athletic status to pulse rate in men and women. *Journal of Physiology*, **76**, 39-51.

*Council for National Cooperation in Aquatics. (Yates, F., Fairbanks, B., Fleming, P., & Thorsen, M., Eds.) (1968). *Swimming and diving: A bibliography*. New York: Association Press.

Counsilman, J.E. (1967). Problems—''dirt'' in interval training. *Swimming Technique*, **3**(4), 112-113.

Counsilman, J.E. (1968). *The science of swimming*. Englewood Cliffs, NJ: Prentice Hall.

Counsilman, J.E. (1969). The role of sculling movements in the arm pull. *Swimming World*, **10**(12), 6-7, 43.

Counsilman, J.E. (1971). The application of Bernoulli's principle to human propulsion in water. In L. Lewillie & J.P. Clarys (Eds.), *Proceedings: First international symposium on biomechanics in swimming, waterpolo and diving* (pp. 59-71). Bruxelles: Universite Libre de Bruxelles Laboratoire de l'effort.

Counsilman, J.E. (1975). Hypoxic and other methods of training evaluated. *Swimming Technique*, **12**(1), 19-26.

Counsilman, J.E. (1977). *Competitive swimming manual*. Bloomington, IN: Author.

Counsilman, J.E. (1979). Biokinetics, the ultimate exercise. In R.M. Ousley (Ed.), *American Swimming Coaches Association world clinic yearbook 1979* (pp. 29-36). Fort Lauderdale, FL: American Swimming Coaches Association.

Counsilman, J.E. (1980). Hand acceleration patterns in swimming strokes. *Big Ten Biomechanics Conference*. Bloomington: Indiana University.

Counsilman, J.E. (1984). The use of goal sets and cruise intervals as a method of balancing high intensity and endurance training as a diagnostic tool. In T. Welsh (Ed.), *American Swimming Coaches Association world clinic yearbook 1984* (pp. 1-9). Fort Lauderdale, FL: American Swimming Coaches Association.

Counsilman, J.E. (1986). Strength training, sprint training and speed assisted training for sprint swimmers. In *Swim 86 yearbook* (pp. 1-16). Brisbane: Australian Swimming Inc. & Australian Swimming Coaches Association.

Counsilman, J.E. (1988). All that yardage. *Swimming Technique*, **24**(3), 19-24.

Counsilman, J.E., & Brown, R.M. (1970). The role of lift in propelling the swimmer. In J.M. Cooper (Ed.), *Selected topics on biomechanics: Proceedings of the C.I.C. symposium on biomechanics* (pp. 179-188). Chicago: Athletic Institute.

Counsilman, J.E., & Favell, E.R. (1980). *Biokinetic strength training: A compilation of scientific papers*. Albany, CA: Isokinetics.

Counsilman, J.E., & Wasilak, J.M. (1982). The importance of hand speed and acceleration in swimming the crawl stroke. *Swimming Technique*, **18**(1), 22-26.

Craig, A.B., & Pendergast, D.R. (1979). Relationships of stroke rate, distance per stroke, and velocity in competitive swimming. *Medicine and Science in Sports*, **11**, 278-283.

Craig, A.B., Skeehan, P.L., Pawelczyk, J.A., & Boomer, W.L. (1985). Velocity, stroke rate and distance per stroke during elite swimming competition. *Medicine and Science in Sports and Exercise*, **17**(6), 625-634.

Cunningham, L. (1980). *Hypnosport*. Melbourne, Australia: Cassell.

Cureton, T.K. (1934). *How to teach swimming and diving* (vols. 1-2). New York: Association Press.

*Cureton, T.K. (1940). Review of a decade of swimming research at Springfield College 1929-1939. *Research Quarterly*, **9**, 68-79.

Cureton, T.K. (1947). *Physical fitness, appraisal and guidance*. St. Louis: Mosby.

Cureton, T.K. (1951). *Physical fitness of champion athletes*. Urbana, IL: University of Illinois Press.

Cureton, T.K. (1974). Factors governing success in competitive swimming: A brief review of related studies. In L. Lewillie & J.P. Clarys (Eds), *International series on sport sciences: vol 2. Swimming II* (pp. 9-39). Baltimore: University Park Press.

Curry, I. (1975). Stroke length, stroke frequency and performance. *Swimming Technique*, **12**(3), 88, 91.

Daniels, J., & Oldridge, N. (1970). The effects of alternate exposure to altitude and sea level on world-class middle distance runners. *Medicine and Science in Sports*, **2**(3), 107-112.

Dellon, A., Curtis, R., & Edgerton, M. (1974). Re-education of sensation in the hand after nerve surgery and repair. *Plastic Reconstruction Surgery*, **53**, 297-305.

Demopoulos, H.B., Santomier, J.P., Seligman, M.L., Pietrogro, D.D., & Hogan, P.I. (1986). Free radical pathology: Rationale and toxicology of antioxidants and other supplements in sports medicine and exercise science. In F.I. Katch (Ed.), *Sport, health and nutrition: 1984 Olympic Scientific Congress proceedings. Vol. 2.* (pp. 139-189). Champaign, IL: Human Kinetics.

De Vries, H. (1974). Warmup, its values and efficient utilisation. In J.W. Taylor (Ed.), *Proceedings of the first international symposium on the art and science of coaching*. Willowdale, ON: F.I. Productions.

Dick, F. (1979). Relevance of altitude training. *Athletics Coach*, **13**(4), 11-14.

Digby [Dygbeio], E. (1587). *De arte natandi libri duo, quorum prior regulas ipsius artis, posterior vero praxin demonstrationemque continet*. London: (s.n.)

Dill, D.B., & Adams, W.C. (1971). Maximal oxygen uptake at sea level and at 3,090-meter altitude in high school champion runners. *Journal of Applied Physiology*, **30**, 854-859.

Dominguez, R.H. (1980). Shoulder pain in swimmers. *The Physician and Sportsmedicine*, **8**(7), 35-42.

East, D.E. (1970). Swimming: An analysis of stroke frequency, stroke length and performance. *New Zealand Journal of Health, Physical Education and Recreation*, **3**, 6-27.

Elyot, T. (1531). *The boke named the governour*. London: Thomas Berthelet.

English, A.W. (1976). Limb movements and locomotor function in the California sea lion (*Zalophus Californianus*). *Journal of Zoology*, **178**, 341-364.

English, A.W. (1977). Structural correlates of forelimb function in fur seals and sea lions. *Journal of Morphology*, **151**, 325-352.

Ewald, R. (1988a). The rise of Romania. *Swimming World*, **29**(3), 35.

Ewald, R. (1988b). World's fastest female. *Swimming World*, **29**(3), 33-34.

Faulkner, J. (1967). *What research tells the coach about swimming*. Washington, DC: American Association for Health, Physical Education, and Recreation.

*Faulkner, J. (1968). Physiological characteristics of swimming. In B. Balke (Ed.), *Physiological aspects of sports and physical fitness: A selection of papers presented at scientific meetings* (pp. 60-63). Chicago: The Athletic Institute.

Feldkamp, S.D. (1985). Swimming and diving in the California sea lion, *zalophus californianus*. *Dissertation Abstracts International*, **46**, 2973B.

Feldkamp, S.D. (1987). Foreflipper propulsion in the California sea lion, *zalophus californianus*. *Journal of Zoology*, **212**, 43-57.

Firby, H. (1975). *Howard Firby on swimming*. London: Pelham Books, p. 15.

*Firsov, S., & Jokl, E. (1968). *Medical research on swimming*. Ann Arbor, MI: Federation International de Natation Amateur.

Fish, F.E. (1984). Mechanics, power output and efficiency of the swimming muskrat (*ondatra zibethicus*). *Journal of Experimental Biology*, **110**, 183-201.

Fitch, K. (1978). Swimming medicine and asthma. In B. Eriksson & B. Furberg (Eds.),

Swimming medicine IV: Proceedings of 4th international congress on swimming medicine (pp. 16-31). Baltimore: University Park Press.

Foley, D. (1987). Swimmer's shoulder—A different clinical approach. *Excel, 4*(2), 9-11.

*Fox, E.L. (1979). *Sports physiology*. Philadelphia: Saunders.

Georges, C. (Ed.) (1981a). Swimming biomechanics/Meet and club administration [Entire issue]. *Swimming Technique, 18*(1).

Georges, C. (Ed.) (1981b). The compleat swimmer [Special issue]. *Swimming Technique, 17*(4).

Gerschler, Rosskamm, & Reindell. (1964, March). Das Interval Training [Interval Training]. *Congress on running*. Duisberg: Deutscher Leichathletic.

*Gilbert, D. (1980). *The miracle machine: The story of the rise of D.D.R.* New York: Sport-Coward, McCanny & Geoghegan.

*Greenwood, F.A. (1935). *Swimming, diving and water sports*. Tuscaloosa, AL: Weatherford.

*Greenwood, F.A. (1940). *Bibliography of swimming*. New York: H.W. Wilson.

Handley, L. de B. (1914, April). The swimming stroke of the future. *Outing*, pp. 99-103.

Handley, L. de B. (1928). *Swimming for women*. New York: American Sports Publishing.

Hansen, P.G. (Speaker) (1980). *Athletic staleness: A clinical perspective* (Cassette Recording). 27th Annual Meeting, American College of Sports Medicine, May 28-30, Las Vegas, NV.

Harre, D. (1982). *Principles of sports training*. Berlin: Sport Verlag, p. 58.

Hay, J.G. (1973). *The biomechanics of sports techniques*. Englewood Cliffs, NJ: Prentice Hall.

Hay, J.G. (1986). The status of research on biomechanics of swimming. In J.G. Hay (Ed.), *Starting, stroking and turning (a compilation of research on the biomechanics of swimming, the University of Iowa, 1983-1986)*. Iowa City: Biomechanics Laboratory, Department of Exercise Science, University of Iowa.

Hay, J.G., Guimaraes, A.C.S., & Grimston, S.K. (1983). A quantitative look at swimming biomechanics. *Swimming Technique, 20*(2), 11-17.

Haymes, E.M., Puhl, J.L., & Temples, T.E. (1983, May). *Training for cross-country skiing and iron status*. Read before the annual meeting of the American College of Sports Medicine. Montreal, Quebec.

Hodge, T. (1988, January). The ancient Olympics: a run for the money. *The Ottawa Citizen*, p. B3.

Hodgson, C. (1984). A stroke description of butterfly. In T. Welsh (Ed.), *American Swimming Coaches Association world clinic yearbook 1984* (pp. 79-83). Fort Lauderdale, FL: American Swimming Coaches Association.

Hoecke, G., & Gründler, G. (1975). Use of light trace photography in teaching swimming. In L. Lewillie & J.P Clarys (Eds.), *International series on sport sciences: Vol. 2. Swimming II* (pp. 194-206). Baltimore: University Park Press.

Hogg, J.M. (1977). Flexibility training. In R.M. Ousley (Ed.), *American Swimming Coaches Association world clinic yearbook 1977* (pp. 32-47). Fort Lauderdale, FL: American Swimming Coaches Association.

Holmer, G. (1972). Development in running. *Track Technique, 50*, pp. 1584-1585.

Holmer, I., & Haglund, S. (1977). The swimming flume: Experiences and applications. In B. Eriksson & B. Furberg (Eds.), *Swimming medicine IV* (pp. 379-385). Baltimore: University Park Press.

Hopper, R.T. (1981). Dragging on about training aids. *Swimming Technique, 17*(4), 13-16.

Hopper, R.T., & Bartels, R. (1980). Getting a grip on strength. *Swimming Technique, 17*(2), 10-13.

Hopper, R.T., Hadley, C.L., & Piva, M. (1980). Specificity of strength testing in swimming. *Abstracts Medicine and Science in Sports and Exercise, 12*(2), 135.

Horwill, F. (1982). Gerschler: The innovator. He was 30 years ahead of his time. *Athletics Weekly, 36*(38), 33.

Howard, S. (1849). *The science of swimming as taught and practiced in civilized and savage countries*. New York: (s.n.)

Isenberg, D.J. (1984). How senior managers think. *Harvard Business Review, 62*(6), 80-90.

Jackson, R., & Balke, B. (1971). Training at altitude for performance at sea level. *Schweizerische Zeitschrift für Sportmedizin, 19*(Suppl.), 19-27.

Jacobson, E. (1938). *Progressive relaxation*. Chicago: University of Chicago Press.

*Jensen, C.R., & Fisher, A.G. (1979). *Scientific basis of athletic conditioning*. Philadelphia: Lea & Febiger.

Jochums, D. (1982). The dissident's view of distance freestyle training. In R.M. Ousley (Ed.), *American Swimming Coaches Association world clinic yearbook 1982* (pp. 139-151).

Fort Lauderdale, FL: American Swimming Coaches Association.

Johnson, R. (1978). Organizing a season program. In R.M. Ousley (Ed.), *American Swimming Coaches Association world clinic yearbook 1978* (pp. 129-143). Fort Lauderdale, FL: American Swimming Coaches Association.

Johnson, R. (1982). Tempo awareness training. In R.M. Ousley (Ed.), *American Swimming Coaches Association world clinic yearbook 1982* (pp. 39-54). Fort Lauderdale, FL: American Swimming Coaches Association.

Karikosk, O. (1983). Altitude training. *Modern Athlete and Coach*, **21**(2), 25-27.

Karpovich, P.W. (1933). Water resistance in swimming. *Research Quarterly*, **4**, 21-28.

Kennedy, J.C., Hawkins, R., & Krissoff, W.B. (1978). Orthopaedic manifestations of swimming. *American Journal of Sports Medicine*, **6**(6), 309-322.

Kimiecik, J., & Gould, D. (1987). Coaching psychology: The case of James "Doc" Counsilman. *The Sports Psychologist*, **1**(4), 350-358.

Kindermann, W. (1978). Regeneration und trainings Prozess in den Ausdauer—Sportarten aus medizinischer Sicht. *Leistungssport*, **4**, 354-357.

Kiphuth, R.J.H. (1942). *Swimming*. New York: Barnes.

Kiphuth, R.J.H. (1950). *How to be fit*. London: Nicholas Kaye.

*Kipke, L. (1986). Research applications in the DDR. In J. Leonard (Ed.), *American Swimming Coaches Association world clinic yearbook 1986* (pp. 8-13). Fort Lauderdale, FL: American Swimming Coaches Association.

Klausen, K., Robinson, S., Michael, E.D., & Myhre, L.G. (1966). Effect of high altitude on maximal working capacity. *Journal of Applied Physiology*, **21**(4), 1191-1194.

Knight, K. (1978). Cryotheraphy in sports medicine. *Relevant topics in athletic training* (pp. 52-59). Torquay, Australia: Author.

Koshkin, I. (1985). The system and methods of Vladimir Salnikov's development, 1980-1984. In T. Welsh (Ed.), *American Swimming Coaches Association world clinic yearbook 1985* (pp. 5-8). Fort Lauderdale, FL: American Swimming Coaches Association.

Lanchester, F.W. (1907). *Aerodynamics: Constituting the first volume of a complete work on aerial flight*. London: Constable.

Lane, H.W., & Cerda, J.J. (1979). Potassium re-quirements and exercise. *American Corrective Therapy Journal*, **33**(3), 67-69.

Leonard, J. (1988, August). An interview with Bud McAllister. *American Swimming Coaches Association Magazine*, pp. 3-4.

Lighthill, M.J. (1973). On the Weis-Fogh mechanism of lift generation. *Journal of Fluid Dynamics*, **60**(pt. 1), 1-17.

Lilienthal, O. (1889). *Der Vogelflug als Grundlage der Fliegekunst*. Berlin: Ouldenberg.

Lyons, J. (1977). From the lotus position to starting blocks. *Swimming Technique*, **13**(4), 124-128.

Madsen, O., & Wilke, K. (1983). A comprehensive multi-year training program. In R.M. Ousley (Ed.), *American Swimming Coaches Association world clinic yearbook 1983* (pp. 47-62). Fort Lauderdale, FL: American Swimming Coaches Association.

Magel, J.R. (1970). Propelling force measured during tethered swimming in the four competitive swimming styles. *Research Quarterly*, **41**(1), 68-74.

Maglischo, C.W., Maglischo, E.W., Higgins, J., Hinricks, R., Luedtke, D., Schleihauf, R., & Thayer, A. (1986). A biomechanical analysis of the 1984 U.S. Olympic team: The distance freestylers. *Journal of Swimming Research*, **2**(3), 12-16.

Maglischo, E.W. (1982). *Swimming faster*. Palo Alto, CA: Mayfield.

Maglischo, E.W. (1983). A three-dimensional cinematographical analysis of competitive swimming strokes. In R.M. Ousley (Ed.), *American Swimming Coaches Association world clinic yearbook 1983* (pp. 1-14). Fort Lauderdale, FL: American Swimming Coaches Association.

Maglischo, E.W. (1985). Constructing workouts with energy system considerations. In T. Welsh (Ed.), *American Swimming Coaches Association world clinic yearbook 1985* (pp. 56-62). Fort Lauderdale, FL: American Swimming Coaches Association.

Magnus, O. (1555). *Historia de gentibus septentrionalibus Romae* [History of the northern people] (s.n.)

Maltz, M. (1960). *Psycho-cybernetics*. New York: Prentice Hall.

*Mathews, D., & Fox, E.L. (1976). *The physiological basis of physical education and athletics*. Philadelphia: Saunders.

Matveyev, L. (1981). *Fundamentals of sports training*. (s.l.): Progress, pp. 55-58.

McArdle, W.D., Katch, F., & Victor, L. (1981).

Exercise physiology, energy, nutrition and human performance. Philadelphia: Lea & Febiger.

McPherson, B.D., & Taylor, A. (1980). Physical activity scientists: Their present and future roles. In F.J. Hayden (Ed.), *Body and Mind in the 90's* (p. 165). Hamilton, ON: Canadian Council of University Physical Education Administrators.

Morehouse, L.E., & Miller, A.T. (1971). *Physiology of exercise*. St. Louis: Mosby.

Morgan, W.P. (Speaker) (1980). *Physiological monitoring of athletic stress syndrome* (Cassette recording). 27th Annual Meeting American College of Sports Medicine, May 28-30. Las Vegas, NV.

Muckenfuss, M. (1985a). Close to the breast. *Swimming Technique*, **22**(2), 9-14.

Muckenfuss, M. (1985b). Making best use of the elements. *Swimming Technique*, **21**(4), 8-13.

Muckenfuss, M. (1986a). Breaststroke Texas style. *Swimming Technique*, **23**(2), 16-22.

Muckenfuss, M. (1986b). Training backstroke. *Swimming Technique*, **23**(1), 17-20.

Muckenfuss, M. (1987a). A steady diet of the four basics—training at Germantown is based on the individual medley and it shows up in the swimming that comes out of Dick Shoulberg's program. *Swimming Technique*, **24**(3), 15-18.

Muckenfuss, M. (1987b). Flying in Virginia—John Flanagan talks about training methods. *Swimming Technique*, **23**(4), 11-16.

Muckenfuss, M. (1989). Tuning up the butterfly. Master technician Dr. Ernie Maglischo is still studying the mechanics of swimming and making new discoveries. *Swimming Technique*, **25**(4), 14-20.

Murray, J., & Karpovich, P.V. (1956). *Weight training in athletics*. Englewood Cliffs, NJ: Prentice Hall, pp. 141-144.

Muths, G. (1798). *Kleines lehrbuch der Schwimmkunst zum selbstunterrichte* (Manual for self-instruction in the art of swimming). Weimar: (s.n.)

Nelson, J. (1973). Distance per stroke—how to swim fast—some call it "sprinting." In R.M. Ousley (Ed.), *American Swimming Coaches Association world clinic talks (first five years) 1969-1973*. Fort Lauderdale, FL: American Swimming Coaches Association.

Nelson, R.C., & Pike, N.L. (1975). *Swimming Medicine IV*. Baltimore: University Park Press.

Nicolle, C. (1932). *Biologie de l'invention*. Paris: Alcan.

Oppenheim, F. (1970). *The history of swimming*. North Hollywood, CA: Swimming World.

Ostrander, S., & Schroeder, L. (1971). *Psychic discoveries behind the Iron Curtain*. Des Plaines, IL: Bantam Books.

Ostrander, S., & Schroeder, L. (1983). *Superlearning*. Pine Brook, NJ: Dell Books.

Pai, Y.-C., Hay, J.G., & Wilson, B.D. (1984). Stroking techniques of elite swimmers. *Journal of Sports Science*, **2**(3), 225-239.

Persyn, U. (1978). *Evaluation in swimming*. Unpublished manuscript, Katholieke Universiteit, Leuven, Belgium.

Platt, W., & Baker, R.A. (1931). The relation of the scientific "hunch" to research. *Journal of Chemical Education*, **8**(10), 1969-2002.

Prins, H. (1978). *Histological changes in human skeletal muscle with isokinetic strength training at two distinct limb speeds*. Unpublished doctoral dissertation, Indina University.

Pursley, D. (1986). Practice makes perfect. *Swimming Technique*, **22**(4), 26-32.

Pyne, D.B., & Telford, R.D. (1988). Classification of training sessions. *Excel*, **5**(2).

Pyne, D.B., & Telford, R.D. (1989, February). Classification of swimming training sessions by blood lactate and heart rate responses. *American Swimming Coaches Association Magazine*, pp. 7-9.

Rackham, G.W. (1975). An analysis of arm propulsion in swimming. In L. Lewillie & J.P. Clarys (Eds.), *International Series on Sport Sciences: Vol. 2. Swimming II* (pp. 174-179). Baltimore: University Park Press.

Reischle, K. (1979). A kinematic investigation of movement patterns in swimming with photo-optical methods. In J. Terauds & E.W. Bedingfield (Eds.), *International Symposium of Biomechanics: Swimming III* (pp. 127-136). Baltimore: University Park Press.

Richardson, A. (1979a). The shoulder in swimming: Part 1. *Swimming World*, **20**(2), 55-58.

Richardson, A. (1979b). The shoulder in swimming: Part 2. *Swimming World*, **20**(3), 33-34.

Richardson, A. (1979c). The shoulder in swimming: Part 3. *Swimming World*, **20**(4), 5-8.

Ronan, D. (1977). *The swimmers' memorandum on mental training*. West Islip, NY: Author.

Rushall, B.S. (1979). *Psyching in sport*. London: Pelham Books.

Sachs, F. (1912). *The complete swimmer*. London: Methuen.

Sauberlich, H.E., Dowdy, R.P., & Skala, J.H.

(1974). *Laboratory tests for the assessment of nutritional status.* Boca Raton, FL: CRC Press.

Scheuzenzuber, H.J. (1975). Cited by R.C. Nelson & N.L. Pike in *Swimming Medicine IV* (p. 360). Baltimore: University Park Press.

Schleihauf, R.E. (1974). A biomechanical analysis of freestyle. *Swimming Technique,* **11**(3), 89-96.

Schleihauf, R.E. (1977). Swimming propulsion: A hydrodynamic analysis. In R. Ousley (Ed.), *American Swimming Coaches Association world clinic yearbook 1977* (pp. 49-81). Fort Lauderdale, FL: American Swimming Coaches Association.

Schleihauf, R.E. (1979). A hydrodynamic analysis of swimming propulsion. In J. Terauds & E.W. Bedingfield (Eds.), *International Symposium of Biomechanics: Vol. 8. Swimming III* (pp. 70-109). Baltimore: University Park Press.

Schleihauf, R.E. (1986). Swimming skill: A review of basic theory. *Journal of Swimming Research,* **2**(2), 11-20.

Schleihauf, R.E., Higgins, J.R., Hinrichs, R., Luedtke, D., Maglischo, C., Maglischo, E.W., & Thayer, A. (1988). Propulsive techniques: Front crawl stroke, butterfly, backstroke, and breaststroke. In B.E. Ungerechts, K. Wilke, & K. Reischle (Eds.), *International series on sport sciences: Vol. 18. Swimming science V* (pp. 53-59). Champaign, IL: Human Kinetics.

Schleusing, G., Rebentisch, J., & Schippel, C. (1964). Research on endurance and interval training. *Medicine and sport, books I and II.* Berlin: Verlag Volk and Gesundheit, V.E.B.

Schoenfield, A. (1987). Going for the gold down under. *Swimming World,* **28**(1), 49, 51.

Schubert, M. (1985). Distance training. In T. Welsh (Ed.), *American Swimming Coaches Association world clinic yearbook 1985* (pp. 205-211). Fort Lauderdale, FL: American Swimming Coaches Association.

Schubert, M. (1987, June). Individual medley training. *American Swimming Coaches Association Magazine,* pp. 11-13.

Selye, H. (1956). *The stress of life.* New York: McGraw-Hill.

Sharp, R.L., & Costill, D.L. (1989). Shaving a little time. *Swimming Technique,* **26**(3), 10-13.

Sheldon, W.H., Stevens, S.S., & Tucker, W.B.

(1940). *The varieties of human physique.* New York: Harper & Brothers.

Shoulberg, R. (1983). Distance freestyle training. In R. Ousley (Ed.), *American Swimming Coaches Association world clinic yearbook 1983* (pp. 209-213). Fort Lauderdale, FL: American Swimming Coaches Association.

Shoulberg, R. (1985). Distance training. In T. Welsh (Ed.), *American Swimming Coaches Association world clinic yearbook 1985* (pp. 205-211). Fort Lauderdale, FL: American Swimming Coaches Association.

Sinclair, A. (1909). *Swimming.* London: Routledge & Son.

Sinclair, A., & Henry, W. (1908). *Swimming.* London: Longmans, Green, & Co.

Smith, A. (1968). *The Body.* London: Allen & Unwin, p. 361.

Smith, J.A., Telford, R.D., Hahn, A.G., Mason, I.B., & Weidemann, M.J. (1988). Training, oxygen radicals and the immune response. *Excel,* **4**(4), 3-6.

Smith, J.A., Telford, R.D., Mason, I.B., & Weidemann, M.J. (1988). Acute effects of exercise on oxidative burst activity of neutrophils and susceptibility of erythrocytes to oxidative stress in trained and untrained human subjects. *Proc of the Aust Biochem Soc,* **20**, SP3 (abstract).

Smith, J.A., Telford, R.D., Mason, I.B., & Weidemann, M.J. (1990). Exercise, training and neutrophil microbicidal activity. *International Journal of Sports Medicine.*

Smith, M.H., & Sharkey, B.J. (1984). Altitude training: Who benefits? *The Physician and Sportsmedicine,* **12**(4), 48-52.

Snelling, D. (1980). Combining stretching and weight work. In R. Ousley (Ed.), *American Swimming Coaches Association world clinic yearbook 1980* (pp. 81-100). Fort Lauderdale, FL: American Swimming Coaches Association.

Staff. (1980). By George! After 30 years on the job, Olympic coach George Haines has coached 'em all—and talks about it. *Swimming Technique,* **17**(1), 8-12, 32-35.

Stampfl, F. (1955). *Franz Stampfl on running.* London: Jenkins.

Stanton, H.E. (1979). *The plus factor—a guide to positive living.* Sydney: Fontana Books.

Starkman, R. (1990, June 2-4). Randy Starkman in East Germany. *The Toronto Star.*

Steedman, C. (1867). *Manual of swimming, including bathing, plunging, diving, floating, scientific swimming, training, drowning and rescuing.* Melbourne, Australia: (s.n.)

Sterrett, J.H. (1917). *How to swim.* New York: American Sports Publishing.

Sullivan, F.J. (1927). *The science of swimming.* New York: American Sports Publishing.

Telford, R.D., Hahn, A.G., Catchpole, E.A., Parker, A.R., & Sweetenham, W.F. (1988). Post competition blood lactate concentration in highly ranked Australian swimmers. In B.E. Ungerechts, K. Wilke, & K. Reischle (Eds.), *International series on sport sciences: Vol. 18. International symposium of biomechanics and medicine in swimming: Swimming science V* (pp. 277-283). Champaign, IL: Human Kinetics.

Telford, R.D., Hahn, A.G., Catchpole, E.A., Plank, A.W., Deakin, V., & McLeay, A.C. (1988). The effect of vitamin/mineral supplementation on athletes: 1. Performance and haematology. *Report to Australian Sports Commission.* Canberra, Australia: National Sport Research Program.

Telford, R.D., Hahn, A.G., & Parker, A.R. (1987). Iron deficiency. *Excel,* **3**(4), 12-15.

Telford, R.D., McLeay, A.C., Deakin, V., Catchpole, E.A., Plank, A.W., & Hahn, A.G. (1988). The effect of vitamin/mineral supplementation on athletes: 2. Vitamin/mineral status. Initial Report. *Report to Australian Sports Commission.* Belconnen, A.C.T.: Australian Institute of Sport.

Telford, R.D., Tumilty, D., & Damm, G. (1984). Skinfold measurements in well-performed Australian athletes. *Sports Science & Medicine Quarterly,* **1**(2), 13-16.

Telford, R.D., Tumilty, D., Kupkee, W.O., Woolston, M.E., Burton, G.R., & Damm, G.R. (1984). Laboratory measures of well-performed male and female swimmers and comparison of two different training programs. *Pre-Olympic Scientific Congress.* Belconnen, A.C.T.: Australian Institute of Sport.

Telford, R.D., Zhang, Z., Carlile, F., Gathercole, T., Hahn, A.G., & Sweetenham, W.F. (1987). Monitoring cardiovascular adaptation using EKG and blood pressure. *Proceedings of the International Coaching and Swimming Science Conference.*

Thevenot, M. (1696). *L'art de nager.* Paris: T. Moette.

Thevenot, M. (1699). *The art of swimming.* London: D. Brown, D. Midurnter, T. Leigh, & R. Knaplock.

*Thierry, N. (1970). A look at East German swimming. *Swimming World,* **2**(2), 5, 8, 9.

Thierry, N. (1972). The world scene. *Swimming Technique,* **9**(1), 2-3, 10.

Thomas, R. (1904). *Swimming.* London: Sampson Low, Marston.

Thornton, N. (1979). The Berkeley Program. In R.M. Ousley (Ed.), *American Swimming Coaches Association world clinic yearbook 1979* (pp. 1-15). Fort Lauderdale, FL: American Swimming Coaches Association.

Thornton, N. (1987, January/February). A few thoughts on training, or a closer look at the path U.S. swimming seems to be currently following. *American Swimming Coaches Association Magazine,* pp. 11-14.

Travers, P., & Watson, R. (1972). Results of altitude training in British track and field athletics. *British Journal of Sports Medicine,* **8**(1), 46-51.

Treffene, R.J. (1978). Swimming performance test: A method of training and performance time selection. *Australian Journal of Sports Medicine,* **10**(2), 33-38.

Treffene, R.J., Alloway, J., & Shaw, J. (1977). Use of heart rates in the determination of swimming efficiency. In *Swimming medicine IV.* Baltimore: University Park Press.

Treffene, R.J., Craven, C., Hobbs, K., & Wade, C. (1979). Differences in sprint and endurance swimmers' lactates. *Swimming Technique,* **15**(4), 120-124.

Troup, J., Plyley, M., Sharp, R., & Costill, D. (1981, April). The age group swimmer: Considerations for training and performance. *Swimming Technique,* pp. 22-24.

Tutko, T. (1976). *Sports psyching.* Los Angeles: Tracher.

Ungerechts, B.E. (1979). Optimizing propulsion in swimming by rotation of the hands. In J. Terauds & E.W. Bedingfield (Eds.), *International Symposium of Biomechanics: Swimming III* (pp. 55-61). Baltimore: University Park Press.

Ungerechts, B.E. (1983). A comparison of the movements of the rear parts of dolphins and butterfly-swimmers. In A.P. Hollander, P. Huijing, & G. de Groot (Eds.), *International series on sports sciences: Vol. 14. Biomechanics and medicine in swimming* (pp. 215-221). Champaign, IL: Human Kinetics.

Ungerechts, B.E., Wilke, K., & Reischle, K. (1988). *International series on sports sciences: Vol. 18. International symposium of biome-*

chanics and medicine in swimming: Swimming science V. Champaign, IL: Human Kinetics.

Van Aaken, E. (1947). Running and record. *Sport und Gymnastik.*

Van Dam, C.P. (1988). In wind and water. *The Sciences,* **28**(1), 37-39.

Vanek, M. (1971). In L. Percival & J.W. Taylor (Eds.), *Proceedings of the first international symposium on the art and science of coaching,* **1** (pp. 254-256). Toronto: Fitness Institute Productions and the Coaching Association of Canada.

Von Holst, E., & Kuchemann, R. (1942). Biological and aerodynamic problems in animal flight (Abridged Translation). *The Journal of the Royal Aeronautical Society,* **46**, 39.

Weis-Fogh, T. (1973). Quick estimates of flight fitness in hovering animals including novel mechanisms for lift propulsion. *Journal of Experimental Biology,* **59**(1), 169-230.

Weissmuller, J. (1930). *Swimming the American crawl.* London: Putnam.

Westcott, M. (1968). *Toward a contemporary psychology of intuition.* New York: Holt, Rhinehart & Winston.

Wilmore, J.H. (1979). The application of science to sport: Physiological profiles of male and female athletes. *Canadian Journal of Applied Sport Sciences,* **4**(2), 103-115.

Wilson, W. (1883). *The swimming instructor.* London: (s.n.).

Wood, T.C. (1979). A fluid dynamics analysis of the propulsive potential of the hand and forearm in swimming. In J. Terauds & E.W. Bedingfield (Eds.), *International Symposium of Biomechanics: Swimming III* (pp. 62-69). Baltimore: University Park Press.

Wynman, N. (1538). *Colymbetes, sive de arte natandi et festivus et iucundus lectu.* (Dutch Copy.) Ingolstadt, Bavaria: (s.n.).

Young, D. (1984). *The Olympic myth of Greek amateur athletes.* Chicago: Aries Press.

Young, P. (1986a). Basic speed essential ingredient. *Swim Canada,* **13**(5), 14-15.

Young, P. (1986b). Only the committed, enthusiastic and hungry need apply. *Swim Canada,* **13**(6), 10-11.

Young, P. (1990). Education is the key. *Swim Canada,* **17**(1), 6-7.

Credits

Quotations and Paraphrases

Material from *The A.S.C.A. Newsletter*, *The A.S.C.A. World Clinic Yearbooks*, and the *American Swimming Coaches Association Magazine* used by permission of the American Swimming Coaches Association.

Material from *The Complete Swimmer* by F. Sachs, 1912, London: Methuen & Co., used by permission of the publisher.

Material from *How to Teach Swimming and Diving* (Vol. 1, chapter 4) by T.K. Cureton, 1934, New York: Association Press, reprinted by permission of T.K. Cureton.

Material from "Distance Freestyle Training" by R. Shoulberg in *American Swimming Coaches Association World Clinic Year-Book 1983* (pp. 209-213) by R. Ousley (Ed.), 1983, Fort Lauderdale, FL: American Swimming Coaches Association. Used by permission of the American Swimming Coaches Association and R. Shoulberg.

Material from "Distance Training" by R. Shoulberg in American Swimming Coaches Association World Clinic Yearbook 1985 (pp. 205-211) by T. Welsh (Ed.), 1985, Fort Lauderdale, FL: American Swimming Coaches Association. Used by permission of the American Swimming Coaches Association and R. Shoulberg.

Material from *Swimming Technique* magazine used by permission.

Material from *Swimming World* magazine used by permission.

Quote on page 5 by Manilius from *Sport in Greece and Rome* by H.A. Harris (1976), Ithaca, New York: Cornell University Press.

Chart on p. 106 from "Development in Running" by G. Holmer, 1972, *Track Technique*, 50, pp. 1584-1585, reprinted by permission of *Track Technique*.

Letter in chapter 6 from Forbes Carlile to Cecil Colwin on early use of interval training for swimming in Australia, June 15, 1988, reprinted by permission.

Material in chapter 6 from "Where Do We Go From Here? American Swimming Coaches Association's First World Clinic, Montreal, 1971" by F. Carlile in *Swimming Technique*, 8(4), 1971, used by permission of *Swimming Technique*.

Material in chapter 7 from *An Introduction to Swimming Coaching* (the Canadian Swimming Certification Level One manual) by C. Colwin, 1977, Ottawa, ON: Canadian Amateur Swimming Association, used by permission of Swimming Canada.

Material in chapter 8 from "A Few Thoughts on Training, or a Closer Look at the Path U.S. Swimming Seems to be Currently Following" by N. Thornton, 1987, *American Swimming Coaches Association Magazine*, January/February, pp. 11-14, used by permission of N. Thornton and the American Swimming Coaches Association.

Material in chapter 8 from "Hypoxic and Other Methods of Training Evaluated" by J.E. Counsilman in *Swimming Technique*, 12(1), 1975, used by permission of *Swimming Technique*.

Material in chapter 10 from *The History of Swimming* by F. Oppenheim, 1970, North Hollywood, CA: Swimming World, used by permission of Swimming World.

Material in chapter 10 from "The Ancient Olympics: A Run for the Money" by T. Hodge, January 9, 1988, p. B3, *The Ottawa Citizen*, used by permission of *The Ottawa Citizen*.

Material in chapter 10 from remarks made by M. Vanek, reprinted in *Proceedings of the First International Symposium on the Art and Science of Coaching* (Vol. 1, pp. 254-256) by L. Percival and J.W. Taylor (Eds.), 1971, Toronto: Fitness Institute Productions and the Coaching Association of Canada. Copyright 1971 by the Fitness Institute and the Coaching Association of America. Used by permission.

Material in chapter 10 from an interview with Bill Sweetenham, May 1987, used by permission.

Material in chapter 10 from a letter by Dale E. Neuburger, October 1990, used by permission.

Material in chapter 11 from "Coaching Psychology: The Case of James 'Doc' Counsilman" by J. Kimiecik and D. Gould, 1987, *The Sport Psychologist*, 1(4), used by permission of Human Kinetics.

Material in chapter 11 from *Super-Learning* by S. Ostrander and L. Schroeder with N. Ostrander, 1983, Pine Brook, NJ: Dell Books.

Material in chapter 11 from *Toward a Contemporary Psychology* (p. 24) by M. Westcott, 1968, New York: Holt, Rhinehart, & Winston, used by permission of Malcolm Westcott.

"Mark Schubert on Training 1,500-Meter Swimmers" in Appendix B from an interview conducted by Cecil Colwin, 1983, used by permission.

"Steve Bultman on Training for the 100-Meter and 200-Meter Backstroke Events" in Appendix B from "Training Backstroke" by M. Muckenfuss in *Swimming Technique*, 23(1), 1986, pp. 17-20, used by permission of *Swimming Technique*.

"Training for Butterfly in the Midseason: An Example From the Curl Swim Club Training Program" in Appendix B from "Flying in Virginia—John Flanagan Talks About Training Methods" by M. Muckenfuss in *Swimming Technique*, 23(4), 1987, pp. 11-16, used by permission of *Swimming Technique*.

"Sample Butterfly Workouts Designed by Coaches Bill Thompson and Mitch Ivey" in Appendix B from "Making Best Use of the Elements" by M. Muckenfuss in *Swimming Technique*, 21(4), pp. 8-13, used by permission of *Swimming Technique*.

"Training for the 100-Meter and 200-Meter Breaststroke" in Appendix B from "Breaststroke Texas Style by M. Muckenfuss in *Swimming Technique*, 23(2), 1986, pp. 16-22, used by permission of *Swimming Technique*.

"Paul Bergen on Breaststroke Training" in Appendix B from "Close to the Breast" by M. Muckenfuss in *Swimming Technique*, 22(2), 1985, pp. 9-14, used by permission of *Swimming Technique*.

"Mark Schubert on Individual Medley Training" in Appendix B from "Individual Medley Training" by M. Schubert, June 1987, *American Swimming Coaches Association Magazine*, pp. 11-13, used by permission of Mark Schubert and the American Swimming Coaches Association.

"Training for the 200-Meter and 400-Meter Individual Medley" in Appendix B from "A Steady Diet of the Four Basics—Training at Germantown Is Based on the Individual Medley and It Shows Up in the Swimming That Comes Out of Dick Shoulberg's Program'' by M. Muckenfuss in *Swimming Technique*, **24**(3), 1987, pp. 15-18, used by permission of *Swimming Technique* and R. Shoulberg.

Figures

Figures 1.1 and 1.3 from *The Complete Swimmer* (pp. 134, 145) by F. Sachs, 1912, London: Methuen & Co. Adapted by permission of the publisher.

Figures 2.11, 2.12, 2.13, and 2.16 from ''Swimming Propulsion: A Hydrodynamic Analysis'' by R.E. Schleihauf. In *American Swimming Coaches Association World Clinic Yearbook 1977* (pp. 51, 53, and 50) by R. Ousley (Ed.), 1977, Fort Lauderdale, FL: American Swimming Coaches Association. Adapted by permission of American Swimming Coaches Association and R. Schleihauf.

Figure 2.14 and accompanying text from ''Propulsive Techniques: Front Crawl Stroke, Butterfly, Backstroke, and Breaststroke'' by R.E. Schleihauf, J.R. Higgins, R. Hinrichs, D. Luedtke, C. Maglischo, E.W. Maglischo, and A. Thayer. In *Swimming Science V: International Series on Sport Sciences* (Vol 18, p. 56) by B.E. Ungerechts, K. Wilke, and K. Reischle (Eds.), 1988, Champaign, IL: Human Kinetics. Copyright 1988 by Human Kinetics Publishers. Reprinted by permission.

Figures 2.19 from ''The Status of Research on Biomechanics of Swimming'' by J.G. Hay. In *Starting, Stroking and Turning* (a compilation of research on the biomechanics of swimming, the University of Iowa, 1983-1986; p. 80) by J.G. Hay (Ed.), 1986, Iowa City: Biomechanics Laboratory, Department of Exercise Science, University of Iowa. Reprinted by permission of James G. Hay, University of Iowa.

Figures 4.4, 4.5, 4.8, and 4.9 from ''Foreflipper Propulsion in the California Sea Lion, *Zalophus Californianus* by S.D. Feldkapm, 1987, *Journal of Zoology*, **212**, pp. 44, 43, 54, and 56. Reprinted by permission of the Zoological Society of London and S.D. Feldkamp.

Figures 8.2 and 8.3 from ''Hypoxic and Other Methods of Training Evaluated'' by J.E. Counsilman in *Swimming Technique*, **12**(1), 1975. Reprinted by permission of *Swimming Technique* and James Counsilman.

Figure 8.4 from ''Controlling the Training of Top Level Swimmers'' by T. Absaliamov in *How to Develop Olympic Level Swimmers* by J.L. Cramer (Ed.), 1984, Finland: International Sports Media; and from ''Classification of Training Sessions'' by D.B. Pyne and R.D. Telford, 1988, *Excel*, **5**(2). Adapted by permission of Richard Telford.

Figure 8.5 from ''Constructing Workouts With Energy System Considerations'' by E.W. Maglischo in *American Swimming Coaches Association World Clinic Yearbook 1985* (p. 62) by T. Welsh (Ed.), 1985, Fort Lauderdale, FL: American Swimming Coaches Association. Reprinted by permission of American Swimming Coaches Association and E.W. Maglischo.

Figures 8.6 and 8.7 from *Theory and Methodology of Training* by T.O. Bompa, 1985, Dubuque, IA: Kendall/Hunt.

Figures 9.1, 9.3, and 9.4 from *Physical Fitness of Champion Athletes* by T.K. Cureton, 1951, Urbana: University of Illinois Press. Reprinted by permission of Thomas K. Cureton.

Figure 10.1 from a section by M. Vanek in *Proceedings of the First International Symposium on the Art and Science of Coaching* (Vol. 1, p. 255) by L. Percival and J.W. Taylor (Eds.), 1971, Toronto: Fitness Institute Productions and the Coaching Association of Canada. Copyright 1971 by the Fitness Institute and the Coaching Association of Canada. Reprinted by permission.

Index